Broken Lives

Broken Lives

SEPARATION AND DIVORCE IN ENGLAND 1660–1857

By
Lawrence Stone

OXFORD UNIVERSITY PRESS
1993

Oxford University Press, Walton Street, Oxford OX2 6DP
Oxford New York Toronto
Delhi Bombay Calcutta Madras Karachi
Petaling Jaya Singapore Hong Kong Tokyo
Nairobi Dar es Salaam Cape Town
Melbourne Auckland
and associated companies in
Berlin Ibadan

Oxford is a trade mark of Oxford University Press

Published in the United States
by Oxford University Press, New York

British Library Cataloguing in Publication Data
Data available

Library of Congress Cataloging in Publication Data
Stone, Lawrence.
Broken lives: separation and divorce in England, 1660–1857 /
Lawrence Stone.
p. cm.
Includes index.
1. Divorce—England—History. 2. Marriage—England—History.
3. Divorce—Law and legislation—Great Britain—History.
4. Marriage law—England—History. I. Title.
HQ876.S728 1993
306.89'0942—dc20 92-31576
ISBN 0-19-820254-7

Typeset by Graphicraft Typesetters Ltd., Hong Kong
Printed and bound in
Great Britain by Biddles Ltd.,
Guildford and King's Lynn

All history that descends to sufficient detail of human actions and characters is useful to bring us acquainted with our species, nay with ourselves.

Lord Bolingbroke, *Letters on the Study and Use of History* (1752), in Lord Bolingbroke, *Historical Writings*, ed. I. Kramnick (Chicago, 1974), 71

I could furnish a series of stories from the annals of Doctors' Commons which should rival the Waverley Novels in interest.

William Scott, Lord Stowell, Judge of the London Consistory Court in *Quarterly Review*, 75 149 (1844), 49

The dedicated social historian is second cousin to the tabloid journalist.

Professor Sir Geoffrey Elton, in *New York Review of Books*, 14 June 1984, p. 39

To

Robert Lawrence Fawtier Stone

Acknowledgements

ANY book published today on the subject of separation and divorce in early modern and modern England is inevitably constructed on the solid foundations of a large body of earlier work, mostly published in the last twenty years. This book would never have been written if some fifteen years ago Dr E. G. W. Bill, Librarian of Lambeth Palace Library, had not asked me to try to put together a consortium of American libraries to provide funds for a period of years, in order to microfilm the Process Books from the records of the Court of Arches. This was done, and microfiches of this enormous, invaluable, and hitherto inaccessible body of archival records, now augmented by microfilms of the bulk of the other records of the court, are deposited at the National Research Library and can be obtained on loan. For about eight years I was therefore able to consult these materials at leisure at Princeton. I am also indebted to Dr Bill and Miss Barber for their generous assistance while I was working on original records of the court in Lambeth Palace Library.

I am indebted to Mr Jorden D. Luttrell of Meyer Boswell Books Inc. for his great generosity in sending me his copy of *The Trial at large of Edward Loveden Loveden Esq. against Thomas Baker Esq.* (London, 1809). It is an extremely rare pamphlet which has since been sold to a library in Australia. I am also indebted to Mr Droh Wahrman for ordering a microfilm for me from the British Museum of a pamphlet written by Lady Westmeath; and to Mr Alastair Everitt of Chadwyck-Healey Ltd. for sending me microfiches of four trial pamphlets from his forthcoming microfiche series of *British Trials, 1660–1900.*

For a systematic survey of the records of some seven Consistory Courts, I am indebted to my research assistant, Dr Timothy Wales. Under my supervision, he spent two years examining selected samples of surviving records, tabulating matrimonial suits for statistical purposes, briefly noting all cases, and xeroxing or microfilming materials which he considered important. I am deeply grateful to him for his devotion to the task, and for the intelligence and historical imagination he exercised.

I am also grateful to Dr Geoffrey Clark. For two summers he combed the microfilm records of the Old Bailey for materials concerning bigamy, infanticide, rape, and similar problems related to separation and sexual relations. He also listed all the cases of Parliamentary divorce in the *Journals of the House of Lords.*

Acknowledgements

My third invaluable helper has been my wife, Jeanne C. Fawtier Stone, who interrupted her own research in order to help me complete this book. She has put into the computer and edited my handwritten drafts of this volume, has commented extensively on the text, and has spent many weeks on the thankless and dreary tasks of checking footnotes and compiling the index.

The fourth person upon whom I have relied heavily for assistance has been my long-suffering secretary, Mrs Joan Daviduk, who typed my almost illegible drafts of many case-studies, and also the flow of correspondence about the book as it took shape over the past ten years.

For financial support of this project I am indebted to the Rockefeller Foundation (G. A. Hum. 8116) and to the National Endowment for the Humanities (Grant R. O.–20220–82). I am also grateful to two semesters of paid leave from Princeton University, for a Rollins Research Grant from Princeton History Department, and for another grant from the Humanities Research Committee of Princeton University.

For the leisure and peace of mind in which thoroughly to revise the contents of this book for publication, I am deeply grateful to the National Humanities Center, which appointed me to an Andrew W. Mellon Foundation Fellowship in the autumn of 1990.

Among the staff of the many libraries and record offices visited for this project, all of whom were extremely helpful, I should like to single out those of Oxford University, both the Bodleian and Law Libraries, the British Library, Hatfield House, and the Huntington Library. For facilitating several days of intensive work on the extremely rich collection of printed pamphlet trial records in the Royal Irish Academy in Dublin, I am very grateful to Ms Brigid Dolan. I have also been helped by the staff of the Buckinghamshire, Norfolk, and Suffolk Record Offices.

Among the many individuals who have helped me in various ways, I am particularly grateful for references supplied by Mr Robin Harcourt Williams, Dr Roger Highfield, Mrs R. E. F. Gough, Dr J. J. Looney, Dr A. P. W. Malcomson, Professor James Pollock, and Mrs Susan Whyman. I also owe a great debt of gratitude to Ms Betty Muirden of the Yale Center for British Art for invaluable assistance in tracking down illustrations for this book, and to Burton B. Fredericksen and Libby Spatz of the Provenance Index at the J. Paul Getty Museum.

Finally, I would like to thank the anonymous reader of this manuscript for the care and good judgement he exercised in suggesting cuts, even if I have not always followed his advice.

L.S.

Princeton, New Jersey
February 1992

Contents

Contents

List of Plates

Between pages 174 and 175

List of Figures

List of Genealogies

Abbreviations

Anderson	S. Anderson, 'Legislative Divorce: Law for the Aristocracy?', in G. R. Rubin and D. Sugarman (eds.), *Law and Society 1750–1914: Essays in the History of English Law* (Abingdon, 1984), 412–40
BL	British Library
Bon Ton Mag.	*Bon Ton Magazine* (3 vols.; London, 1791–3)
Calvert Diary	Princeton University Library, Frances Calvert's MS diary
Campbell, *Lives of the Chief Justices*	J. Lord Campbell, *Lives of the Chief Justices of England* (2 vols.; London, 1848–9)
Crim. Con. Gaz.	*Crim. Con. Gazette* (2 vols.; London, 1838–9)
Eng. Rep.	*English Reports* (187 vols. [1220–1865]; London, 1900–30)
Fratricide	Anon., *The Bristol Fratricide* (London, 1741)
Gent's Mag.	*Gentleman's Magazine*
Genuine Trial	Anon., *The Genuine Trial of Samuel Goodere Esq.* (London, 1741)
Greville Memoirs	L. Strachey and R. Fulford (eds.), *The Greville Memoirs 1814–60* (London, 1938)
JH Lords	*Journal of the House of Lords*
LPCA	Lambeth Palace, Court of Arches MSS
MacQueen, *House of Lords*	J. F. MacQueen, *A Practical Treatise on the Appellate Jurisdiction of the House of Lords and the Privy Council, together with the Practice of Parliamentary Divorce* (London, 1842)
Memoirs	S. Foote, *Genuine Memoirs of Sir John Dineley Goodere, Bart.* (London, 1741)
Narrative of the Case	*A Narrative of the Case of the Marchioness of Westmeath* (London, 1857) (BL 6497 c 13)
NC Trials for Adultery (1797)	*A New Collection of Trials for Adultery* (3 vols.; London 1796 [*sic*])

NCC Trials for Adultery (1780)	*A New and Complete Collection of Trials for Adultery* (2 vols.; London, 1780)
Peerage	G. E. Cockayne, *Complete Peerage of England* (14 vols.; London, 1910–65)
Plowden	F. Plowden, *Crim. Con. Biography* (2 vols.; London, 1838–9)
RIA/AP	Royal Irish Academy, Academy Pamphlets
RIA/HP	Royal Irish Academy, Haliday Pamphlets
Reply to the Narrative	[George Nugent, Marquis of Westmeath], *A Reply to the 'Narrative of the Case by the Marchioness of Westmeath'* (London, 1857) RIA/AP (1857) and BL 1417 g 57
Shelford	L. Shelford, *A Practical Treatise of the Law of Marriage and Divorce* (London, 1841)
Sketch	*A Sketch of Lord Westmeath's Case* (Dublin, 1828), BL 1609/4162 and Hatfield House, Westmeath Papers
State Trials	W. Cobbett, *Complete Collection of State Trials*, ed. W. B. Howell (London, 1809–28)
Stone, *FSM*	L. Stone, *Family, Sex, and Marriage in England 1500–1800* (London, 1977)
Stone, *Road to Divorce*	L. Stone, *Road to Divorce: England 1530–1987* (Oxford, 1990)
Stone, *Uncertain Unions*	L. Stone, *Uncertain Unions* (Oxford, 1992)
T & C Mag.	*Town and Country Magazine* (London, 1769–93).
Trial	*Trial of an Action by Edward Loveden, Esq., against Raymond Barker, Esq., for criminal conversation* (London, 1810)
Trials	*Trials of Samuel Goodere Esq., Matthew Mahoney and Charles White for the Murder of Sir John Dineley Goodere, Bart.* (London, 1741)
Trials for Adultery at Doctors Commons	*Trials for Adultery at Doctors Commons or the History of Divorces, being Select Trials at Doctors Commons . . . from the Year 1760 to the Present Time* (7 vols.; London, 1779–80)

Walpole's Correspondence	*Horace Walpole's Correspondence*, ed. W. S. Lewis *et al.* (48 vols.; New Haven, Conn., 1937–80)
Wharton	J. J. S. Wharton, *An Exposition of the Laws Relating to the Women of England* (London, 1853)

I
Introduction

1. Purpose, Structure, and Evidence

This volume of case-studies illustrates, through detailed narratives of individual lives, just how marriages broke up in early modern England. It is a companion volume to the set of case-studies about how marriages were formed, entitled *Uncertain Unions: The Making of Marriage in England 1660–1753*. The analytical background to both volumes of case-studies is provided by *Road To Divorce: England 1530–1987*, which examined in detail the nature of the evidence and its reliability; the structure of the courts, and the complex and changing technicalities of the laws regulating private separations, judicial separations, Parliamentary divorces, and suits for criminal conversation (crim. com.) against a wife's lover; the laws concerning debt, inheritance, and married women's property; changes in attitudes to privacy, honour, shame, and cruelty; the importance in the regulation of marital and sexual behaviour of surveillance, gossip, and denunciation by bystanders and interest groups who constantly recur in these documents, notably relatives and 'friends', neighbours, domestic servants, the dark underworld of easily perjured witnesses, and the parsons who made a dubious living by performing clandestine marriages. Finally, the book examined the slow drift of case law, made by the lawyers and judges, away from compliance with the strict rules of canon law, as well as the causes and consequences of the first Divorce Act of 1857.

Since this volume of individual case-studies is intended to be read on its own, for illumination and pleasure, without reference to this material contained in *Road to Divorce*, it is therefore provided with an introduction which supplies an abbreviated summary of the social, moral, and legal background. Those who have already read *Road to Divorce* can move straight on to the case-studies, omitting Sections 2–7 of this Introduction.

Telling stories should require no justification from the historian. After all, literature is nothing but fictional stories, which are avidly read for the light they throw both on the changeless qualities of human nature and on the very different types of human thought and behaviour and general conditions of life at the time and place in which they are set. Freud once wrote: 'It still strikes me myself as strange that the case histories I write should read like short stories and that, as one might say, they lack the

3

serious stamp of science. I must console myself with the reflection that the nature of the subject is evidently responsible for this, rather than any preference of my own.'[1] If the historian's prime task is to explain change over time, another equally important function is surely to bring the past alive to contemporary readers. As any anthropologist who has done field-work will testify, other people are other. Those whose thoughts, whose speech, and whose behaviour are recorded in the stories in this volume had very different values and beliefs from ours; and they lived in a quite different political, legal, moral, economic, and technological environment. If Marc Bloch was right when he asserted that 'in the last analysis it is the human consciousness which is the subject matter of history',[2] then the case-study has an irreplaceable role to play. The human mind is so constructed that it comprehends the inwardness of things more easily by the concrete example than by the theoretical generalization. As John Aubrey observed in the seventeenth century: 'The retrieving of these forgotten things from oblivion in some sort resembles the art of the conjuror, who makes those walk and appear that have been in their graves many hundreds of years; and represents as it were to the eye the places, customs, and fashions that were of the old time.'[3]

The stories in this volume are based on what for England appears to be a uniquely rich set of documents. Under the procedures used in the ecclesiastical courts, witnesses were interrogated in private and their depositions taken down in notes or shorthand. The result is a full, and sometimes more-or-less verbatim, account of what was said by dozens, or hundreds, of persons, protagonists, witnesses, lawyers, and judges, who gave evidence or argued in a given case. As a result we can eavesdrop on the conversations of men and women of all sorts and conditions who lived in southern England in the long eighteenth century from about 1660 to 1820.

It must be admitted that this volume is inescapably concerned almost exclusively with marital breakdowns among the very rich. This is not the result of deliberate choice, but of the nature of the evidence available. The court records tell us very little about the experiences of marital breakdown among the poor, for the reason that they could not afford the enormous costs of a full-scale long-drawn-out legal battle, involving the transport and maintenance of dozens of witnesses, often three times in three different courts, and the payment of squadrons of lawyers, legal clerks, and detectives. Even the middling sort of artisans, shopkeepers, cottagers, and husbandmen could not afford such legal extravaganzas, and, although they

[1] S. Freud, *Studies on Hysteria* (London, 1895), 160–1.
[2] M. Bloch, *The Historian's Craft* (London, 1949), 151.
[3] J. Aubrey, *Wiltshire: The Topographical Collection*, ed. J. E. Jackson (Devizes, 1862), 4.

appear frequently before the courts, their cases are brief and their witnesses few. As a result their cases do not provide the historian with the depth and richness of evidence produced by major disputes among the very rich.

Towards the end of the eighteenth century, as the litigation became exclusively concerned with the breaking rather than the making of marriage, and as costs rose, the litigants became even more exclusively persons of property, that is members of the landed élite and rich merchants and professional men, and the smaller 'middling sort' almost disappear.

Some hints of the scale of marital breakdown among the poor, and even of its causes, can be gleaned from other sources, namely those concerned with poor relief. This is because, for a husband among the poor, the natural, and indeed often the only, avenue of escape from a failed marriage was simply to run away, either to join the armed forces or to set up a second household. The loss to the family of the main wage-earner often forced the abandoned wife and children to apply for poor relief from the parish. It is, therefore, possible from a study of applications for poor relief to calculate the proportion of those seeking relief who were wives and children who had been abandoned by their husbands and fathers. In one village it is even possible to calculate what proportion of all marriages resulted in abandoned wives seeking poor relief. At Colyton in Devon, applications for poor relief indicate that about 10 per cent of all marriages between 1741 and 1769 ended in desertion, mostly by husbands of wives. About a half of the deserting husbands went into military service, while many of the others abandoned their families in order to set up new households in another county with some other women, by whom they produced illegitimate children. In all cases, poverty seems to have played a large role in causing marital separation.[4]

In the countryside generally, between 4 and 6 per cent of all applications for poor relief consisted of deserted wives, a figure which remained remarkably stable between 1700 and 1830.[5] In the great anonymous city of London, the proportion of abandoned wives thrown on to the charity of the parish was much higher; for example, in St Martins-in-the-Fields in the last half of the eighteenth century the proportion was 12 per cent.[6] In times of war, men took advantage of easy recruitment into the army or navy to abandon their family responsibilities. Arthur Young observed in 1801 that, under pressure of poverty, a man 'enlists for a soldier, and leaves the wife

---

[4] P. Sharpe, 'Marital Separation in the Eighteenth and Early Nineteenth Centuries', *Local Population Studies*, 45 (1990).

[5] K. D. M. Snell, *Annals of the Labouring Poor* (Cambridge, 1985), 359–64.

[6] D. A. Kent, ' "Gone for a Soldier": Family Breakdown and the Demography of Desertion in a London Parish, 1750–91', *Local Population Studies*, 45 (1990), 29.

and children to the parish'.[7] The accuracy of his observation is proved in London by the fact that service-related desertions in war years, such as 1755–61 or 1780–1, were as high as 20–35 per cent of all those reported to the parish. If one includes those husbands who ran away to sea, either in the navy or merchant marine, the proportion of families applying for poor relief which had been broken up and driven into destitution by war over the whole of the eighteenth century amounted to nearly one-third of the total.[8]

Those abandoned wives who fell into abject poverty and sought relief form an unknown proportion of all deserted wives, many of whom either could support themselves and their families for a while by their work, or could sometimes form another household with a second, illegal, spouse. But everything points to the fact that, for most poor women, marriage was an economic necessity for survival. They were caught in a poverty trap, and could only afford to abandon a marriage if they could find another spouse or male companion to add to the family income.

Since abandonment and enlistment in the armed forces was such an easy way out of a bad marriage for a man, it is hardly surprising that war had a devastating effect in breaking up marriages, although some of the destitute families may have come together again among that minority whose husbands returned alive. As a result, among the factors which caused marriages among the poor to fail, poverty and war were clearly the most important. Others were migration and urbanization, causing the poor relief rolls in London to swell far faster than those of the countryside. Marriages among the poor were formed late, and often did not last very long, over half of the break-ups occurring within the first ten years. Before the abolition of Fleet marriages in 1754, nearly 60 per cent of all recorded broken marriages of the poor had taken place there, which is a suggestive indicator of the extreme fragility of these clandestine arrangements.[9]

These largely statistical glimpses of a drifting underclass, many of whose marriages seem to have been unstable, will have to serve as a substitute for the wealth of psychological, social, and economic detail revealed by the records of the courts about the matrimonial disasters of the rich. It is not much, but for the present it is the best the historian can do.

On the other hand, the records of litigation are packed with testimony provided by the very lowest strata of society, in many cases including brief accounts of their lives. This was because in all matrimonial cases witnesses were inevitably mostly domestic servants, many of whom belonged to the

[7] Quoted by Snell, *Annals*, 360.
[8] Kent, ' "Gone for a Soldier" ', 39.   [9] Ibid. 30–1.

very poor. Another group of witnesses were individuals from the crime-prone pauperized underclass of London, who for a few shillings would cheerfully perjure themselves on oath in court.

It is not pretended that stories derived from ecclesiastical court records reveal the full and unvarnished truth, although the claim can be made that they offer a deeper and more intimate insight into the psychology, behaviour, and even speech of actors in the past than can be obtained from any other source. In recording the depositions and answers of witnesses, the clerks of the court, usually, but not always turned direct speech in the present tense into indirect speech in the past tense. For example, one record reads: 'the deponent said that she was married to Mr Williams, and that he was her husband.' In cases where a brisk exchange of dialogue is recorded, this indirect speech formula has sometimes been converted back into direct speech, but only when it seemed appropriate and when there is no possibility of ambiguity. Thus in telling the story the recorded statement has been adjusted to read: 'I am married to Mr Williams and he is my husband.' The purpose of the conversion is to recapture the immediacy and sharpness of the dialogue, much of which is so like that in a contemporary novel or play. It can be claimed with a very high degree of certainty that the statement as presented in the case-study now reads exactly as the witness spoke it before the clerk, and before he had turned it into indirect speech in the past tense.

The reader needs to be reminded, however, that these case-studies are not one but two steps away from that mythical beast 'the Truth'. First, the huge mass of raw data—in some cases amounting to a quarter of a million words, and in one case half a million words—have necessarily been compressed so as to present a more-or-less coherent story. Secondly, the contradictions have been sorted out, the repetitions eliminated, the chronology reconstructed, and a new narrative created, albeit one which makes careful mention of any inconsistencies in the record. This volume of case-studies, therefore, is made up not of raw data but of a series of narratives constructed from those data which appear to a twentieth-century author, and usually to contemporary judges, to offer the most plausible interpretation of the evidence.

The story of what really happened has to be pieced together from two semi-fictitious constructs created by the prosecution and the defence, each buttressed by the often coached, and occasionally false, sworn evidence by their respective posses of witnesses. It should be noted that the large and growing disparity between the income of the litigants and those of the witnesses—servants, neighbours, and professional oath-takers for money—made bribed testimony and perjury almost an inevitability, despite every effort by the court to curb it. As a result, perjury, alas, was all too common in the early modern courtroom. For example, case-studies reveal that at least some clandestine marriage claims were based on forged documents and perjured testimony. They were the product of the desperation of a battered wife from a propertied family, determined to win a marital separation, such as Lady Westmeath; or a husband determined to find evidence for a Parliamentary divorce, such as Sir John Dineley. What is astonishing about these cases is the brazen fabrication of evidence based entirely on fraud, forgery, and perjury. Even more astonishing, however, is the high detective skill of the agents of the defendants in these cases, who somehow contrived to expose the frauds, identify the perpetrators, and even reconstruct their life histories. In doing so they reveal a seamy London underworld of venal and drunken clergymen and easily corrupted witnesses, all willing to swear to anything if they were adequately rewarded. These were men and women on the very edge of destitution, and driven by a combination of poverty, greed, and a total absence of moral principle.

But if we assume, as I think we must, that in most cases most sworn statements were perhaps evasive but at least not downright lies, then it can plausibly be argued that the truth usually emerges as clearly as it does in any court of law today.

A second qualifier is that some of the testimony has been tailored to fit the law, and some things we would like to know, or witnesses we would like to hear from, are therefore often missing. Witnesses could not be forced to incriminate themselves, although one can draw one's own conclusions from the questions they refused to answer. The third qualifier is that, although we have detailed records of the evidence of the litigants, we usually do not have the speech of the judge, giving his reasons for his verdict.

On the other hand, the mass of accusations, answers, and testimony of witnesses is often of enormous bulk. This huge, chaotic, and often repetitious outpouring of raw data has had to be compared, sorted out, rearranged, reorganized, and compressed into a coherent narrative, with allowances made for possible alternative interpretations. Some comfort may be derived from the fact that the interpretations of the evidence presented by me in these secondary narratives are usually—not always—supported by the opinions of at least the appeal judges. But, of course, other readers of the same documents might come to different conclusions.

The safeguard against any twisting of the data by the author is that the records of the Court of Arches, from which most of these stories are largely constructed, can be found on microform in both the United States and England. Printed transcripts of many of the more sensational trials in the London Consistory Court are also readily available in the seven volumes of

Trials for Adultery at Doctors Commons, recently reprinted by Garland Press. Moreover, every effort has been made to avoid applying twentieth-century moral judgements to episodes occurring in a pre-modern society. The exact speech of witnesses, whether for praise or blame, has been carefully cited, although the precise meaning of words, like 'divorce', has sometimes changed over the last two hundred years. Modern words have to be used to describe situations, but authorial manipulation has been reduced to the minimum possible. And sometimes, as in the Middleton case, after hundreds of thousands of words of testimony have been produced, at prodigious cost, over a period of several years, it is still not quite certain to the modern author whether or not justice was in fact done to the defendant. The Westmeath case provides an even more dramatic example of the assemblage of a vast body of evidence, resulting in factual ambiguity and, in this particular case, in judicial indecision and contradiction.

Unfortunately it is in the nature of evidence drawn from records of the courts of law that the resulting accounts of the lives of the protagonists are both partial and episodic. The actors in the drama emerge from the shadows, strut a while upon the stage, expose in intimate detail a story that may cover only a few years or decades of their lives up to that moment, and then, once the trial is over, vanish abruptly into the darkness of unrecorded history. What we have, therefore, are slices out of people's lives, illuminated for an instant in the beam of an immensely powerful searchlight. For a little while we can eavesdrop upon our forefathers, listen to them, and watch them travelling, drinking, courting, making love, and negotiating, threatening, and manœuvring in order to break a marriage and obtain either a separation or a divorce.

2. The Courts and the Law

The prime legal responsibility for all matters concerning sexual behaviour, marriage, and separation lay with the ecclesiastical courts. The lowest of these were the Consistory Courts, one for each diocese, run by a chancellor and staff appointed by the bishop. Appeals from the Consistory Courts in the southern province of England under the jurisdiction of Canterbury, that is south of a line including the dioceses of Lichfield and Coventry and Lincoln, were made to the Court of Arches in London. It is from the hitherto largely untapped records of this court that the bulk of materials for this volume are drawn, since for various technical reasons its transcripts of Consistory Court trials are more complete and easier to assemble than those of the Consistory Courts themselves. Very occasionally litigants would appeal a sentence from the Court of Arches to the Court of Delegates, composed of an *ad hoc* group appointed by the Lord Chancellor, and consisting of common-law judges, and three civil lawyers, whose verdict was final.

The law administered by the ecclesiastical courts was the medieval canon law, which had been left unaltered at the Reformation except for a drastic reduction in the number of proscribed degrees of incest. Thus England was unique in Europe since it preserved the medieval canon laws about marriage, which had been swept away in Catholic Europe by the Council of Trent. And yet it failed, largely for accidental reasons, to adopt the laws for full divorce with permission to remarry, usually on grounds of female adultery, or male cruelty, or desertion for seven years or more, which had been introduced into all other Protestant countries. England thus had the worst of all worlds: marriage was all too easy legally to enter into, but all but impossible legally to get out of.

But, thanks to changes created by case law, the courts slowly modified their position on a number of issues. The most important of these changes in judicial interpretation was probably the shift in the definition of cruelty from life-threatening damage as a result of physical abuse, as defined by canon law, to the inclusion after 1790 of 'a reasonable apprehension of future bodily harm', to a reinterpretation by 1860 which defined cruelty as mere verbal abuse and insults, even if not accompanied by a single blow. There was thus a slow concession by judicial pronouncements to the new ideal of the companionate marriage, made under a cloak of conservative rhetoric. The result was a subsequent rise of cruelty as the principal cause offered for marital separation by wives, slowly overtaking the older combined charges of adultery and cruelty. The second shift in judicial interpretation of the law involved a tightening-up of the rule defining proof in cases of adultery, which also worked in favour of wives, who were the ones most commonly sued for adultery.

If the canon law (now administered by men trained in the civil law) and the ecclesiastical courts ruled over all matters of law concerning marriage and divorce, secular courts held jurisdiction over property, the disposal of which was intimately bound up with marriage. Thus Chancery had jurisdiction over trusts and contracts, and the disposal of personal property, and was therefore the court which dealt with trusts to secure married women's property, marriage settlements, and the like. It also had jurisdiction over claims for debt, and was therefore drawn into deciding whether or not a marriage was valid, simply in order to ascertain whether the alleged husband was responsible for his alleged wife's debts.

The common-law courts also became increasingly involved, especially after the rise in the late seventeenth century of breach-of-promise suits for damages, which slowly replaced marriage-contract suits before the ecclesiastical courts. In the late seventeenth, eighteenth, and early nineteenth centuries there flourished a form of common-law action for trespass, which allowed an aggrieved husband to sue his wife's lover for damages for crim. con., that is sexual relations. Most of these cases were tried in King's Bench.

The criminal courts could also become involved if either of the parties chose to sue the other for such statutory penal offences as bigamy or sodomy, as mentioned in the Calvert case. Parliament was drawn in when, in the late seventeenth century, it began to permit the passage of private bills of full divorce with permission to remarry to very wealthy husbands whose wives had committed adultery. These various courts interlocked, overlapped, and not infrequently returned contradictory verdicts.

3. Separation and Divorce in a Pre-Modern Society

Marital breakdown, separation, and divorce are traumatic and tragic events, occurring at the bottom end of the spectrum of marital felicity, unravelling ties between kin groups, rearranging or annulling property transfers, forcing friends and relatives to adjust to a new situation, often threatening the stability of another family through adultery, and generally upsetting the life of the community. It is hardly surprising that in most advanced civilizations, Church and State have made every effort to regulate these events, and in many cultures full divorce has been virtually forbidden. Early modern England was no exception to these generalizations, since it did not acquire an official system of legalized divorce followed by remarriage until 1857. On the other hand, as we shall see, significant numbers contrived to escape their marital bonds in one way or another. There was a wide gap between the law and human behaviour.

There are good reasons for making a close investigation of marital breakdowns. These were rare events, but when they occurred they brought sharply together the family, the law, and the legal machinery, the three elements which together shaped domestic values and behaviour in the centuries under discussion. Most marital breakdowns, of course, occurred outside the law, or rather in its shadow, and only about 10 per cent of those involving legal proceedings came to trial and sentence. Then, even more than today, litigation was more a form of blackmail than a machinery for dispute resolution.

Cases of judicial separation reveal the shifting and competitive positions of these three rival systems of law—canon, equity, and common—which jostled for control over moral and material aspects of marital strife. It was judicial decisions handed down with careful explanations by distinguished judges, mostly in appellate jurisdictions, which in fact contrived, under a smoke-screen of faithful adherence to precedent, significantly to change the content of family law. Intervention of Parliament to change statute law occurred, not only very rarely, but also very belatedly, merely bringing the law into line, not only with public opinion, but also, to a considerable extent, with legal practice. There was a lag of about seventy years between shifts in élite and legal opinion and changes in statute law.

That small minority of bitter marital disputes which were fought to a finish are of importance only because they gave rise to crucial judicial reinterpretations. They also offer posterity a unique window into the past, allowing actors and observers from many walks of life to tell us in their own words about their values, their aspirations, and their ideals. Like a revolution in the polity, a bitterly disputed marital separation provides us with a unique and privileged view into otherwise hidden areas of thought and behaviour. Depositions in the ensuing litigation reveal, as no other data can, changing ideas among different layers of society about such matters as marital fidelity, marital cruelty, sexuality, patriarchal authority, individual autonomy, the expected roles of the two genders, and the rival responsibilities and claims of husband and wife for child custody, care, and maintenance.

It has to be emphasized that England in the sixteenth and seventeenth centuries, and even the eighteenth and nineteenth, was not only not a divorcing society—which is a legal condition; except perhaps at the very bottom of the social structure, among the very poor, it was also not much of a separating society, which is a behaviour pattern. The annual total of court-ordered separations and divorces in the mid-eighteenth century was only about 0.1 per cent of all marriages. A reasonable guess would be that this represented at most a fortieth of all forms of marital break-up. This gives us an outside maximum of about 4 per cent of all marriages which somehow came apart in early modern England, as compared with the 33 per cent that in 1993 are projected to end in divorce in England.

This does not sound very much by modern standards, but it has to be remembered that the high adult mortality rate meant that many marriages were cut short prematurely by the early death of one or other of the spouses. Even among the élite, the median duration of marriage in the seventeenth and eighteenth century was only between twenty and thirty years, and that for the poor more like twenty. Apart from the fifty-year gap between 1900 and 1950 after mortality declined and before divorce replaced it, the median duration of marriage did not change very much over time— at any rate before the 1960s. All that happened before 1960 was that divorce became a modern substitute for death.

It can also be argued with some confidence that marital breakdowns, although rare, were by no means uncommon, and that the subject was much on people's minds in the late seventeenth and eighteenth centuries. Thus, the only way to explain the passage of the first Divorce Act of 1857 is by seeking its roots in marital breakdowns over the previous two centuries, and by identifying the changes in moral attitudes to separation and divorce which were becoming increasingly clear after about 1750, affecting first the middle and upper classes and a little later showing up in judicial opinions which substantially altered case law.

There were both structural and particular reasons for the relatively low level of marital breakdown in early modern England. There can be little doubt that the institutional marriage, in the arrangement of which parents and 'friends' played a large part and financial considerations loomed large, tended to create marital stability. This was because the ties that bound the spouses together were more numerous and more permanent than those ephemeral psychosomatic experiences, romantic love and sexual passion. The couple were inextricably linked together in a many-sided joint enterprise, with a variety of reproductive, educational, economic, and social functions to perform; they were supported and kept in line by the watchful care of relatives and neighbours; and time, sex, habit, and children normally led to some sort of more-or-less satisfactory partnership.

The ideology of patriarchy also helped to consolidate marriage. The overwhelming ideology of female subordination and inferiority, drilled into every member of the society by clerical sermons, state regulations, marital handbooks, and both élite and popular culture, induced a certain docility in most wives, and thus reduced the tension level of the inevitable power struggle within the household.

If these economic, social, and ideological forces were not sufficient to hold a marriage together, the deterrents to a wife suing for separation were so severe that few would choose to go through such an experience unless driven by desperation. The first of these deterrents was the near-certainty of severe financial hardship and, if poor, the probability of destitution. If the husband was the guilty party, the alimony awarded by the ecclesiastical courts was generous, amounting to about a third of the husband's declared net income. Then as now, however, the courts found it extremely hard to enforce regular payments over a long period of years. Moreover, even after a judicial separation, a husband would continue to have the power to take possession of and enjoy the income of any property his wife might inherit from relatives as well as any fixed capital and earned income from any business activity in which she might engage to support herself. There are cases on record of a husband sweeping down years later upon the home of his separated wife, ransacking it, and removing every stick of furniture, money, and other goods. The Calvert case provides an example of such a raid. And the husband was entirely within his rights to do so.

In many cases, an even more severe deterrent from seeking separation by a wife trapped in a miserable marriage was the strong probability of losing all contact whatsoever with her children. However outrageous in terms of physical cruelty and promiscuous adultery the behaviour of the husband might have been, well into the nineteenth century the common law still granted him absolute control of all the children. The situation only began to change in the late eighteenth century when the Court of Chancery, and later the common law, began to allocate custody of small children to wives on grounds of equity. Until then, the husband not only had sole control of the children, but also could, and usually did, forbid any contact whatsoever with the mother. The Grafton and Westmeath cases are typically tragic examples of what could and did happen over child custody.

The third great deterrent to a wife from seeking a separation was fear of the publicity involved. Since before about 1790 the only grounds for a suit in the ecclesiastical courts were gross physical cruelty or adultery, all the sordid details both of the sufferings of a battered wife and of the promiscuous sexual activities of an unfaithful husband had to be displayed in open court. For persons in the high and middling ranks of society, the embarrassment was aggravated after about 1740 by the flood of published pamphlets containing the stenographic record of the most scabrous and sensational of these court cases. The whole world could—and did—read all about it.

The courts certainly tried to act as *moral* theatre, the cases of the two spouses being couched by their lawyers in terms of good versus evil, and the judge prefacing his decision by a long public speech about the need to uphold the moral order, to preserve the marital union whenever possible, to redefine the tolerated boundaries of legal patriarchy, and to identify and punish sexual deviance. On the other hand, thanks to this widespread reporting after 1740 of the sordid details of intimate marital life, the courts also involuntarily acted as *immoral* theatre, feeding juicy raw material to the booming pornographic market. This publicity acted as a strong deterrent to many couples from launching a suit for judicial separation after a court trial. The opposition in the Westmeath case of Lady Westmeath's family to her desire to sue her husband for judicial separation for fear of scandal shows the strength of this sentiment.

Despite these powerful forces at work to hold marriages together, some of them did break up, for the usual variety of economic, social, and cultural and psychological reasons. The anomie of urban life in a big city is clearly one, at least among the lower classes, particularly among those fresh from the provinces. This explains why Londoners bulk increasingly large in separation suits, so that by the very late eighteenth century they represent the great majority of all court cases. War and the dislocations of war have always generated a large crop of marital breakdowns, largely because of the physical separation of spouses by the absence of husbands at sea or abroad.[10] Breakdowns were also partly caused by the billeting in home towns of unattached bachelor officers and soldiers with little to occupy their time other than sexual intrigues. Interminable wars, like those between England and France from 1689 to 1712 and from 1793 to 1815, divided hundreds of thousands of husbands and wives for years or even decades at a time, thus encouraging adultery and consequent marital separation or divorce.

Expectations of marital sexual fidelity also differ over time and space. Adultery by the husband obviously has less effect upon the break-up of marriage in cultures, such as that in England in the early modern period, where male philandering is accepted as normal, and something to which a sensible wife turns a blind eye. Once the companionate marriage had become the ideal by the mid-eighteenth century, however, there was greater hostility among wives to marital infidelity by their husbands. There can be little doubt that the rising expectations at that time of what marriage involved in terms of personal commitment more frequently led to disappointment, resulting in more frequent marital breakdowns. Higher expectations of marital felicity engendered not only greater wifely resentment of a husband's adultery, but also greater resentment of verbal and physical abuse.

In general one might surmise that, in a culture which trains women to adopt a posture of total submission to a husband's wishes—for example, in sixteenth-century England or nineteenth-century Japan—there is less likelihood of marital breakdown than in one which encourages female independence, and offers more egalitarian access to legal remedies and financial self-sufficiency. Obviously, the real division of authority in any household depends in practice very much upon the relative strength of character of the two spouses, but the legal and moral framework necessarily exerts a powerful influence on the outcome. It is not—I hope—reactionary to argue that, until masculine cultural expectations have adapted to the new situation, the ideology of feminism is likely to put many marriages under exceptional strain. That is what seems to have happened after the 1790s, as a result of the romantic movement and the liberalizing tendencies first of the Enlightenment and then of the French Revolution.

The unions most likely to break down in the eighteenth century seem to

[10] LPCA, D.1761; E.36/61; Ee.10/107; Eee.15 ff. 53–61; B. 19/2.

have been those at either end of the spectrum, from the romantic love-match to the marriage arranged entirely by the parents in the interests of family prestige and property. Statistically, the most fragile were either sudden love-matches at a very early age, without consent or advice of parents and friends, or marriages arranged by parents and friends without any consultation about the wishes of the spouses. That is understandable, if at bottom most marriages foundered on temperamental incompatibility or indifference.

The most specific causes of breakdown were ostensibly fairly restricted in number. One was financial quarrels between the husband and wife, and another ruptures between the husband's kin and that of the wife, usually caused by disputes over financial settlements. Many cases included gross physical cruelty by the husband, and there appear to have been at least as many horribly battered women in the early modern period as there are today. Finally, there was adultery by the wife, which in most cases was preceded by a long period of indifference, neglect, and adultery by the husband. Husbands undoubtedly committed adultery much more frequently than did wives, but it was also much more frequently condoned. Sexual problems were far less in evidence in cases of marital separation in early modern England than they are nowadays, but this is probably merely a consequence of a greater reticence about such matters. The Westmeath case is exceptional in this respect. On the other hand, it is very striking how many loving wives and dutiful mothers, after a decade or more of apparently tranquil marriage, suddenly found themselves swept away by a wave of irresistible sexual passion, as happened to Mrs Middleton and Mrs Loveden. Moreover, there are signs of friction arising in the early nineteenth century over methods of controlling fertility, whether by *coitus interruptus*, as husbands preferred, or by abstention, as preferred by many wives. This seems to have been a cause of serious friction in the Westmeath case.

4. The Methods of Making a Marriage

A striking feature of early modern England is the extraordinary freedom from parental interference which is revealed in the daily lives of many of the young women concerned. One would expect such freedom to be found among the poor, since they married late, at 25–7; most had long ago shaken off parental controls by moving into service away from home, as apprentice or farm labourer if a boy, or into domestic service if a girl; and in any event their parents did not have sufficient economic resources to enforce a veto by denial of money for marriage. What is much more surprising is to find that such liberty in courting extended, at least from the mid-seventeenth century, as high up the social and economic scale as the lower ranks of the gentry.

There were several ways of making a marriage in early modern England. One was both legal and valid, others of questionable legality, others clearly illegal but still valid, and others both illegal and invalid. Based on the medieval canon-law doctrine that mere voluntary consent makes a marriage, a private verbal contract of marriage made in the present tense before two or more credible witnesses could create an indissoluble lifelong marriage. Slowly, over a period of several centuries, however, the church courts increasingly rejected suits for marriage based on verbal contracts, unless they were very securely witnessed, so that in 1640 both contract marriages and suits over contracts had become quite rare. But the collapse of church discipline in the Interregnum between 1640 and 1660 caused a revival of contract marriages, which had to be suppressed all over again after the Restoration in 1660.

In the early seventeenth century there sprang up the practice of clandestine marriages, conducted by clergymen who used the ritual laid down by the *Book of Common Prayer*, but carried out the ceremony without banns or licence, in secret, and often in a private house. Although the officiating clergyman could be tried by an ecclesiastical court and suspended from his functions for three years without pay, the marriages were none the less legally binding, so long as they could be proved by verbal witnesses or written records. By 1700 vigorous efforts by the church courts to punish offenders had done much to reduce the numbers of clergy in the countryside who were willing to perform clandestine marriages. But such marriages flourished more than ever in privileged sanctuaries in London throughout the late seventeenth and the first half of the eighteenth centuries. The most notorious and most popular were the Fleet marriages, carried out after 1710 by parsons operating in the Rules of the Fleet prison. It was not until 1753 that Parliament finally legislated to put a stop to this intolerable abuse, by which time up to one in five of all marriages in England were conducted in this manner. As a result, clandestine marriages loom large in all stories about matrimonial problems in the first half of the eighteenth century.

The third and last mode of marriage was according to canon law, in the church of the parish where one spouse was resident, within canonical hours of 8 a.m. till noon, conducted by a parson, based on banns or a licence, performed before witnesses, and duly entered in the parish register. After 1753 this was the only legal method of marriage, except in Scotland, where contract and clandestine marriages were still perfectly legal.

5. The Methods of Breaking a Marriage

(i) *Desertion and Elopement*

The most obvious method of breaking a marriage, for those with little or no property, was simply to leave home. Some wives were forcibly ejected or locked out by their husbands, and obliged to take refuge with parents or friends. Others felt that they had no alternative but to leave home in order to escape from persistent and even life-threatening cruelty. Among the poor most of this cruelty was merely a product of customary brutality, frustration, and alcohol. But among the propertied classes cruelty was often either pathological—the result of sadism—or else calculated—either to drive the wife out of the house, or else to force her to surrender control over her own property, which increasingly after 1700 was secured to her by a trust deed before marriage. The Turst case provides a dramatic example of the use of cruelty for this purpose. In 1792 one English heiress was cynically reminded that 'women having power over their own property is in general of little avail—they are either kissed or kicked out of it'. This was a gross exaggeration, but some women were indeed induced by 'kicking' to surrender their property rights to their husbands. Some of these brutalized wives left home and sued their husbands in an ecclesiastical court for a legal separation, with alimony, on grounds of adultery and life-threatening cruelty, or sometimes—less successfully—for cruelty alone. If they won, they were assured court-ordered maintenance, enforceable by the Court of Chancery. But a wife in this position lost all contact with her children, and ran the risk that her husband might offer to take her back, and that she would be ordered by the Court to comply. If she refused, the husband was within his legal rights to abduct his wife by force and lock her up, as indeed sometimes happened. By the late eighteenth century Chancery would protect the wife from such forcible abductions, but it could act only if alerted to the wife's predicament.

The options for an unhappily married man were more extensive. For the poor, the simplest was just to abandon his family, to walk out of the house one day and never come back.

(ii) *Wife-Sale*

Among the poor, amicable separations by mutual consent were presumably quite common, but the problem in all these separations was how to cut the legal financial obligations of husband to wife and wife to husband. How could the husband be sure that he might not find himself liable to arrest for debts run up unbeknown to him by his separated wife? How could he be sure that after his death his legal wife would not suddenly reappear and put in a claim for a third of his estate as dower? On the other hand, how could the separated wife prevent her husband from intermittently raiding her home and seizing all her goods and earnings, which by law were still his? Moreover, after about 1700 how could she be certain that, if she started a new household, her ex-husband might not decide to sue her lover for crim. con. and levy crippling damages?

There is evidence of husbands making informal arrangements for the sale of their unwanted wives since as far back as the sixteenth century, and probably long before, but, so far as we can tell, the numbers were small and the success rate low. During the eighteenth and early nineteenth centuries a more formal and public procedure of wife-sale is recorded all over southern England, especially in the West, and has been immortalized by Thomas Hardy in *The Mayor of Casterbridge*. It was, however, rarely employed, and has earned a notoriety that far exceeds its real importance. The fact that whenever it occurred huge crowds collected, and the event was widely reported in the newspapers, is certain proof that it was a relatively unusual occurrence. Only some three hundred or so cases are known and many of these are probably fictitious.

The procedure was set in motion when a man and wife decided to part company, the wife having fallen in love with another man. The problem was how legally to transfer from the husband to the lover all financial responsibility for, and all financial claims upon, the wife. Some poor people— artisans in the eighteenth century and labourers in the early nineteenth— realized that one solution was to obtain maximum publicity from the transfer, and to imitate exactly the procedure of a cattle sale. After the husband, the wife, and her lover had agreed on a nominal price, a ritualized public sale took place. The husband tied a halter around his wife's neck, led her into the cattle market or fair in front of a large crowd, and put her up for auction. The lover duly put in his nominal bid for her, paid his money, and led her away by the halter, often after a friendly drink with the ex-husband in a tavern. These wife-sales were merely a public method of divorce by mutual consent, a development of what had long been customary proced- ure among the poor, that is to extract a bribe from a wife's lover in return for not prosecuting him in the church courts, and thus exposing him to shame and ridicule.

(iii) *Separation by Private Deed*

For those who rejected desertion or wife-sale—and that meant all persons of property and standing—the first option for winding up a failed marriage was by private agreement to separate. The key clauses in all private agree- ments were those by which the husband assured his wife alimony—that is an assured annual allowance for life, which was usually about or rather less than one-third of his net income. In return she indemnified him against any suit by creditors for future debts run up by her, for in common law a wife's debts were the responsibility of her husband. The most important reason for the popularity of the private separation deed in the eighteenth century was that in most cases it came to include three more very important clauses.

As a logical extension of the grant of maintenance by the husband in return for the wife assuming responsibility for any future debts, separation deeds declared that the wife was free to act financially as if she were a single woman, and so have full power to buy and sell property and make contracts. The clause first appears in the early eighteenth century, but it took a long time to gain full acceptance in the common-law courts. But by 1800 it had done so. Thus, once again, legal ingenuity and judicial flexibility had been used to modify existing law and bring it into conformity with changing standards of natural justice long before the statutory laws concerning Married Women's Property were changed in the 1870s.

The second clause was tantamout to granting to the wife (and the husband) full freedom to cohabit, commit adultery, or remarry at will, without running the risk of prosecution by the spouse in any court of law. This was an attempt to bar the husband from launching any suit either in a civil court for crim. con. against his wife's lover, or in an ecclesiastical court for restitution of conjugal rights or for separation for adultery, or in a civil court for the penal offence of bigamy. This clause was not enforceable in any court of law, but, if adhered to by both parties, it provided the equivalent of a full divorce by mutual consent, by tacitly allowing the wife and the husband to live in concubinage, or even in bigamy.

Despite the fact that the clause was unenforceable in law, it is remarkable that it continued to be inserted routinely in separation agreements for 150 years. One can only conclude that in most cases the clause was indeed respected, if only because it paid both parties to do so, so that advantage was rarely taken of the refusal by the courts to enforce it. Private separation agreements containing these two clauses were thus tantamout to collusive agreements to set up new households. They were in practice the equivalent of full divorce by mutual consent.

The third important clause in these private separation agreements concerned child custody. According to the common law, the husband had absolute and inalienable power to dispose of his children as he wished, however disgraceful his own conduct might have been. He was free to take custody of an infant at its mother's breast, and to forbid the mother ever to see her children again, or even to write to them. This remained the legal situation until 1839. In practice, however, attitudes were changing, even if the law was not. Under the influence of Rousseau and others, even upper-class women were beginning to breast-feed their own children, and fathers were beginning to acknowledge that the mother was the best custodian of very small children, up to about 7, and especially of the girls. By the end of the eighteenth century the Court of Chancery was beginning to award custody of the younger children under 7 years to the mother. As a result, separating wives now normally bargained with their husbands to obtain the custody at least of small children. They used the carrot of claims to superior qualifications for looking after small children, and also of willingness to accept a smaller financial settlement in return for custody and access; and the stick of threatening to reveal the husband's own adultery and so put a stop to any separation. As Lady Westmeath found to her cost, however, even in the early nineteenth century a clause in a private separation deed giving her custody of her child was not sufficient to stop her husband from exerting his common-law right to seize custody by force.

We do not know just how many private separations there were among the élite, but it is likely that the numbers were substantial. Many such agreements survive in family archives, but most of them only come to light because they were brought into court after the arrangement had broken down, as in the Boteler, Dineley, or Beaufort cases.

(iv) *Judicial Separation from Bed and Board*

Before 1657 the ecclesiastical courts had sole jurisdiction over the legal break-up of a marriage. According to medieval canon law, the most they could grant was separation from bed and board, with no permission to remarry—a situation which inevitably led to concubinage or bigamy, and the production of bastard children. The sole grounds for such judicial separations were life-threatening cruelty and adultery by the husband, or adultery by the wife. On the other hand, even if a wife were clearly guilty of adultery, her husband would normally be refused separation if she could demonstrate 'recrimination', that is that he was also guilty of the same marital offence.

The Church of England continued to interpret the rather ambiguous words of Christ, as recorded in the Gospels, as meaning that marriage was legally indissoluble. The only exception was if it could be proved to have been invalid in the first place, in which case the ecclesiastical courts could declare it null and void. Apart from such improperly conducted affairs as contract marriages and some clandestine ones, a legally valid marriage could be dissolved only if it was not consummated for two years or more because of impotence or frigidity (which very rarely happened); or if it was

21

incestuous, since the parties were close kin within the prohibited degrees. This usually took the form of a marriage between a man and his deceased wife's sister, or occasionally between an uncle and a niece.

A marriage could also be declared null and void if it was proved bigamous, since one of the parties had a spouse still living. Bigamy seems to have been a quite common occurrence in the period of flourishing clandestine marriages before 1753. It was a penal offence, which meant that a vengeful spouse could bring a suit in the civil court on a charge of felony, as did the Duchess of Cleveland in the Calvert case. Although the punishment was theoretically death, it was a clergyable offence, which meant that anyone who could read had the sentence commuted to burning in the hand. This was a painful but minor punishment, and by the middle of the eighteenth century it was usually done with a cold iron. There is good reason to believe that thousands, perhaps tens of thousands, of marriages in eighteenth-century England were in fact bigamous.

In cases of cruelty and adultery by the husband, the ecclesiastical courts would grant the wife legal separation of bed and board, and provision of generous alimony, as in the Boteler case. But in cases of adultery by the wife, the court would decree legal separation of bed and board, without any alimony, thus leaving the wife penniless.

Between 1660 and 1860 there is a clear trend towards ever greater ingenuity in trickery, perjured evidence, and collusion. After a century of exploiting the ambiguities of the pre-Tridentine marriage system, the guile and ingenuity of suitors, witnesses, lawyers, and clergymen had stretched beyond exploiting the ambiguities in the medieval marriage system to include the wholesale manufacture and manipulation of evidence to prove whatever was needed to void a marriage. Thus a false claim of bigamy could be used to dissolve a marriage (with no maintenance due to offspring illegitimized *ex post facto*); or documents could be forged and witnesses bribed to give false evidence about a fictitious earlier marriage, in order to invalidate the marriage of a former lover;[11] or a victim could be tricked into committing bigamy, by counterfeiting the death of one of the spouses and inveigling the survivor into marrying a second time.

(v) *Crim. Con. Litigation*

In the late seventeenth century there developed at common law a new legal procedure, which as time went on began to achieve considerable notoriety, even if in fact it was fairly rarely employed. This was an action by which a husband sued his wife's lover for damages in one of the major civil courts

---

[11] See *Mordaunt* v. *Mordaunt*, in Stone, *Uncertain Unions*.

in Westminster Hall, King's Bench, or Common Pleas. The action was a writ of trespass, the theory being that, by using the body of the wife, the seducer had damaged the property of her husband, for which he could sue for damages, like any other tort. The second legal principle involved, which had applied since the sixteenth century to breach-of-promise cases, was that the common law was empowered to award financial damages not merely for economic losses but also for emotional pain and suffering.

To distinguish it from the many other actions for trespass, the suit was known as an action for 'criminal conversation'. Both words are misleading, since sexual relations with a married woman were neither criminal nor a conversation. Its origin lay in the practice by a husband of the middling sort, certainly in the seventeenth century and probably earlier, of demanding monetary satisfaction from the lover of his wife by private negotiation and arbitration. What was new about the crim. con. procedure was, first, that it took the form of legal action rather than private blackmail; secondly, that after the mid-eighteenth century it was largely confined to the central courts rather than the local assizes; and, thirdly, that it involved gentlemen and noblemen. These were classes among which the injured husband in the sixteenth and early seventeenth centuries had been accustomed to resorting to murder, open violence, or a challenge to a duel in order to obtain satisfaction for his own honour and his wife's shame. After the late seventeenth century a non-landed kind of property, a monopoly right over the body of one's wife, was transformed into an object with a price-tag, to be paid for by monetary damages publicly awarded in a court of law. The transition took place despite the inevitable notoriety given to the husband's cuckoldry. It is difficult to imagine a clearer sign of a change from an honour-and-shame society to a commercial society than this shift from physical violence against, or challenge to a duel with, one's wife's lover to a suit for monetary damages from him.

There were three possible motives why a plaintiff should launch such a suit. The first was the primitive desire for revenge for a psychologically wounding injury, by financially crippling or even imprisoning the lover: in some cases, especially in the period 1740–1820, the damages awarded were so much beyond the defendant's capacity to pay that the verdict was tantamount to a sentence to life-imprisonment for debt. This motive was very clear in the Middleton, Loveden, and Cadogan cases. The second motive was to raise the money to cover the legal costs of the lengthy litigation involved in either separation or divorce cases at that time. The third motive was to prepare the way for a Parliamentary divorce, the successful prosecution of a crim. con. suit being a preliminary step which had become normal by the 1780s and obligatory in 1798.

The costs of prosecuting a crim. con. suit, especially a contested one, were such as to put it out of reach of any but the landed élite and the upper levels of the middling sort. In consequence the plaintiffs in these suits were all rich men, though the defendants might range from duke to stable boy. The number of cases and the amount of damages both rose sharply in the 1790s, when the whole process was given an additional stimulus by the appointment of Lloyd Kenyon as Lord Chief Justice. Inspired by his own brand of Puritanism, reinforced by the moral panic among the élite aroused by the French Revolution, he urged juries to award damages not merely in reparation to the husband for mental suffering and loss of companionship, but also of sufficient size to set an example to the nation, and act as a deterrent to future adulterers. He thus transformed a civil suit into a semi-criminal one in a manner which was quite illegal. As a result of his influential rhetoric, juries began awarding larger and larger damages running to thousands of pounds. Some awards were for £10,000, £20,000, and even very occasionally £25,000. Damages so far beyond the capacity of the defendant to pay meant, in practice, the condemnation of the latter to a life in prison for debt unless the plaintiff chose to free him.

In a growing number of cases, however, indeed probably a majority, the actions were by now merely collusive. These huge damages were paid by the defendant to the plaintiff, but then secretly returned back to him. This procedure developed, partly due to a growing moral repugnance at taking such tainted money, but mostly as the result of a secret agreement between the plaintiff husband, his wife, and her lover the defendant to win an uncontested crim. con. suit, and to use the victory to obtain an uncontested Parliamentary divorce, thus allowing all three parties to remarry. This was tantamount to a conspiracy for divorce by mutual consent. It was clearly evident in the Grafton case in 1769, and became very common indeed after 1790. This widespread collusion was a clear indication of how far élite opinion had moved in favour of full divorce by 1790, sixty years before there was a serious move towards statutory reform.

Between 1560 and 1860 élite public opinion had undergone three quite startling reversals over the way to treat the seducer of a married woman. In the sixteenth and seventeenth centuries he had been forced by ecclesiastical courts publicly to confess his guilt, clad only in a white smock, and carrying a candle, a penalty based on concepts of shame. At the same time, upper-class ideas of honour justified violent revenge on the seducer, and in the early seventeenth century both personal violence and a challenge to a duel were morally acceptable.

From about 1700 to 1800 it was thought perfectly acceptable to make money out of one's wife's dishonour by a crim. con. suit, even at the cost of publishing one's own cuckoldry. After 1800, however, a reaction set in, as the concept of wifely adultery as a breach of male property rights, so prevalent in the eighteenth century, was replaced by the concept of wifely adultery as a violation of the ideal of Victorian domesticity. A logical consequence of this shift was the abolition of the crim. con. suit in 1857, accompanied by serious talk of making adultery a criminal offence, punishable by imprisonment.

(vi) *Parliamentary Divorce*

In the late seventeenth century there also began a trickle of cases of divorces granted by Parliament, with permission to remarry, an option at first being confined to men with great estates and titles, adulterous wives, and no heirs. Men in this situation were, rather reluctantly, permitted by Parliament to divorce and remarry, in order to beget male heirs to their estates and titles. But even after 1750, when wealthy men without such pressing need to re-marry were allowed to take advantage of this loophole, the numbers never rose above three or four a year, largely because so few could afford the enormous cost. The procedure was so expensive, because it involved three separate lawsuits, one in an ecclesiastical court, for separation from the adulterous wife; one in a common-law court, for damages for crim. con. against the wife's lover; and a private bill before Parliament, for full divorce. Examples of this procedure are provided by the Beaufort, Loveden, and Cadogan cases.

6. Marriage and Property

At every step, not only of entry into marriage but also of exit from it, the way was strewn with issues of property. On her marriage, the family of the bride paid a dowry to the family of the groom, in return for which the latter settled property for the maintenance of the couple (if they had any to settle), and made provision for a jointure, which was a life annuity for the widow if she survived, usually assured by settlement of property. On marriage, the husband gained possession of all the wife's personal property, and control over as much of her real property as had not been previously put in the hands of trustees for her own exclusive use. He could do what he liked with the personal estate, including furniture, jewels, and money, and could enjoy the income of the real estate.

He could use any or all of this property to pay off his own debts, but at marriage he also became liable for all his wife's debts run up before or during marriage. This issue of debt loomed very large indeed in eighteenth-century English life, since the society increasingly depended on credit, and since the ultimate penalty for non-payment was arrest and indefinite imprisonment. It is hardly surprising, therefore, that there are many cases of men marrying women merely in order to seize their property and use it to pay their own debts. On the other hand, some women could play the same game.

7. Marriage and Moral Values

The most striking feature of married life in eighteenth-century England was the theoretical, legal, and practical subordination of wives to their husbands, epitomized in the concept of patriarchy. It was a domination mitigated only by the skilful resistance of many wives, and the compassion and goodwill of many husbands. Even worse than the condition of the unhappily married, however, was the lot of those women who were separated or divorced. They automatically lost all contact whatsoever with their children, unless their husbands were willing to allow it, and they were also financially reduced to very small allowances, even if they were innocent parties.

Another feature of the age is the near-total absence of privacy in domestic life. Servants and neighbours were everywhere, and prying eyes and listening ears were constantly on the watch for any hint of marital discord or disorder. Concepts of privacy and individualism were certainly developing during the eighteenth century, but the areas of physical and emotional space they had conquered by 1800 were severely limited by the constant presence of inquisitive servants, and the age-old tradition of neighbourly surveillance and gossip. It was a world far removed from the isolated, detached, servantless, nuclear home of the late twentieth century.

All stories of female adultery in high society prove that it was virtually impossible for persons surrounded day and night by servants who waited on them hand and foot to conduct a love-affair without it becoming known below stairs. Indoors, the servants were constantly coming into the rooms to carry out some chore, while outdoors a lord or lady was never unaccompanied by at least a groom, or a footman, or a lady's maid. The only hope of any degree of secrecy was reliance upon the absolute discretion of one or two personal servants, but this loyalty needed careful cultivation if it was not to end in blackmail and possible betrayal. The lovers were more-or-less safe only if the woman had long ago taken the precaution of seeking the friendship of these servants, by the daily exchange of banter, and confidences, and a generous flow of gifts of clothes and other marks of appreciation. Contrast the warm relations with her servants of Mrs Middleton in the Middleton case, with the haughty indifference exhibited in the

Beaufort case by the Duchess in her dealings with the many servants of one sort of another who were involved in covering up the birth of her and Lord Talbot's baby. The same distancing is true of Mrs Loveden in the Loveden case, who could not even rely on the support of her own lady's maid.

If no such bond had been formed before the love-affair started, if she found herself under threat of denunciation, the lady inevitably resorted to lavish bribes, often as much as a year's wages, in return for promises of silence. But this rarely worked for long. The servant either turned to blackmail and demanded more and more money in return for his or her silence, or else betrayed the secret to the husband in expectation of even greater rewards.

Apart from the failure to cultivate the loyalty of the domestic servants, the other cause why so many adulterous wives were found out in the eighteenth century was the lack of care they exercised to obliterate traces of sexual intercourse. Unaccustomed to lifting a finger to help themselves, they could not be bothered to plump up and remake or turn over the feather beds, so as to remove the tell-tale depressions left by the weight of two bodies. When intercourse took place outside the bedroom, as it usually did, dining-room chairs placed together to form a bed were not replaced. When it took place on a sofa or the carpet, dirt from muddy boots, hair-powder, or stains of sperm were left to be found by the servants. There was a constant underestimation of the cunning and curiosity of the servants which, again and again, was to cost the lovers dearly in the end. On the other hand, in cases of brutal cruelty by a husband to his wife, the servants —especially the female servants—usually interposed themselves between the couple and comforted and succoured the victim, though never to the extent of stopping the treatment altogether. Striking examples are provided by the Boteler and Dineley cases. By the end of the eighteenth century, when a marriage began to show signs of breaking up, some servants went so far as to take upon themselves the role of counsellor. They would try to prevent the dissolution of the household, which was likely to be disbanded if the marriage fell apart, thereby putting the servants out of work. Such behaviour, which illustrates most vividly the close interdependence of masters and servants, can be observed in both the Middleton and the Loveden cases.

Finally it should be noted that, in the period between about 1680 and 1710, the country, both high and low, seems to have lost its moral moorings. Story after story, whether about the making or the breaking of marriage, provide evidence of an abnormally cynical, mercenary, and predatory ruthlessness about human relationships, which is deeply offensive to modern sensibilities. The same traits are visible in the plays of Shadwell and the novels of Defoe, and are well displayed in the 1982 film, *The Draughtsman's Contract*. The explanation for this moral collapse is obscure, but there cannot be much doubt about its reality.

This moral breakdown did not go unnoticed by contemporaries. Monarchs, from Charles II to Anne, saw fit to issue Proclamations denouncing the spread of vice; in about 1700 a fierce attack was made upon the obscenity and amoral cynicism of the theatre; at the same time the newly founded Society for the Reformation of Manners undertook to identify and prosecute sabbath-breakers, prostitutes, and other moral backsliders. Except for the attack on the stage, none of these efforts had much long-term effect.

More significant is the sense of moral decay displayed in the popular literature of the age, especially in Mary de la Rivière Manley's *New Atlantis* of 1714–20, and Mrs Haywood's *Memoirs of a Certain Island* of 1725–6, both of which were bestsellers.

The first was a veiled attack on the Whigs as the prime exponents of male aristocratic debauchery, based on a philosophy of atheism or epicureanism, and an obsession with money, lust, and personal advancement. Virtue is made to lament that

Innocence is banished by the first dawn of early knowledge. Sensual corruptions and hasty enjoyments affright me from their habitation. . . . By a diabolical way of argument they prove the body is only necessary to the pleasures of enjoyment; that love lies not in the heart but in the face . . . Hymen no longer officiates at their marriages . . . Interest is deputed in his room, he presides over the feast, he joins their hands.

Virtue goes on to lament that 'avarice, contemptible covetousness, sordid desire for gain . . . have quite extinguished the very glimmerings of [love]'.[12]

These popular writers saw moral collapse as taking place in two stages: first came the unbridled libertinism of the Court of Charles II, a relatively innocent sexual promiscuity for the sake of physical pleasure. This hedonism was said to include homosexuality, so that 'man with man, woman with woman sins'. Secondly, after about 1690, the pleasure principle was over-ridden by an overpowering lust for money and power, which turned sexuality into a mere instrument for self-advancement. As a Countess advised a young woman: 'The first thing a woman ought to consult was her interest, and establishment in the world; that love should be a handle towards it.'[13] This involves so much dissimulation that 'these are not times when the

[12] M. de la Rivière Manley, *New Atlantis* (London, 1714–20), i. 2–4; cited in J. J. Richetti, *Popular Fiction before Richardson: Narrative Patterns, 1700–39* (Oxford, 1969), 133–4.
[13] De la Rivière Manley, *New Atlantis*, i. 73, 53.

heart and the tongue do agree'.[14] Thus the world as seen by these popular writers of the early years of the eighteenth century was a bleak one, dominated by avarice, lust, and duplicity. This is exactly the same world as is revealed in the Calvert case.

[14] E. Haywood, *Memoirs of a Certain Island* (London, 1725–6), i. 155–6; cited in Richetti, *Popular Fiction*, 143, 146, 156.

II
Case-Studies

I

Boteler v. Boteler
The battered wife, 1656–1675

The story of Lady Anne Boteler provides a good example of how much a woman was prepared to endure in the late seventeenth century before seeking to separate from her husband.[1] The daughter of Sir Robert Austen, a Kentish baronet, in 1656 she made what at the time would have been thought of as a very good marriage to Sir Oliver Boteler, the heir to another and rather richer baronet family of Kent. Both families had been Royalist, and Sir Oliver's father had been killed fighting in the Civil War. The marriage was thus an alliance between two prominent Royalist families in the largely Parliamentarian county of Kent.

Anne's marriage portion was £5,000, and her jointure after her husband's death assured by the Botelers was set at £650 a year. Lady Anne claimed that Sir Oliver's gross income was over £3,000 a year, while Sir Oliver put it at £2,100, exclusive of fines, goods, and debts due. Since the latter statement was made on oath, it is likely to be more-or-less correct.

Like so many wealthy squires at that time, the Botelers did not own a town house in London, and when, in 1664, they moved permanently from their Kentish seat into the metropolis, they rented lodgings in the still fashionable area of Bloomsbury. There they stayed for the next seven years, except for a nine-month gap during the Great Plague, when they fled back to Kent. It was during these seven years that relations between Sir Oliver and Anne deteriorated to a point that eventually he came positively to hate her. At the same time he was still sleeping with her sufficiently often to keep her almost constantly pregnant, and she gave birth to nine children in sixteen years, only four of whom are recorded as reaching adolescence. The reasons for Sir Oliver's hatred of his wife are obscure. She made no attempt to explain it, while he claimed that it was because, when he quarrelled with her mother and other relatives, she took their side, 'contrary to her duty' to obey and support him under all circumstances. Quarrels with in-laws were indeed a very common cause of marital friction, especially at a period when kin ties were very powerful. But his

---

[1] LPCA, D.206 (unpaginated).

own mother and stepfather sided with Anne against him in the estrangement between them, and it seems unlikely that the real cause of the trouble was a quarrel with *her* relatives. Sir Oliver also claimed that Anne behaved 'disrespectfully' towards him, but he gave no examples.

Marital cruelty occurred intermittently, but with an increasing degree of seriousness, from 1664 to 1671. It took several forms, both physical and mental, and involved attacks not only upon Anne but upon her children. In the first place, Sir Oliver attacked her physically in all the usual ways. He kicked her out of bed and left her shivering in the cold; he turned her out of the house in the early hours of the morning; he repeatedly beat and kicked her, often on the breast, or the belly when she was pregnant; once he punched her in the face, giving her a black eye. He twice threw a chamber-pot at her, and once a chair. Once he dragged her by her smock along the ground about the house, and several times he threatened her with his sword.

All this brutal behaviour was partly a product of alcohol, carried out after returning home drunk, and partly a product of a naturally hair-trigger temper. The servants advised Anne never to argue with her husband, 'because of his aptness to fall into a rage'.

Anne complained that he treated her in 'a rigid, harsh and cruel manner', and that all the servants knew about his 'very fierce and angry nature', so much so that they hid all the knives and swords whenever he came home drunk. The servants did indeed give evidence supporting everything of which she accused him, whereas he was unable to get a single one of them to testify on his behalf.

But these frequent physical assaults were only part of what Sir Oliver admitted to be a campaign to wear her down and drive her to suicide by systematic cruelty. He once told her: 'I hate you the more because you love me so well, and I will never leave till I have broke your heart.' A large part of his tactics therefore took the form of mental cruelty. He treated her more like a servant than a wife and forced her to perform such menial chores as pulling off his boots and fetching him a chamber-pot. Once in 1666 he discharged her maid, the nursemaid, and all her attendants while she was pregnant, thus forcing her to dress herself and the children—an unheard-of duty for a woman of her position. Many times over several years he made her sit up all night and watch over him, although he was quite well and she far gone with child. Once he called her out of her closet and made her lie face down on the floor, saying: 'You are my domestic servant, and I will make you as humble as a spaniel.' All this insulting treatment was accompanied by a constant running barrage of verbal abuse: he called her 'whore', 'vile and base woman', 'base damned woman', 'jade', 'damned woman', and so on. The recurrence of the adjective 'base' seems to refer to the fact that Anne's parentage was not quite as grand as that of the Botelers.

Other forms of torment were more refined. Once he threw the meat in the fire in a rage, as a way of complaining about her housekeeping. Once he beat her since she refused to drink a glass of wine—apparently she did not touch alcohol. When she took refuge from her misery in the comforts of religion, he became still more enraged. She spent much time reading the popular devotional tract *The Whole Duty of Man*, until one day he seized and burnt it. He was always angry when she retired to her closet to say her prayers; or alternatively he forced her to pray in his presence and then mocked her, saying: 'I hate a wife that says her prayers.'

But this is not the end of the list of her torments. Sir Oliver's favourite tactic from 1667 onwards was to threaten to beat, or actually severely to beat, the surviving children, the older boy, Philip, the 7-year-old Elizabeth, and even the 2-year-old John. He several times told her: 'I wish that you and the children were all dead.' Once he threatened to drop Elizabeth down the stairwell, but instead beat her so severely that she was unable to sit or stand for several days. He also beat the 2-year-old John, telling him: 'I do this to be revenged of that base woman your mother, and I have no other way to break her heart but this.' When in 1667 Anne miscarried because of his ill-treatment, he said he was glad of it, and later told her: 'I hate you and anything that comes of you.' Once in a rage he said he wished 'the child you are pregnant with may be a rat'. Finally he threatened to kill both the new infant and the child Elizabeth, which so terrified the nursemaid that she fled with them to the house of his own mother, Lady Warwick.

Sir Oliver's final refinement of cruelty to Anne through her children was to terrorize them into abusing her. In 1669 he made the 7-year-old Elizabeth strike her mother on the stomach while she was pregnant, and made little John say he hated his mother under threat of whipping him if he said he loved her. He also taught them both to spit in their mother's face.

Sir Oliver's final way of tormenting his wife Anne was through sex. Her constant condition of pregnancy proves that she performed her wifely duties punctually, but this was not enough for Sir Oliver. Once he ordered her to watch as an apothecary inserted a glyster into his anus. When she refused, he was furious with her and forced her to apologize to him on her knees. On another occasion he stripped himself naked and ordered her to come to him in the presence of his manservant, which again she refused out of modesty. Finally, in 1670, according to her unsupported testimony, he ordered her to have intercourse with him in the presence of his male servants, which she also refused.

Meanwhile, Sir Oliver had been consorting with 'several lewd and debauched women and whores', a fact of which he boasted both to Anne and to his doctor. According to the latter, it was early in 1665 that Sir Oliver first contracted 'a violent and pocky gonorrhoea'. The doctor treated him for it for two years, and then gave up, since his 'disorderly and debauched life' was constantly causing him to be reinfected and so nullifying the effect of the medicine. But it was not until May 1668 that the inevitable happened, and Anne began to manifest symptoms of infection, passed on by him.

The crisis in the marriage came in 1670. Anne went off to Tonbridge to complete her cure for the gonorrhoea, and while she was away Sir Oliver again became reinfected. He complained crossly to his doctor that it was impossible for this to be so, since he and another man had used the same woman on the same occasion and only he had become infected. Anne knew nothing of this, and on her return from Tonbridge she allowed him to sleep with her again, and once more was reinfected. The result was a violent row at the dinner-table, as Sir Oliver and Anne exchanged accusations of giving each other the pox. When she accused him, he replied: 'Damn me, then we will part beds,' and swore never to sleep with her again. He worked himself up into a tremendous rage, threatened to disinherit her children and settle the Boteler estate on a chambermaid's bastard (presumably one of his making), struck her about the face, and knocked her down. He would have continued the attack, but was pulled away from her by the servants. He announced: 'I will lock you in a dark hole and feed you with bread and water,' upon which Anne fled to the house of her mother-in-law—Sir Oliver's mother, Lady Warwick, who was already taking care of the children.

But Sir Oliver asked her to return home, promising to treat her kindly in future, and she was rash enough to give him one last chance. The moment she set foot inside the house, however, he locked her in a room without fire or food, and told her darkly that: 'I will do your business with a bodkin or a needle and will not be hanged for you'—in other words that he would murder her without leaving a mark on her body. Anne somehow escaped—probably released by the servants—and returned to the safety of the house of Lady Warwick.

At this point Sir Oliver's stepfather, the Royalist administrator and politician Sir Philip Warwick, stepped in and arranged for a private separation. Sir Oliver signed a deed promising to pay Lady Anne £300 a year, settled on two trustees, one of whom was Sir Philip.[2] Even this, however, did not bring peace, since in 1672 there occurred the death of Lady Warwick, who had been giving shelter to Anne and her children. Sir Oliver thereupon

[2] *Eng. Rep.* 23: 39.

tried to repossess his wife, by suing for restitution of conjugal rights from the London Consistory Court. To defend herself from this threat, Lady Anne countersued for separation with alimony on grounds of cruelty. She won the case for separation, but appealed the sentence about the size of the alimony up to the Court of Arches. She told the judges that she refused to return to her husband, not only because of long-time cruelty but also because of his recent threats 'to kill her or to beat out her brains, if he could get her again'. The case dragged on and it was not until 1675 that Anne at last won her suit and the court ordered an official separation of Sir Oliver and Lady Anne, on grounds of cruelty, with provision of adequate alimony.[3]

But this victory did nothing to solve the financial problem of enforcing the separation agreement of 1670. While the case was still in progress in the ecclesiastical courts, the trustees of the separation agreement, Sir Christopher Turner and Sir Philip Warwick, were suing Sir Oliver in Chancery on four counts: for his refusal to fulfil the agreement to pay Anne the £300 a year; for non-payment of £300 in legal costs; for future payment of the £300 a year; and for a further allowance for the maintenance of her daughter. Chancery appointed two eminent arbitrators, Lord Shaftesbury and Sir William Coventry, who agreed on the following terms: Sir Oliver was to pay all the arrears of the £300 allowance to Lady Anne, and to pay it regularly in future. He was also to pay £80 a year to maintain his daughter, who until her marriage should remain in the custody of her mother and be educated by her. Sir Oliver should accept the sentence of separation in the ecclesiastical courts, and pay the scheduled costs. In return, the trustees promised to give bonds that Lady Anne would not appeal the case up to the Court of Delegates for an increase in her alimony, and that Sir Oliver would cease harrassing Lady Anne in her person, and would not try to seize any goods she might acquire in the future.[4]

There is nothing uncommon about the cruelty in the case, even the details of which figure with sickening regularity in other court records. What is so striking is that, even in so clear-cut a case, with overwhelming evidence of life-threatening abuse, with no defence witnesses, and with even his relatives siding against the husband, it still took the ecclesiastical courts some three years to decree a separation with adequate alimony. The legal breaking of a marriage on grounds of cruelty was not easy in late seventeenth-century England, however extreme the circumstances.

[3] LPCA, Ee.3, fos. 738, 745; Eee. 4, fos. 613–15, 807–8, 816–17, 821, 850–9; B.8/183(1).
[4] *Eng. Rep.* 23: 39.

2

Blood v. *Blood*
Separation for cruelty, 1686–1704

Of all the implausible adventurers thrown up by the English Revolution, there is none to equal Colonel Thomas Blood. The son of a rich Irish blacksmith, he allegedly first became a Royalist, and rose to the rank of captain 'in the old king's army'. In about 1650 he switched sides, wormed his way into the favour of Henry Cromwell, then the military commander of the Parliamentary forces in Ireland, rose to the rank of lieutenant, and after the conquest received large grants of confiscated Irish estates. But he lost all these ill-gotten gains in 1660, and thereafter became a professional conspirator against the Restoration monarchy, being apparently a devout Calvinist.

In 1663 he plotted to seize Dublin Castle and the Lord-Lieutenant, the Duke of Ormonde, but he was betrayed, and was obliged to flee to Holland. In the late 1660s Blood seems to have become a government agent, or perhaps a double spy. Arlington hired him to try to lure the regicide Edmund Ludlow out of his safe retreat in Switzerland, so that he could be kidnapped, shipped to England, and executed, a project which failed. At about the same time, he carried out a daring rescue of an imprisoned radical dissenter, so he was working actively for both sides. His private diary is full of moral precepts for a virtuous life, and declarations of his faith in providence to look after him.

After various adventures, in 1670 he and his highwayman son Thomas waylaid and abducted his old enemy the Duke of Ormonde in St James's Street, London, his plan being to hang the victim publicly at Tyburn. The abduction, for which he was rumoured to have been hired by the 2nd Duke of Buckingham to satisfy a personal vendetta, was bungled by his associates while Blood—who by now was calling himself Colonel—was riding ahead to Tyburn to prepare the rope; as a result Ormonde escaped with his life. Next year Colonel Blood attempted his most famous coup of all, an almost successful attempt to steal the Crown Jewels from the Tower of London. He nearly killed a guard in the process, but, when captured, demanded and obtained a personal interview with Charles II. Once in the royal presence, he either captivated the King with his astonishing stories, or more likely convinced him of the valuable services he could render to the Crown by keeping a close eye on his radical religious friends, some of whom were suspected of conspiring to assassinate the King. As a result of the interview, he was freed and allegedly restored to his Irish estates of £500 a year.

For the next few years he lived a raffish life in London, a friend and client of the debauched Duke of Buckingham. Eventually, however, he joined in yet another plot, this time to ruin the reputation and career of his old patron the Duke of Buckingham. He was said to have bribed witnesses to accuse the Duke of sodomy, and as a result was imprisoned for several months. The imprisonment broke his health, and he died soon after release, while being sued by the Duke for £10,000 damages for defamation.[1]

Colonel Blood's eldest son, Holcroft Blood, clearly inherited some of his father's talents for landing on his feet. For obvious reasons the boy found it prudent to conceal his ancestry, and in 1672 at the age of 12 he enlisted in the Navy in order to fight in the third Dutch War. Later, under the false name of Leture, he drifted into the French army, where he stayed for seven years and studied engineering. In the 1680s he returned to his native Ireland, where he served as a mere foot-soldier, apparently now under his own name.

After about five years of this, he came back to London, where in 1686 he met and courted a widow, Elizabeth Fowler, the daughter of a barrister called Richard King. Although Elizabeth was still a Catholic and her brother a Catholic priest, whereas Blood was the son of a former Parliamentarian dissenter, they none the less were married in St Pancras Church by the rites of the Church of England. Holcroft had no property (his father's Irish estates seem to have been lost) and no prospects, and Elizabeth brought nothing to the marriage either. They were a penniless pair. She did, however, have influential contacts, that essential ingredient for getting on in the early modern world.

At first Holcroft lived off Elizabeth, but he soon obtained a part-time job 'to draw draughts in the Tower', thus using and displaying his engineering talents. Then came the Glorious Revolution of 1688 and one of his wife's first cousins, Richard Biddulph, became very influential with the new King William III. It was Biddulph who got Holcroft his start, by arranging for his appointment as Captain of the Pioneers under Lord Dartmouth, the Master of the Ordnance. During the next fifteen years Holcroft distinguished himself in siege after siege, at Carrickfergus, Namur, Hochstadt,

[1] A. Marshall, 'Colonel Thomas Blood and the Restoration Political Scene', *Historical Journal*, 32 (1989); *DNB*, s.n. Thomas Blood; W. C. Abbot, *Colonel Thomas Blood: Crown Stealer* (London, 1911).

and elsewhere, rose to be Colonel of the Regiment of the Train of Artillery, and gained a reputation as one of the best military engineers in Europe.[2]

In 1693, however, he was accused of robbing the post-boy of the mails. He was imprisoned in Winchester Castle, where Elizabeth joined him, but he was acquitted when brought to trial at the Old Bailey. William III was both convinced of his innocence and impressed by his technical abilities, and the main result of the episode was rapid promotion to Major and then to Lieutenant-Colonel.[3]

In the 1690s Holcroft's public career as a military engineer was a dazzling success, but his private life was becoming quietly unravelled. His wife Elizabeth proved to be a very difficult woman to live with. One of her mother's servants, who had known her since childhood, described her as 'of an unquiet, discontented and unsatisfied temper, and seldom pleased, subject to jealousy and sometimes whimsical'. Holcroft later denounced her as 'a woman of a perverse, froward, peevish and ill-natured, passionate disposition, jealous and whimsical, much addicted to be angry'.[4]

On the other hand, she certainly had a good deal to be discontented about, especially her husband's sexual infidelities. One of the chief witnesses for his defence in his trial for robbing of the mails was a Mrs Mary Andrews, the wife of Robert Andrews of London. The two families were friends at the time of the trial, and afterwards Mrs Andrews became a regular overnight visitor to the house—and also Holcroft's mistress. Elizabeth complained that her husband would get out of her bed at three, four, or five o'clock in the morning, go into Mary's room, and stay there behind locked doors for anything from three to six hours at a time. On other occasions all three went to bed together, and Elizabeth got up and left the couple to it, later excusing her action on the obscure grounds, first that she had no option and, secondly, that she 'knew Mrs Andrews to be an old whore and fit for Holcroft's purpose'.[5]

By 1696 she became suspicious that Holcroft was planning to get rid of her by poison in order to be more free to cohabit with Mary Andrews. She searched his pockets and found some mercury wrapped up in a cloth, which an apothecary told her was 'rank poison'. She told Holcroft's great crony Captain Pittman of her suspicions. According to her, when Pittman remarked to Holcroft that he assumed he was planning to poison her little dog, he replied, 'No, God damn me, the poor homeless dog had not deserved it; it was for the bitch herself.' It seems likely that this whole episode was a product of Elizabeth's vivid imagination, and, if Holcroft

---

[2] *DNB*, s.n. Holcroft Blood; LPCA, D.187: 272, 303–6.
[3] LPCA, D.187: 369–70.   [4] Ibid. 224, 226.   [5] Ibid. 66, 309, 320.

did have any mercury in his pocket, it was probably to treat himself for venereal disease.

Thereafter, things went from bad to worse. Holcroft twice abandoned Elizabeth at their lodgings, leaving her to eat her 8*d.* meals alone, while he 'sat with his doxy Mrs Andrews abroad'. Matters did not come to a head, however, until 1699–1700, when she and Holcroft, by then Colonel of the Train of Artillery, were living in a rented house in Hornsey. Holcroft was still regularly visited by Mary Andrews, but, according to Elizabeth, his eye was turning to other women. He told his wife frankly that he 'had a mind to debauch or lie with Dorothy Green', the daughter of a nearby victualler. He sent for Dorothy to stay the night and sleep in the same bed as Elizabeth, who took the precaution of telling the young girl of what was planned for her, and warning her that, if Mary Andrews got to hear of it, she would publish it to the world. As for herself, she professed that 'she did not care if Holcroft lay with all the women in Highgate and Hornsey'.

A few nights afterwards Holcroft came in his shirt at midnight to the bed where Elizabeth and Dorothy were sleeping, and tried to ravish the latter, who fought him off, 'begging mercy for her soul at the point of death'. When Holcroft later reproached Elizabeth for encouraging Dorothy to thwart him, she replied: 'I think it a very wicked thing for me to consent or be privy to my husband lying with another woman while I am in bed with him, whatever you may do unknown to me which I cannot prevent.'[6] Three in a bed was not uncommon in the early eighteenth century, even though Elizabeth's attitude seems to have been the conventional one.

That Christmas Elizabeth fell extremely ill, a condition she blamed on a clumsy attempt by her husband to poison her, so far as can be seen an accusation entirely without justification. Soon after she had recovered, there was a fresh row, this time over her habit of reading the Bible. Holcroft exploded: 'God damn me, if ever you read more in that book, I will burn it. It is not a book fit for you, for you have a goose's skull.' To which Elizabeth retorted (according to her): 'If I had not applied myself to reading, the treatment I have received from you had made me mad.' Holcroft then launched into his usual flow of abuse, calling her 'bitch' and 'whore'. This was the sort of episode (if it occurred) that led Elizabeth to describe Holcroft as 'more like Nero than a husband'. Soon after a fairly violent episode of marital rape in May 1700, Elizabeth, who was evidently a woman of spirit and resource, left the house and withdrew to London, taking with her a good deal of the family plate, pictures, hangings, medals, linen, and other goods.[7]

---

[6] Ibid. 312–19.   [7] Ibid. 330–8, 139, 146–8, 206, 271, 274, 291, 343, 356.

Case-Studies

It has to be remembered that by now Holcroft was quite a wealthy man. Estimates of his net income vary, but there is general agreement on the gross. He was a pluralist, holding four offices. He was Second Engineer at the Tower of London, at a gross salary of £250 a year, or £200 net of tax and deductions, an office which he lost on the accession of Queen Anne. Secondly, he was Lieutenant-Colonel of a Regiment of Foot (and also Captain). This carried with it a salary of £356 a year, but he claimed that he received only £200 a year, after deduction of agent's fees and poundage for the maintenance of hospitals. Thirdly, he was Colonel (soon to be Brigadier-General) of the Train of Artillery in Flanders, on active duty as soon as war broke out again in 1702. This brought him in £456 a year gross, and an alleged £400 a year more in perquisites. Fourthly, he was Engineer General to the Army at a gross salary of £780 a year. In addition, while travelling he drew a personal allowance of £1 a day, and while on campaigns an extra 2s. a day each for four servants.

His wife claimed that his gross income from all his offices (during wartime) came to £2,400, and his expenses to £300–£400. This seems to be a fairly accurate estimate of his gross income, but he claimed that his expenses, in order to live in the style expected of him, absorbed between £800 and £1,000 a year. This included agency fees for payment of salary, poundage for maintenance of hospitals, the cost of subsistence and entertainment in the field abroad, and maintenance for five guards and twelve horses, as well as for himself and a personal servant. Other witnesses, however, challenged these claims to expenses, saying that he kept only two French servants and four horses, and was too mean to keep a public table for the entertainment of brother officers.[8]

After a series of estrangements, returns, and elopements during the spring and summer of 1700, on 11 October Holcroft decided to try to effect a reconciliation with his wife. Since he did not know where she was living, he called on a friend of hers, Jane Loggin, a tailor's wife, to ask her to fetch Elizabeth. The latter, however, was so suspicious that she left her gold watch behind before going to the meeting, 'for fear her husband would take it away', as he was legally entitled to do. Knowing Elizabeth's temper, Mrs Loggin warned her 'not to fall into a passion when she came to him', since he wanted to make peace.

Holcroft began the discussion by asking Elizabeth: 'Is it not time to come home? Have you not done rambling yet?' Elizabeth retorted sullenly: 'I do not ramble without a just cause.' Mrs Loggin urged them to withdraw to the next room 'and not be in a passion together, but sit down and argue

[8] Ibid. 75–7, 100–1, 174–7, 213–16, 235–6, 239, 262–3, 289, 412, 478; Eee.9/10, 11.

the matter between you civilly'. She then went off to the kitchen to prepare the dinner. For a description of what happened next, we have to rely on a patchwork composed of the often contradictory testimony of Elizabeth and Holcroft. He asked her to come home, but she refused unless he gave security to keep the peace and not abuse her. She then began cursing him, dragging up the Mary Andrews affair and describing her as Holcroft's whore. Working herself up, she began calling him 'rascal', 'rogue', and 'dog'. Provoked by these epithets, Holcroft completely lost his temper and began hitting her on the face and nose. Elizabeth screamed 'Murder!', Mrs Loggin and others rushed into the room, and a large crowd gathered in the street outside.

Mrs Loggin found Elizabeth with her nose streaming blood down into her mouth. She was spitting the blood directly into her husband's face and over his cravat, crying loudly and calling him names. Holcroft told her to hold her tongue and come home with him, but she said she dared not, for he would murder her. Holcroft then gave her a great blow across the ear which knocked her down. By now there was quite a crowd in the room, including a constable who had been summoned to the scene by a neighbour. Elizabeth demanded that Holcroft be taken immediately before a Justice of the Peace, so that she could swear a charge of assault against him. Holcroft flatly refused to go along, declaring, 'I am Justice of the Peace over my own wife,' an assertion of husbandly authority that, in view of his elevated position as a colonel and a gentleman, the constable did not have the courage to contradict. The meeting then broke up in confusion, and Holcroft departed alone.[9]

A day or two later Elizabeth went before Justice Thomas Boteler, told her story of the public assault, and 'swore the peace against Holcroft her husband and Mary Andrews', asking for warrants to be issued to bring them both before the Justice for physical assault and adultery in her own house and bed. The Justice and his wife later testified that 'both sides of her jaw (were) black and blue, from the lower part of her forehead almost to her mouth, her eyes black and swelled, and she had clods of blood in one of her ears'. Even so, Justice Boteler had a proper respect for social proprieties and was unwilling to issue the warrants before first talking to Holcroft's brother Charles, who was a barrister and a friend of his. He warned Elizabeth that 'the Colonel will not suffer such a matter to come before the Sessions'. He was right. He ran into Charles Blood soon afterwards in the Whitehall Coffee House near Charing Cross, and told him that Elizabeth had sworn the peace against his brother Holcroft. The latter, however, had already

---

[9] Ibid. D.187: 95–7, 152–3, 158–64, 170, 197–8, 202–3, 260, 278.

taken action, and Charles pulled out of his pocket two writs of *supersedeas*, signed by another JP, a military captain and friend of Holcroft. This blocked the warrants, the justification being that Holcroft and Mary Andrews had given bonds to appear before the Quarter Sessions when summoned. In fact, however, when Boteler searched the court records, he found that there were no such bonds on file. Holcroft had used legal trickery, friendship, and pulling rank to protect himself from court proceedings.[10]

Even so, Holcroft was still not quite certain of his position, and a few weeks later he visited Justice Boteler and told him that, if his wife did not drop the suit, he would indict her for bestiality, namely 'lying with a horse and a dog', alleging that his friend Captain Pittman, JP, would testify to it (a matter of which Pittman later denied all knowledge). Elizabeth confirmed that Holcroft had threatened her that, if she would not quietly agree to his plans for a formal separation, 'he would get people to swear she had lain with a dog and a horse'.[11]

Holcroft certainly had his own grievances against Elizabeth. She had gone off with large quantities of his household goods, to much of which she had no right at all; she had tried to disgrace him by leaving in a meat-cart and by planning to sell eggs at a market stall in order to expose to the world his alleged meanness and ill-treatment of her; and, worst of all, she was running up large debts, as a result of which he was in danger of being arrested by one of her creditors, egged on by her.

He therefore offered her a variety of options, in order once and for all to settle the matter before he left for the coming campaign in Flanders. He began by warning her that he had settled all his personal estate out of her reach by acknowledging a fictitious debt to a friend of £2,600. His language, if Elizabeth is to be believed, was nothing if not frank.

By the laws of this land I am obliged to maintain you—not that I value you any more than the next bitch in the street. I have acknowledged a judgment of six and twenty hundred pounds. The rest is yours, if you know where to find it, not that I owe anything, you know; it is but to trick the law. There is a house, but God damn me if I ever took it for you. And no longer than Mrs Andrews can be easy can you have one over your head.[12]

In other words, it was useless for Elizabeth to sue him for maintenance, since he had conveyed all his movable property out of her reach; while, if she sued Mrs Andrews for fornication, he would leave her homeless.

The options Holcroft offered her were as follows: first, she could retire to a nunnery in France, accompanied by her brother the priest, which she

[10] Ibid. 98–9, 133, 141–8.   [11] Ibid. 136–7, 145, 261, 360, 383.
[12] Ibid. 347–8.

refused on the grounds that she had not been a Catholic since 1687 and had no desire to become one again. Alternatively, she could retire into the country on a small annuity of £30–£40 a year. Elizabeth wavered for a while, but finally refused the offer over a trivial detail, namely whether Holcroft would give her her side-saddle. This he was unable to do since he could not find it, but Elizabeth believed that he had given it to Mary Andrews.

The third option, which he forcefully pressed upon her, was to get the marriage annulled by the ecclesiastical courts, by colluding with him to bribe witnesses to swear falsely that one of them had been bound by a pre-contract, and that the marriage was therefore bigamous. In return he offered to pay all her debts, £400 in cash, and a life annuity of 16*s.* a week. He said he would 'find out the persons that were to swear what that court required where these proceedings were to be made'. Elizabeth rejected this risky, and wholly illegal proposal, and instead offered to accept a private separation which would give her £500, in return for security not to run him into debt nor ever lay claim to anything he possessed. But he refused this proposal, the negotiations thus collapsed, and he left for Flanders with the matter still up in the air.[13]

While he was away, Elizabeth lodged with her friends Justice and Mrs Boteler. She continued to run up debts both for maintenance and for sheer extravagance, and the moment Holcroft returned to England she arranged to have him arrested for a debt to her milliner for £23. She told the bailiff exactly where to find him, and exulted that 'I have just got the rogue and caused him to be taken up'. She chose her creditor badly, however, since it was easy to show that her expenditures had been grossly extravagant, and not merely for necessities, and at a trial in the Guildhall Chief Justice Holt non-suited the plaintiff.

Elizabeth was not to be put off by this set-back, and in 1702 she launched a suit in the Consistory Court of London for separation with alimony on grounds of cruelty and adultery. While the suit was in progress, the Court, as usual, awarded her a comfortable maintenance allowance from her husband of £60 a year, while she was secure in the knowledge that he would also be held responsible by the Court for her taxed legal costs. Her accusations, however, were mostly both wild and unsupported by any evidence. She claimed that Holcroft had fathered six illegitimate children since the marriage: two by Mary Andrews; one by a Jane Morton (whose child Elizabeth claimed to have looked after for the nine months it lived); one by Nell Strong; one by another woman; and one by 'a wench that quilted at

[13] Ibid. 239–43, 386–95.

his sister's, was brought to bed in the street'. But she was unable to produce any witnesses even for the Mary Andrews affair, much less for the other alleged episodes.

Perhaps since Holcroft had been threatening to accuse her of bestiality, she also made various rather elliptical remarks about 'some indecent things I have taken him in the acting of, and lewdness that he hath told me he hath committed with lewd women'. Talking to Holcroft's maid, whom she found in bed with another woman in their house in Hornsey, she commented 'sure you are turned an Italian boy, or does your master use you after his Irish fashion?' The first national sexual slur clearly suggests sodomy, but the meaning of the second has not survived the centuries.[14] On another occasion, when Elizabeth was being coaxed by Holcroft to go to bed with him with the words 'bitch, kiss and be friends', she replied tartly, 'I am an English woman and not of a Spanish nature, and am sorry to find you a perfect Irishman who uses me at his pleasure,' an observation which is rather easier to interpret.

As for the cruelty, the public assault in October 1700 at the projected reconciliation meeting was beyond dispute, since there were many witnesses, although the chief objective witness to the scene said she thought that Elizabeth had provoked Holcroft 'by words to wrath and anger'.[15] Moreover, Holcroft was able to produce a small army of witnesses testifying to his general courtesy and easy manners, and his kindness to Elizabeth in particular. He was, they all said, 'a gentleman, a man of honour, courteous and civil in his carriage, peacable and quiet in his humour and conversation, and obliging to all persons', besides behaving 'very kindly and civilly to Elizabeth'. All this was in sharp contrast to the total failure of Elizabeth to produce a single character witness in her favour, and to her description of her husband as 'more like a tyrant than a husband, and one' whose 'language is generally rude and brutish'.[16] The picture she tried to paint of Holcroft as a perpetual lecher and a cruel and tyrannical husband simply did not ring true in the courtroom, while her allegations of attempted poisonings seemed pure fantasy.

Holcroft had no difficulty in proving her repeated refusals of invitations to return home, her removal behind his back of much of his household goods, her running up of £500-worth of debts, much of it on sheer extravagance, and her plot to have him arrested for these debts of hers.

Because of Holcroft's lengthy absences in Flanders in the field, the case dragged on until early 1704, and, just before the case came to judgment,

[14] Ibid. 156, 232–3, 286–7, 410–11, 300, 364, 338.
[15] Ibid. 164.   [16] Ibid. 77, 80, 306; see also ibid. 186, 192, 213, 238.

he told the Court that he had discovered important new evidence about adultery by Elizabeth. He produced a detailed account of how six months before, between September and November 1703, Elizabeth and a man called Brome, formerly footman to a nobleman, had lived together in a rented house as man and wife. They were, he claimed, discovered by pure chance, when a visitor to the landlord was sitting in the kitchen and happened to recognize Elizabeth. The pair moved out hastily the next day, but were seen and followed by a friend of the landlord, to whom they still owed 8*s*. 6*d*. When challenged, Brome paid up quickly enough, but Elizabeth's cover was blown. Whatever may have been the sexual peccadilloes of Holcroft, evidence of his wife's infidelity would have destroyed her legal case, by the doctrine of 'recrimination'—that is that two adulteries cancel one another out.

As a result of the new and plausible-seeming evidence of adultery by Elizabeth, her suit for separation was rejected by the Consistory Court. Despite this serious set-back, Elizabeth was obstinate enough to appeal her case to the Court of Arches.[17] There she turned the tables on her accusers by having them summoned to an identification line-up. She appeared with six other women, and, when asked to pick her out, the three key witnesses to her alleged adultery with Brome all failed the test. Moreover, Mrs Boteler and her maid swore that Elizabeth never slept out of the house a single night during all the period she was supposed to have been living with Brome.[18]

Notwithstanding this convincing evidence of perjured testimony, Elizabeth lost her case. It seems likely that Holcroft's unanimously attested reputation for good temper and courtesy, and his eminent military career, all swayed the judge in his favour, while Elizabeth's obvious extravagance and ill-temper told against her. Promoted to Brigadier-General, Blood returned to Flanders in 1705, at last legally separated from his unquiet and troublesome wife. But he did not live long to enjoy his victory, since he died on campaign two years later in 1707.

This is a story peculiar to the time of the late seventeenth and early eighteenth centuries. It begins with the improvident marriage of a couple of penniless adventurers; and it shows the critical importance of patronage by a relative in getting a man his start up the professional ladder, in this case the military career which was rapidly growing in importance in English society. But above all it offers more evidence of the disorderly and promiscuous sexuality, and the wild swings of the pendulum of fate—in

<hr />

[17] Ibid. 416–28; E.15/11.   [18] Ibid. Eee.9/3–5, 14, 18, 19.

gaol one day on a felony charge, pardoned and promoted major the next—
that were so remarkable features of the post-Restoration era.

Also peculiar to the period are the brutality of the language used in
domestic quarrels, and the wholly amoral manipulation of the law. Examples
of the latter are how Holcroft evaded a prosecution for assault on his wife
through the legal machinations of his brother; how his wife tried to get him
gaoled for her own debts; his plan to bribe witnesses to swear to a pre-
contract in order to annul the marriage as bigamous; his threat to bring
witnesses to support an improbable charge of bestiality against his wife;
and, finally, his use of apparently perjured witnesses to her alleged adultery.
The whole story reads like a novel written by Daniel Defoe.

3
Calvert v. Calvert
Multiple adultery and bigamy, 1698–1710

In 1698 Benedict Leonard Calvert, eldest surviving son and heir of Charles Calvert, 3rd Lord Baltimore, former proprietor of the Colony of Maryland, was contracted in marriage to Charlotte Lee (Plate 1). She was the daughter of Edward Lee, 1st Earl of Lichfield, and Charlotte Fitzroy, the illegitimate daughter of Charles II by Barbara Villiers, Lady Castlemaine and Duchess of Cleveland (see Genealogy of the Calvert family). It seems more than likely that the marriage was arranged by the parents and that the children had little or no say in the matter. The bride's own father and mother had been contracted by Charles II at the ages of 4 and 3; they were both only 19 when they were married; they certainly did not know each other's character very well to judge by what was to follow; and one parent, Lord Baltimore, continued to play a major part in their lives. It was a Catholic marriage on both sides.

Under the terms of the marriage contract, Lord Baltimore agreed to settle £600 a year on the pair for maintenance for life, £150 of it going directly to Charlotte for her personal use.[1] Pin-money, as a wife's personal allowance was called, had only fairly recently become normal, and it was very exceptional for as much as a quarter of the joint allowance to be placed directly into the hands of the wife. In return for the annuity the Earl of Lichfield offered £6,000, £2,000 of it cash down, £2,000 on the marriage of his eldest son, Viscount Quarendon (the money to be taken out of the marriage portion of the latter's wife), and £2,000 on the death of the Earl's mother, the Countess of Lindsey. Alternatively, he offered Lord Baltimore the office of Ranger of Woodstock Park, which he valued at £3,000 and was in his gift as a result of a grant to him for three lives by the Crown of the Lieutenancy of Woodstock. This grant had apparently been made in 1674, when at the age of 11 he was actually married to Charlotte Fitzroy, Charles II's illegitimate daughter, and was created Earl of Lichfield. Lord Baltimore accepted the Rangership for his son, since it involved little or no duties, free use of a substantial house in the Park, Woodstock Lodge, the

---

[1] LPCA, D.355: 611.

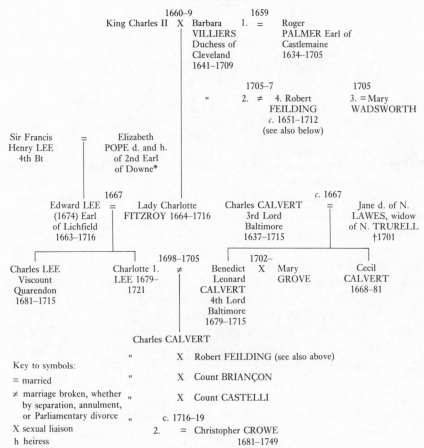

1. Genealogy of the Calvert family

run of the 1,800-acre royal park, and certain quite valuable fees and perquisites, including venison from the park to distribute to patrons, kin, and clients.[2] The exercise of a piece of patronage that happened to be at the Earl of Lichfield's disposal thus enabled him to dispose of his daughter and to provide his son-in-law with an income and a house to live in, all at no cash cost to himself.

The pair were married in 1698 by the Catholic Bishop of Kilmore in the town house of the bride's father in Petty France in Westminster.[3] Within

[2] Ibid. 586, 620; E. Marshall, *Early History of Woodstock Manor* (London, 1873), 258, 269; I owe the information about gifts of venison to Susan Whyman.
[3] LPCA, D.355: 91.

a year the couple moved into Woodstock Lodge, which became their main country residence, while they also rented a town house for the winter season, first in Covent Garden and later in Bloomsbury. Unprotected by any form of contraception or by the breast-feeding of her infants,[4] and at the peak of her fertility in her early twenties, Charlotte produced a child a year over the next six years, four sons and two daughters.[5] The first three were all born in Leonard's father's house and the rest at Woodstock Lodge. Charlotte was described at about this time as 'a comely, portly, fair woman . . . a very little pitted with smallpox'. She was generally thought to be 'of a sweet and courteous humour and disposition' and 'a tender and affectionate mother to her children'. The children 'scarce . . . ever went to bed but she went up to them or had them brought down to her, and the nursery was generally the first place she went after she arose in the morning'. She was obedient to her husband, and was careful to be amiable to his relatives and friends—a matter which proved so often a source of marital discord. In particular, one witness noted that she went out of her way 'to ask blessing of the present Lady Baltimore, purely at the request of and to oblige her husband'.[6] This was a practice already falling into disuse, but may have been kept up longer in Catholic circles. The evidence for her attachment to her children, and for her obedience to her husband's wishes in receiving his friends and relatives during the early years of the marriage, seems fairly secure, and to all appearances she conformed precisely to the model of the ideal wife and mother.

In 1702, some time between the birth of the first and the second child, Leonard's attitude towards his wife began to change. He treated her 'coldly', became 'very morose with her', and fairly soon was showing open hostility towards her. He was later on to have a reputation as a habitual lecher, and it may be that his wife's unwillingness or inability to satisfy him sexually during her constant pregnancies was an initial cause of the marital discord. He was certainly soon frequenting a whore at Islip near Woodstock, and no doubt others in London.

The major reason for the breach between them, however, was that in 1702 Leonard fell in love with Mary Grove. She belonged to a respectable and well-to-do family, and was the eldest of four daughters who all lived with their widowed mother in a substantial house within Woodstock Park, and were reputed to have £1,500 a year each settled on them after certain lives. Leonard's attention was first attracted to Mary on his initial call on her mother. As he was being shown over the house, he noticed portraits of the four daughters hanging in the parlour, and his eye was caught by that

---

[4] Ibid. 470.   [5] Ibid. 590.   [6] Ibid. 553, 503, 831, 832, 1020.

of Mary, who was then away in London. Leonard 'in a sort of rapture cried out: "Now I could stab myself for this woman"'. His enthusiasm is a little surprising if Mary was really as plain as Charlotte later described her: 'a little slender woman, her hair and complexion fair, her nose sharp and rising up, her lips thin, and her fore-teeth standing out and somewhat black and discoloured.'[7]

Mary soon became a close friend of Charlotte and would often stay at Woodstock Lodge for two or three weeks at a time to keep her company. They often went for drives together with Leonard in the coach. Exactly when Charlotte discovered that her husband was pursuing Mary is not clear, but the two women seem to have quarrelled in about 1703, and Mary was no longer invited to stay. Thereafter Leonard haunted the house of Mrs Grove, and his coachman, who drove him to and fro, testified that he was there several times a week and usually stayed until the early hours of the morning, leaving Charlotte all alone at home. Inevitably, all this became common knowledge at Woodstock, and the gossip concluded, not unreasonably, that Leonard and Mary were lovers. One witness said it was well known in the district that 'they were naught together' and three years after the liaison began, on 20 September 1705, they were observed taking 'very indecent familiarities and freedoms towards each other'.[8]

Meanwhile, Leonard was showing more and more hostility towards his wife. By general agreement, he was an extremely hot-tempered man. He was 'very passionate' towards Charlotte, falling into 'great rages', especially when he was in drink. One witness, a laundry maid called Jane Johnson, either had a vivid imagination, encouraged perhaps by bribery and coaching, or else had total recall of conversations she had overheard six or seven years before. She testified that when Charlotte once said to Leonard, 'My dear, how do you do?', he replied, 'God damn you, Madam, hold your peace, and eternal damnation light on you.' Charlotte continued, 'My dear, what shall I do to please you?', to which he answered, 'I will make you humble as a worm.' When Charlotte meekly said she would do so, he retorted, 'Damn you, that you shall not do neither.' He once told her, 'I had rather drink a glass of your blood than the best wine in the world.'[9]

When he was drunk, this verbal abuse would turn into physical attack. Charlotte once took refuge in Jane's bed, saying: 'Lord, Jenny, your master is in one of his freaks tonight, and nothing will serve him but to kill me.' While Charlotte cowered in Jenny's bed, Leonard searched the house with a drawn sword, shouting: 'God damn her, I will have the blood of her this

---

[7] Ibid. 851, 825, 677; another witness described her as 'a very little slender woman' (ibid. Eee. 3/317).
[8] Ibid. D.355: 1151, 827, 630.   [9] Ibid. 495, 833–5, 641, 519.

night before I sleep.' Many witnesses testified that he would often roam around the house 'with drawn sword or pistols under his gown', enquiring where she was hiding. He often lay in bed with her 'with a pocket pistol, case knives or pen knives by him', and threatened he would stab or shoot her. Once she found a case knife concealed under his pillow. Although he never actually put these threats into practice, Leonard certainly succeeded in terrifying Charlotte. He once searched the house for her with a knife in his hand, while she hid, pale and trembling, in the laundry room. Failing to find her, he went back to his room, got his pistol, and shot it off twice. Charlotte in the laundry room heard the shots, as she was intended to, and screamed, ' "Lord, Lord, he hath shot himself, he is dead, he is dead", and thereupon fell into a fit' and fainted.[10]

The physical violence, when it occurred, took various forms, of which the mildest was to kick Charlotte out of bed in the middle of the night and leave her shivering in her shift in the cold until morning. Once when he did this she had to spend the night in the laundry; another time she fled into the park in her shift to get away from his fury; and once 'he came to her bedside, drew his sword upon her, forced her out of bed and downstairs, and followed her with his sword drawn' while she fled through the house to take refuge with the servants. On yet another occasion, he pushed her out of bed so violently that she fell on the floor, breaking a quart bottle of strong water (spirit) which was lying beside the bed—presumably for his own consumption.[11] Perhaps the most dramatic of these repeated violent expulsions from the marriage bed took place very early on, in 1702, when Charlotte was pregnant with her third child and they were living in their town house in Bloomsbury for the winter. Leonard became so furious with her that he not only turned her out of bed, but thrust her out of doors into the night streets of London in her petticoat and gown at one o'clock in the morning, locking the door in her face. He was still so enraged that he fetched a loaded pistol and began following her through the streets. Charlotte was taken under the protection of the night-watchman, who escorted her to the nearby house of her father-in-law, Lord Baltimore, from which she returned home in his chariot the next morning.[12]

Even after this episode, however, Charlotte still did not tell her mother what was going on, or allow anyone in the household to do so, much to the annoyance of her old nurse, Mrs Vancove, who told her own daughter that the trouble had started soon after the birth of the first child, back in 1700, and that she blamed Charlotte for putting up with it and not enlisting the

[10] Ibid. 839–41, 519, 641, 465, 840, 409.   [11] Ibid. 842, 411, 638, 520.
[12] Ibid. 640, 867, 1024, 1142.

help of her influential relatives. Charlotte was often in tears 'from the un-
kindness and ill temper of Mr Calvert towards her'. By 1703 or 1704 Mrs
Vancove reported that Leonard had become 'very cruel and barbarous'
towards her, and seldom visited her during her lying-in with her fourth
child. When Mrs Vancove urged him to visit her, Leonard replied: 'Damn
you for an old bitch, and your lady together. I will drag you through the
horse-pond if you ever speak to me about her.'[13] Physical violence seems to
have got worse before the birth of the fourth child in 1704. Once Leonard
dragged her down the stairs by her hair, and once there was a painful
struggle while they were returning home in the coach from a party at
Sarsden with Sir John Walters. The coachman heard Charlotte 'complain
and squeal most part of the way', and he later found her ear-rings lying in
the coach. Charlotte told him that Leonard 'tore them out of her ears', but
offered no explanation for this action. By now Leonard seems to have lost
what little self-control he ever had, and was seriously maltreating her.
Witnesses testified to seeing her neck black and blue one day, clearly from
Leonard grabbing her by the throat, while on another occasion, when they
were in bed together and Charlotte was six-months pregnant with her
fourth child, he began beating her savagely. She cried out, 'Murder', begging him, 'for God's sake, if you murder me, don't murder my child'. The
servants heard her cries and came to her rescue, but her arms were bruised
next day. Witnesses testified that she often had bruises on her arms, legs,
and thighs as a result of pinches she received from Leonard while in bed.[14]

It is difficult to know exactly what to make of all this testimony. Leonard
was clearly an extremely choleric man, who had become cold and indifferent
towards his wife within two years of marriage. Slowly this indifference
turned into passionate hatred, apparently because he had lost interest in
her sexually (except to keep her continually pregnant) and was enraged and
frustrated by the insurmountable obstacle she presented to his living with
Mary Grove, with whom he was in love, and with whom he was spending
most of his evenings. That sexual difficulties played a part (as well as
alcohol) is suggested by the fact that so many of the outbursts of rage took
place late at night while they were in bed together. Charlotte put up with
the ill-treatment without complaint, and was careful to conceal her domestic
difficulties from her parents, although his parents were much more alert to
the situation. One must assume that she kept this silence because of her
acceptance of the traditional 'double standard', by which the husband was
free to commit minor adulteries and to maltreat his wife without her
protesting. After 1704 one of the reasons for Leonard's increasing brutality

[13] Ibid. 1021–3.   [14] Ibid. 465, 1159, 638, 520, 836–8, 863–5.

was that he was beginning to suspect Charlotte of excessive familiarity with a close friend of his, Tom Thayer, *alias* Johnson, 'a middle-sized swarthy sort of man [who] wore a periwig and had a long nose and a poking out chin', who lived close by in a rented house in Woodstock and was said to be on bad terms with his wife. The latter later declared that 'his going to the Lodge was the ruin of me', while Charlotte excused his interest in herself by the fact that 'he had such a life with that beast of a wife that he was not able to bear it'. No boubt there is some truth in both versions.[15] At all events, at first the two husbands and the two wives were very close, but later Charlotte's friendship with Mrs Johnson was broken off, and thereafter Tom continued to visit the Lodge alone.[16]

By the middle of 1704 Tom Johnson was spending more and more time with Charlotte, despite Leonard's orders that she should see him no more. Lonely in the big house in the great park, constantly pregnant, abandoned and abused by her husband, it is hardly surprising that she should have fallen in love with her new suitor. What seems clear from the evidence is that Leonard's infatuation with Mary Grove and his physical abuse of his wife had both started long before Charlotte met Johnson. The marriage was on the rocks by 1702 because of Leonard's behaviour, and it was only two years later that Charlotte became involved with Johnson.

Johnson's pursuit of Charlotte and her warm response inevitably attracted the attention of the servants. Some of them saw Johnson lurking about outside the house, usually while Leonard was away. Three times the coachman saw them walking alone in the park together. Once, when he was deliberately spying, he saw Johnson standing outside Charlotte's bedroom window at two o'clock in the morning, while she leaned out and talked to him.[17]

The most circumstantial evidence about how the romance developed in late 1704 and early 1705 came from Mrs Clements, the young wife of Leonard's bailiff at Woodstock. While Leonard was away in London or elsewhere, Charlotte organized several jaunts on horseback for herself and the Johnsons, and persuaded the Clements to come along as well. One autumn morning the five of them rode off in a party through the park. They first visited a friend and had dinner with him. Then Charlotte persuaded them all to ride on to Chipping Norton and back. When they got near home she said she would spend the night at the Clements' house and asked Mrs Clements to send a message to her woman, Mrs Carter, at the Lodge to send over some clean shifts and night-clothes. When they reached the Clements' house, however, she changed her mind and said she would spend the night with the Johnsons instead.

[15] Ibid. 453, 378, 363.   [16] Ibid. 344, 498, 363, 378.   [17] Ibid. 207, 450.

At five o'clock next morning Charlotte and the Johnsons were back at the Clements' house to get them to go on another expedition, this time to Abingdon. They set off together, but Charlotte and Tom Johnson soon left the others behind and galloped off into Port Meadow, the huge grassy common land by the river on the outskirts of Oxford. The Clements and Mrs Johnson stuck to the road, and did not see the missing pair again until they reached Abingdon. There they found them at an inn, all alone upstairs in a private room with a bed in it. The party was not a great success, since Mrs Johnson was—not unreasonably—'displeased' at having been abandoned by her husband on the journey. In the afternoon they set out for home, and the same thing happened again. Charlotte and Johnson immediately galloped off ahead towards Oxford, but they were soon overtaken, since Charlotte was having trouble with her saddle. As soon as that was fixed, they again took to their heels, and the others only caught up with them at the George Inn at Oxford, from which they all rode sedately home together.

In February 1705, while Leonard was away in London, Mrs Clements allowed herself to be badgered, against her will, into agreeing to go on yet another trip with Tom and Charlotte. She took care to tell Mrs Johnson about it, who was furious at being left behind. The three of them rode all day and spent the night at an inn at Banbury, where they each took separate rooms, rather than the two women sharing a bed, which would have been the normal thing to do. Mrs Clements noticed that Charlotte and Tom Johnson had adjoining rooms, and that the former refused either to allow herself to be undressed or to let Mrs Clements lock her in her room for safety, which was also a normal precaution at that time for women sleeping alone. At seven in the morning Charlotte's room was still locked on the inside, and it was not until ten o'clock that Mrs Clements entered and found her dressing. They then all rode home, Mrs Clements deeply suspicious that she had been gulled into acting as a cover for an adulterous night out.

A week later Charlotte suggested another trip to Mrs Clements, but by now rumours about the liaison were flying about the village and the latter declined to go, pretending she had a cold and that one of the horses was lame. Charlotte would not accept the excuses and told her to arrange for horses anyway. They rode to Chipping Norton, where Mrs Clements lay down on a bed for a while, since she was feeling unwell. When she recovered she found that Charlotte had locked her in. When after two hours a servant finally released her, she was dismayed to find Charlotte and Johnson alone together in another room with a bed in it. They then took horse again and rode home, Mrs Clements now more suspicious than ever.

Charlotte was now so deeply in love that she had lost all sense of prudence, and a few days later she proposed yet another trip to Mrs Clements. The latter's husband had warned her that the liaison was 'a town talk and a matter of joke among people living thereabouts', and she therefore flatly refused to accompany them. But Charlotte was determined to go, if necessary alone with Johnson. She ordered two horses to be got ready at three in the morning and picked them up at four, but found the park gates all locked (perhaps on Mr Clements's orders) and so was thwarted in her plan. Soon afterwards Charlotte told Mrs Clements that Johnson was abandoning his wife and going off to London, and Mrs Johnson told her that her husband had already left. Mrs Clements hurried back to the Lodge, found Johnson there, and told him to go home to his wife. Charlotte 'wept and told Mr Johnson he should be gone'.

Mrs Clements, who was clearly a young woman of considerable personal strength, persuaded Charlotte to have a face-to-face confrontation with Mrs Johnson, to discuss both the money Johnson had spent on the trips and the scandal they had caused. So the two women talked in Mrs Clements' presence.

CHARLOTTE. Why then, you desire I should never see your husband more?
MRS JOHNSON. Yes madam, I don't care what becomes of me, so you never see him more.
CHARLOTTE. The Devil take me if I ever do see him more.

But the promise was more than she could—or perhaps intended—to keep, and a week later Mrs Clements caught her talking to Johnson in a wood in the Park. By now Charlotte had lost all sense of prudence, and was admitting Johnson secretly into the Lodge while her husband was away. The children's nurse, Anne Rogers, testified that once she spied and caught Johnson climbing into the drawing-room window one evening, and on another occasion saw him sneak into the house at 11 p.m. and stay there all night. Once she looked through the keyhole of the drawing-room, saw Johnson sitting there, and called out: 'You damned dog, what do you there?' Charlotte's woman, Mrs Carter, told her that she thought that someone 'was in bed with her lady'. They went into a low-ceilinged room immediately under the bedroom, and distinctly heard the sound of voices overhead. Other witnesses testified that it was all managed by Charlotte's personal servant, Mary Cockerell, who admitted Johnson to the house, cut food for him, and carried it up on a plate to the bedroom. Inevitably all this became 'the daily discourse and table-talk of the servants'.[18]

---

[18] Ibid. 341–80, 475–80.

At this point in early 1705, when the Charlotte–Tom Johnson liaison was becoming notorious, and the Leonard–Mary Grove liaison had been in progress for about two years, the lives of the Calverts were changed by a battle fought many hundreds of miles away, at Blenheim on the Danube. This stunning victory by English troops under the command of the Duke of Marlborough induced a grateful Parliament to grant him Woodstock Park, and money with which to build himself a palace on the site. Leonard had never liked living in the Park and for years had been trying without success to find a purchaser for his office at the original assessed price of £3,000. Suddenly the price of all the Park offices doubled overnight, and Lord Baltimore and Leonard were able to sell the Rangership back to the Crown for presentation to the Duke for 6,000 guineas. Lord Baltimore generously let his son keep the money and Leonard moved house to Middle Aston, eight miles away.

The move took place in June 1705, while Leonard escaped from the upheaval by going off to Bath. Meanwhile, Johnson abandoned his wife and rented a house nearby in order to be close to Charlotte. The story of what happened next is told by the London upholsterer who was sent down to Woodstock lodge to remove the hangings and to put them up again in the house at Middle Aston. He spent three weeks at Woodstock and seven at Aston, during which he had plenty of time to observe what was going on. The servants in the Aston house consisted of John Smith, the lady's butler, Mr Cherry, the master's gentleman, William Ashley, the groom, 'a black whom they generally called Billy', Mary Cockerell, the lady's personal maid, Mrs Carter, the lady's woman, Anne Clements, the nursery maid, Lydia Ricketts, the housemaid, and Sarah Ashley, the laundry maid. Some of them were deliberately on the watch to see Johnson slipping into the house and up to Charlotte's bedroom, and they gossiped endlessly to one another about the fact that Johnson was living secretly in the house with Charlotte while Leonard was away in Bath. Mrs Carter even showed the upholsterer the imprint of two bodies in the feather bed in which Charlotte had slept.

Mrs Carter and Mr Cherry were genuinely upset by this evidence of adultery, and it was probably they who sent two anonymous letters to Leonard at Bath, informing him of what was going on in his absence. On receipt of these letters, Leonard hurried home, arriving so unexpectedly that Johnson barely managed to slip out of the house in time. A few days later Leonard spotted his wife and Johnson talking together in a grove nearby. He rushed back into the house to rouse the servants, who pursued Johnson but lost him in a cornfield. A few weeks later, Mary Cockerell was discharged by Leonard for abetting his wife's adultery and a week later, in

August 1705, Charlotte eloped. She was eight-months pregnant with a child whose paternity was a very open question, but she was apparently already disillusioned with Johnson. Sarah Ashley listened at her dressing-room door at Aston and heard her say to Johnson: 'You are a rogue, and I never found out but yesterday.'[19]

She fled to her parents, who now at last intervened actively to arrange a private separation agreement. As was customary at the time, her husband retained full control over all the children, the schooling and maintenance of whom was mostly paid for by their grandfather, Lord Baltimore. Leonard agreed to pay Charlotte a third of his income—£200 a year out of the £600 annuity allowed him by his father under the original marriage agreement. Charlotte later complained that Leonard had pocketed the 6,000 guineas he received for selling the Rangership, which had originally been purchased with her marriage portion. This was true but irrelevant, and in fact she was treated reasonably by the standards of the day.[20] Although her own adultery was not in doubt, she presumably already knew enough about her husband's long liaison with Mary Grove to be able to prevent him from suing her in an ecclesiastical court for separation without maintenance. Since both parties had committed adultery, they were probably only too happy to go their own way.

Until 1704 Charlotte appears in the record as a dim, docile, colourless figure, a model of the obedient, long-suffering wife and devoted mother. She was constantly pregnant and assiduous in the loving care of her many children; she never questioned her husband's orders, was respectful to his relatives, and hospitable to his friends. When he took a fancy to Mary Grove, Charlotte accepted her as a friend and companion, and had her to stay in the house for weeks at a time. When he struck up a close friendship with Tom Johnson, Charlotte became equally friendly with Mrs Johnson. Moreover, she was, by all accounts, almost unnaturally submissive to the habitual verbal abuse and physical threats she received from Leonard from 1702 onwards. In 1704, however, something snapped in her, and other aspects of her character began to appear. Leonard later accused her of financial extravagance, and claimed that he had to pay off £3,000-worth of her debts run up between 1705 and 1707 'by her extravagant way of living'. The struggle in the coach, during which he tore her ear-rings off her ears, may have been caused by the fact that she had bought them without consulting him. By all accounts Leonard was equally reckless with money, but this extravagance in consumption by Charlotte after 1704 seems to

[19] Ibid. D.356: 568–76, 426–30, 779.   [20] Ibid. 100, 590–4, 618, 623–5.

have been something new. If she did indeed run up £3,000-worth of debts between 1705 and 1707, she was living at a rate vastly in excess of her £200 annuity.

Another feature of Charlotte's character change in 1704 was the awakening of her libido. Once she had fallen in love with Tom Johnson, she went to almost any lengths to be alone with him in a bedroom several times a week. Her jaunts with Mrs Clements display a determination and ingenuity animated by overwhelming sexual desire. Her willingness not only to let Johnson lurk about the Lodge, but also to admit him into the house and up to her bedroom during her husband's absence, was little short of folly. The servants were bound to notice, and they did. In her recklessness, her financial extravagance, and her insatiable sexual appetite she revealed herself at last as a true granddaughter of Charles II and Lady Castlemaine.

Charlotte's tragedy was that, by the time she fled the house in August 1705, eight-months pregnant with a child whose father could be either her husband or Johnson, she was no longer in love with either. She took shelter with her influential court relatives, and for her lying-in was installed in the London house of her paternal grandmother, the Countess of Lindsey. There in October a baby girl was born. The midwife was old Mrs Watson, who had attended Charlotte's mother's confinements. She testified that both before and after the birth Charlotte was in the deepest despair, and 'wept so much that I did apprehend that she should have fallen into a fit'. She had reason to despair. She was indeed rid of Leonard, but she had no access to her many children on whom she had doted, she was no longer in love with Johnson, she was not free to remarry, and in future she would have to live on a mere £200 a year. It was not a pleasant prospect. Neither she nor any one else particularly wanted the new baby of uncertain parentage, and it soon afterwards died, to no one's surprise or regret, at the house of its wet-nurse in Bridge Street.[21]

After she had recovered from her confinement, Charlotte moved to the house in Bond Street of her maternal grandmother, Barbara Villiers, Duchess of Cleveland, where she stayed for five months from November 1705 to March 1706. The Duchess was now 64 years old, and had been better known to history forty years before, when she was Lady Castlemaine and Charles II's favourite mistress (Plate 2). Since then she had run through an assortment of lovers, and had squandered huge fortunes on dissipation and gambling for high stakes. Even now her house in Bond Street was still the centre of a raffish social circle. In March 1706 Charlotte moved out of the Bond Street house of her grandmother and set herself up in a small rented

[21] Ibid. 103, 415, 417, 245.

furnished apartment in Westminster, where she lived modestly with two servants, one lady's maid, and one footman/butler.

The reason for her move was that she was now sleeping with her grandmother's new husband. In 1705 the 64-year-old Duchess of Cleveland found herself at liberty to marry again, thanks to the death of her husband of convenience, the Earl of Castlemaine, whom she had not seen for decades. Despite her age, her wealth and influence were enough to attract the attention of a man called Robert Feilding, generally known as 'Beau Feilding' or 'Handsome Feilding' (Plate 3). He came from a respectable Warwickshire family and had clawed his way to success in London high society by using his remarkable charm to captivate and seduce rich and pretty women. In the 1670s he had even seduced the mistress of James, Duke of York, the King's brother, and then swapped off-colour jokes with King Charles about the details of her sexual anatomy. He had been married twice, the second time to Viscountess Muskerry, who had died in 1698 and whose considerable fortune he had by now dissipated in riotous living.

During the reign of James II he had become a Catholic, had remained loyal to James, and had allegedly fought for him in Ireland, whence he derived the title of Major-General and a promise—so he boasted—of the earldom of Glasgow (or Feilding). Only in 1696 did he make his peace with the new regime of William III and return to England. Although in his choice of wives he was governed by strictly financial considerations, he was also an insatiable and promiscuous sexual athlete and had run through many mistresses in high society, including one enterprising courtesan, Elizabeth Price, who passed successively from his bed to those of two knights, the colonel of a regiment, and an earl. In 1709 Swift wrote a character sketch of him for the *Tatler* as 'Orlando the Handsome'. After describing his remarkable physical beauty, he went on to say that these qualities 'made Orlando the universal flame of all the fair sex; innocent virgins sighed for him as Adonis; experienced widows as Hercules ... However the generous Orlando believed himself formed for the world and not to be engrossed by any particular affection. Woman was his mistress and the whole world his seraglio.' Swift curtly dismissed him as 'the meanest figure in history'.[22]

By 1705 Major-General Robert Feilding was 54 years old. He was well known as a bully, repeatedly embroiled in duels and acts of violence in the streets, as a lecher with whom no woman's virtue was safe, as an unscrupulous fortune-hunter, and as a spendthrift in urgent need of a

---

[22] *Tatler*, 50 (1709); P. W. Sergeant, *My Lady Castlemaine* (London, 1912), 292–7; *NCC Trials for Adultery* (1780), i, pp. xxviii, 55–64; *Cases of Divorce for Several Causes* (London, 1715), pp. ix, xxii; LPCA, Eee. 1, fos. 55–9, 67, 70, 86.

fresh supply of funds. His eye now lighted on two possibilities. The first was the 64-year-old Duchess of Cleveland, who was still immensely rich, and as ruthless, extravagant, avaricious, and sexually promiscuous as himself. She was also, like himself, a Catholic. So he set out to woo her despite her age and her gout, and throughout the summer of 1705 paid her assiduous court, being in and and out of her Bond Street house day after day and week after week.

The second possibility Feilding had his eye on was a recently bereaved young widow, Mrs Anne Deleau, who had inherited from her late husband the huge fortune of £60,000—a fact which Feilding took care to check by obtaining a copy of her husband's will. But the widow was in deep mourning and living in extreme seclusion, besides being carefully watched over by her father in order to keep her from falling a prey to fortune-hunters. Feilding had no doubt that, if only he could obtain an interview with her and exert on her his well-tried charms, he could sweep her off her feet. The problem was how to obtain access to her.

In this dilemma he turned for help to a friend, who located a Mrs Villars (or Villiers) who was the widow's hairdresser. Mrs Villars was the illegitimate daughter of the second Duke of Buckingham, and a hairdresser by profession, but also a demi-mondaine on the fringes of the fashionable world, who boasted to intimates of having had two bastards by Lords Torrington and Stamford. She was said—perhaps falsely—to have served time in Bridewell, a prison for prostitutes. Feilding pressed Mrs Villars to arrange a meeting with Mrs Deleau, promising her £500 for her pains. Mrs Villars was well aware that she could not possibly induce the reclusive Mrs Deleau to meet Feilding, so, in order to lay her hands on the £500, she decided to pass off a woman called Mary Wadsworth in her place. Mary had a bad reputation as 'a common bitch', a thief, and a professional prostitute who had 'clapped some of the Guards' (i.e. given them gonorrhoea). Nevertheless, Feilding (who should have known better) fell right into the trap. He had obtained only a very distant and blurred glimpse of the real Mrs Deleau through a window from her garden. He was therefore entirely taken in when eventually a demure Mary Wadsworth, all dressed in black widow's weeds and ac-companied by Mrs Villars, came in a black mourning coach to visit him at his lodgings.

Mrs Villars's later deposition provides a vivid account of Beau Feilding's courting tactics. For several weeks he bombarded 'Mrs Deleau' with letters elegantly tied up 'with green sewing silk', and addressed in a high romantic style to 'the countess of my heart'. The letters sent through Mrs Villars —who had also to read them since Mary Wadsworth was illiterate— were accompanied by a series of presents, including a rich apron and handkerchief and a pair of gold and white garters. 'Mrs Deleau' graciously received these gifts, for which she thanked him in notes drafted by Mrs Villars and written by a friend. Finally Feilding arranged for 'Mrs Deleau' to see the Lord Mayor's show from the balcony of a linen-draper cousin of his in Cheapside, and invited her back afterwards to his lodgings, which consisted of a dining-room and bedroom over a milliner's shop in St James's Street, conveniently situated next door to the Bagnio.

When 'Mrs Deleau' and Mrs Villars arrived there, they were ushered upstairs into the bedroom. Feilding was late, being detained by the Duchess, and hurried in a quarter of an hour afterwards. He bounded upstairs, rushed into the bedroom, threw his hat on the bed, took 'Mrs Deleau' in his arms, and kissed her warmly. He then dropped on one knee and said: 'My life, my soul, why would you stay from me so long, that love you more than life itself? Sure you must be mine.' He then got up, sat down beside her, and asked how she had liked his gifts. He then put his hands about her waist and kissed and nuzzled her for about a quarter of an hour, until 'Mrs Deleau', acting smitten but modest, gently reproved him, murmuring, 'I think you go too far.' Feilding was quick to reassure her: 'Pray, my dear, don't take it ill, for we want nothing but the holy man to join our hands and make us both one.' He then sent out for a playhouse singer, 'Little Margaretta', to sing some sentimental songs, one beginning 'Charming creature, the Goddess I adore', and the other 'Ianthe the lovely . . . the longer they lived the fonder they grew'. At this line Feilding clapped his hand on 'Mrs Deleau''s knee and said 'that will be you and I, my dear, we'll strive which can love most'. He then offered her plum cake and wine, and urged immediate marriage, but 'Mrs Deleau' demurely put it off for a week, besides raising some objections to the use of a Catholic priest since she was a Protestant. Altogether it was a highly successful charade, played by both parties with consummate skill.[23]

Throughout October and early November 1705 Feilding was extremely active, courting the Duchess almost every day, and at the same time pressing Mrs Villars to arrange another meeting with 'Mrs Deleau' intended to culminate in a prompt and secret marriage. With this in mind, he had the brazen impudence to buy a gold wedding ring inscribed at his specific instructions 'Tibi soli' (to thee alone). At their next meeting in his lodgings in November 'Mrs Deleau' seemed reluctantly persuaded to consent to a secret marriage. Feilding hastily went out of the room, locked the door in case she changed her mind, and took a coach to fetch a Jesuit priest, popularly known as 'the Father in Red'. He performed the marriage before

[23] LPCA, Eee. 9/250: 6–10.

Mrs Villars the same evening in the bedroom and Feilding made haste to consummate it that night (while his manservant went to bed with Mrs Villars in another bedroom). He then sent his new bride out of town, pretending the need for deep secrecy in order to keep the news from her father, who controlled part of her estate. He also told her that he did not want to offend his important patron the Duchess. Mary Wadsworth therefore withdrew to the country, returning to her new husband's lodgings only three times in six weeks for three more nights of strenuous love-making. On each occasion Feilding was always very late for the encounter, arriving invariably after midnight. When Mary complained that 'it was hard he should be with the Duchess all the week and when I come too', Feilding's reply was nothing if not frank: 'My dear, these are early days to find fault. The Duchess of Cleveland is so good she has willed me all that she has, and one would not disoblige such a friend.'

Even so this was hardly the way to treat a new bride, and a sexually frustrated wealthy widow at that, as Feilding supposed her to be. And so, in order to keep her quiet and happy and out of the way of the Duchess, he wrote her a series of letters, addressed to 'The Countess of Feilding', and expressing in gross terms his enjoyment of her person on the last occasion they had slept together and his hopes and intentions for the next. These letters the Duchess later obtained from Mary Wadsworth, either by purchase or by bullying, thereby thwarting Feilding's offer of five guineas to have them stolen back. She then took malicious pleasure in having them read out in court and later published them in a pamphlet to be read all over town. In one of them Feilding wrote to his secret wife: 'Methinks I fucked you again with the height of pleasures, and fucked and fucked till I dissolved with pleasure.' In another letter he wrote: 'I shall be very jealous any one should peep into Nanette's backside but myself. I assure you when I have got you once more back in my arms I'll so belabour it I'll make it black and blue, and cram it full of my elixir to nourish young Lord Tonbridge'—an allusion to the son and heir to the alleged earldom he hoped to conceive upon her. Since he was in fact writing to a professional prostitute rather than, as he thought, to a sex-starved widow, these clumsy pornographic effusions, when read aloud by Mrs Villars to Mary Wadsworth, must have been received with laughter rather than excitement.

The real reason why Mary Wadsworth saw so little of Feilding was that less than two weeks after his marriage to 'Mrs Deleau' his siege of the Duchess suddenly came to a successful conclusion, and on 25 November he was married to the Duchess by another Catholic priest, this time the chaplain of the Portuguese Ambassador. He naturally moved into the Duchess's Bond Street house, but retained his old lodgings for one more rendezvous with Mary Wadsworth, for which he carefully arranged that his night-gown, night-cap, and slippers should be sent over from Bond Street.

At this juncture, not content with these two new wives, both married for money, Feilding became sexually involved with the Duchess's granddaughter Charlotte, who was then living in her grandmother's house. By March 1706, when she moved into lodgings of her own, they were already lovers. So Feilding had now at least three women to satisfy. Two of them were his wives—the first a prostitute, the second the elderly but insatiable ex-mistress of Charles II—and the third the granddaughter of the second and the same monarch. Nor was this all, for the solicitor employed to draw up his marriage contract with the Duchess reported that, when he visited Feilding's lodgings, he met there 'an abundance of common women of the town'. These women catered to his various needs, such as the Mrs Fletcher who supplied him with both pornographic pictures and young virgins.

In May 1706, however, Feilding at last discovered that he had been duped in his marriage with the supposed 'Mrs Deleau'. This came out when she began pressing him for money, which should have been flowing in the reverse direction if she had been the wealthy heiress she pretended to be. Once suspicion was aroused, it did not take him long to discover her real identity. Feilding summoned Mrs Villars to the Bond Street house of the Duchess, locked her in a closet, secured her with five locks, and gave vent to his rage by brutally beating her about the head and face, shouting: 'God eternally damn you, you bitch, how could you think that woman a wife fit for I, Major-General Feilding?' When Mrs Villars retorted, 'Your honour liked her well enough, or else why did you marry her?', he beat her again, saying, 'You bitch, she is not the woman of that fortune.' He then held up to her face a large steel hammer and chisel and threatened that, if she uttered a word about the marriage with Mary Wadsworth, 'I will slit your nose off and I will get two blackamoors (belonging to the Duchess) to whip you and strip your skin over your head.' 'Suppose', he asked, 'I should send for the Duchess of Cleveland down and tell her of this fine wife that you have helped me to, do you think she would thank you for it.' Mrs Villars replied coolly, 'I cannot tell but her Grace might thank me' (meaning she might be pleased to find that her marriage to Feilding was bigamous and so null). As they parted, Feilding warned Mrs Villars again that, 'if ever you mention my being married to that bitch my wife, I will have your flesh stripped from your bones, and your bones bruised'.[24]

---

[24] *The Arraignment, Tryal and Conviction of Robert Feilding for Felony* (London, 1708); *State Trials*, xiv. 1327–370; Bodl. MS Rawlinson B. 379, fos. 81–2; LPCA, Eee. 9/278; for more about Feilding, see *An Historical Account of the Life . . . of Beau Feilding* (London, 1707), and *An Elegy on the Death of Robert Feilding* (London, 1712); see also the article in *DNB*.

Soon afterwards Feilding had a violent confrontation with the now pregnant Mary Wadsworth in the street in Whitehall as she got out of a coach. He called her 'bitch', to which she boldly replied: 'You are a rogue. I am your lawful wife.' This so enraged Feilding that he struck her across the mouth with his cane, making her bleed, and then gave a sentry a crown to hold her while he stalked off alone. This physical and verbal violence may have relieved Feilding's feelings, but it was exceedingly unwise. Mrs Villars was alleged to have said: 'If I sell my soul to the Devil, I will be revenged of Robert Feilding.' To this end she and Mary Wadsworth conveyed their story to the Duchess via her grandson the Duke of Grafton, and the storm broke. There was a fearful scene in June in the Bond Street house, when the Duchess accused Feilding of bigamy and of breaking into her closet and stealing £400 from it. He lost his temper and began beating her up too, despite her age and rank, until she screamed 'Murder!' out of the window. When the watch arrived, Fielding fired a blunderbuss to frighten it off. For this uncontrolled act of violence the Duchess had him committed to Newgate, but he soon got out on bail. Before he returned to the Bond Street house, however, she fled on 25 July, taking with her all the most valuable clothes and furniture, since by law the house and the contents belonged to her husband until he was convicted of bigamy. With supreme effrontery, Feilding had an advertisement placed in the newspapers, denouncing the Duchess for refusing to return and cohabit with her lawful husband, and for making off with property which belonged by right to him, and declaring that, as her husband, he would no longer be responsible for her debts. He also took the precaution of having the Jesuit who had married him to Mary Wadsworth hastily shipped off as a missionary to China, so that he could not serve as a witness in any future lawsuit.[25]

Meanwhile, he spent most of his time making love with the Duchess's granddaughter, Charlotte Calvert. He visited her in her lodgings almost every day from morning until ten or eleven at night, where they were closeted alone together in a room with a bed in it, and it was not long before Charlotte was pregnant again by her new lover.[26] In September 1706 Charlotte was ejected from her lodgings by her landlady, who was afraid of scandal, and she moved into an unfurnished rented house in Stratton Street in Westminster. She must have had to borrow the money with which to furnish the house and pay the rent, since Feilding was in no position to supply cash, being himself arrested for debt on 4 October. She had by now evolved into a woman with strong and unrestrained sexual

---

[25] Bodl. MS Rawlinson B. 379, fos. 81, 86.
[26] LPCA, D.356: 1-4-05, 244-7, 384, 216, 1166.

appetites and a taste for an opulent way of life. Clearly she needed a new and wealthy protector who would give her the sex and luxury for which she craved. Beau Feilding could provide only the first of these things, and then only when he was out of gaol; moreover, time was running out if she were to find a new patron before her pregnancy became too obvious.[27]

After about three weeks in her new house, Charlotte one day brought home 'a tall lusty brown man and a very civil and well bred gentleman', called Count Briançon. She had met him through Beau Feilding's nephew, but whether this was a deliberate arrangement between Feilding and Charlotte is not clear. At all events the next few months were hectic for Charlotte. Beau Feilding, who was now once more out of gaol, visited her every day and stayed from about two in the afternoon until ten in the evening. As soon as the coast was clear, Count Briançon would arrive, slip into bed with her, and stay till four or five next morning. Sometimes he stayed until the next day, and once, when the charwoman hit the bedroom door with her mop, the door flew open and she saw them in bed together. This almost round-the-clock sexual activity went on until Christmas, by which time Charlotte's pregnancy was very visible, the Count was spending most days as well as some nights in the house, and Beau Feilding had dropped out of the picture.[28]

The latter was probably tired of Charlotte by now, and anyway was far too busy defending himself from the Duchess, who was bent on revenge. Not only had she been tricked into a marriage with a bigamist, but she had been beaten up, publicly insulted, and—perhaps the bitterest blow of all for an elderly courtesan—had been supplanted in her own house by her granddaughter in competition for the sexual services of her new husband. In late October she not only launched a suit against Feilding in the London Consistory Court for annulment of the marriage on grounds of bigamy; she also brought an action against him in the Old Bailey on a criminal charge of bigamy, which could in theory cost him his life. The latter was a test case as to whether the English common-law courts would recognize the legality of a marriage on English soil performed by a Roman Catholic priest. The lawyer for the prosecution, Mr Raymond, persuaded the court that the marriage was valid, and in doing so made himself so famous that he went on to become Lord Chief Justice.[29]

After this decision of principle, Feilding's only hope of avoiding conviction was to prove that his first marriage with Mary Wadsworth was invalid since she was already married at the time. He therefore bribed the daughter of

---

[27] Ibid. 216–18, 249, 419.   [28] Ibid. 249, 389, 238, 567.
[29] Campbell, *Lives of the Chief Justices,* ii. 191.

the keeper of the marriage registers in the Fleet to allow him to insert an item about an earlier marriage of a Mary Wadsworth. But the prosecution got wind of this scheme and searched all the clandestine marriage registers in London. Two of the Duchess's lawyers testified that they had examined that particular register some weeks before, had found no entry for Mary Wadsworth, but had noticed a blank space at the bottom of the page where the entry now appeared. It was a clumsy forgery, clearly in a different ink and by a different hand. The jury therefore ignored it and brought in a verdict of guilty. Before the judge could pass the death sentence, Feilding pleaded benefit of clergy. When the judge therefore sentenced him to be branded in the hand, Feilding coolly produced from his pocket a warrant from Queen Anne to suspend the execution of the sentence, and walked out of the Court a free man. How he obtained the warrant is a mystery, since the Queen was unlikely to have looked with favour on a man of his character. On the other hand, she may have been pleased to see the Duchess of Cleveland humiliated, or it may be that Feilding exercised a little blackmail on one of his many influential former conquests in order to obtain the warrant. Feilding's story thereafter is soon told. The revelations at the trial exposed him to the ridicule of London society, particularly since a full transcript, including the obscene letters to 'Mrs Deleau', went into several editions between 1706 and 1708. More serious, his plans to recoup his fortunes by a rich marriage were clearly destroyed for ever. His creditors therefore closed in for the kill, and had him arrested for debt and imprisoned in the Fleet. Resilient as ever, however, Feilding soon obtained his release, and from then until his death in 1712 lived quietly in London in Scotland Yard. The last bizarre twist to his story is provided by his reconciliation with his legal wife, Mary Wadsworth, to whom on his death he bequeathed his estate.[30]

Meanwhile on 23 April 1707 Charlotte had given birth to a baby girl, delivered by old Mrs Watson and her daughter. Both testified that Count Briançon was present in the delivery-room, which they clearly considered very scandalous. His attendance at the confinement is all the more remarkable as the child could not possibly have been his, since he had met Charlotte only seven months before: the father had to be Beau Feilding. The child was thus as unwanted as her previous one, and was immediately removed that same night to the house of Mrs Watson's daughter, Mrs Canning. It was thought to have been maintained by Beau Feilding, was several times brought to Stratton Street to be seen by Charlotte, and was still alive in 1709.[31] Charlotte and the Count now settled down in the daytime in the

[30] Sergeant, *My Lady Castlemaine*, 298–316; *Cases of Divorce*, pp. xlii–xlv.
[31] *The Arraignment of Robert Feilding*, 108–9, 218–19, 258, 277.

Stratton Street house, although for fear of discovery by her husband, Leonard, they continued to take rather feeble precautions to keep the liaison secret.

The cook–maid who served in the house for three months testified that the Count dined and supped there most days, but left the house at eleven or twelve in the evening and did not normally sleep there overnight. One night she was ordered by the lady's woman to go to bed at once, and to leave the dishes unwashed. She was suspicious and watched the staircase and entrance hall to see what would happen. At two in the morning the Count knocked gently on the front door, was admitted by the lady's woman, given slippers and a night-gown, and escorted up to Charlotte's bedroom. But normally the pair had to take their pleasure in the daytime. One afternoon the maid opened the door of the bedroom to find Charlotte vomiting into a chamber pot held for her by the Count. Both were in bed in their night-gowns. When she reported this below stairs, the butler commented crudely: 'She is a beast of a woman for going to bed so soon after dinner.'[32]

Between November 1707 and May 1708 the Count also rented and furnished a little house with two bedrooms in Knightsbridge which he and Charlotte occasionally used for a night of love-making, uninhibited—so they thought—by the prying eyes of servants. They established a maid, Maria, in the house in order to keep it ready for their visits, which occurred about once every six weeks. To keep up appearances in front of the maid, they pretended to be uncle and niece and kept one bed in each room, a large one for Charlotte and a field-bed for the Count.

Once when they arrived unexpectedly Maria aired the sheets in front of the fire, and the Count helped her to make the beds. Charlotte explained that the Count was her uncle, and asked 'whether she thought it was cordial for uncles and nieces to be together', to which Maria replied that 'she thought not, but had taken the said gentleman to be her husband'. Charlotte told her that she had had a husband and one child. The latter was now kept by her father, who had 'beat and misused her sadly, but she thanked God he was now dead, and that ever since his death she had lived with her uncle, who used her very kindly'. The maid did not fail to note that Charlotte had had a lock fitted to the outer door leading into the two bedrooms, so that there could be no witness to the actual sleeping arrangements. She also noted that the Count's bed was never used and that there was always the imprint of two bodies in Charlotte's bed. She testified that she had seen the Count 'frequently kissing her and having his hands

[32] LPCA, D. 356: 528–34, 222.

in her bosom' and calling her 'my dear'.[33] They were clearly a very affectionate couple, at any rate on the Count's side.

By the spring of 1708, when the Count gave up the Knightsbridge house, Charlotte was pregnant once more, and gave birth to a baby boy on 16 June, the Count again being present at the delivery. As usual, the child was immediately removed to the wet-nurse hired by Mrs Canning, the daughter of the old midwife, Mrs Watson. Mrs Canning remained with Charlotte to look after her while she recovered, but left after a month when she heard that the child was sick. The footman sent to enquire about the health of the child met Mrs Canning in St James's Park and was given two letters for the Count and Charlotte announcing the baby's death. The news was witheld from Charlotte for fear of upsetting her, but she guessed what had happened and began to cry.

During the summer months of 1708 the Count and Charlotte hired two rooms in a house on Hampstead Heath from a Mr Fothergill in order to escape the heat and stench of the city, and did not return to Stratton Street until September. Around Christmas the Count fell ill and they moved out to Brentford, where he died.[34] Exactly how Charlotte had felt about the Count is not clear. She was undoubtedly fond of him and upset when his child died, but he was older than she—she passed him off as her uncle—and was absolutely necessary to her for financial support. The Count had recently complained, not only that her first illegitimate child had not been his since he had not known her when it was conceived, but that she had cost him £2,000 in cash and £300 in household goods over a period of two-and-a-half years. She told a neighbour that 'she must have starved but that she took the Count for a boarder'. She also frankly told a friend that 'when she was free from Count Briançon she would never be tied to any other man, for that she was as much confined to him as ever she was to Mr Calvert'. It looks very much as if he was far more attached to her than she to him, and she was in some measure using him largely for financial reasons.[35] On the other hand, too much should not be made of the discrepancy between their ages. Nothing is known about Tom Johnson's age, but Beau Feilding was nearly twice her age, so perhaps she had a taste for older men.

By January 1709 Charlotte was left all alone with her five servants, in her luxuriously furnished Stratton Street house, the mother of one live and two dead illegitimate children by three different men, but now without a protector, patron, or lover, and with nothing to live on but her £200 annuity from the separation agreement. Moreover, she could not even

---

[33] Ibid. 299–314, 328.   [34] Ibid. 228, 390.   [35] Ibid. 260, 421, 233.

count on this, since from late 1708 Leonard had been letting it fall heavily into arrears. As his knowledge of his wife's adulteries increased, so he more and more cut off her funds.[36] It was at this point, when she was at her most defenceless, that Leonard struck, launching a suit against her in the Consistory Court for separation on grounds of adultery. If he should win, he would free himself from all responsibility for her debts, reduce her allowance to the pin-money of £150 a year, and make it possible to go on to obtain a full divorce in the House of Lords, if his Catholic faith would allow him to do so. On the other hand, if Charlotte contested the suit, Leonard would inevitably run the risk of having his own marital infidelities laid open to public scrutiny, besides being made responsible for at least part of his wife's legal costs.

Charlotte's counter-attack took three forms: to accuse him of intolerable and life-threatening cruelty towards her, to impugn his moral character by showing that he was a promiscuous lecher, and to prove that he had had a long and continuing liaison with Mary Grove dating back to before her own adulteries. The cruelties have already been described. As for the lechery, one witness had been living in lodgings at Islip in 1708, where she had met a professional prostitute, Rebecca Blay, who reminisced very freely about her encounters with Leonard Calvert in about 1702–3 at Jeremiah Cooper's house at the Sign of the Black Boy. Rebecca said that 'Mr Calvert had there lain with her several times'. At their first encounter Leonard told her that she was 'the best bedfellow that ever man lay with'. When Rebecca pointed out that he had a very fine wife of his own, he retorted, ' "She is not lewd enough for me," ' adding ' "now you little devil, be as lewd as you can", and satisfied himself three times with her before he departed'. As a reward, he gave Rebecca 'a piece of cherry coloured and silver ribbon which had cost him two or three guineas at Oxford'.[37]

Charlotte also collected evidence of numerous attempts by Leonard to seduce or rape servant girls. There was a circumstantial story about how in 1705 he had visited a parson's house near Henley, had followed the maidservant out into the fields when she went to milk the cows, had tried to rape her, and had then beaten her when she resisted. News of the affair put all the servants into an uproar the next day, and Leonard was forced to ride back to the parson's house and pay money to hush the matter up. During most of 1707 Leonard had been very ill, and Charlotte alleged, without proof, that he was suffering from venereal disease. This is not unlikely, since there is a year-long gap at just this time in the chain of evidence linking him to Mary Grove. Charlotte alleged, but again offered

---

[36] Ibid. 421, 604.   [37] Ibid. 775–6, 784–8.

no proof, that several times he 'confessed that he had been clapped' and that he did indeed 'have the French pox'. All that she could prove, however, was that he nearly died in 1707 at Aston, that the rumour among the servants was that the disease was venereal, and that in early 1708 he was still ill, and drinking nothing but cow's and ass's milk.[38]

In 1708 Leonard was living in a rented house at Richmond, where he soon got a reputation as 'a lewd man and much addicted to women'. A young maidservant in the house testified that, while she was warming his bed, 'he would often kiss me and put his tongue into my mouth and has several times thrown me down on the bed and endeavoured to debauch me, and I was always forced to make a noise to get away from him'. On one occasion, she had a very narrow escape. 'One morning he shut me in the parlour and began to be very rude with me, and I endeavouring to get from him, he . . . said: "God damn you for a bitch, I will fuck you", and then the butler coming in to lay the cloth, I got away from him.'[39]

All this was very damaging to Leonard Calvert's general character but not critical to his case. Charlotte's best legal defence was to prove that her husband had also committed adultery with Mary Grove before the separation. She was able to show that Mary Grove came to London in 1705–6, immediately after the separation, and was living in rooms in the house of Ralph Green in Bloomsbury at a time when Leonard was at his own house in King Street, Bloomsbury. All she could prove, however, was that his coachman had several times driven Leonard to Mr Green's house in the afternoon, and that he had stayed there about three hours.[40] The more incriminating evidence related to 1708–9, after Leonard had recovered from his long sickness. From April to September 1708 Leonard rented for the summer a small house on Richmond Hill, where Mary joined him a month later. Mary and Leonard always dined together so long as there was no company, but whenever there were visitors Mary discreetly withdrew. She thus led the socially isolated life of the secretly kept mistress. On the other hand, Mary had ordered Leonard's servants about, and had gone for drives in his calash.[41]

The only concrete evidence of adultery, however, came from the fact that, during the stay at Richmond Hill, Mary became pregnant. She suffered from morning sickness, swelled up, left off her stays, and began making baby-clothes. When they got back to London in September, they began enquiring for a midwife. Bart Hyatt, the *valet de chambre*, was told

---

[38] Ibid. 680–1, 895; Leonard suggested that Charlotte had tampered with witnesses on this issue (ibid. E.20/36).
[39] Ibid. D.356: 1162, 806, 890–3, 756–7.   [40] Ibid. 643, 1037, 1094–5, 8.
[41] Ibid. 882, 926, 893, 1081.

by his sister about a midwife in Lincoln's Inn Fields who needed work, but she was rejected since she lived too near Leonard's tailor, who might recognize him when he visited Mary. For Leonard was extremely anxious to keep his liaison secret, so that it would not come to the ears of either his father, on whom he depended for financial support, or his wife, who might use the information to damage him. In late September Mary was installed for 30s. a week at the house of a 60-year-old midwife at the Sign of the Unicorn in Paternoster Row, where she lived under the name of Mrs Moore, and in December gave birth to a girl christened Mary.[42]

After the birth, Mary was frequently visited there by Leonard, but in a vain attempt to throw any detectives hired by Charlotte off the scent he took the precaution of leaving his coach some distance from the house, walking the rest of the way, and returning either on foot or in a hackney coach. As for the infant, five days after it was born it was sent away to a wet-nurse in Camberwell. She was the 30-year-old wife of a gardener and for four to five years had 'taken in children to nurse', and she agreed to look after the baby for 5s. a week. Mary was often melancholy 'to think what would become of the child and how it would be provided for', but she visited it only three times before it died four months later, in April 1709. The sad little funeral took place in Camberwell, attended only by Mary's friend and confidante Mrs Courtney and her maid; the death was registered in the name of Mary Grove, daughter of John Grove, although the sexton admitted that he knew it was said to be the bastard of a gentleman. Mary's final comment was that 'she was glad the child was dead for she would have been under a concern how it would have been provided for'.[43]

During the early months of 1709 Mary was living in lodgings in Hampstead, rented by Leonard from a widow for her and her maidservant for £1 a week. Leonard, who was at his town house in Bloomsbury, often visited her and stayed the night, but allegedly in a bedroom far removed from hers. In the spring Leonard again rented a secluded house out of London for the summer, this time in Banstead, Surrey. He remained desperately anxious to conceal the liaison, and there was a panic one day when he was unexpectedly visited by his father, Lord Baltimore. Mary was whisked out of sight, but her clogs stood by the street door and Leonard had to whisper to a servant to remove them quickly. Moreover, Mary almost always dined alone when there was company present. Apart from this one alarm and these precautions against detection, the two seem to have spent a happy

---

[42] Ibid. 654–8, 798–805, 1101, 1068, 1073, 1000–4, 1013–15.
[43] Ibid. 1000–4, 1030–5, 1038–40, 664; Eee. 10/317.

and adulterous summer together. The neighbours were under no illusions about the relationship, and once, when she went to church with their landlord (Leonard as a Catholic stayed at home), she was pointed out as Mr Calvert's 'whore'.

There is a little testimony about Mary's state of mind. On the one hand, she said 'that she did love him to distraction, that she was not easy a minute when he was from her, and that she would follow or go with him wherever he went'. On other occasions, however, she was less happy with her lot. Charlotte alleged that Mary had often told witnesses that Leonard 'had ruined her or debauched her, and had taken her from her friends and country'—which was certainly true. Once at Banstead she burst into tears and said to him: 'I was happy when I lived with my mother, but it was for your sake that I left my mother, friends and relatives at Woodstock.' It must indeed have been a lonely life if she had to eat by herself whenever there was company, especially if Leonard was at the same time making indecent assaults upon the maids. It is hardly surprising that she suffered from insomnia, and took 'sleepy potions' almost every night, supplied to her by Leonard's apothecary. The most sinister view of their relationship was supplied by Leonard's valet, Bart Hyatt, who told his sister that his master 'had debauched her when she was young, and that therefore she was obliged to live with him, for if she went from him he believed Mr Calvert would expose her'.[44] This would certainly fit the brutal character ascribed to Leonard by his wife and the maids, but not his eight-year liaison with Mary, even if he was constantly unfaithful to her. She clearly had some emotional hold over him, as well as he over her.

During late 1709 Leonard's lawsuit against his wife for adultery ground its leisurely way through the ecclesiastical courts. As has been seen, Charlotte fought back vigorously and, since both parties were accusing each other of adultery and some at least of the forty-five witnesses in the suit were clearly perjured, the verdict remained in doubt. Before the decision was handed down, Leonard resorted to another sudden act of violence, although one that was fully justified under existing laws. A husband had a right to all the property of his wife which was not separately vested in trustees, and Leonard therefore had a legal claim to everything in Charlotte's Stratton Street house which had not been bought after the separation with her own allowance of £200 a year.

In December 1709 Leonard, who was clearly having Charlotte closely watched by detectives, learnt that she had taken on a new lover, another foreign nobleman called Count Castelli. He determined to pull off a triple

[44] Ibid. D.356: 683, 673, 997, 1067, 1100.

victory against his wife: to shame her publicly by exposing her in bed with a lover; to bolster his legal case for separation by adding indisputable evidence of Charlotte's adultery with yet another man; and to seize every piece of her property in the house. On the afternoon of Christmas Eve, having presumably received word from a servant inside the house that the Count was preparing to spend the night there, he sent for the bailiff of St Martin's-in-the-Fields, told him that he had reason to believe that his wife was committing adultery with a foreigner, and asked him to go with him to the house early the next morning and help him to force his way into the bedroom 'to see if they could catch his wife and the foreigner together'. Money must have changed hands, and the bailiff agreed. Leonard then assembled the rest of his gang of about eight men: one of them had been a servant of Charlotte since her infancy, and most of the others were familiar with her. All no doubt were handsomely rewarded for their morning's work.

The party assembled at a house in Bloomsbury at five o'clock on Christmas morning, and proceeded to Charlotte's house in Stratton Street, where they arrived at about six and were let in quietly by a servant who was in the plot. At about seven they forced the lock on Charlotte's bedroom and rushed into the room, to find Charlotte and Count Castelli 'in naked bed together' as the contemporary phrase went. It does not mean exactly what it seems, since men and women very rarely stripped naked in the eighteenth century, even for sexual purposes in bed. The Count was dressed in his shirt and a night-cap (to cover his shaven head that in daytime was concealed under his wig), and Charlotte was in her shift and head clothes. Evidence that they had spent an energetic night together was provided by two empty pint bottles of sack and ratafia and four empty jelly glasses on the table next to the bed. All this was viewed by Leonard Calvert and the other men at his back, who all crowded into the room to witness the spectacle.

The bailiff seized Count Castelli, who was trying to conceal himself behind the bed-curtain, saying, 'You are the gentleman we are looking for, I suppose,' and told him to 'surrender himself to Mr Calvert'. Leonard Calvert proceeded to strip Charlotte of all her personal possessions. He removed the diamond ring from her finger, and asked her about a second, which she said she had pawned to Count Castelli. He emptied her purse of the twenty guineas he found in it; he even took the buckles off her shoes. An hour later he bundled her out of the house, stripped of everything she possessed 'saving what was on her back'. Over the next twelve days he had the contents of the house inventoried, appraised, and removed to his own house. His victory over Charlotte appeared to be complete.[45]

[45] Ibid. Eee. 10/309, 311, 314.

The property he seized was substantial, as we know from the detailed inventory of the household goods that Charlotte promptly filed with the Court and claimed to be her own (in fact many of them must have belonged to, or been paid for by, Counts Briançon and Castelli, but of course she could hardly admit that).[46] The large quantity and the high quality of the goods indicate that Charlotte and Count Briançon, and later Count Castelli, had been living in an opulent style, and at first Leonard was no doubt well pleased with his coup. But he reckoned without Charlotte, who was a determined and resourceful woman with influential relatives and skilled lawyers. What Leonard forgot was that, although by law he had a right to all his wife's property, he was also liable for all her debts for maintenance in a style suitable to her degree. After her expulsion, Charlotte directed her many creditors to send their bills to Leonard, and they soon began to pour in: £77 from the poulterer, unpaid since the separation in 1705, £77 from the mercer, £23 from the linen-draper. The creditors were angry and 'threatened to arrest or sue me for the same'. Leonard alleged that the total debts accumulated by Charlotte since the separation (presumably including the £3,000 run up from 1705 to 1707 which he had already paid) amounted to £8,000, for all of which he now found himself liable.

Leonard thought that he was beaten. He was afraid that the court might throw out his case against Charlotte on grounds of 'recrimination' because of his own adultery, and he was now entangled in lawsuits and under threat of arrest by his wife's creditors. He went so far as to offer to continue to maintain Charlotte 'according to my estate and quality, provided she will live in some house of credit and reputation such as my Lord and Lady Lichfield and his Grace the Duke of Northumberland and all her trustees shall think proper and appoint her'. All that he now asked for, and here he hoped to enlist the support of her relatives, was that she should stop taking new lovers and constantly getting pregnant, thus bringing disgrace not only on herself but on him; and also that she should be restrained from running up enormous debts which eventually he had to pay.[47] It was not an unreasonable request, but it was not at all what he had originally set out to achieve when he first launched the suit. In fact, however, the Court favoured Leonard in the end. Despite the overwhelming evidence of his own adultery, the Consistory Court decreed a separation, presumably on the grounds that, although Charlotte's prior proven adulteries had started after his, thereafter she had run through a long succession of lovers. Although Charlotte appealed the case to the Court of Arches, she lost again in December 1710.[48] Both

---

[46] Ibid. D.356: 1170–9; G.79/11.   [47] Ibid. D.356: 1210–17; see also E.20/27.
[48] Ibid. E.20/27; B.14/180.

Calvert *v.* Calvert

Courts seem to have been applying the double standard with a vengeance: they clearly had no sympathy for a promiscuous wife.

Because both parties were adulterous, Charlotte did not give in, but appealed the case up to the ultimate court of appeal, the Court of Delegates, which also finally gave a verdict against her. She was able to pursue the lawsuit, since, as long as the case continued, her husband was obliged to pay not only her allowance, but also her taxed (assessed) legal costs, which amounted to perhaps half or more of the whole. A century earlier or later, the verdict would very probably have gone the other way, the two adulteries being taken to have cancelled each other out, and Leonard's petition for divorce would have failed. He would have been forced to come to terms with Charlotte and to continue to provide her with adequate maintenance.

Although he was still a Catholic, in 1710 Leonard began a suit for full divorce in the House of Lords, on the grounds of the more recent adulteries of Charlotte after the formal private separation. The House delayed action while the separation suit was still before the Court of Delegates, and in the end Leonard dropped it. One can only surmise that either the Catholic clergy put pressure on him to do so, or that, in view of the overwhelming evidence of his own adultery, he realized that his bill had no chance of passing in Parliament.[49]

In 1713 he finally abjured the Roman Catholic faith of the Calverts and declared himself a convert to Anglicanism, in reward for which he was restored to the Proprietorship of Maryland, of which his father had been deprived. Next year he turned up in Parliament as Tory MP for Harwich in the critical 1714 Parliament. A year later his father died and he inherited the title and estates of Lord Baltimore. But he did not live to enjoy them for more than a mere three months, dying at the early age of 36. Whether or not his liaison with Mary Grove continued until his death is unknown.

As for Charlotte, after the legal separation in 1711 she still kept the £150 pin-money assured her in her marriage contract. But she was a grossly extravagant woman and Leonard was no longer responsible for her debts. It is most likely that she stayed on with Count Castelli, or found herself another rich protector. She was certainly not reduced to penury, for some time between Leonard's death in 1715 and 1719 she married Christopher Crowe Esq., who had been consul at Leghorn. But she, too, came to an early end, dying of rheumatism in her husband's house at Woodford in Essex in 1721 at the age of 42. Within eleven years of the separation both parties were dead.

---

[49] *JH Lords*, 19: 226a, 272a; Private Act 9 Anne.

There is a peculiarly brutal and exploitative quality about gender relations in the period 1680 to 1720, which is reflected both in this and other legal cases and also on the stage and among the writings of pamphleteers. Violence, perjury, rape, and obsessive promiscuous sexuality are the hallmark of this age, when gender relations were on the turn, when women were at last beginning to assert themselves, and when contractual theories were starting to spread even into domestic relations, modifying the patriarchal power of parents and friends and raising the aspirations for the happiness of children. For a while, however, this period of conflicting values led to extremes of behaviour patterns, all of which are exhibited in rich detail in the unedifying story of the Calverts, Beau Feilding, and the Duchess of Cleveland.

4
Turst v. Turst
Marital cruelty and the wife's separate estate,
1725–1738

In 1725 Thomas Sebastian Turst, one of the Sergeants-at-Arms and Mace-Bearer to King George I, agreed to marry Catherine Jane Mary Peltier, from a well-to-do Huguenot family. Thomas's official salary was only £100 a year, whereas Catherine had inherited £3,000 in stock from her father's estate. Since Thomas could provide no jointure to match it, it was agreed that her whole estate should be settled on trustees for her exclusive personal use. Five years later her mother died, leaving her another £400, also in trust for her exclusive personal use. She later claimed, not only that she paid for her own wedding clothes, which was normal, but that after marriage she often paid for the housekeeping and the rent, and that on the death of George I she lent her husband £80 to renew the patent of his office. So she could argue that she paid her full share of the family expenses.[1]

Thomas soon proved to be a brute who, when drunk, was in the habit of hitting her and calling her names. In 1729, after four years of marriage, they agreed to separate, and she was persuaded by her trustees to give Thomas an allowance out of the income from her fortune. After ten months the couple were reconciled, but the beatings soon started again, especially when Thomas was drunk. But now the beatings had a purpose, which was to force Catherine to surrender to her husband the settlement of her property on trustees, so that he could gain control of her fortune. This was something which she obstinately refused to do. To increase the pressure, Thomas threatened to take her off into the country where her relations could not trace her, and to lock her up there. At other times he threatened 'to lock her up in a madhouse'. Worst of all, he removed all three of their children and put them somewhere where their mother could not find them; and, as a final refinement of cruelty, he told her (falsely) that the baby was dying. At home, he put her more or less under house arrest, in the charge

---

[1] LPCA, D. 2124: 61–6, 303, 311, 319–25, 334–5, 340.

of a wardress called Dolly, who often kept her locked up in her room for a week on end. But she still would not surrender her fortune, and in 1733 she managed to escape from the house and flee.[2]

By now she was so frightened of her husband that she went into hiding in Spitalfields, passing herself off as Mrs Thomas, and visited only by her brother. As a result, she entirely lost contact with her children. Meanwhile Thomas settled down in a bizarre *ménage à trois* with a Mr and Mrs Vandrick. For a while he slept in the same room as they did, in a separate bed. Mr Vandrick would complaisantly get up early every morning and leave his wife and Thomas in bed together for hours on end behind locked doors. Catherine later collected overwhelming proofs of Thomas's adultery, supplied by a continuously changing stream of maidservants in the Vandrick household.[3]

For nine years Thomas kept looking for his wife, his intention being to seize her by force and renew the pressure to force her to turn over her fortune to him. But it was not until February 1738 that he finally ran her to ground. He suddenly appeared at her house one day accompanied by two strong men, who seized her and carried her off to the Vandrick house, where she was put in a locked bedroom, the windows of which had been nailed up. He also seized all her movable goods, including £70 in banknotes, £130 in cash, silver objects, eight family pictures, clothes, and a spinet. Once he had got her into his power at the Vandricks' house, he stripped her naked, equipped himself with a thick birch rod taken from a large broom, and began whipping her ferociously to force her to agree to surrender her estate in trust. She screamed 'murder' every time she was beaten, which was up to ten times a day, and cried most of the rest of the time, but the Vandricks encouraged Thomas in his brutality, and none of her friends or relatives knew where she was.[4]

Exactly how long it was before she was rescued is not clear, but it was certainly at least four days. She was saved by a maidservant, who after three days could no longer stand the repeated sounds of the blows of Thomas's birch rod on Catherine's body, and of the latter's screams. The maid gave notice and quit the house after only five days of service, and immediately reported the situation to Catherine's brother. On the basis of an affidavit by the maid, the latter obtained a writ of habeas corpus from the Chief Justice, and so secured his sister's release into his custody. She was badly cut and bruised, but still stubborn in her refusal to surrender her fortune. Even when her trustees urged her to make some compromise

[2] Ibid. 69–72, 77, 79–82, 313, 327, 337–9.
[3] Ibid. 82, 100–13, 212–16, 228–33, 260–2, 268–9, 278, 293, 326.
[4] Ibid. 84–5, 88–94, 242–6, 253, 256, 304–9, 330.

agreement with Thomas in return for concessions such as access to her children, she would not give an inch.[5]

Instead, she gathered her evidence and sued her husband in the London Consistory Court for separation on the grounds of adultery and cruelty, and easily won her case both there and on appeal to the Court of Arches. This put her in a position to obtain alimony from Thomas, but she still could not obtain access to the children.[6] The ecclesiastical courts had no jurisdiction over child custody, and the common-law courts followed the ancient rule that the father had absolute power over the disposal of his children, regardless of the wishes of the mother and however badly he might have behaved to her.

Whether Catherine could successfully have sued Thomas for damages for kidnapping, assault, and battery is far less clear, for the powers of a husband to punish his wife were legally still very extensive, although indeterminate. But even by early eighteenth-century standards Thomas had gone too far in the calculated brutality of his treatment of his wife.

This story is unusual only in the degree of brutality used by Thomas in his efforts to force his wife to surrender to him her property, which had been settled on trustees for her exclusive use. Fathers of daughters had first begun to make these trusts in the late seventeenth century, and almost at once Chancery began to protect them. But many husbands naturally resisted, and the struggle to obtain possession of the trust estates of wives was fought out in household after household from then until the late nineteenth century, when Parliament at last legislated to provide secure protection for married women's property.

In these struggles to force a wife to surrender to her husband control over property vested in trustees on her behalf, the three weapons that a husband had at his disposal were consistant wheedling or bullying—being 'kissed or kicked' as it was later described; the removal of the children from the house and a refusal to allow their mother any access to them; and kidnapping followed by indefinite incarceration at home or in a madhouse, sometimes, as in this case, accompanied by physical torture. Only the last was subject to legal intervention, and then only if the wife's friends could find out where she was confined, and also obtain a writ of habeas corpus for her release.

[5] Ibid. 95–6, 248. [6] Ibid. B. 16/171, 17/117.

5

Dineley v. *Dineley*
Cruelty, adultery, and murder, 1717–1741

In the seventeenth century, the Gooderes were a middling gentry family living in a substantial Elizabethan country house at Burhope in Hereford-shire.[1] The first to break out of this obscure provincialism was John Goodere, who after the Restoration sought his fortune in India. He ended his career as Deputy-Governor of Bombay and died in about 1685. It was this success-ful career in India that set the family on a rapidly upward social trajectory. It enabled John in 1679 to marry his son and heir Edward to Eleanor, the 18-year-old only daughter and heiress of Sir Edward Dineley, the last of a wealthy family seated at Charleton in Worcestershire, where they could trace their pedigree back for ten generations.[2] By combining the Goodere for-tune with the much larger fortune of the Dineleys, Edward Goodere was able to enter the ranks of the national élite (see Genealogy of the Goodere 'Dineley' family). From the death of his father-in-law in about 1706 until the death of his wife in 1714, he enjoyed part of the Dineley fortune, which helped him to acquire a baronetcy in 1707, and get elected as Tory MP for the town of Evesham near Charleton from 1708 to 1715. He later served as Knight of the Shire for his home county of Herefordshire from 1722 to 1727, and lived to the ripe old age of 82, not dying until 1739.[3]

Sir Edward had three sons and one daughter, besides a son who died in

[1] The principal documentation for this chapter is: LPCA, D.601 and E.9; *Genuine Trial*, which is described as 'taken in shorthand by the order and direction of S. Foot of Worcester College, Esq, and nephew of the late Sir John Dineley Goodere'; *Memoirs; Fratricide;* and *Trials.* Samuel Foote wrote his pamphlets when he was 21, soon after he had been expelled from Worcester College, Oxford, where he had been a Founder's Kin Scholar, and even sooner after a disastrous marriage, apparently made merely to recoup his tottering fortunes. The pamphlets were a way to make some money in a hurry, and some of his more far-fetched stories about the Gooderes and Dineleys may well be inventions, concocted to help sales (S. Trefman, *Sam Foote Comedian, 1721–1777* (New York, 1971) 6–11).

There is an engraving of the Burhope house at the end of *Memoirs*; it was nine miles out from Hereford on the Leominster road.

[2] J. and J. B. Burke, *Extinct and Dormant Baronetcies* (London, 1838), s.n. Goodere; Sir Thomas Phillips, *Pedigree of Dineley of Charleton* (privately printed, 1842) (Bodl., Cap. 6.19 (98)).

[3] G. E. Cokayne, *Complete Baronetage* (Exeter, 1900–9), v. 5; M. L. Stephen, *State Trials Political and Social* (London, 1899), ii. 283; R. Sedgwick and J. Brooke, *History of Parlia-ment, The House of Commons, 1715–54* (London, 1970), ii. 68.

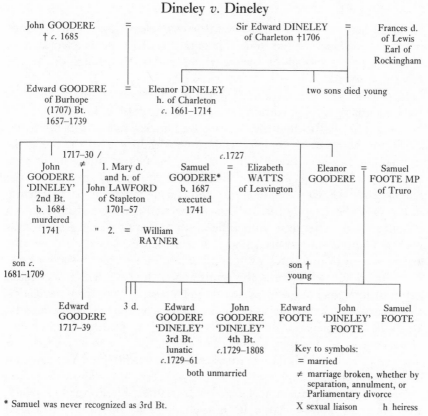

Dineley v. Dineley

John GOODERE † *c.* 1685	=	Sir Edward DINELEY of Charleton †1706	= Frances d. of Lewis Earl of Rockingham

Edward GOODERE of Burhope (1707) Bt. 1657–1739 = Eleanor DINELEY h. of Charleton *c.* 1661–1714

two sons died young

1717–30 /

John GOODERE 'DINELEY' 2nd Bt. b. 1684 murdered 1741 ≠ 1. Mary d. and h. of John LAWFORD of Stapleton 1701–57

" 2. = William RAYNER

*c.*1727

Samuel GOODERE* b. 1687 executed 1741 = Elizabeth WATTS of Leavington

Eleanor GOODERE = Samuel FOOTE MP of Truro

son *c.* 1681–1709

son † young

Edward GOODERE 1717–39

3 d.

Edward GOODERE 'DINELEY' 3rd Bt. lunatic *c.*1729–61

John GOODERE 'DINELEY' 4th Bt. *c.*1729–1808

both unmarried

Edward FOOTE

John 'DINELEY' FOOTE

Samuel FOOTE

Key to symbols:
= married
≠ marriage broken, whether by separation, annulment, or Parliamentary divorce
X sexual liaison   h heiress

* Samuel was never recognized as 3rd Bt.

2. Genealogy of the Goodere 'Dineley' family

infancy. The daughter married Samuel Foote Esq. of Truro, an attorney, JP, and MP, and had three sons, but they will only reappear at the very end of this story. In 1705 Edward's third son, Samuel, entered the Royal Navy, where he had a somewhat chequered career. He will play a key role in the story, but only towards the end.

The eldest son was born in about 1681 and was killed in a duel in Ireland in 1709, leaving no children. This unexpected death radically altered the configuration of the family by making the second son, John, the heir to the combined Goodere and Dineley estates. Up to this time John had lived the life of a younger son with no expectations. His maternal grand-father, Sir Edward Dineley, who apparently had the direction of the education of the children, 'was determined not to adhere to that false principle which had so much prevailed amongst the English gentry, of rather letting them starve than derogate from the dignity of their family by putting any of them to trade'. He therefore sent John to sea in the

merchant service, where he followed the example of his Goodere grandfather and made his way to India. There he apparently made a fair amount
of money, partly through his own exertions, and partly through the help of
influential friends.[4]

In 1708 he quit the merchant marine to serve as a volunteer on HMS
Diamond during the war with France. But, on the death of his elder brother
the next year, he became the heir to the Dineley estate, and his father
called him home. With some reluctance he withdrew from the life at sea
to which he had been bred. Five years later his mother died, and in 1714
at the age of about 33 he found himself the owner and occupier of the
rambling old Dineley family house and 1,600-acre estate at Charleton,
in the parish of Cropthorne, half-way between Pershore and Evesham in
Worcestershire. This shift from a life at sea to that of a landed squire was
not easy for him, since, as his nephew Samuel Foote explained apologetically,
he 'succeeded to the estate without an education suitable to such a rank.
For with all due deference to the gentlemen of the navy, a ship was not at
that time thought a proper academy for politeness, nor the art of navigation
a necessary ingredient towards composing a social character.' Consequently,
'any little negligences in his conduct' were to be ascribed to 'the prejudice
of his education'. He was, Foote admitted, 'neither polite in his dress or
behaviour', and even his father remarked that he was fitter to be a boatswain
than a baronet.[5]

His first obligation was to look after his father, Sir Edward Goodere.
Ever since his father-in-law's death in about 1706, Sir Edward had been
living off his wife's Dineley estate, and the transfer of that property to his
son John on her death in 1714 meant a serious financial loss to him. He was
a man with the extravagant tastes of a newly created baronet and was an
MP at a time when elections were both frequent and expensive. To ease his
father's financial position, John was obliged under the Dineley trust deed
to transfer part of the property worth £500 a year to his father for life,
which enabled the latter to maintain himself in the style to which he had
become accustomed.[6] Even after this compulsory transfer, however, John
was still a very wealthy landowner, and to mark his change of status he
substituted the name of Dineley for that of Goodere, signed his name 'John
Dineley alias Goodere', and was henceforth known as Squire Dineley.
Even after he finally succeeded to the Goodere baronetcy, he continued to
call himself Sir John Dineley, Bt.

---

[4] T. R. Nash, *Collections for the History of Worcestershire* (London, 1799), i. 272–3;
Memoirs, 6–7.
[5] *Memoirs*, 7, 16; *Fratricide*, 26.   [6] *Memoirs*, 8.

Dineley *v.* Dineley

Soon after inheriting his fortune, John set about finding himself a wife, which he did with a single-minded concentration on wealth rather than psychological compatibility. His choice fell upon a fatherless 14-year-old heiress, Mary Lawford, and he succeeded in persuading the girl's mother (who was also her guardian) that Mary was ripe for marriage and that he would make her a suitable husband. According to Mary's own later testimony, she brought with her an estate of £600 a year in hand at Tockington, and another £1,000 a year or so at Stapleton, to come on the death of her mother. John claimed that her estate amounted only to £400 year and anyway was mortgaged to two Bristol merchants for £3,200. Despite these allegations, it is clear that in fact the property was worth a great deal more than John was willing to admit, and twenty-five years later a sworn witness in court testified that Mary's fortune amounted to £20,000. In return, John promised to settle on Mary a jointure as widow of £600 a year, but this promise was never fulfilled, since when he died the estate was still not settled.[7]

John's description of Mary's social status, however, was closer to the truth than her own. She claimed to be 'by birth a gentlewoman, and descended from an ancient gent's family'; he said she was 'of mean and low extraction'. Although her father had indeed passed as a gentleman, the Lawfords do not appear in any genealogy or heraldic visitation, and the maker of the family fortune had been her grandfather, a successful businessman and alderman of Bristol. She was, moreover, uneducated to a degree that was very unusual indeed for one of her station and income by the early eighteenth century.[8] In that respect she and John were well matched.

In January 1717 the 34-year-old ex-merchant seaman John Dineley married the 14-year-old semi-illiterate heiress Mary Lawford. For a while they lived with Mary's mother at Stapleton, where in December 1717 Mary gave birth to a son. Two years later the family moved, with seven or more servants to attend to their needs, back to Charleton. According to Mary, the Dineley estate was worth at least £3,200 a year, while the goods and personal property amounted to at least £10,000. There is independent testimony that this was not too far from the truth.[9] It would appear that by 1726 John was in possession, in his own right or that of his wife, of some £4,800 a year and three houses. This would have put him well into the upper ranks of the squirearchy, while even a substantial scaling-down of

[7] LPCA, D.601: 399, and E.9/200; *JH Lords*, 25: 378a; *Bill of Divorce of Sir John Dineley* and *Case of Dame Mary Dineley* (BL 357 c 7 (38 and 40)).

[8] LPCA, D.601: 394, and E.9/200.

[9] LPCA, D.601: 401; *JH Lords* 25: 378a; *Gent's Mag.*, 11 (1741), 50; *Trials*, 5.

these estimates to £3,000 a year would still leave him a man of considerable affluence.

At this point John's prospects looked very good indeed. In course of time the combined estates of the Gooderes, the Dineleys, and the Lawfords could be expected to descend to him and his son and heir. If all had gone well, and the family had switched their political loyalties to the Whig party and retained the respect of the community, this income might have been sufficient to have pushed the Dineley Gooderes up into the peerage. But things did not go well, and by 1770 the family had utterly destroyed itself, primarily because of matrimonial disputes and arbitrary changes in property dispositions. Exacerbating factors were personal flaws of character, violent family quarrels, and more than a touch of hereditary mental instability. The end of the baronetcy by the failure of the male line in 1808 merely served to mark the demise of the family, the ruin of whose fortunes and reputation had already taken place half a century before.

The first evidence of John's eccentricity and lack of suitability to fulfil the role of an eighteenth-century landed squire occurred as early as 1716. As soon as he settled at Charleton in 1712, John was appointed a member of the Bench by a Tory Lord Chancellor. Although his younger brother was later to be a staunch Whig, John was a Tory like his father, and it is quite possible that it was dislike of his political views and of his ostentatious contempt for the Church that lay behind the collection four years later of a series of scandalous charges against him. They were assembled by a nearby clerical JP and led to his permanent dismissal from the Bench by the Whig Lord Chancellor Cowper in 1716.[10]

The actions of which he was accused, however, have a ring of truth about them. One minor accusation was of public breaking of the Sabbath both by hunting with hounds and by helping physically to get a long-sunken boat of his pulled out of the river. Another was his refusal to pay his share of the assessment on the parish for repair of the highways, or to allow one of his tenants to contribute more than three of the four days' labour that were due. More serious was his treatment of a spinster who lived and worked at home to look after and support her poor aged mother. She had annoyed John by testifying against him in a lawsuit with his cousin—for he was already feuding with his relatives. To revenge himself against her, John, in his capacity as JP, issued a warrant for her arrest as 'an idle, dissolute and disorderly person', and ordered her confinement in

---

[10] The following three paragraphs are taken from: Hertfordshire Record Office, Panshanger MSS D/EP/F154, fos. 60–64v; N. Landau, *The Justices of the Peace 1679–1760* (Berkeley, Calif., 1984), 90–1.

the county gaol, with instruction to the gaoler to put her to work and punish her 'by putting fetters upon her and by moderate whipping her'. When she eventually appeared before the Bench, the Justices immediately discharged her.

This was bad enough, since the warrant was both illegal and immoral, but the final accusation added weird magical and sexual overtones to the range of allegations against him. One day in 1716 John arrested a woman on suspicion of being a witch, and made her submit to the ancient, but now officially discredited, ordeal by water. The procedure consisted in hog-tying the suspect, wrists to ankles, and throwing her into deep water, with a rope round her waist with which to pull her out. If she floated, it was proof she was aided by the devil; if she sank, it was proof she was innocent, but she was in danger of drowning if not hauled out in time.

Before a large crowd of both sexes assembled on the river bank, John had the suspected witch stripped to her shift; a rope was tied around her waist, but she was not, apparently, hog-tied as well. He then ordered her to be pulled into the deep water below the mill sluice, where she struggled about on the surface until she was exhausted, and was finally hauled out. John commented: 'By God she swims like a cork!' Then, for some unknown reason, perhaps because he was very drunk, he stripped himself naked, jumped into the water, and swam about on his back with his private parts exposed to public view. When he came out of the water, he went into the mill and pulled on his breeches in front of several women, asking as he did so which of them wanted to be 'knocked'. When a woman asked why he had ordered the suspect to be pulled into the water, he replied that it was 'because the hair of her cunt is too long and reaches under her feet'. This remark is so wildly implausible that it is hard to believe that the witness made it up.

It is not easy to interpret this bizarre episode. Belief in witchcraft was on the decline in educated circles, while trial by ordeal had long been regarded by lawyers as obsolete. Both, however, survived as a part of popular culture. The 'swimming' of witches was an ancient legal practice of the early Middle Ages, when it had been used for settling many otherwise insoluble cases of justice. Rejected by the more rationalist authorities in the late seventeenth century, ordeal by water continued to be used by lynch mobs well into the eighteenth, the evidence being especially plentiful between 1690 and 1720.[11]

But John is the last English public official known to have supervised such as ordeal—if ordeal it was, since the woman was not hog-tied. It

---

[11] K. Thomas, *Religion and the Decline of Magic* (London, 1971), 453, 551.

remains unclear, however, why he himself plunged into the water and swam about. Why did he expose himself naked to a large mixed audience? Why did he make such crude sexual overtures to the women in the crowd, and why did he make such a peculiar remark about the suspect's pubic hair? It should be remembered that witches were commonly suspected of having sexual relations with the devil, and it was therefore customary to inspect their pudenda for abnormalities. It is therefore quite possible that an exceptionally long mat of pubic hair could have aroused suspicions of witchcraft.

The most plausible explanation of the events is that John was adopting the folklore mentality about witches of the lower classes, in whose company he had been brought up in the merchant service at sea. The case is unusual since it was the legal authority—that is John in his capacity as JP—rather than the mob who was taking the lead in organizing the ordeal, and this probably seemed as serious a charge to the rationalist Whig Lord Chancellor as John's undignified and obscene sexual antics.

It was not until early 1720, soon after the birth and immediate death of a second boy, that there appeared the first evidence of serious marital friction between John and Mary. The ostensible cause of the quarrel, as of so many other subsequent ones, was Mary's taste for gadding about the countryside, while her husband preferred to stay at home. The violent form it took, however, was caused by flaws in John's character. By universal consent he was reputed in the neighbourhood to be an extremely choleric, ill-tempered, and brutal man, who habitually lost his temper with both servants and wife, especially when in liquor. A few witnesses claimed that John's moods oscillated, and that he could sometimes be amiable and even kind, but all agreed that his flash point was abnormally low, and his rages abnormally violent.[12] In 1724 a boy called Joseph Baker bound himself to serve John as his personal servant for seven years, but he quit his service after six and a half years. He complained that John was 'a hard cross master . . . frequently beating him and using him ill'. It is very noticeable that, apart from the gardener and butler, none of the many servants who later gave evidence had lasted longer than three years in John's service. Several stated that they had quit in disgust at his behaviour.[13]

One evening in February 1723 Mary came home very late, after having promised to be back early. At midnight, soon after they had gone to bed, John worked himself up into a rage, kicked her out of bed, turned her out of the house into the cold winter's night, and bolted all the doors. He told

[12] LPCA, D.601: 76, 118, 134, 153, 158, 189, 245, 251, 252, 262, 276, 278, 284, 287, 288, 297. [13] Ibid. 99.

her to go back to where she had come from, and forbade the servants to let her in again. Still in a fury, John afterwards turned out the nursemaid, together with his young son Edward, saying, 'Take the child and carry it to its mother, or I will break its neck.' At one in the morning Mary, the maid, and the little boy arrived at the door of a nearby cottage belonging to a wheelwright, William Andrews. He and his wife obligingly got out of their bed, gave it to the nurse and the little boy, and went into the only other bed with their children. Mary sat up all night in the kitchen, complaining about her mistreatment to her housekeeper, who had hurried over from the big house to comfort her mistress. The next morning Mary appealed for help to a neighbour, an elderly gentleman, Captain Jacob Meyrick, who acted as mediator between husband and wife. He successfully reconciled them, and John actually apologized for his outburst of temper.[14]

In the summer of 1726 Mary went on a two-month visit to her mother at Stapleton, leaving John to be looked after by the housekeeper, Elizabeth Atkins. On her return Mary learnt that there had been 'greater freedoms and familiarities between John and Atkins than were common'. Although she herself had brought Elizabeth Atkins into the house as her companion, she was naturally jealous, and bitter quarrels soon broke out between the two women. Mary dismissed Elizabeth, but the latter—who was universally regarded as 'a person of very vile character' and 'of mean extraction'— refused to leave, asserting that she could be dismissed only by John, who encouraged her in her truculent defiance of his wife. John, however, soon became more and more exasperated at these constant altercations between Mary and Atkins, and one day his temper finally snapped. His servant Joseph Baker met John in the passage between the parlour and the hall, pulling Mary along by the arm, cursing her, and saying that he would lock her up in a closet in the hall. But he changed his mind, and dragged her up to a garret under the roof of the house where the cheese was kept, Baker 'lighting them with a candle'. When they came to the garret, John told Baker to fetch a chain used to stake horses when put out to grass. Baker refused to obey the order, so John locked Mary in the garret and, still convulsed with fury, threw his slipper at Baker, who fled. John went outside, fetched the chain and two horse padlocks, returned to the garret, and chained his wife by one ankle to a post. He did have the humanity to order a bed to be brought up to the garret, but he also threatened 'to keep her there and beat her to death if she would not carry herself civilly to Elizabeth Atkins'. Mary alleged that the chain was fastened so tightly around her leg that it swelled and turned black and blue. John relented

---

[14] Ibid. 31–2, 154–5, 297, 306, 375; *JH Lords*, 25: 377b.

only after thirty-six hours and then only thanks to the intervention of neighbours. Soon afterwards Elizabeth Atkins seems to have left the household, since nothing more is heard of her.[15]

The next year, in 1727, there was another great quarrel, as a result of which John went up to London to see the Coronation of George II by himself, leaving Mary behind at Charleton.[16] This must have been a bitter blow to so habitual a party-goer as Mary. By 1728 the pair were on more-or-less continual bad terms, and Mary was the subject of a steady barrage of verbal abuse, especially when John was fuddled with drink, as he often was.

There seem to have been three main causes for John's irritation with her. The first was her love of gadding about.[17] The circles in which they moved ranged from a local baronet and his sisters, who had come to live in a big house two miles away, to the keepers of local alehouses and inns. They were a wholly uncultivated, idle, and disreputable crowd, who apparently spent most of their time either hunting and coursing in the fields, or drinking themselves almost insensible in each other's houses and in nearby alehouses and inns. Women participated as equals in both the sports and the drinking parties, and Mary was always prominent in both. John was also a hard drinker, but he was far less sociable, and mostly preferred to toss off bumpers and get drunk at home. He was noticeably anxious to get on the record that he was generally regarded as 'a careful man'.[18] Mary, on the other hand, was much more convivial. She spent her days galloping about in largely male company on the hunting field, and part of her nights carousing for hours on end in alehouses. John complained a good deal about her taste for strong liquor, although alcohol mostly seems to have made her drowsy.[19] But one witness in later litigation hardly helped her case by swearing that he had never seen her too drunk to walk or talk.[20]

John's second grievance against Mary was what he regarded as her slovenly, dirty, and unladylike habits and tastes. He blamed her for 'making her maids familiar with her', instead of keeping her social distance. He disliked her habit of 'going a-milking', telling her rather 'to go and sit in your parlour, which is a place much more proper for you'. He objected to Mary 'doing some servile work' in the kitchen, and told her that 'it is a shame for you to do such dirty work.' He asked her 'to keep yourself neat and clean as other ladies of your fortune'.[21] This particular grievance came to a head in 1727 when John fell sick. He was convinced that Mary's

---

[15] LPCA, D.601, 35–8, 77–82, 331, 375.   [16] Ibid. 320, 380.
[17] Ibid. 339.   [18] Ibid. 262, 284, 292, 302, 370.
[19] Ibid. 101, 104, 130, 144, 168–70, 214, 283, 347.
[20] Ibid. 103.   [21] Ibid. 103, 269, 292, 302, 310, 338–9; E.9/199.

careless and dirty habits made it unsafe for him to be nursed by her, and so removed himself for three weeks to the neighbouring alehouse, the Golden Fleece at Bengeworth, where he thought he could be better cared for by the owners, Mr and Mrs Smith. He complained to everyone he met, including the servants, casual employees, and visitors, that Mary did not look after him properly. He told them that 'I could not get anything that was convenient, and my wife would not allow me so much as a little wine in my cordial.' He explained to a wheelwright and his wife, 'if I had stayed at home I would have been poisoned with nastiness'.[22]

Another complaint, which he made to Mrs Chappell, the woman who kept his other favourite alehouse, the Sign of the Angel at Pershore, was that 'my wife keeps common whores in my house, and my house is no better than a bawdy house'.[23] Just what he meant by this wild sexual accusation is not clear. What is certain, however, is that he complained about his wife to a wide circle of acquaintances, who ranged from his social equals to a wheelright, servant girls, and keepers of inns and alehouses. Every detail of the Dineleys' domestic difficulties therefore became common knowledge throughout the area.

John's last grievance, which in the end broke up the marriage, was his jealousy of Mary's growing friendship with Sir Robert Jason, Bt. Sir Robert and his three sisters appeared on the scene only in 1728, living at a big house at Hinton-on-the-Green, a few miles down the road from Charleton. The background of the Jasons was very much like that of the Dineley Gooderes. The sixth baronet, Sir Robert, was also a younger son who had unexpectedly inherited the family estate in 1728 on the premature death of his 23-year-old elder brother. His father had also been a younger son, a Londoner who late in life had inherited first the estate on the death of his stepgrandmother in 1713, and then the title on the deaths of his brother and nephew in the same year. Robert Jason and John Dineley were younger sons who had not been educated for the positions they had unexpectedly inherited. Robert Jason was at most only 21 when he came into estate and title in 1728, and was not married. He consequently brought along with him a rather older unmarried sister to run the house for him, while two others paid them long visits.

At first John Dineley actively cultivated the friendship of these new neighbours, with whom he shared a common enthusiasm for hunting, coursing, and the bottle. The Jasons were frequent visitors to Charleton, often staying for days at a time. But he soon grew extremely jealous of Mary's evident liking for Sir Robert's company, as well as her close friendship with

---

[22] LPCA, D.601: 261–2, 309.   [23] Ibid. 339.

Robert's evidently rackety sister Anne. One day Sir Robert came over to Charleton to dinner, and after the meal he and Mary were sitting close together by the fire. John watched them suspiciously for a while, then stalked across the room in a passion, said to Mary, 'Why don't you thrust your nose in his face,' and asked Sir Robert abruptly, 'don't you know the penalty of lying with other men's wives?' He pressed the point home by telling him 'the story of Lord Abergavenny and Lyddell', a recent and famous adultery case in which Lord Abergavenny was awarded no less than £10,000 damages against Lydell for criminal conversation with his wife.[24] On another occasion, when Sir Robert accidentally shot himself, Mary at once prepared to go to Hinton to sit up with him at his bedside. But John flatly forbade her to go, and, when she tried to leave anyway, he stopped her by force. Finally he ordered her never to see the Jasons any more, but, since these were now her closest friends, she deliberately ignored his orders.[25]

Objective witnesses, like the gardener at Charleton and the wife of a wheelwright, testified that Mary had once been mild, affable, and obedient, but that by now her behaviour had deteriorated. The former admitted that 'by reason of keeping ill company she is much altered from what she was', and the latter confirmed this impression.[26] She was drinking more and more heavily, and her ever closer association with Sir Robert Jason and his friends in 1729–30, including late night drinking parties at alehouses, aroused widespread public condemnation. Most people thought her conduct imprudent and disobedient, but not necessarily criminal.[27] But it did not help matters that Mary referred to Sir Robert in public in such familiar terms as 'the dear man of Condercop' or 'Bob of Condercop', or that late one evening after a lot of heavy drinking Sir Robert was observed in the parlour at Charleton with his arm round Mary's neck, admittedly in the presence of his sister and others. Another witness once saw them in the Angel Inn at Pershore, Mary sitting on Robert's lap, and Robert with one hand into her bosom and the other under her petticoats.

John may have been a little mad, but in his eyes Mary was disobedient, imprudent, neglectful of her duties, sluttish in her ways, and too fond both of the bottle and of Sir Robert Jason. It is hardly surprising that John was very suspicious of her relations with the latter, even if Anne Jason, who was not the most reliable of witnesses, was wrong to accuse him of being 'jealous of any man she [Mary] spoke to'. Mrs Chappell, the keeper of the inn at Pershore, who knew all parties very well, often prophesied that

[24] Plowden, i. 26–36.
[25] LPCA, D.601: 340–3, 279–82.   [26] Ibid. 272, 296–7.
[27] Ibid. 101–2, 130, 289, 300, 350; *JH Lords*, 25: 376b–377a.

Dineley v. Dineley

'there would be the Devil to pay between Mr Dineley and his wife upon the account of [her] keeping company with Sir Robert Jason, after she had been so often reprimanded for the same by her husband'.[28]

Her prophecy came true in the early months of 1730, as Mary became more and more reckless in her behaviour. One evening during the winter Sir Robert and his sister came over with his hounds to Charleton in John's absence, and stayed the night there in order to be ready to go hunting early next day. The three spent the evening drinking in Anne Jason's room, and then went to their separate beds. As was common in the eighteenth century, Mary usually took another woman to bed with her if her husband was away, either her maidservant, or another gentlewoman. It was apparently a prudent and normal insurance policy against possible accusations of adultery or attempts at rape. Whether Mary slept with her maidservant that night is not known, but Anne Jason certainly slept alone. However innocent it may in fact have been, Sir Robert's stay in the house overnight in John's absence did not look at all good.[29]

One evening in April 1730 Mary stayed out very late indeed. She came home very drunk from the house of Sir Robert Jason about four or five o'clock in the morning, 'and being in so weak a condition as not being able to stand to be undressed, did lie down on the bed with all her clothes on'. John noticed that she had a red cap on. A red cap seems to have carried connotations of whoredom: in 1820 there was a brothel in Camden Town called Mother Redcap's; in the same year the adulterous Queen Caroline was also satirized as Mother Redcap. John was therefore right to interpret the cap as a mark of whoredom, clapped on her head by her drunken companions after a night of debauchery. When she woke up in the morning, John asked her where the red cap was, and, when she denied all knowledge of it, he began beating her in a fury, cursing her for having exhibited herself in this manner.[30]

The outing was probably the cause of a nasty episode a few weeks later at Sir Robert Jason's house at Hinton. A drinking party was in progress in the kitchen in front of the servants, on the eve of a hunting expedition. Present were Sir Robert, his sister Anne, Mary, and Mr John Acton of Bengeworth. Mr Acton got extremely drunk and started abusing everyone present. He also told Sir Robert that, if he did not turn his sister Anne out of his house, she would be the ruin of him. This infuriated Anne, who called him a rogue and a rascal, picked up a candlestick, and threw it at him. Despite the drinking, her aim was good, for she hit him, but it did

[28] LPCA, D.601: 350, 168, 348.   [29] Ibid. 107–8, 175–7.
[30] BM Satirical Prints 14071, 13975; see also *OED*, s.n. 'redcap'; LPCA, E.9/199; D.601: 39, 136–7.

93

not stop his tongue. He went on to make a remark that, passed on by the servants, was soon spread over the neighbourhood and became the common talk of all Pershore and Evesham. He said 'Mr Dineley is a cuckold. He should go to Hinton and look after the drunken whore his wife.' So drunk was the party and so casual their manners that little offence seems to have been taken. At all events the next morning Mary, Sir Robert, Anne Jason, and Mr John Acton all went out hunting together, although it was observed that Anne was still cool towards Mr Acton.[31]

Inevitably, the story of Acton's remark much have got back to John, which perhaps explains the next episode, which took place shortly after, in the same month of April. Anne Jason and her sister Catherine were sitting in the parlour with Mary when John came storming in, with a horsewhip in his hand. After a curt 'Your servant, ladies,' addressed to the Jason sisters, he turned on Mary and said, 'God damn you, you bitchington, I have a great mind to whip you this moment, but I'll let it alone till tomorrow morning, and then, by God, you shall have some of the oil of this whip.' His complaint was that Mary had gone out that afternoon instead of staying at home to supervise the workmen, who were making internal alterations to the house.[32]

In May things went from bad to worse, and there was another scene in which John came into the kitchen at Charleton, swore at Mary in front of the servants, kicked her, and threatened to beat her and chain her up in a garret.[33] By now John suspected that his wife was planning to elope with Sir Robert Jason, and rumours were flying about that the two were meeting alone in an alehouse in the village.[34] Jealousy drove John to the bottle and provoked more frequent and more violent rages, during which he cursed and swore at his wife in public, both at inns and alehouses and in his own house before the servants. He called her 'slut', 'trollop', 'hell-fire bitch', and 'drunken, nasty draggle-tailed bitch in Hell'; he told her that her mother was 'broiling in Hell'; and he threatened 'to slit one of her legs to put through the other in order to keep her at home'. Again and again he threatened either to chain her up in a garret or to carry her off to a private madhouse where none of her friends or relatives could find her. He often said to her: 'God damn you, I will send you to Bedlam or some other madhouse'.[35]

One day in early June 1730 Mary came home from the Jasons so drunk that she fell off her horse several times, badly bruising herself in the

---

[31] Ibid. 113–14, 184–5, 261, 284.   [32] Ibid. 159–61.
[33] Ibid. 41–2, 83–4.   [34] Ibid. 289, 291.
[35] Ibid. 30, 56, 135, 190, 277, 328, 365; Bedlam, of course, was a public madhouse, and he could not have had Mary confined there.

process.[36] But the most scandalous episode so far took place on 21 June, when Mary stayed out all night with her maid, Sir Robert, and his sister Anne at the nearby alehouse, the Golden Fleece at Bengeworth—the same alehouse to which John had moved when he had been ill. Mary wanted to go to the alehouse to visit her friend, the daughter of the proprietors, Mr and Mrs Smith. She sent a message over to Anne Jason at Hinton to say that she was walking to the alehouse and inviting her to join her. Anne asked Mary to Hinton to dinner on the way, but she refused and waited outside with her maid until the meal was over. The three women then walked to the alehouse, where they were later joined by Sir Robert, and perhaps others. A drunken party developed, and at 11 p.m. Mary sent word home that she was staying the night there. The alehouse-keepers, Mr and Mrs Smith, did what they could to make their unexpected guests comfortable. The bed in the main guest room was shared by Mary and Anne Jason. Mary's maid, who is the only witness for what happened, was provided with a mattress on the floor in the same room, while Sir Robert was allocated a small bedroom elsewhere. But he had drunk 'very plenti-fully of punch, so much so that he was very drunk therewith'. In this inebriated condition he came staggering into the room after the three women had retired and sat heavily on the bed, complaining that this was the room in which he normally slept. Mrs Smith came up to see what the noise was all about, and then went away again.

There are two versions of what happened next. Mary admitted that Sir Robert stayed in the room all night, but claimed that 'he fell asleep in the great chair there and continued in the chamber till next morning'. The story that was much later told by the maid was different. According to her, Sir Robert lay down on the bed with Mary and Anne Jason, and, since the bed was a narrow one, there was a lot of pushing, so much to that Anne Jason cried out crossly: 'is the Devil in you? You will push me out of bed.'

Thereafter things quieted down, but once there was a lot of movement and the curtains round the bed parted, at which Mary cried out in alarm: 'draw the curtain, draw the curtain.' At three in the morning Sir Robert got out of the bed with his breeches down to his knees, buttoned himself up, and went down to fetch some cider. At six Anne Jason and the maid got up and went downstairs, leaving Mary and Sir Robert alone together in bed.[37] These highly incriminating details did not come to light at the time, but the general story of the night out at Mrs Smith's was soon all over Evesham. John complained to everyone who would listen, including trades-people such as a milliner from the town, that his wife had got drunk and

---

[36] Ibid. E.9/199.   [37] LPCA, D.601: 101–11, 179–83, 256–60.

stayed all night in the Golden Fleece in the same room as Sir Robert Jason.[38]

Matters came to a head in late July 1730. At Mary's suggestion, John agreed to go with her to the horse races at Chipping Campden. John's version of the affair, which is the more plausible of the two, is that it was inconvenient for him since he was busy supervising the harvest, but he nevertheless agreed to go later on, ordered an early dinner, and went out into the fields. When he came back and found that Mary had already left, he jumped to the conclusion that she had gone off to a rendezvous with Sir Robert Jason. Frantic with jealousy, he searched her room, only to find that many of her clothes and jewels were missing. Told by the servants that she had removed them some time before, he concluded that she and Sir Robert had already eloped or were just about to do so.[39]

Mary's story was that, since John was not ready, and since she had to go out to a paddock a mile away to pick up her horse, he told her to go on ahead, promising to catch up with her on the road. So at eleven o'clock she set out on a draught horse for the paddock, accompanied by John's servant William Dancock, who carried her saddle. But Mary had no housing for her side-saddle, since a new one was being made. She had borrowed a saddle from the Jasons, but John in his jealousy had locked it up to prevent her from using it. So she decided to go via the Jason house of Hinton to borrow another housing.

Thereafter, both accounts agree. Mary was overtaken on the road by John, who angrily asked, 'What have you done with your own clothes? I can find none of them.' When Mary replied that they were scattered in several rooms in the house, John's fury burst out. 'There are none there, God damn you for a bitch. Come back and show them. What rogue are you going to?' As he spoke, he struck her as hard as he could three or four times across the head and shoulders with the thick end of his horsewhip. Mary turned and proceeded home at a brisk trot, John whipping her horse and swearing he would chain her up 'so I will then know where to find you'.[40]

When they got to Charleton, John said, 'Come, Madam, show me your clothes,' and led her indoors, ordering William Dancock to walk the horses. Mary was unable to prove to John's satisfaction that she had not smuggled out some of her clothes and jewels, which drove him into a fresh paroxism of fury, for he was now convinced that she was about to elope. The stairs to the garrets had been temporarily removed by the workmen who were

---

[38] Ibid. 356–7, 368.   [39] Ibid. E.9/199.
[40] Ibid. D.601: 42–5, 190–6.

altering the house, so that the only way up was by two vertical ladders. John dragged Mary to the foot of the ladders and ordered her to climb them. When she said she was afraid, he retorted that he would beat her to death if she did not, and began striking her with full strength across the shoulders with the thick end of his horsewhip. This forced her up the first ladder, and further savage blows drove her up the second. John locked her in the garret, and went off to fetch a chain, a staple, and padlocks. He nailed the staple to the floor, and attached one end of the chain to it and the other to one of Mary's ankles. He swore to her that 'he would keep her chained for eight years' until she confessed what she had done with her clothes and jewels, then locked the door of the garret and went off to the Campden races, taking with him the keys of both garret and cellar, and ordering the servants not to go near Mary.

No sooner was John out of sight than the servants took action. William Dancock climbed out on to the leads of the roof, and got into the garret through the window. Mary complained that she was choked with thirst, but, since John had taken the keys of the cellar, they could get no drinkable liquid for her (to drink water from the well was obviously regarded as unthinkable). William therefore went to the nearest alehouse called the Sign of the Horseshoes, Hammer and Pincers, bought a quart bottle of ale, and returned with it to the garret. There he found Mary's maid Jane Broughton, the dairy maid, and a neighbour, Mrs Dingley, who had all climbed over the roof and in at the window. Mary was 'sitting on a chair in a sorrowful and melancholy manner with a chain fixed to her leg with a padlock' in a garret containing nothing but some lumber and old iron. She was in great pain across her arms and shoulders from the horsewhipping, and Mrs Dingley went home to fetch some spirits of wine with which to bathe the wounded flesh. Mrs Dingley, an elderly matron of 52, was apparently a friend of Mary's, although she was both poor and illiterate, unable to sign her name.

When John got back home from the Campden races at 11 p.m., he ordered a bed to be put in the garret for Mary's use. He kept her chained up there from Thursday morning to Sunday morning. On Friday he tightened the chain around her ankle 'to her great pain and torture', and kept swearing at her and threatening, 'I will murder you in case I can do so conveniently'. She told the servants that she was in genuine fear that, if he got drunk, he might do so. Every time John left the house, the servants climbed up on to the leads and into the garret to comfort Mary sitting there in chains. According to John, they brought her 'great quantities of ale, brandy and other strong liquors, of which she drank very plentifully'. They also spread the news of her imprisonment, and the neighbourhood was soon buzzing about the affair. The neighbours remonstrated with John, telling him 'it is very hard and barbarous that a gentlewoman should be so served', but his only reply was to threaten to lock her up in a madhouse. He also claimed that 'he gave her several good books to read, and desired her to reflect upon her present folly and resolve to amend in her future behaviour'. It was not until Sunday morning that the mounting pressure of public opinion persuaded him to release her.[41]

Mary lost no opportunity to show her bruises—according to John caused by her falling off her horse while returning drunk from the Jasons a few days before—and to tell her tale to Mrs Chappell, the innkeeper, and to Captain Meyrick. But she cannot have been as badly injured as she claimed, and some of the sympathy of the neighbourhood was clearly misplaced, for a few weeks later she was again out most of the day and half the night drinking with Sir Robert Jason and others at the Angel Inn at Pershore. She and Sir Robert left the inn together after midnight, and she did not get home to Charleton before four in the morning—in a very drunken condition, according to John. Soon afterwards, on 30 August 1730, Mary left Charleton, moved to London, and launched a suit in the Worcester Consistory Court for separation with alimony on grounds of cruelty, and for recovery of those of her personal possessions she had not already removed.

The inventory of these possessions shows something of the style in which she had lived. On the one hand, she was an eager participant in the activities of the vulgar, uncultivated, hard-drinking, hard-riding squires and lesser gentry of the neighbourhood. On the other hand, she was the wife of the heir to a baronetcy and the granddaughter of a wealthy Bristol alderman, and had inherited much valuable jewellery. Amongst other things, she owned one six-pound and one four-pound ingot of gold, two gold chains with pictures set in gold, one pearl necklace, four diamond rings, one gold ring and two mourning-rings, a silver coffee pot, lamp, and canister, a gold medal of Queen Anne, and silver counters for playing quadrille. She may have spent much of her life in the kitchen, the alehouse, or the hunting field, but her inherited personal belongings were undoubtedly those of a lady of substance.[42]

The last personal contacts between John and Mary took place a year later in the autumn of 1731, by which time Mary had moved back into lodgings with her friends the Smiths, the owners of the Golden Fleece alehouse at Bengeworth. At three o'clock in the morning on 7 September, as Mary was lying sick in bed with her maid in the alehouse, John rode up, cursing at

---

[41] Ibid. 46–58, 86–90, 197–204, 265–7, 334–5, 378.
[42] Ibid. 405–6.

the Smiths, and ordering them to 'pull her out of bed and turn her out of doors', or else 'I will raise the posse and pull the house down about your ears within an inch of the ground.' Mrs Smith was so terrified that she fell into fits, 'and screamed out in a frightful manner'. Meanwhile John kept threatening Smith and swearing, 'By God, I'll indict you for keeping a bawdy house and entertaining that whore my wife.' Since the alehouse was within walking distance of Sir Robert Jason's house, and had been his favorite tippling place, John had some reason to be suspicious and angry.[43]

A week later John and Mary accidentally ran into each other in the Angel Inn at Pershore. John again lost all control of himself, and publicly called her a whore, saying that she and Sir Robert Jason 'had jockeyed him'. He threatened that if he met her on horseback he would shoot her, and if he met her on foot he would strangle her, adding that he did not care if he hanged for it. Even he later admitted that 'much foul and abusive language did at that time pass on both sides'. Mary left the inn, pursued down the town street by John, who attracted a crowd by publicly shouting and swearing at her and crying 'Hollow, boys', 'Hollow, boys', which Mary interpreted as an invitation to the mob to duck her in the town pond.[44]

After Mary left him in 1730, John showed increasing signs of both alcoholism and mental instability, the two being clearly connected. The former vice grew on him more and more until 1739, when he forswore the bottle altogether, and thereafter until his death drank nothing but water. It was a change that did much to improve his mental balance. During the 1730s, however, his alcoholism and eccentricity became more and more pronounced. He was neglecting his houses at Charleton and Tockington and exhibiting signs of pathological meanness. A London woman who was hired as housekeeper at Tockington, and was promised rule over a fine mansion full of servants, found herself in 'a poor shattered house ready to tumble down about one's ears, and the household goods all to pieces', while at times there was only one servant. John was exhibiting even graver signs of mental derangement; and one witness declared that 'he hath been quite raving mad'.[45] This deterioration in John's mental state has to be borne in mind in order to understand his behaviour towards his relatives from 1730 until his switch to total abstinence in 1739.

Mary's lawsuit for separation from John with alimony was begun in the Consistory Court of Worcester in December 1730. It was the first salvo of a legal war that was to be carried on for nine years on many fronts, at a cost

---

[43] Ibid. 407–10; E.9/201; Eee.14/1, 2.   [44] LPCA, D.601: 401–12; E.9/201.
[45] *State Trials*, xvii, cols. 1059–60.

so gigantic that ultimately it almost consumed the great Dineley fortune. It was fought before one JP, three ecclesiastical courts, including the highest in the land, as well as the Court of Common Pleas, the Court of King's Bench, the Court of Chancery, and finally the House of Lords. And yet it was almost stopped in its tracks before it ever began, for, two months after Mary launched her suit in the Consistory Court, the two parties reached a private settlement.

Under the articles of agreement, John agreed to drop all lawsuits, to pay Mary £150 to clear her current debts and a maintenance allowance of £200 a year for life, and to hand over her personal clothes and jewellery. In return, Mary agreed that John could not be held legally responsible for any of her debts incurred after the day she left him in August 1730. But the conditions of the agreement were not met by John, presumably because he had begun piling up damaging evidence of Mary's adultery. So he paid her neither the £150 in cash nor the £200 a year, nor did he return her clothes. He also refused to pay her debts, and allowed himself to be sued by Mary's creditors. His purpose was to run up the costs to be charged against her allowance, 'having frequently declared that he would starve her by spending her allowance in law'.[46] Mary therefore widened the battlefield by suing John in the Court of Chancery to enforce the terms of the separation agreement. Since she had received no allowance for six months, the Court imprisoned John for four weeks until he gave a bond of £4,000 that he would in future pay her the allowance and cease all harrassment.[47]

Meanwhile John was equally active in pursuing Mary through the courts, regardless of the cost. By 1732 he had collected what seemed like convincing proof of her adultery with Sir Robert Jason, both before and after she had left Charleton. Armed with this new evidence, he sued Sir Robert Jason in the Court of Common Pleas for damages on the grounds of the latter's adultery with his wife. In this crim. con. suit he produced a lot of evidence of public sexual fondling, while the more damaging version of the drunken night at the Smith's alehouse in June 1730, evidently taken from a deposition by Mary's maid, was also brought in as evidence.

To clinch the matter beyond all dispute, Sir John finally produced two new witnesses, who testified that they had seen Mary and Sir Robert in the act of committing adultery. Henry Grove said he saw them under a tree in a field near Charleton on 23 June 1730, two days after the night at the alehouse, in the usual eighteenth-century posture with Mary on her back with her petticoats up, and Sir Robert on top of her with his breeches

---

[46] LPCA, G.106/19; *Case of Dame Mary Dineley*.
[47] Ibid; LPCA, G.106/22; *Bill of Divorce of Sir John Dineley and Case of Sir John Dineley* (BL 357 c 7 (39)).

Dineley *v.* Dineley

down. Mrs Esther Grove (presumably Henry's wife) testified to seeing them at it again in a field on 15 August, a fortnight before Mary finally left. Given this direct evidence by the Groves, it is hardly surprising that John won his case against Sir Robert Jason in the Court of Common Pleas, and was awarded by the jury damages of £1,000.[48]

Meanwhile, since the agreement of 1731 had broken down and she was not receiving her allowance, Mary encouraged her creditors to bombard John with suits for payment of her debts. He implausibly alleged that it cost him £14,000 in legal fees to fight off these debts, as a result of which he 'with some difficulty escaped being totally ruined'.[49] Mary also renewed her lawsuit in the Worcester Consistory Court for separation from John with alimony on grounds of his cruelty. The Court decided that Mary's charges about John's cruelty, although true and proven, did not constitute a life-threatening situation, which in strict canon law they had to do to justify separation with alimony. On the other hand, although John had produced solid evidence of her adultery with Sir Robert Jason, the Court decided that this defence of 'recrimination' could not serve as a bar to the original suit by the wife for separation on grounds of cruelty.[50] Mary promptly appealed the sentence against her to the Court of Arches, but was defeated again there. The Court upheld the validity of John's recrimination about her adultery which seemed proved, thanks to the testimony of Mr and Mrs Grove. Defeated in the two lower courts, Mary then took the very unusual and expensive step of appealing the case to the final court of appeal, the High Court of Delegates.[51] There she hoped to fare better, for the evidence of the two key witnesses to her adultery, Mr and Mrs Grove, now appeared to be worthless. There had always been something odd about their story. First, it was strange that Mary and Sir Robert should have risked having sexual relations in broad daylight in the open air, when they had the privacy of his house and rooms in various alehouses at their disposal; and, secondly, it was at the very least a remarkable coincidence that the witnesses to the two occasions should have been man and wife. But Mr Grove had recently confessed in an affidavit before Justice de Veil in London that he had been bribed by John to give false testimony, on a promise of a three-life lease of a farm let at over £70 a year, 'but that after the job was done, the performance of the promise was but indifferently observed, and the man never received what he expected'.[52]

Although there was still a good deal of circumstantial evidence to

---

[48] LPCA, E.30/132; *Gent's Mag.* (May 1732), 772.
[49] *Bill of Divorce of Sir John Dineley* and *Case of Sir John Dineley.*
[50] Suffolk RO, HA 5/4/89.   [51] LCPA, G. 106/39.
[52] *Fratricide,* 29–30; *JH Lords,* 25: 386b–87a.

support a charge of adultery against Mary, this revelation that the key witness had been bribed to perjure himself did much to undermine John's position. The Court of Delegates sat on the case for five years, the judges being split about how to decide it, and by 1737 it was clear that they never would pass sentence.[53] Thus these enormously expensive suits in the ecclesiastical courts petered out inconclusively after some nine years.

Thwarted in the ecclesiastical courts, John and Mary turned to the secular courts. In March 1736 Mary accused John in the Court of King's Bench of subornation of witnesses, but he was acquitted for lack of evidence. In August of the same year John indicted Mary and Sir Robert Jason in the same court on a charge of conspiracy to accuse him of attempting to murder her. The chief and only witness against her (possibly suborned like the Groves) was her maidservant. But the evidence was found sufficiently plausible for the Court in November 1737 to convict Mary and sentence her to a year in prison, although Jason was acquitted. Since John was still witholding her allowance, Mary was now reduced to penury. Her response was to run up debts for fees and diet in the Golden Lyon Sponging House (an annexe of the King's Bench Prison) and persuade the Master to sue her husband for payment. But in 1740, when the case came to trial, the Court found that much of the debt was for extravagant parties to entertain her visitors. In any case, the Court decided that Mary had no right to be in the Sponging House rather than the Prison, since she was not entitled to the freedom of the Rules of the Prison.[54] It therefore dismissed the case.

In 1739, while Mary was still languishing in prison, John moved in for the kill, introducing into the House of Lords a bill for full divorce from Mary, on grounds of the conviction in King's Bench of Sir Robert Jason for crim. con. with her. As drafted, the bill would have freed John from responsibility for any of her debts run up since her first conviction for adultery by the Worcester Consistory Court; bastardized any children born by her since the day she left Charleton in 1730; cut off all her rights to dower of the Dineley and Goodere estates; and have granted him full divorce with freedom to remarry. If passed, the bill would have ruined Mary and caused her to be thrown into prison for debt; have deprived her of any claims on the inheritance after John's death; and have enabled John to marry a new wife to beget another heir, thus possibly defeating the rights of inheritance both of their son Edward and of John's brother Samuel.

[53] Suffolk RO, HA 513/4/89; *Eng. Rep.* 162: 146.
[54] *Bill of Divorce of Sir John Dineley*; *Fratricide*, 30; *Eng. Rep.* 93: 1072 (*Fowles* v. *Sir John Dineley*).

Dineley v. Dineley

John had every hope of success, since he believed that Mary lacked the money to fight back, in addition to the moral and practical handicap of still being in prison for conspiracy. Indeed by her own admission she was reduced to a deplorable state. She declared to the Lords that she

has been left in a starving condition ever since [her imprisonment], having received no more than almost five guineas from her husband since her confinement, which is 11 months, although she was ill of a fever for about a month; and it was thought she might have died if a physician of great eminence had not attended her *gratis*; and must have starved if some persons out of mere charity had not supplied her with common necessities.

Although the sworn confession of Harry Grove about his perjured testimony about Mary's adultery was not admitted on technical grounds, it still told heavily against John. Secondly, Mary's evidence of John's cruelty was incontrovertible and was taken by the House of Lords to be a bar to divorce. Thirdly, the Lords were very uneasy about passing a divorce bill without prior sentence of separation in an ecclesiastical court. So in the end the House rejected John's bill and ordered him to pay all Mary's legal costs, amounting to £230. The end result of the nine-year legal war between Mary and John was thus a stalemate, while the costs were not merely heavy but ruinous. John claimed that his legal costs alone amounted to £14,000 and those of Mary could not have been much less.[55]

The final episodes in this prolonged and bitter war between John and his wife Mary overlapped the first episodes in an equally prolonged and bitter war between John and his younger brother, Samuel. The two battles were linked, since, if John had not suspected the paternity of his and Mary's only son, Edward, the main cause for the enmity between John and Samuel—namely a dispute about the inheritance of the great estate—would not have existed. Samuel was a ruffianly and unscrupulous fellow, who, if his nephew Samuel Foote is to be believed, had displayed his violent nature from an early age. While still a schoolboy at Henley School, he and some companions are said to have gone to Charleton and robbed the house of his maternal grandfather, and in the process 'clapped a pistol at his own mother's breast'. There was also said to survive a letter from him to his father asking for money, and threatening that in the case of refusal he would 'wait on him in the country and send a brace of bullets through his heart'. These may be inventions, but what is certain is that,

[55] *JH Lords*, 25: 360, 372, 376–8, 386–7, 411, 412; Suffolk RO, HA 5/4/89; *Bill of Divorce of Sir John Dineley*, *Case of Sir John Dineley*, and *Case of Dame Mary Dineley*; *Fratricide*, 30; J. Roberts, *Divorce Bills in the Imperial Parliament* (Dublin, 1906), 56, 361, 372, 411.

after a stint in the merchant service, Samuel joined the navy in the later years of the reign of Queen Anne, getting a post thanks to the influence of his Tory MP father. In 1715, when the Whigs were once more in the saddle, he was promoted to Lieutenant, and in 1719 to Captain, after distinguishing himself in some fighting with the Spaniards in San Sebastian. There followed a set-back, and he seems to have spent the next twenty years or so retired on half-pay, and demoted back to Lieutenant.[56]

In 1733 he tried to recover his fortunes by launching a complicated scheme of his own devising to get himself returned to active service as Captain. The Dineleys of Charleton traditionally exercised great influence over the election of MPs in the nearby borough of Evesham. One candidate, presumably a Tory, approached Lieutenant Samuel and promised to get him promoted to Captain if in return the latter would obtain the support of his father, Sir Edward, and brother John for his candidacy in the forthcoming election at Evesham. Samuel agreed, but later discovered that his candidate was in no position to make good his promise, while another more influential candidate, presumably a Whig, was equally prepared to nominate him for a captaincy in return for the family support at the election. He therefore switched sides, but Sir Edward and John refused to break their word to the first candidate, which led to a violent quarrel between the two brothers. In order to obtain control of the electoral process, both Samuel (who was presumably now a Whig) and John (who was certainly a Tory) contested the office of Mayor of Evesham, and both were elected by rival factions in the town. The Sunday after the Mayoral election, John Dineley arrived at the city church and took his place of honour in the Mayor's pew. But Samuel arrived soon after the service had begun, ordered his servants to eject John from the seat by brute force, and enthroned himself in his place. The result of this public insult was 'an open declaration of war' between the two brothers. Their father, Sir Edward, sided with John and refused to see Samuel for several years. Samuel's reward for this victory was small, merely a very temporary appointment as Captain of HMS *Antelope* for a few months.[57]

In 1739 there occurred four interrelated events which brought to a shattering climax the great family row, which by now involved sexual jealousy between spouses John and Mary; disputes over inheritance and politics between brothers John and Samuel; and apparently a personal quarrel between father and son, Sir Edward and John. At the heart of the matter lay the succession to the extensive Goodere, Dineley, and Lawford

---

[56] J. Charnock, *Biographia navalis* (London, 1796), iv. 241–4; *Memoirs*, 9–10.
[57] *Memoirs*, 10–11.

estates, worth about £4,000 a year. The first was supposed to be entailed on John Dineley and his heirs male, and failing them his brother Samuel Goodere; the second, by far the largest item, on John and his heirs male by Mary, and failing them his brother Samuel; and the third on Mary herself for life on the death of John, and then to their heirs.

The first event in 1739 was the defeat of John's attempt to push through the House of Lords his private bill of divorce from Mary. Shortly after, there occurred the death of his father, old Sir Edward Goodere, Bt. On hearing the news of his father's illness, John hurried off to the family home at Burhope to take charge. On his father's death, he opened the will and was very annoyed to discover that he was tenant only for life of the Goodere estate, and even more annoyed to find that the reversion went not to his heirs but to Samuel. It was in a fit of anger at discovering these limitations that John (now Sir John Goodere, Bt.) shuffled the old man unceremoniously into a pauper's grave, without the solemn ritual appropriate for a baronet, an act which 'drew a general odium upon Sir John Dineley's character'.[58]

Meanwhile Sir John, who had been nominally reconciled to his brother by their sister (Mrs Foote), sent a message to summon Samuel, who arrived at Burhope the same day their father died, accompanied, as usual, by a bodyguard of ruffians. Samuel had no sooner arrived than he dropped the temporary mask of amity and ordered Sir John out of the house, claiming that he was entitled to the estate by virtue of a lease which he alleged the old man had made in his favour long ago, presumably before the 1733 quarrel over the Evesham election. Samuel refused to show Sir John the lease, and threatened that, if he did not immediately leave the house, he would have him beaten up and thrown out by six 'sturdy fellows' under his command. Samuel's wife fell on her knees and begged her husband not to molest or kill his brother, which gave Sir John time to slip upstairs. He reappeared on the landing armed with a blunderbuss (which in fact lacked powder and shot) and, by threatening to shoot the first man who mounted the stairs to attack him, forced Samuel and his gang to retreat.[59]

Enraged by the loss of ultimate inheritance of the Goodere estates, and by this armed confrontation with his brother, Sir John now determined to deprive Samuel and his heirs of any hope of inheriting the extensive Dineley estates. To accomplish this he had to break the entail, which must have given him a life estate and his son an estate in tail. The need to obtain the boy's consent drew his attention to yet another object of his hatred, his only son and heir, Edward. Everything indicates that neither John nor Mary had ever shown much interest in the child. He first appears in the

---

[58] Ibid. 8.   [59] Ibid. 12–13.

story in 1723, at the age of 6, when he and his nurse were ejected from the house in the middle of the night by his father, who was in a rage with his mother. Thereafter no one seems to have bothered with the child. His mother and father continued hunting, drinking, and quarrelling, and Edward was presumably left to be brought up by the servants. He was 13 when his mother left him and his father, and went off to London. A little later his father had him apprenticed to a saddler in London—an extraordinary thing to do to a child destined to inherit a baronetcy and a huge estate. The boy fell into dissipation, and by the late 1730s his father had abandoned him altogether, leaving him to struggle on alone in poverty in London. The reasons for this neglect are wholly obscure, and the only explanation that makes any sense is that John had somehow convinced himself—without a shred of evidence except Mary's subsequent behaviour—that the child was not his.

In order to disinherit his brother by breaking the entail, Sir John needed the formal written consent of Edward, since the latter was now of age. He therefore ordered a search for the boy, and found him living in London in miserable poverty, in danger of arrest for debt, and very near death. He hastily removed the boy to his own attorney's house in Fetter Lane, and, in return for a promise of a life annuity of £200 towards the discharge of his debts, he managed to persuade the boy to join with him in executing a legal document called a recovery. This effectively barred the entail, and freed John to dispose of the Dineley estate by will. Two days after signing the document which deprived him of his inheritance, the boy died. Samuel Foote alleged that, to save the burial fees, Sir John himself drove the hearse which carried the corpse to a pauper's grave. Sir John at once made a will, settling the bulk of his estate on the second son of his sister, his nephew John Foote—who accordingly changed his name to John Dineley Foote.[60]

The state of mind of Samuel Goodere in late 1739 can easily be imagined. Thanks to the successful legal manoeuvring of his brother Sir John Dineley, he found himself deprived not only of his hopes of immediate possession of the Burhope house and estate, but also of any hope of succeeding to the much larger Dineley inheritance, which was now destined to pass to his nephew John Foote. When his brother Sir John died, Samuel now stood to inherit nothing but the run-down Goodere property and the bare title of a baronet. His dreams of becoming a wealthy country squire and influential political figure, based on the substantial Dineley estates at Charleton, had been totally frustrated. But he persistently asserted that 'my

---

[60] Ibid. 14–16; J. Latimer, *Annals of Bristol in the Eighteenth Century* (Bristol, 1893), 233.

brother has no power to cut off the entail, and I will set aside the recovery', an illusion which was to lead to the final tragedy.

If the injury done to Samuel was great, the revenge he planned was out of all proportion.[61] In late 1740 Samuel had at last been given a naval command, and was Captain of the sixty-gun HMS *Ruby*, then stationed down-river from Bristol at King Road. Captain Samuel approached his brother's Bristol lawyer and agent, Jarret Smith, and asked him to arrange a meeting of reconciliation order to put an end to the long and ruinously expensive lawsuits between them. A meeting was arranged to take place on 13 January 1741, at the Bristol office of the lawyer. Meanwhile, Samuel hired a gang of Irish ruffians from a privateer, the *Vernon*, under the orders of a 21-year-old Irish seaman from the *Ruby* called Mahoney, and stationed them in a room in an inn opposite the lawyer's office. Their instructions were to kidnap Sir John when he emerged. The plot was aborted, however, when Sir John appeared on horseback with a servant, both of them riding through the streets of Bristol with pistols drawn and at the ready. Samuel called off the attempt, saying, 'Look at him well, Mahoney, and watch him, but don't touch him now.' Since Sir John was in a hurry, the meeting was postponed until he returned the next week, after a visit to Bath for his failing health.

On Sunday, 18 January, Sir John returned to Bristol and informed Jarret Smith of his arrival. Smith notified Captain Samuel, who prepared to meet his brother at three in the afternoon. Before entering the lawyer's chamber, he again posted his men in the inn opposite, and ordered the barge of the *Ruby* to be moored at a quay about half a mile away. The meeting between the two brothers lasted for an hour and was ostensibly very friendly. Samuel kissed John 'as heartily as ever any two persons who had real affection for each other', and Mr Smith opened a bottle of wine, saying, 'John, give me leave to drink love and friendship.' 'With all my heart,' replied Sir John, 'I don't drink wine, nothing but water; notwithstanding, I wish love and friendship.' An amiable talk followed, during which Samuel reminisced about the beauties of Burhope, where they had both grown up. Finally, Sir John got up to go, saying, 'Brother, I wish you well.' But Samuel, after a pause for reflection, followed him out, muttering to himself, 'By God, it will not do.'

As soon as Sir John came out of the door, dressed like a gentleman in a scarlet cloak, but alone and armed only with a sword, Captain Samuel's men (three ruffians from the privateer, and eight men under Mahoney's

---

[61] The following account is based on the trial proceedings, published in State Trials, xvii, cols. 1003–94; this reprints *Trials* and *The Genuine Trial*.

command from his own ship the *Ruby*), came tumbling out of the inn. Told by Samuel to 'look sharp', the three privateersmen seized Sir John by both arms and began dragging him through the streets of Bristol towards the quay. Sir John shouted, 'Murder, murder, for God's sake save me, for they are going to kill me,' and a crowd collected. But Captain Samuel, who was following close behind, told them that the prisoner was being taken back on board ship for trial by court martial as a thief and deserter, while his men brandished formidable bludgeons and cudgels, and shouted, 'Damme, stand off, or else we will knock your brains out,' at any one who attempted to interfere. The gang half-dragged, half-carried the old man for over half a mile through the centre of Bristol on a Sunday afternoon without any interference from the authorities. A curious crowd attended their progress, but was afraid to interfere, 'having lately seen the sad effect of opposing the authority of a press-gang'.

When the party arrived at the quay, the steersman of the *Ruby* barge objected to receiving the prisoner, but the privateersmen threatened to 'throw him over the quay into the sea'. To satisfy the crew, Captain Samuel changed his story, and told them that Sir John was his own brother, 'a poor crazy man who has been the ruin of himself and his family'. He said to Sir John, 'I am going to carry you on board, to save you from ruin and from lying rotten in gaol' (arrested for debt). Sir John, however, was very frightened and replied, 'I know better things, I believe you are going to murder me. You may as well throw me overboard and murder me right here as carry me on board and murder me.' Samuel retorted, 'No brother, I am going to prevent you rotting on land, but however I would have you make your peace with God this night.' When the barge stopped by the shore to deposit the ruffians from the privateer, Sir John managed to shout to a friend, asking him to tell Jarret Smith what had happened to him. He got out most of the message before Captain Samuel silenced him by throwing his cloak over his head and clasping his hand over his mouth.

At about 7 p.m. the barge arrived at the *Ruby* and Sir John was dragged up the ladder on board and bundled down into the purser's cabin. Two strong bolts were nailed on the outside of the door to shut him in, and a guard was posted. Sir John's clothes were wet and Captain Samuel ordered Mahoney to pull off his stockings, only to be stopped by his saying, 'Don't strip me, fellow, until I am dead.'

Samuel spent the rest of the evening getting two of the crew sufficiently drunk to obey his instructions to go into the cabin and strangle his brother. His motive was not pure revenge, but a crazy idea that, once his brother was dead, he could overthrow the recovery by another lawsuit, and so inherit the Dineley estates. Mahoney, lured by a promise by Samuel of several hundred pounds, kept his head. But the second sailor got so drunk as to be incapacitated, and yet another sailor, a 36-year-old Irishman called Charles White, had therefore to be roused from his hammock in the middle of the night, summoned to the captain's cabin, and promised £150 to play his part in the murder. Between them Samuel, Mahoney, and White proceeded to drink a bottle and a half of raw rum to screw up their courage for the task ahead.

At about two in the morning Mahoney went into the cabin to see the victim and bring him a bucket in which to ease himself. Mahoney had a long talk with Sir John, who reminisced about his early life as a merchant seaman in the East Indies. He said, 'I myself have been at sea, and might have been a Commander.' He also told Mahoney, 'What, does he say I am mad? I used to be so, but I have not tasted anything stronger than water these two years.' He also said, 'I know I am going to be murdered,' and, when his brother also came in, he asked, 'Brother Sam, what do you intend to do to me?'

By three o'clock in the morning Mahoney and White were sufficiently drunk to carry out the murder. Captain Samuel, armed with a sword and a pistol, relieved the guard on watch outside the cabin, and the two sailors went in. Mahoney first throttled Sir John with his hands while the latter cried out and groaned, and blood gushed out of his mouth and nose. After some time they finally finished him off by tightening a rope about his neck, the whole business taking up to half an hour. They then went through his pockets and robbed him of his money and his watch. After it was all over, Captain Samuel went in with a candle to view the corpse, saying, 'By God, I will be sure he is dead,' and laid his hand on his brother's neck. Before he retired to bed, the two murderers came to his cabin, Mahoney exclaiming cheerfully, 'Damme, Captain, we have done it, boy.'[62] Samuel gave the murderers the £8 or so they had taken from Sir John's pockets, but kept the latter's silver watch and instead gave Mahoney his own gold one. He then ordered a boat to leave the ship at 4 a.m. and set them ashore, his plan being to set sail the same morning, and to throw the body overboard when out at sea.

What he did not know, however, was that the ship's cooper had smuggled his wife on board that night, and that they were using a cabin divided from the one occupied by Sir John by no more than a thin deal partition. The noise of the prolonged murder woke the cooper's wife, who in turn woke her husband. He peered through a chink in the partition and was

---

[62] This remark is recorded in Captain Samuel's later confession to a clergyman (Charnock, *Biographia navalis*, iv. 249).

horrified to witness the slow strangulation taking place by the dim light of the candle. He was afraid to cry out, but at first light he felt safe enough to emerge from the cabin. He hastened to inform the carpenter, the lieutenant, and the master of the ship that 'about three o'clock this morning they went down and murdered Sir John'. But the strength of naval discipline still held, and the lieutenant stubbornly refused to order the arrest of his Captain until the cooper forced his hand and did it himself.

At about noon there arrived the water bailiff, dispatched by the Bristol magistrates on the urgent plea of Jarret Smith that his client was on board and in grave danger. The two murderers were searched for and soon found dead drunk in Bristol. Both of them very readily confessed to the crime. At the trial it was revealed why Samuel had pocketed Sir John's watch and had instead given his own to the murderer: his own was a very incriminating piece of evidence. Warned of his imminent arrest, the murderer Mahoney had given the watch to his landlady, who had thrown it down the privy hole 'for fear I should come into trouble'. But the cesspool was emptied by order of the magistrates and the watch discovered. It was then found to have been custom-made for Samuel, and, instead of the usual numbers 1 though 12, it had the twelve letters: 'DEATH DINELEY'. Every time he had looked at his watch Samuel had been reminded of the need to wreak vengeance on his brother, and its manufacture to order is revealing evidence of his state of mind.

The trial of the two murderers and of Captain Samuel took place amid great publicity at Bristol two months later, on 26 March 1741. The trial lasted eight hours—a long time even for a murder trial in those days—but the inevitable verdict of the jury, after being out for half an hour, was guilty. Samuel was sentenced to death by hanging.

As Captain Samuel returned to gaol, he put on a brave face and went on foot, wearing the scarlet cloak of a gentleman and bowing graciously to his acquaintances among the gentry whom he recognized in the crowd. At first he was optimistic, and spent his time in gaol agitating for a pardon. He was a notorious figure, and women paid a shilling for the thrill of shaking the hand of such a villain. Meanwhile, his wife obtained access to King George II and presented a petition for mitigation of the sentence to transportation or imprisonment for life. But the crime was so heinous, and the evidence so overwhelming, that her plea was rejected. Failing that, the Captain and his friends tried to hire a gang of colliers—notoriously a lawless and violent lot and 'a terror to the City of Bristol'[63]—to attack the gaol and release him.

[63] R. W. Malcomson, '"A Set of Ungovernable People": The Kingswood Colliers in the Eighteenth Century', in J. Brewer and J. E. Styles (eds.), *An Ungovernable People* (London, 1980), 126.

But the authorities posted a strong guard both day night, and strengthened the prison door with iron plates. By 8 April, one week before the execution, his friends decided that Samuel was doomed, and, as a *memento mori* to turn his thought to his approaching end, they sent into his prison cell his coffin with the forbidding inscription:

SAMUEL GOODERE, Aged 53 years,
who departed this life April 15, 1741

The appearance of the coffin greatly depressed Samuel, and the local clergy set to work on him to persuade him to make an appropriately pious and repentant end. They were successful, and, after he had confessed his guilt, he was given holy communion. His wife visited him in gaol, took the sacrament with him, and then left the city before the execution. Samuel's behaviour in gaol before his execution exactly matched the standard trope deployed in current popular literature on the life and death of notorious rogues and murderers.[64]

On Wednesday, 15 April, at 11 a.m., Samuel and a clergyman entered a mourning coach and four, followed by his hearse carrying the coffin, and proceeded under heavy escort through the streets to the place of execution, watched by 'the greatest crowd as ever was known in Bristol'. Behind came Mahoney and White, rattling along in chains in a cart, sitting on a single coffin and accompanied by a clergyman. On the scaffold Samuel publicly confessed his guilt; asked the massed spectators to pray for his soul; explained to them that Sir John's action in cutting off the entail had unhinged his mind; sang a psalm; and prayed 'Lord, do not reward me according to my deserts'. Finally he was turned off the cart, and the noose tightened around his throat. By eighteen century standards it was a good end to a bad life.

A hanged man's fingers were supposed to have magical powers, and, as Samuel dangled twitching in the last slow agonies of death, women crowded round to touch him. One of them drew one of his fingers nine times across a wen on the neck of her child in the hope of performing a cure. After he was cut down, a friend laid two crowns upon his eyes, but they were soon stolen by the mob. To complete the humiliation of the family, Samuel's corpse was then publicly exhibited for some hours in the Bristol Infirmary, where a surgeon opened his breast with a scalpel and displayed his heart to a large crowd, before sewing up the body again to be removed for burial in

---

[64] A. Smith, *History of the Lives and Robberies of the Most Noted Highwaymen* (London, 1720), iii. 47, quoted in J. J. Richetti, *Popular Fiction before Richardson: Narrative Patterns, 1700–39* (Oxford, 1969), 55.

the family vault at Burhope. Several of the onlookers expressed surprise on finding that his heart was not black.[65]

The bodies of Samuel's fellow conspirators met various carefully regulated fates. That of Mahoney was removed from the scaffold, chains were riveted around it, and it was hung up to rot slowly on the shore near where the murder had taken place. The body of White was placed in the coffin on which he and Mahoney had sat on the way to the scaffold, and taken for burial. In contrast to these exemplary punishments, the three privateersmen who had abducted Sir John by force on the streets of Bristol got off amazingly lightly. They were charged only with a misdemeanour, and were sentenced to a fine of 40s., a year in prison, and a year on security for good behaviour. It was a sentence which speaks volumes about the state of law and order, and the relationship between the two, in eighteenth-century England.[66]

After her husband's murder, Mary's first thought was to order elegant mourning clothes for herself from London to celebrate the occasion. Her letter shows that her spelling was purely phonetic—a very unusual situation for the wife of a baronet by the mid-eighteenth century.[67] Her next move was to tell her attorney to file a claim on the whole estate in the name of an 11-year-old boy, whom she suddenly produced and claimed was the lawful son of herself and her late husband. She alleged that she had given birth to the child secretly two months before she had fled from Charleton in 1730, that all witnesses to the birth were now dead, and that the boy's existence had been concealed from his father. This was too much even for her own lawyer to swallow, and he endorsed the document: 'This was the fictitious case Lady Dineley made me draw and take opinion on when she wanted to set up and pretend she had a son by Sir John then living, and which was all false.'[68] All the same, the executors of the will were sufficiently disturbed to ask the Court of Chancery to investigate whether any such child existed. The Lord Chancellor, however, refused, saying, 'You cannot bring a bill in here to discover whether there is such a person, or where he is, in order to make him a party to a suit in this court'.[69]

---

[65] *Memoirs*, 34–6; Latimer, *Annals of Bristol*, 231–32; *Fratricide, passim*. These last two details are taken from an unknown contemporary source, probably a newspaper. Belief in the curative power of hanged men's hands was widespread at the time. At an execution in London in 1785 Boswell saw 'no less that four diseased persons who had rubbed themselves with the sweaty hands of malefactors in the agonies of death, and believed this could cure them' (*Boswell: The Applause of the Jury*, ed. I. S. Lustig and F. A. Pottle (New York, 1981), 319).

[66] *State Trials*, xvii, col. 1094.   [67] *Gent's Mag.*, 11 (1741), 163, 218.

[68] Latimer, *Annals of Bristol*, 232.   [69] Ibid. 234.

Dineley v. Dineley

Although this crude plot to grab the whole estate ultimately failed, since there was no son, Mary did succeed in asserting her right to about £500 a year and the house on the Charleton estate as dower by common law, since John had never settled the estate, while she also succeeded in keeping the Lawford family estates of Stapleton and Tockington, which Sir John had illegally tried to entail on his nephew, Samuel Foote. With this fortune at her disposal, she had no trouble finding a second husband, a London printer William Rayner, who presumably was prepared to overlook her rather dubious past. But he himself was not much of a catch, and Mary does not seem to have chosen her second husband much more wisely than her mother had done her first, John Goodere. In 1733 Rayner had been tried for seditious libel in an article against Walpole, which he had printed in the Tory paper, the *Craftsman*, for which he had been imprisoned for two years and fined £40. To have attacked Walpole is no blot on a man's character, but it was later reported that a journeyman printer and his sister, while infants, were left a substantial inheritance from their aunt, the printer of the *St James's Evening Post*, 'of which they were deprived by the chicanery of Mr Rayner, their guardian'.[70]

By 1750 the Dineleys and the Jasons, who had been the source of so much gossip and scandal in 1728–30, had totally disappeared from the local scene. As for Mary, she died in 1757 at her Lawford family home at Stapleton, where she had been born. It is hard to disagree with the verdict of a pamphleteer in 1741, that 'her life has not been always agreeable to the rules of the strictest modesty and virtue'.[71]

After the murder of the 2nd baronet, Sir John Dineley, and the execution of his brother and murderer Captain Samuel Goodere, the Burhope estate of the Gooderes, which was all that was now left to go with the title, passed to Samuel's eldest son, Edward, the 3rd baronet (see Genealogy of the Goodere 'Dineley' family). In Sir Edward the streak of hereditary insanity was particularly pronounced and he was a recognized lunatic, who died unmarried in 1761 at the age of 32. The Goodere estate and the title of 4th baronet then passed to his twin brother Sir John, who although not mad was certainly mentally unbalanced. He soon ran through what was left of the estate and sold the ancient seat of the Gooderes at Burhope in about 1770. After this, he was left literally penniless, and was only saved from starvation when friendship with the Pelham family and the influence of Lord North got him a place as one of the Poor Knights of Windsor, which gave him a free lodging and a small pension.

[70] *Eng. Rep.* 62: 638.
[71] H. C. Timperley, *Encyclopaedia of Literary and Typographical Anecdotes* (London, 1842), 651, 763.

For thirty years thereafter Sir John built up a reputation as a notorious eccentric, whose life was wholly devoted to the single-minded pursuit of a wealthy heiress. Dressed in the antique costume of the reign of George II—velvet embroidered waistcoat, satin breeches, silk stockings, and full-bottomed wig—he haunted the pastry shops of Windsor and the theatres of London. He would approach any likely-looking young lady and, with a great show of gallantry, offer her a printed handbill. These handbills explained quite frankly that his plan was to obtain money by marriage with which to launch a lawsuit, which he claimed would enable him to recover his ancestral estates, estimated by him as worth £11,000 a year. All he sought was a woman of child-bearing age and an income of £1,000 a year.

He even advertised in the newspapers, for example in the *Ipswich Journal* of 21 August 1802:

To the angelic fair of the true English breed Sir J. Dineley, of Windsor Castle, recommends himself and his ample fortune to any angelic beauty of good breed fit to become, and willing to be, a mother of a noble heir, and keep up the name of an ancient family, enobled by deeds of arms and ancestral renown. Ladies at a certain period of life need not apply, as heirship is the object of the mutual contract offered by the ladies' sincere admirer, Sir John Dineley. (Plate 4)

When he at last died in 1808, still without finding the bride he had so long and so earnestly sought, the line of the Dineley Gooderes finally became extinct.[72] The first two baronets had elevated the family by the capture of two heiresses; the fifth finally ended the line still attempting to emulate their success. In the long run, however, the obsessive greed behind this pursuit of heiresses brought first tragedy and then ruin upon the family.

It cannot be claimed that Sir John Goodere Dineley was typical of the country squire of the age. Indeed he was in most ways the exact opposite of what was expected of one of his position. He broke almost every rule in the code of honour which was supposed to govern the behaviour of the élite in the early eighteenth century. He was boorish and wholly lacking in either cultivation or—what was more important—good manners. He married purely for her money a 14-year-old girl who was barely literate, and then treated her with a physical brutality which shocked even the most patriarchal of his contemporaries, despite the provocation. His manners, his willingness to perform menial chores, and the squalor in which he lived in his latter years offended traditional ideals of gentility and hospitality.

---

[72] G. E. Cokayne, *Complete Baronetage*, iv. 231, B. Burke, *The Romance of the Aristocracy* (London, 1855), ii. 19–25; Phillips, *Pedigree of Dineley of Charlton*.

Dineley v. Dineley

The shabby way he shuffled both his father and his son into their graves without funeral rites suitable to their degree was a grave offence to society's concepts of family obligation. His violent quarrels with his wife, his son, and his brother were a public scandal. His breaking of the entail in order to allow him to deprive his brother and his brother's children of their rightful inheritance was a shocking breach of the conventions about hereditary succession. The dissipation of much of his estate in extravagant and endless vindictive lawsuits with his relatives made him contemptible in the eyes of the neighbourhood. The only way in which he conformed to the ideal of the country gentleman of the early eighteenth century was that he was fair and honest with his tenantry. In all other respects he was the paradigm of what a gentleman ought *not* to be, and even the horror of his end did not stifle the criticism of his life and character. The best that could be said about him was that his brother and murderer was worse. Even his principal defender, his nephew Samuel Foote, was obliged to admit that 'he was reckoned a very sad fellow, lived almost universally hated, and died unlamented'.[73]

The story highlights the great importance in the generation of family feuds of any violation of traditional norms for the transmission of property. The issue which destroyed the Goodere Dineleys was the prolonged quarrel about the inheritance of the properties so arduously put together by the marriage of heiresses. The first baronet began the quarrel by diverting the ancestral Goodere estates from the children of his heir to those of his younger son, Samuel, presumably on the grounds that the Dineley and Lawford estates were quite enough for the former. The second baronet, John, brought the family dispute to a shattering crisis by breaking the entail and disinheriting his brother and his son altogether in favour of one nephew, and trying to leave his wife's property to another. This playing fast and loose with the normal rules of primogeniture, in an age when such behaviour was both rare and legally difficult, was at the root of the family troubles. Not only did the pursuit of heiresses by the first two baronets produce its own nemesis in a destructive family feud. The single-minded greed behind these marriages also brought their own psychological punishment in the torments of jealousy that plagued John when he contemplated the suspiciously indiscreet behaviour of his flighty wife. This family policy of marrying heiresses was finally parodied by the grotesque efforts of the fifth and last baronet to find himself a rich wife by publicly advertising for one in the newspapers.

Nor was this the end of the costs involved in this policy of family

[73] *Fratricide*, 31.

aggrandizement. We do not know exactly how the Goodere Dineleys managed to dissipate their large inheritance, but it seems certain that the expense of the endless lawsuits between John and Mary consumed most of it. Law was not merely an instrument of justice for this family; it was a means of waging war, of obtaining revenge, and of finally destroying an enemy. Sir John tried to starve out his wife Mary this way, but he also ruined himself by his obsessive litigation, since in the ecclesiastical courts he had to pay her legal costs as well as his own. When he was in the barge being kidnapped by his brother, Samuel was heard to say to him, 'Have you not given the rogues of lawyers money enough already? Do you want to give them more? I will take care that they shall never have any more of you; now I'll take care of you.'[74] And take care of him he did!

[74] *State Trials*, xvii, col. 1062.

6
Beaufort v. Beaufort
The impotent duke and the adulterous duchess,
1729–1742

Henry Somerset, 3rd Duke of Beaufort, was born in 1707 with a golden spoon in his mouth. He was heir to one of the greatest estates and noblest titles in all England. His father owned extensive property in Wales and the West Country, a great house at Badminton in Gloucestershire, two or three smaller houses nearby, and a London house in the newly built Grosvenor Street. He was also a Plantagenet, a direct descendant of John of Gaunt, and therefore had royal blood in his veins. To add to his good fortune, his father died at the early age of 31 in 1714, so that this vast inheritance and the accumulated titles of Duke of Beaufort, Marquis and Earl of Worcester, Earl of Glamorgan, and Barons Herbert, Raglan, and Beauford of Caldecot-Castle all descended upon him at the early age of 7. He did not even have to wait for his inheritance (Plate 5).

In 1729, at the age of 21, this child of fortune was married to the heiress to an almost equally vast inheritance. On whose initiative the match was made we do not know. His own mother had died in childbirth in 1709 and his stepmother was also dead, as were both his uncles. Since he had no close relatives to advise him, it is certainly possible that the initiative was his, but it seems unlikely. In any case the choice fell on Frances, the 17-year-old only daughter of the late 2nd Viscount Scudamore, and the heiress not only of the rich Scudamore estates and mansion at Holme Lacy in nearby Herefordshire, but also, through her mother, of some of the estates of the Digby family around Coleshill in Warwickshire (Plate 6). If an heir male were to come from this union, he would by any calculation be one of the very richest noblemen in England, and thus in Europe, and the greatest political and social patron not only of south Wales but also of the four contiguous English counties of Gloucestershire, Herefordshire, Monmouthshire, and Warwickshire. He would be 'King of the West'. No doubt these prudential calculations of power and money—'interest' as it was called in the eighteenth century—were paramount in driving the 17-year-old Frances to accept the Duke's offer, 'at the instances and requests of relations and friends'. It was pretty clearly an arranged marriage in the traditional pattern which prevailed in aristocratic circles in the sixteenth and seventeenth centuries. No one ever pretended that the affair involved much personal attraction between the parties, but both seem to have been quite willing to go along. The complex legal and financial negotiations occupied March and April and the wedding took place in Holland House on 8 June 1729. In accordance with the will of the late Viscount Scudamore, Henry, Duke of Beaufort, was obliged to make the sacrifice of changing his ancient surname from Somerset to Scudamore in order to lay his hands upon this great inheritance.[1]

For the next ten years the Duke and Duchess journeyed regularly back and forth with their retinue of servants between their Grosvenor Street house in London, the great palace at Badminton, still only some forty years old, and smaller houses at Lavington and Netheravon in Wiltshire. Many servants declared that, so far as they could see, the Duke and Duchess got along perfectly well until the late 1730s. One claimed that they seemed 'a very happy couple', several others more cautiously declared that they 'lived comfortably together'.[2] On the other hand, the Duke was sickly, despite his youth, and the Duchess remained childless. This last was a matter of no small importance, since the whole object of the marriage had been to unite the two great estates of the Somersets and the Scudamores. If no male heir was born and survived, this purpose would be frustrated. Both families must have been worried, and the spouses themselves embarrassed, by the continued failure of the Duchess to conceive. They may well have consulted doctors, as the Duchess later alleged. If so, they were wasting their time and money, since in those days the medical profession knew almost nothing about the functioning of the reproductive system. The advice given by doctors about the optimum time for conception in the female ovulation cycle was the direct opposite of the truth: they recommended just after menstruation.

The relations between the Duke and Duchess were showing signs of strain before 1740, and it is clear that by then each was going his and her own way, and that they were seeing relatively little of each other—which was easy enough considering the number of houses at their disposal. It was in February 1740 that Duchess Frances first met William, Lord Talbot of Hensol (Plate 7). He was the 2nd baron, his father having acquired the family fortunes and title by a very successful legal and political career, ending as Lord Chancellor, and by marrying a wealthy heiress. Having

---

[1] LPCA, D.136: 47; Private Acts of Parliament 3 Geo. II, cap. 10.
[2] LPCA, D.136: 48, 345, 375, 433, 437, 482.

succeeded to his father's estates in 1737, William was now a very wealthy gentleman of leisure, made even richer by marriage. He had followed the pattern set by his father, marrying in 1734 the sole heiress of Adam de Cardonnel, Secretary of State for War, who was said to be worth £70,000. Like the Duchess, he seems to have married for money rather than affection, and until the year before they met his marriage also had been childless. In 1739 his wife had with great difficulty given birth to a son, and some years later Lord Talbot excused his seduction of the Duchess on the grounds that his wife was 'a weakly woman and that the midwife had told him that if she had any more children it would kill her'. He was therefore, he explained, 'deprived of her sexual services'.[3]

Lord Talbot was therefore married to a sickly wife whom he did not love and with whom sexual relations were excluded on medical grounds, while the Duchess was a childless woman married to a sickly husband whom she had never loved, and with whom relations were already strained. The Duchess was looking primarily for love, Lord Talbot for a sexual partner, and they were both of them young, healthy, self-centred, and reckless. They were made for each other.

By May 1740, within four months of their first meeting, they had become lovers. Lord Talbot visited the Duchess two or three times a week in her Grosvenor Street house when the Duke was away—as he frequently seems to have been. Inevitably it was not long before the ever-watchful servants found them out. As was usual in almost all cases of adultery at that time, a sense of propriety and a fear of discovery prevented the woman from taking her lover into the matrimonial bed, as a result of which clumsy couplings took place in the dining-room or the drawing-room. Moreover, since these were rooms into which servants were continually entering to remake the fire, draw the shutters, or carry out some other routine chore, the lovers were faced with a dilemma. Either they could lock the door, which would immediately arouse the suspicions of the servants, or they could leave it unlocked and run the risk of a surprise discovery. The Duchess and Lord Talbot tried both options, with unfortunate consequences either way.

The first act of adultery to be observed by any of the servants took place in the Duchess's Grosvenor Street dressing-room one day in May. One of the Duke's servants entered the room unexpectedly, and found the Duchess sitting on Lord Talbot's lap. She jumped up and smoothed down her petticoats, but the servant noticed that 'her head clothes and handkerchief (which covered her bosom) were very much tumbled'. He also noticed that Lord Talbot immediately crossed his legs and thighs and turned away from

---

[3] Ibid. 268.

him, clearly to prevent the servant from seeing that 'his breeches were un-buttoned' and his member exposed.[4] This aroused the servant's curiosity, and a few days later he deliberately set out to catch them at it. When he and the butler found the door to the dining-room locked, they went next door in the great drawing-room and put their ears to the keyhole. They heard the sound of kissing, and then the Duchess saying, 'You make me very hot. I am not able to bear it. What would you have me do? My precious Lord, I am afraid the servants suspect us.' Later, when Lord Talbot had gone and the Duchess had retired, the servants went into the dining-room, where they found five or six chairs set side by side to form a kind of couch. On the chairs and on the floor they found bits of silver lace, which had evidently been rubbed off the back of the Duchess's 'gown flowered with silver', as she had laid on her back on the chairs with her dress and petticoats pulled up to her waist with Lord Talbot on top of her.[5]

Thereafter the lovers were more careful about their behaviour inside the house. The Duchess would ride out on her horse, escorted inevitably by her groom, would meet Lord Talbot on the outskirts of London driving his own chaise, and would dismount from her horse and get into the chaise with him. Her groom, who followed at a respectful distance leading her horse, observed the chaise drive into some secluded by-lane, where it would stop to allow Lord Talbot to leave the driver's seat and get inside. The chaise would then jerk rhythmically on its springs for a while, and once their love-making was so energetic that the back of the chaise broke loose so that the groom could see inside. When it was all over, Lord Talbot would return to the driver's seat, and they would drive home. On other occasions the chaise would stop in a park such as Moor Park, or near a wood, and they would get out and disappear into the bushes. Once they went off to the Epsom races for three whole days.[6]

All this inevitably became the subject of excited gossip below stairs, and on 21 May John Pember, the groom, took it upon himself to warn the Duchess that the servants were talking about her and Lord Talbot. At first she was furious, saying, 'How durst the servants talk of me,' but she soon realized the danger she was in, and burst into tears. The next day she gave Pember ten guineas to keep his mouth shut. Soon after, Lord Talbot spoke to him, told him to warn the servants to be very careful what they said, and gave him another five and a half guineas. Since Pember's wages as groom were only £7 a year, he had received two years' income in two days as a result of his knowledge. In order to keep his mouth shut, he was later taken on by the Duchess as her own groom, his wages were doubled to £15 a

---

[4] Ibid. 69, 349.   [5] Ibid. 71, 323, 352, 486.   [6] Ibid. 74–5, 37.

year, and he was given some horses, which he sold for about £40. In view of these potential rewards for the giving or witholding of information, it was hardly surprising that all the servants kept a keen look-out for any misbehaviour by their superiors. It was certainly not moral indignation, nor was it mere human curiosity which led them to spy so assiduously upon their employers.

At this stage, the Duchess and Lord Talbot presumably thought that Pember was the only witness against them, since they knew nothing about the two servants listening at the dining-room door, nor about the tell-tale evidence they had found of the silver lace on the chairs and floor. Despite Pember's silence, therefore, the news of the Duchess's relations with Lord Talbot soon came to the ears of the Duke, who decided on a private separation. A month later, on 17 June, their respective lawyers presented formal articles of separation for them to sign. The arrangements were very simple: the Duke ceded all claims he might have on the real and personal property of the Duchess, which, since the couple had not produced an heir and were about to separate, was no great sacrifice on his part. In return the Duchess surrendered all claims on the Beaufort estates as either jointure or thirds in her right as widow in case she outlived the Duke. Thus in 1740 the Somersets and the Scudamores parted company and finances, as neatly and as cleanly as they had come together eleven years before. The only difference was that they were still married, and the Duke now bore his new surname of Scudamore.

Two days after they had signed the documents, the Duke and Duchess drove down to an inn near Slough in separate coaches, dined together for the last time, apparently on reasonably polite terms, and then went their separate ways, he to Badminton, she to the Scudamore seat of Holme Lacy. Between this day in June 1740 and June 1742 when the Duke launched a suit against the Duchess, the movements of both parties can be followed in detail. The Duke, as befitted his grandeur, moved restlessly between his many houses, as well as making frequent journeys to Bath to try to restore his failing health. The summer and autumn he spent in the West Country at his houses of Badminton and Netheravon, at Bath, or visiting such friends as the Countess of Coventry at Smithfield in Warwickshire or Lord Lichfield at Ditchley in Oxfordshire. December to June were spent at his London house in Grosvenor Street, with brief jaunts to the Epsom races and elsewhere.[7] As for the Duchess, she spent the summer from June to October at her family residence at Holme Lacy, and then went for a month to Coleshill, the principle seat of her great-uncle Lord Digby, who was

---

[7] Ibid. 83–92, 361–7, 444–51, 457–65, 490–4.

then residing at his other seat at Sherborne in Dorset. At the end of November she settled in for the winter in a rented house in Cavendish Street in London, where she stayed till the end of May. In early June 1741 she moved for the summer to a rented house in the country belonging to Lord North, at Chipping Warden in Northamptonshire, where she stayed —unwisely as it turned out—until the middle of October, when she returned to another rented London house in New Bond Street.[8]

The Duchess and Lord Talbot must have guessed that the Duke would be keeping a fairly close eye on them. After all, his honour was at stake and if he could obtain proof of adultery he could get his revenge by suing Lord Talbot for punitive damages for crim. con. in a civil court, and could blast the reputation of the Duchess by a suit for separation on grounds of adultery in an ecclesiastical court. Moreover, Lord Talbot had his own wife to deal with, from whom he was anxious to conceal the liaison. Throughout the summer, therefore, the two were very discreet. Letters were exchanged through the trusted hands of the groom, John Pember, who, as will be recalled, had been rewarded handsomely.

As soon as the Duchess returned to London in October 1741, however, discretion was thrown to the winds. Lord Talbot visited her in her rented house in New Bond Street about three times a week, staying for up to five hours at a time, often until two or three in the morning behind locked doors in the drawing-room or dressing-room. The footman had strict orders to let no one enter until the bell was rung. As late as thirty years afterwards people still remembered that 'in this engagement they were both so very indiscreet as to subject themselves to much censure'.[9] After the Duchess became pregnant, the only precaution Lord Talbot took was to give the butler two guineas to keep his mouth shut as he slipped into the house one day in January.[10] By February the Duchess knew she was pregnant, which meant that they were both in serious trouble.

Lord Talbot at last made a serious effort to keep things quiet. He again hired for the summer on the Duchess's behalf Lord North's house in Chipping Warden, which was within riding distance of his own residence at Barrington in Gloucestershire. The birth of the child was expected in early September, and Lord Talbot also hired a house in Golden Square in London for the lying-in, and engaged a discreet and experienced 61-year-old midwife for the purpose. Golden Square was not exactly an obscure area of London, but Lord Talbot apparently believed that the birth could be kept secret there.[11]

---

[8] Ibid. 92–147.   [9] *T & C Mag.* 3 (1771), 514.
[10] LPCA, D.136: 96–9, 330–4.   [11] Ibid. 377–9.

Beaufort v. Beaufort

While the Duchess was at Chipping Warden he visited her from time to time, using what he thought to be reasonable precautions. He never came into the house, but arranged to meet her walking alone in the fields. He was not, however, an inconspicuous figure. He always rode the same horse, and wore a bright red hunting coat, so that he hardly passed unnoticed by the villagers. At ten o'clock on a bright summer morning on 6 June, John Pargiter, a young farmer at Wardington near Chipping Warden, observed Lord Talbot riding along in his red coat to meet the Duchess, who was walking on foot in the great common field of the village. He watched Lord Talbot dismount from his horse, and followed them as they walked together along the river bank. They came to a lodge, where Lord Talbot tied up his horse before he and the Duchess withdrew behind a hedge. By now Pargiter had picked up a day labourer working in the field, and a tailor. He urged them to follow him through the hedge and round the lodge to see what Lord Talbot and the Duchess were up to, but they refused and went back to their work. Pargiter pushed through the hedge and found himself within ten yards of the couple, who were busy making love on the ground under the hedge, the Duchess on her back with her petticoats pushed up to her waist. Pargiter then went home and made a written memorandum to himself about what he had seen.[12] He clearly hoped one day to make some money from his discovery.

Meanwhile the effort to maintain secrecy within the household was becoming more difficult. The key witness to the early adultery, John Pember, had had his mouth effectively shut. He had already made about £70, on a starting salary of £7, out of his capacity to speak out or keep silent. The trouble was, however, that there was no way of ensuring his continued silence, and like most blackmailers he did not know when to stop. He had quarrelled with the Duchess's saddler, and threatened that, if the latter continued to be employed, he would give notice and leave. Moreover, he had grown very careless about his duties and was neglecting the horses. In her impetuous way Duchess Frances did not stop to think, but sent him word by her butler that 'he had spoiled all her horses and that if he did not mend his ways she would give him warning'. This message enraged Pember, who replied: 'If I am discharged, you'll have the discharging of me and paying me my wages, but as to the money I have at interest in the Duchess's hands, I paid it into her own hands and I'll have it from her own hands again, and then I shall have an opportunity of telling her her own, for I know enough to blow her.' Pember had evidently deposited with the Duchess the money he had made from selling the horses, which is

[12] Ibid. 107–8, 247–9, 285–90.

interesting evidence of the complicated web of relationships that bound mistress and servant. His threat to 'blow' the Duchess had the desired effect, and he was quickly restored to her favour. Because of what he could tell, the groom now had the whip hand over the Duchess.[13]

June turned to July, and July to August, and August to September, and still Lord Talbot could not persuade the Duchess to return to London, where the house was ready and waiting for her lying-in. Despite her swelling belly, she delayed for week after week. She was happy at Chipping Warden, and no doubt was reluctant to face up to the inevitability of childbirth. She had a female attendant now to keep her company, a Miss Barnes, whose father had been steward at Holme Lacy. Frances Barnes was one of those unfortunate women of indeterminate status in a hierarchical household, who fitted in nowhere. As she herself explained, she was employed 'not as a servant nor strictly as a companion, for that I do not dine at her Grace's table, but sit and work with her at such times as she has no other company'. She was now a 30-year-old spinster whose face was spoilt by recent smallpox, and her prospects of marriage were small.[14] The Duchess finally decided to leave Chipping Warden for London on 13 September, but her plans collapsed when on the the eve of her departure she began to feel labour pains. She called for Elizabeth Franklin, a 43-year-old waiting woman who had been with her since she was a child at Holme Lacy, and had moved with her on her marriage, staying on as her waiting woman after the separation. When the Duchess asked her, 'Betty, you must surely know what is the matter with me,' Betty replied briskly, 'Yes, to be sure, Madam, you are in labour.' A bed was immediately set up in the dressing-room next door to the bedroom, and frantic makeshift preparations for the delivery were put in train. There was not even any childbed linen in the house, and the Duchess had to borrow some from the gardener's wife, Mrs Duffell. Richard Duffel was immediately posted off to Banbury, four miles away, to fetch a midwife. He arrived at Mrs Stiles's house at eleven in the evening, put her behind him on his horse, and took her back. Obeying the Duchess's orders, he went by a circuitous route in a clumsy and inevitably vain hope of concealing the identity of the house. They got back to Chipping Warden at midnight, and Duffell was immediately sent off again to Daventry, some fifteen miles away, to fetch Dr Adams, the nearest qualified physician and man-midwife. He rode all night and started back towards Chipping Warden with Dr Adams early the next morning. At the same time the Duchess sent John Pember to tell Lord Talbot that she was in labour, and to summon him to her side. This was a thirty-mile ride

---

[13] Ibid. 101–3.   [14] Ibid. 396–9.

each way, so that they did not get back until two in the afternoon on the next day.[15]

Meanwhile back in the house the Duchess lay in labour all night attended by the midwife Mrs Stiles, her waiting woman, Elizabeth Franklin, and her companion, Miss Barnes, while Mrs Duffell, the gardener's wife, hovered in the background making herself useful. Between them they managed very well, and a healthy baby girl was safely delivered between eight and nine o'clock the next morning, Sunday, 13 September. The invaluable Mrs Duffell was roped in to act as nurse for the time being. As soon as she had recovered herself, the Duchess asked Mrs Stiles how she did, and, on being assured that she was in no danger, she sent a messenger out on the road to intercept John Pember and Dr Adams. The latter was told to go home and given ten guineas for his pains, thus being kept ignorant of her identity.[16] His was one less mouth which would have to be kept shut. Subsequent events show that the Duchess and Lord Talbot were almost irrationally optimistic about their chances of keeping the birth a secret. As the Duchess later explained, they hoped to conceal it until the Duke died, 'which should not be long, since he is an infirm man'. She planned to claim part of the great inheritance in the name of the child, apparently hoping to be able to pass it off as the legitimate heir of the Duke. She openly said during labour, 'if it is a boy, it will be heir to the whole; if it is a girl, she will have a portion from the Duke and will have Holme (Lacy) estate' from the Scudamores. It seems likely that this far-fetched scheme of passing off Lord Talbot's child as the Duke's and so claiming his inheritance was the brain-child of the Duchess, for Lord Talbot must surely have realized how unlikely it was that they could get away with a bogus claim on one of the greatest estates in England. In any case, his heart was not in it. As soon as he arrived at Chipping Warden he asked the sex of the child, and, on being told it was a girl, remarked, 'I am glad of it, for I don't desire to get heirs to other men's estates.'[17]

Lord Talbot seems generally to have been exasperated with the Duchess that morning for her obstinacy and her folly. He was furious with her for having delayed so long at Chipping Warden that the delivery had had to take place there rather than in the safe house he had prepared for her in Golden Square in London. It was then that he offered to Mrs Duffell, the gardener's wife who was acting as nurse, a very lame and crude excuse for his seduction of the Duchess. He explained to her that another birth would endanger his wife's life, so that he could no longer sleep with her. He then

---

[15] Ibid. 417–18, 262, 278–9, 223–5, 251–2, 309.
[16] Ibid. 119, 228.   [17] Ibid. 110, 424.

added: 'Upon that account I had occasion to go abroad, and I heard that the Duchess of Beaufort had a passion for me, and I thought it was better to make use of her in that way than common women.' This frank reference to the Duchess as a substitute for a whore boded ill for their future relationship.[18]

Meanwhile, the Duchess made every effort to keep the knowledge of the birth a secret. Lord Talbot was smuggled into the house by Mrs Duffell by the bowling-green door, and up to the Duchess's room. There he was introduced by Miss Barnes to Mrs Stiles as the Duchess's brother. He asked Mrs Duffell to keep silent about the child and promised a bribe to Mrs Stiles. He asked her if she could keep a secret, to which she replied, 'I have kept many, and I am not fit for my business if I cannot.' The Duchess then gave her twenty guineas for her work, and they both promised twenty more every year that she kept silent. The Duchess instructed her to say nothing about it to her husband, and only to give him one or two of the guineas so that he would not become suspicious. Noticing some trunks lying in the room addressed to the Duchess of Beaufort, Lord Talbot tore off the labels in a futile effort to prevent Mrs Stiles from finding out the identity of her client. Since the Duchess's attendants, her maid Sarah and Mrs Duffell, had been calling her 'your Grace' during her labour, and since Mrs Stiles had had an opportunity to talk to the cook and the laundry maid below stairs, these efforts at concealment were worse than useless.

Mr Duffell was told to take Mrs Stiles back home to Banbury on his pillion in a roundabout way so that she would not be able to identify the house or village. Needless to say she knew very well where she was, and as soon as she got home she told the whole story to her husband. They both realized that the secret delivery of an illegitimate child by a Duchess was not an everyday occurrence, and that the twenty guineas already paid proved that there was money to be made from their knowledge. Mrs Stiles therefore 'made a memorandum in writing of the day she delivered the Lady Duchess', just in case it might come in useful in the future.[19]

Over the next few days the cover-up proceeded more or less according to plan. Miss Barnes went for walks or out in the chaise, wearing 'a remarkably rich mantle worked with gold and other coloured flowers' which belonged to the Duchess, 'with an intent that the neighbourhood might imagine it was her Grace herself taking the air'.[20] The most critical problem was how to get rid of the baby. On Monday the 14th, the day after the birth, the hard-worked John Pember was sent to London to get the

---

[18] Ibid. 268.   [19] Ibid. 280, 122, 268, 254–63, 271.
[20] Ibid. 313–14, 408.

childbed linen and to bring the wet-nurse down to fetch the child. When she arrived, however, the Duchess was unwilling to part with her baby at once, and the wet-nurse went back to London alone. On Tuesday the 15th, two days after the birth, everyone agreed that the Duchess should not breast-feed the child any more. Lord Talbot said to Mrs Duffell, 'Nurse, I hope the child is of a right shape and make' (it was presumably tightly swaddled so that nothing was visible except the face). 'Yes,' replied Mrs Duffell, 'it is a very fair child and a very pretty child.' Lord Talbot then kissed it and said complacently, 'I have never had one that was not pretty,' which was presumably a reference to two illegitimate children he was said to have fathered on two of his housemaids at Hensol.[21] He then went into the Duchess's bedroom and set about draining her breasts of milk by personally sucking at her nipples and spitting out the milk into a basin held by Mrs Duffell (the emphasis laid upon this act by the prosecution suggests that it was unusual and thought liable to shock the judges). In the following days it was Lord Talbot who held the basin while the sucking was done by the Duchess's maidservant.[22]

Who fed the baby in the meantime is not clear, for it was not smuggled out of the house until Saturday. Long before dawn broke, Mr and Mrs Duffell set out for Northampton with the baby in the chaise, while the ubiquitous John Pember rode on ahead. Soon after daybreak they arrived at Northampton, where they transferred to a private hired coach to go to London. Mr and Mrs Duffell went in it with the child, while John Pember returned home with the chaise and the horse. It was a swift and secret operation. The Duffells travelled all day and all Sunday, not reaching London until the evening, when they went directly to the midwife Mrs Bennen in Jermyn Street. Mrs Bennen at once had the baby transferred to the house in Golden Square, where the wet-nurse who had been hired for the purpose was waiting. A few days later the baby was baptized by a clergyman, two servants in the house acting as godfather and godmother. It was named Fanny Matthews, the surname being that of Lord Talbot's mother.

The baby was still alive a month later when the Duchess returned to London, since the latter tried to get the wife of her butler Thomas Garland to nurse it. She sent a message to him by Miss Barnes asking if his wife suckled her child. Thomas, who presumably had not seen his wife for the whole summer while he had been at Chipping Warden, answered that 'he believed not'. When Miss Barnes asked him if his wife's milk was dry,

---

[21] *T & C Mag.* 3 (1771), 514.
[22] LPCA, D.136: 111–12, 128, 226, 312, 269–70.

he said he did not know, so she told him to go at once to find out. He found that his wife 'had plaisters applied to her breasts to stop her milk', but reported that in his opinion they had not 'been on so long as to hurt her milk'. Miss Barnes took the message to the Duchess, who decided not to pursue the idea 'for fear her milk should not be good'.[23] At this point, at least, she was very anxious that the baby should live, and perhaps still had lingering hopes of passing her off as a legitimate child of herself and the Duke, and therefore as the potential heiress to some of the Scudamore estates. But this is the last that is recorded of poor little Fanny, and we must conclude that, like so many other babies at this period, and especially illegitimate ones, she succumbed to irregular feeding from her wet-nurse or some infantile malady. The fact that she was baptized Fanny Matthews and not Fanny Scudamore suggests that neither of her parents had by then much confidence in their ability to foist her off one day as a legitimate child of the Duke.

During the winter of 1741-2 the Duchess stayed in London in rented houses. By November she had renewed sexual relations with Lord Talbot, but throughout the winter his visits became more and more rare and more and more brief. It was clear that he was getting tired of her. The Duchess was very upset at this neglect, and told her attendants, 'you don't know what it is to part with a man by whom you have had a child,' and said that Lord Talbot 'slighted her now he had got his end of her'—an observation that was probably close to the mark in the light of his comment to Mrs Duffell the day after the birth about treating her as a sexual convenience.[24]

In any case he never forgave her for her obstinacy in remaining so long at Chipping Warden, and so ruining all his plans for a secret delivery in London. He was also angry at the wasted expense. Mrs Bennen presented the Duchess with a bill for no less that £170 for renting the house, buying the linen, hiring the servants and a wet-nurse, and for her own trouble in attending her to treat a sore breast. He abused her both for the extravagant size of the bill, and also for presenting it to the Duchess rather than to himself. He asked her 'whether she distrusted his pay'. It was, after all, one of the gentlemanly conventions of the age that the man should pay for the lying-in of his mistress. Mrs Bennen was angry at the abuse, and also because her efforts had been wasted since the Duchess had given birth in the country after all. There was danger in her anger, and the Duchess hastily sent Miss Barnes to stop her mouth with a handsome present of fifty guineas for herself and ten for her maid. Mrs Bennen alleged implausibly

[23] Ibid. 131-2, 231-4, 273, 281-2, 279-80, 134-6, 399-41.
[24] Ibid. 237-40, 138-44.

128

that she tried to refuse it, but that Miss Barnes had thrown the money into a writing box and then left.[25]

It was not until May 1742, by which time Lord Talbot seems to have more or less broken off relations with the Duchess, that the first hint reached the latter that her husband the Duke was preparing to sue her for adultery in the ecclesiastical courts. One by one her domestic servants were summoned by the Duke and grilled by his lawyer to disclose what they knew. Almost all were quick to change sides and tell all. There is some reason to suspect that Thomas Garland, who had been the Duke's butler and joined the Duchess in the same capacity at the time of the separation in 1740, may have been deliberately planted in the household as a spy. William Fidoe her coachman testified that Garland had told him to take careful note of exactly when Lord Talbot visited her. Garland specifically denied that he had been ordered to observe the Duchess or that he had ever made memoranda about what he saw and heard, but his denials are not altogether credible in view of the amount of detail that he was able to recall under interrogation. John Pember may also have been playing the same double role.

It is certainly suspicious that so many witnesses made written memoranda for their private use. It is clear that in some cases the note-taking was spontaneous, the product of a realization that observation of the adultery of a Duchess might one day have a cash value. This was certainly true of the notes taken by Mrs Stiles the midwife as soon as she returned from the delivery. The zeal with which the farmer dogged the footsteps of the lovers through the fields of Wardington, his creeping to within ten yards of them to watch them making love under a hedge, and the prompt recording of what he saw in a memorandum, might all be merely the result of prurient curiosity. On the other hand, he might have been asked by one of the Duke's agents to keep his eyes open. The same doubts apply to the note-taking of Richard Duffell, the gardener at Chipping Warden, who 'for his own satisfaction made memorandums of the times when the transactions happened'.

Note-taking about adultery *before* the separation, however, was almost certainly the unsolicited response of the individuals themselves. Robert Croucher, the Duke's Groom of the Chamber, who first surprised the Duchess and Lord Talbot in the act of adultery on a chair in May 1740, probably made the note of the time and place on his own initiative. James Phillips, the Duke's butler, who listened at the door to hear them kissing and later saw the silver lace on the floor, explained that he took notes 'by

[25] Ibid. 145–7, 241, 381–4.

reason he did not know but that some time or other he might be called upon to give an account of what he knew'. This seems plausible. At this high social level the servants were both literate and intelligent, and they knew very well the value of precise and documented testimony in a court of law. They were doing no more than investing in the future, expecting that one way or another, one day or another, they might be rewarded for their pains.[26]

There is some reason to think that, from the moment the separation occurred, the Duke, who was no fool, had plans for a lawsuit in mind. As we have seen, it is certainly possible that one or two of his old servants were deliberately encouraged to take service with the Duchess in order to keep an eye on her. And it is certainly odd how careful he was to see that several of his servants kept a daily log of every night he spent after the separation, so that he could prove conclusively that after that moment he had never slept with the Duchess and so could not possibly be the father of any future child.[27] A strong suspicion emerges that the Duchess's household was so riddled with spies that the half-hearted attempts at concealment by her and Lord Talbot were utterly futile. The Duke had no trouble in finding the farmer who had seen them making love in the field, nor the Banbury midwife who actually delivered the baby, nor the London midwife who had been hired to do so in the first place. He knew all about the Duchess's companion, Miss Barnes. Nor did his lawyer find it difficult to obtain information from the Duchess's servants, almost all of whom had been hired by the Duke and had been in his service for many years, often since his marriage and setting-up house in 1729. Since his household was so large, and his financial resources were so great, he had far more to offer them than the Duchess. He could promise them money and a secure position in his household after the trial was over, and as a result nearly all of them promptly told all they knew.

As soon as she learnt what was going on, the Duchess got rid of those of her servants whom she thought had most grossly betrayed her. John Pember was discharged through a message from Miss Barnes, the ostensible reason, according to him, being 'to prevent the world saying spiteful things and reflecting on her Grace by saying that she kept him to prevent his speaking the truth by declaring what he knew with regard to her conduct and behaviour'. In view of the rich rewards he had reaped from his silence over the past two years, and his open threat of blackmail to which the Duchess had succumbed, this final act of betrayal by Pember must have been an

---

[26] Ibid. 376, 345, 262, 249, 284, 355, 501.
[27] Ibid. 361–7, 445–51, 457–65, 490–9, 501.

especially bitter blow. Thomas Garland, the butler, was also let go 'on account of [the Duke's] sending for him and asking him questions concerning her Grace'. William Fidoe, the coachman, was also discharged, 'on account of her selling off her horses', presumably to raise money to pay for the prospective lawsuit. But the Duchess retained her waiting woman, Elizabeth Franklin, and her companion, Miss Barnes, who were loyal to the end and gave away very little on the witness stand, and also her cook and her new groom, who gave away nothing at all.[28]

In June 1742 the Duke finally launched his suit in the ecclesiastical court for separation from bed and board on the grounds of his wife's adultery with Lord Talbot. He could not upset the legal separation agreement of 1740, which gave the Duchess the Scudamore estates in return for the surrender of her jointure, but he could achieve three things. He could get revenge on both her and Lord Talbot by publicly humiliating them; he could finally scotch any plans they might have had to foist Fanny on the world as his child; and he could prepare the way for an action for crim. con. against Lord Talbot in order to collect damages. This would be followed by a private bill for full divorce by Act of Parliament, which would allow him to remarry and beget an heir to the Somerset estates and titles. His case was watertight, for he had overwhelming evidence both of repeated acts of adultery since May 1740 and of the illegitimate birth in September 1741. The first results of the suit were very gratifying to him. The details of the story, as laid out in his 'libel' or bill of particulars, were soon the talk of London, since at least one verbatim copy was in circulation, being obtained by Lady Townshend and passed around among her friends, including Horace Walpole. The latter hastened to spread the news of the juicier items, such as the love-making on the chairs in the dining-room when the silver lace was rubbed off, and under the hedge in Wardington field. Moreover, in July Lord Talbot's wife, outraged at the publicity given to her husband's liaison with the Duchess, and no doubt depressed by the death of her only child, demanded and obtained a formal private separation agreement, with an allowance to her of no less than £3,000 a year. This stimulated the Duke to comment acidly that 'I pity Lord Talbot to have met with two such tempers as our two wives.'[29] The first round clearly went to the Duke.

But he had reckoned without the Duchess, who, as we have seen, was a bold, impetuous, and obstinate woman. In July, just as his suit for separation was getting under way, she launched a counter-suit against him for nullity

[28] Ibid. 316, 344, 375, 396, 432, 510, 516.
[29] *Walpole's Correspondence*, 17: 453, 486.

on the grounds that he was impotent and that his eleven-year childless marriage with her had never been consummated. It was a master-stroke. In normal impotence suits the issue was settled by a physical examination of the wife by experienced midwives and doctors to see whether or not her hymen was intact. In this case, where the wife had already given birth to an illegitimate child, the burden of proof of his virility was inevitably transferred to the husband. To prove virility in a court of law was far from easy. And the Duke, as the Duchess knew, was a sick man, as is proved by his frequent trips to Bath after the separation to take the waters. The Duchess, who as never one to mince her words, claimed that throughout her marriage 'the privy members of the Duke were never to my knowledge turgid, dilated or erected in such a way as (in my opinion) may be usual and necessary to perform the act of carnal copulation'. As a result, the Duke 'never did penetrate into or enter my body'.[30]

The Duke's first line of defence was that they had always slept in one bed together for ten years, except when he was sick with gout. Secondly, he claimed that he had often had sexual intercourse with her. To prove this, he introduced as witnesses three chambermaids who had made their bed over the years, and who testified that there were often stains and marks on both the sheets and the Duchess's shift which could only have come from intercourse. Two of the witnesses had long since left the Duke's service and were already young widows in their thirties, and therefore presumably knew what they were talking about; the other was a spinster of 47, who was still a servant of the Duke. Thirdly, he introduced a letter from the Duchess to the dowager Duchess of Richmond, written five months after the marriage. In it she declared, not only that she found Badminton 'the most agreable fine place I ever saw', but also that 'the lord Duke does everything he can think of to make me happy, and indeed he succeeds in it, for he makes me one of the best husbands in the world. . . . I truly am completely happy.' The Duke claimed that this proved that she was sexually satisfied with the marriage.[31]

The Duchess fought back fiercely. She brushed aside the letter as a mere façade of formal politeness, which did not at all mean that her husband had succeeded in consummating the marriage. She did not deny that they had normally slept in one bed for ten years, but she claimed that the stains on the sheets were hers, not the Duke's. She swore that, whenever the Duke tried to sleep with her, 'I never did perceive the least matter to proceed from his Grace which could occasion such marks or stains.' She then asked the chambermaids a set of increasingly embarrassing questions. 'Do you

[30] LPCA, C.5/73; E.36/138, 139; Ee.10/74.   [31] Ibid. Ee. 10/73; 35/13.

not know that the Duchess and her sex are subject to disorders whereby stains or marks may appear on her and their shifts and sheets . . . without having had carnal copulation with any man?' Leucorrhea and vaginal discharges were indeed common among women in the eighteenth century, but the maids insisted that the Duchess was healthy, and anyway that they had never seen similar stains on the sheets of single women or widows. The second question ran: 'Can you take upon yourself upon viewing the stains . . . whether such stains proceeded from man or woman?' The maids had to admit that they could not be certain about that. The third question was even more difficult: 'May not married women be provoked by the teasing of their husbands so as to cause an emission from the woman without her husband having had at such times carnal copulation with her?' Faced with this suggestion of manual or oral stimulation to orgasm by the Duke, the maids said a little uncertainly that they did not *think* this could have produced the stains in question without male emission as well.[32]

Although the maids were clearly on shaky ground in answering these indelicate questions, the Duke had made a good defence, and the Duchess's suit for a nullity on grounds of impotence was therefore rejected by the London Consistory Court. But it was upheld on appeal by the Duchess to the Court of Arches in December 1742,[33] although the judges were clearly in two minds about the case. The Duke was now desperate, and, in order to obtain a reversal of the sentence, in March 1743 he surprised the world by volunteering to undergo the medieval canon-law test of virility in the presence of eminent witnesses appointed by the Court. The surviving court records make no mention of this test, and for a vivid description of what happened, we have to turn to a letter from Horace Walpole:

I have no victories to tell you, but the Duke of Beaufort's; you have heard all that story of his wife and Lord Talbot: when they had got such proofs of her gallantries, she took a bold step, and swore impotence to his Grace. He, with more than mortal courage, stood the trial. T'other night was appointed for the action; the lists were at Dr Meade's house: he, another physician, three surgeons and the Dean of the Arches, all very matron-like personages, were inspectors. I should never have been potent again!—well, but he was. They offered to wait upon his Grace to any place of public resort—'No, no he would only go behind the screen, and when he knocked, they were to come to him, but come that moment'. He was some time behind the scenes: at last he knocked, and the good old folks saw what amazed them—what they had not seen many a day! Cibber says 'His Grace's—is in everybody's mouth'. He is now upon his mettle, and will sue Lord Talbot for fourscore thousand pounds damages.

---

[32] Ibid. Ee.10/74; 35/13; Eee.14/419, 420, 421.
[33] Ibid. B.17/142A.

Walpole's correspondent Sir Horace Mann, the British envoy in Florence, commented in reply:

The Duke of Beaufort's victory, I think, was very great. I should certainly never have been potent behind the screen, on such an occasion. But after all, it sounds odd that such great personages should turn such matters to profit. Lord Talbot, by such damages, will lose as much as he got with his rich wife; he that was the pattern for all husbands! Her Grace's was a bold stroke truly.[34]

Walpole's letter provides one of the very rare accounts of how such tests for nullity were conducted. The examiners were the leading judge of the ecclesiastical court, two physicians, and three surgeons. Although they offered to accompany the Duke to a brothel, he chose to masturbate to erection and ejaculation, and did so successfully. Like so much of English early modern canon law, this procedure dated back to the rules of the pre-Tridentine medieval Catholic Church. In one case of alleged impotence, at York in 1433, the test prescribed by the court had been for seven women to try to arouse a man to erection by kissing him, exposing their breasts, and masturbating him (in this case, all in vain). In another test in Venice in the 1470s a man accused of impotence successfully demonstrated his virility before a clerical audience, this time by successful intercourse with two prostitutes.[35]

In the ecclesiastical courts of England in the seventeenth century, evidence of virility had to be displayed before at least two men over the age of 60 and of sound doctrine and pure conscience. But the Beaufort test best fits the rules only fully developed in France after the Council of Trent in the late sixteenth and early seventeenth centuries. It was then established that a husband accused of impotence had two choices to prove his virility. Both accorded with the growth at that time of the Baconian stress upon experimental proof rather than deductive reasoning, and of a demand by the lawyers for an increasingly high standard of evidence to settle a case. The first test was visual evidence of erection and ejaculation by masturbation, the candidate being allowed five or six tries and choice of time and place. The witnesses were two surgeons to feel the engorged tissue, and two doctors to draw the theoretical conclusion. Two well-known tests identical to that of the Duke of Beaufort took place in France in the early seventeenth century. The second method of proof was by public copulation with a

[34] *Walpole's Correspondence*, 18: 185, 199; LPCA, D.136: 45–56. It should be remembered that Lord Talbot's wife, when he married her in 1734, was reckoned to be worth £70,000 (*Peerage*, s.n. Talbot of Hensol).

[35] R. H. Helmholz, *Marriage Litigation in Medieval England* (Cambridge, 1974), 88–9; G. Ruggiero, *The Boundaries of Eros: Sex Crime and Sexuality in Renaissance Venice* (New York, 1979), 146–7.

prostitute before an assembly of doctors and ecclesiastical lawyers, a test urged by plaintiff wives, who were rightly confident that most men would fail under such conditions.

The recorded evidence suggests that the men did indeed usually fail, despite the fact that sexual performance in the presence of others was by no means rare in the early modern period. The use of this demanding test culminated in France, in the M. de Langey affair of 1659. Accused of impotence by his wife, he tried to have sexual intercourse in the presence of no fewer than five matrons, five doctors, and five surgeons, but not unnaturally failed before such a large and intimidating crowd. His marriage was consequently annulled, whereupon he remarried and proceeded to give his new wife seven children in as many years. When his first wife died in 1670 the case was consequently reopened and in 1677 the French courts abandoned the 'congress' test as both indecent and inefficient. But it survived in Italy, and apparently remained a very rarely used option in England, to judge by this Beaufort case.[36]

Faced with this proof of the Duke's sexual capacity, in May 1743 the Court of Arches reversed itself, threw out the Duchess's suit for impotence, and gave victory to the Duke in his suit for separation on grounds of his wife's adultery.[37] Encouraged by this victory, the Duke determined on revenge for being made to undergo this humiliating ordeal. The result of this vindictive suit by the Duke for crim. con. damages of £80,000 against Lord Talbot is unknown. If it ever came to trial, the jury certainly would not have awarded such exorbitant damages, especially since Lord Talbot kept insisting that when he first seduced the Duchess he genuinely believed she was *virgo intacta*, as she claimed. The jury could well have awarded up to £5,000, but the absence of any mention of a trial suggests that in the end none took place. It is clear that public opinion at this early stage was very uneasy about making money out of a wife's adultery by bringing a suit for heavy damages for crim. con. in a common-law court against her lover. Lord Orrery commented uneasily: 'Alas, what money can make amends for such injuries? However, of course, his [the Duke's] expenses ought to be defrayed upon this unhappy occasion.'[38]

Fortified by a judicial separation from his duchess, and perhaps the award of heavy damages from Lord Talbot, the Duke introduced a private Act of Parliament to secure a full divorce with freedom to remarry, which finally passed in March 1744. Although unopposed by the Duchess, it did

---

[36] P. Darmon, *Le Tribunal de l'Impuissance* (Paris, 1979), 193–201, 207–20.

[37] LPCA, B.17/147, 142B.

[38] *Walpole's Correspondence*, 18: 185, 189; Countess of Cork and Orrery (ed.), *Orrery Papers* (London, 1903), ii. 172–3.

not go through without a fight, since Lord Ilchester introduced a clause, which was defeated, prohibiting the Duchess from remarrying. His object was to prevent her producing a legitimate male heir, since, if she died without one, his brother-in-law Lord Digby stood to inherit the great Scudamore estates.[39]

The rest of the story is soon told. For a short while the Duchess and her lover, Lord Talbot, were inseparable: 'She seemed to glory in her intrigue, and often appeared with his lordship in the character of a huntress.' But Talbot was in fact already tired of her, and was soon busy pursuing other women, building up over the next twenty-five years a reputation for 'gallantry'. After parting with the Duchess he lived with a succession of mistresses, one of them Elizabeth Pitt, the sister of Lord Chatham, and on his death left his estate and barony to a nephew, who beat off the claims of yet another illegitimate daughter called Mary Ann Talbot.[40]

As for the Duke, six months after the passage of the Divorce Act he was rumoured to be planning a second marriage to a Miss Windham. But in fact he did not live long enough to exploit his many legal victories, for he died in February 1745 at the age of 39, 'worn out by a complication of disorders'. Mrs Delany wrote the most succinct and accurate epitaph upon him: 'he was unhealthy in his constitution and unhappy in his circumstances, though possessed of great honours and riches.'[41]

Some time after the Duke's death, his former wife, who still retained the great Scudamore inheritance, married Colonel Charles Fitzroy, an illegitimate son of Charles, 2nd Duke of Grafton. This was presumably a marriage for love rather than money, since Fitzroy cannot have been a rich man. She died at Holme Lacy in 1750, while giving birth to her only daughter and heiress by her second husband. Thus within six years of the conclusion of the lawsuit both the Duke and the Duchess were dead, neither of them living into their fortieth year.

This story illustrates the intolerable strains placed on marriage in England in the mid-eighteenth century when the old practice of choice of a spouse based almost exclusively on considerations of financial and political advantage was now having to compete with the new ideal of free choice by those involved, based on settled affection. Where, as in his case, there were gigantic economic interests at stake, the patriarchal tradition still persisted

---

[39] LPCA, C.5/72, 73; B.17/147; Private Acts of Parliament 17 Geo. II, cap. 2.
[40] *T & C Mag.* 3 (1771), 513–15; *Peerage*, s.n. Talbot of Henson.
[41] Countess of Cork and Orrery (ed.), *Orrery Papers*, ii. 172–3; Lady Llandover (ed.), *Autobiography and Correspondence of Mary Granville, Mrs Delany* (London, 1861), ii. 235, 344.

at the ducal level. The almost inevitable result was adultery by one or both sexes. The old system worked perfectly well in a place like Italy, where everyone accepted the conventions. After a sufficient number of children had been born, husband and wife had separate bedrooms and separate coaches, lived quite separate lives, and did not interfere with each other's sexual arrangements. It was what nowadays is called an 'open marriage'. In England, however, once affection was being demanded as an essential bonding of marriage, these easy arrangements were not tolerated. Married couples slept in the same bed and were expected to go about together. When the marriage failed at the emotional level, one side or the other was likely to demand formal separation, either by private treaty, as was most usual, or by a suit in the ecclesiastical courts if relations became really bitter and the object was humiliation and financial ruin rather than merely separation. If the Duchess had produced a male heir to unite the two estates, it is very possible that the Duke would have overlooked her adultery. As it was, he needed an excuse for a full divorce and permission to remarry in order himself to beget a legitimate heir.

The situation of the Duchess was exacerbated since there were so few servants in the house whom she could trust. Only her own waiting woman, Elizabeth Franklin, had come with her from her childhood home at Holme Lacy, and she does not seem to have been close to any of the other servants.

In a ducal household, unlike that of more modest ranks, there was considerable security of tenure for servants and good prospects of promotion up through the ranks of a large and complex bureaucratic organization. This resulted in the prime loyalty of servants going to the master of the house, who controlled their future. John Pember, for example, had first been taken into the Duke's service in 1728 as a stable lad at the age of 23, with no fixed wages. He was soon promoted to groom at £7 a year, and it was only his blackmail hold over the Duchess that got his wages raised first to £12, then to £15, a year, while he served as her groom from 1740 to 1742. Thomas Garland, the other betrayer of the Duchess, had been with the Duke since the latter's marriage in 1729. He started as under-butler at £8 a year, and in 1737 was promoted to butler at £20. Robert Croucher was the highest paid servant of all. He too had been taken on in 1729, as confectioner and groom of the chamber with a salary of £40 a year. In 1741 he was promoted to be steward at Badminton, in charge of all the household arrangements, at a salary of £50. If one includes the substantial 'vails' (tips from visitors) and perquisites and gifts from tradesmen, he must have made a very comfortable living. The next highest paid servant was the cook, at £30 a year, who had also been with the Duke since 1729. William Fidoe first took service at the same time, as a helper in the stable for no certain wage, like John Pember. He then became coachman to the Duke at £10 a year, and finally coachman to the Duchess at £12. At the bottom of the scale was young Robert Rivers, who had begun in the household at the age of 12 looking after some pet birds for no fixed wages, and then rose to be footman to the Duke at £7 a year. Even the Duke's gentleman secretary, John Perfect, who was only 22, had been with him for five years at a salary of £20 a year.[42]

This stability of tenure and the possibility of upward mobility contrasts markedly with most households of the squirearchy and bourgeoisie where the servants were all too often poorly paid casual transients, hired and fired for a few months at a time or at most a few years and with no fixed loyalties to anyone. As a result they were far more open to bribery by their mistress, whereas ducal servants had more to lose by betraying their master and more to gain in keeping him informed. It was thus only a matter of weeks before the liaison of the Duchess with Lord Talbot came to the ears of the Duke, whereas in other households the adultery of the wife might be the subject of knowledgeable salacious gossip and joking below stairs, but stay unknown to the husband for months or even years. It is, of course, quite possible that there were dozens of marriages which went quietly and dis-creetly on the rocks, the wife's adultery being concealed by servants and friends and relatives. Like so many of the wives who were found out, the Duchess seems to have had no friends upon whom she could rely not to betray her.

Finally her great wealth and lavish staff of servants made it extremely difficult for her to give birth in secret. From every point of view, therefore, an English duchess in the 1730s and 1740s was particularly strongly tempted to take a lover, but particularly likely to be discovered and disgraced if she did. This was the misfortune of Frances, Duchess of Beaufort, although it cannot be denied that she brought her troubles on herself by her reckless and arrogant folly.

[42] LPCA, D.136: 315–16, 318, 344, 347, 354–5, 503, 510, 367, 375, 438, 452, 357, 368.

7

Grafton v. Grafton
Private separation and public divorce, 1756–1769

(i) *From Marriage to Private Separation, 1756–1765*

Augustus Henry Fitzroy, 3rd Duke of Grafton, was the third in direct line of descent from the second bastard son of Charles II by the latter's mistress Barbara Villiers, Lady Castlemaine, later Duchess of Cleveland in her own right. Of all Charles's many mistresses, she was the most sexually and financially voracious, and she took good care to see that her younger son was handsomely rewarded for his paternity. He was created Duke of Grafton and married at the age of 9 to a 5-year-old heiress, the only daughter of Henry, Earl of Arlington, from whom he and his descendants inherited the great house of Euston in Suffolk and all the Arlington estates, including Wakefield Lodge in Whittlebury Forest in Northamptonshire. At the same time he was endowed by the King, his father, with two huge perpetual annuities from the public funds, one for £7,194 a year on the Excise, and the other for £3,384 a year on the Post Office, together with the prizage and butlerage of wine imports, worth about £500 a year, and the Receiver-Generalship of the profits of sales of offices in the King's Bench and Common Pleas, which was bringing in £843 a year when it was finally abolished in 1843.[1]

At his birth in 1735 Augustus Henry was merely the eldest son of the third son of the 2nd Duke, and so had minimal prospects of succeeding to his grandfather's fortune. But first the eldest son of the 2nd Duke died in infancy; then the third son, Augustus Henry's father, died at a relatively early age in 1741; and finally the second son and prospective heir died childless in 1747 at the age of 22. In consequence of this series of accidents, at the age of 12 the boy Henry became the heir to a great title and estate.

To fit him for his new responsibilities, he was carefully educated in the classics at Westminster School and Peterhouse College, Cambridge. In 1756, when he was barely 21, he married Anne Liddell, the 18-year-old only daughter and heiress of Lord Ravensworth; she brought him a fortune

---

[1] Peerage, s.n. Grafton.

of £40,000 in cash and the expectation of much more on the death of her parents (Plate 8).[2] There is every reason to suppose that this was a match warmly approved for financial and political reasons by both Henry's guardian and Anne's parents. But later on Anne said she had married for love, and a well-informed commentator claimed that Henry also had married 'from pure devotion'.[3] A year after the marriage, the 2nd Duke died, and Henry inherited the dukedom and a great estate, and plunged into the political arena as a loyal Whig follower of the elder Pitt, and vigorous opponent of Lord Bute. Between 1763 and 1766 he was a prominent member of Pitt's ministry, and in 1766 he reluctantly took over the reins as First Lord of the Treasury after Pitt fell ill, went into total seclusion, and was elevated to the peerage.

It was just at this period, however, that Henry's private life began to unravel. Although a cultivated man promoted to high office, and the holder of liberal views both about taxing the American colonies and about the tenets of the Church of England (he later became a Unitarian), he nevertheless was not possessed of great strength of character, and had no great enthusiasm or even aptitude for politics. He preferred his private pleasures, and when he resigned from Secretary of State in 1766 he was obliged to deny the rumours that he did it only 'from a love of ease and indulgence to his private amusements'. It was his misfortune that both his public and private life in the late 1760s were subjected to the scrutiny of the two wittiest and the cruellest pens of the age, namely those of Horace Walpole and of 'Junius' (now generally agreed to have been the pseudonym of Sir Philip Francis). Walpole was quite friendly with Henry, but was brutally frank about his defects of character, observing at an early stage that he always felt 'that the world can be postponed to a whore and a horse-race' (Plate 9).[4]

There can be no doubt about Duke Henry's addiction to horse-racing. As early as 1760 he postponed joining a house party at Chatsworth in order to visit the Derby races,[5] and thereafter consistently put races before politics, even after he became Prime Minister. He regularly attended the races at Newmarket, and Junius's comment that Pitt had drawn the Duke away from Newmarket and Whites—the famous London gambling club—was not strictly true. Thus, at the height of the intense debate over the Regency Bill in 1765, he deserted Parliament to go off to the Newmarket races.[6] It was only decades later, in 1789, that it was finally reported that the Duke

---

[2] Suffolk RO, HA 513/4/30.   [3] *T & C Mag.* 3 (1769), 115.
[4] *Walpole's Correspondence*, 38: 101.   [5] Ibid. 63.
[6] J. Cannon (ed.), *Letters of Junius* (Oxford, 1978), 69; *Walpole's Correspondence*, 38: 543.

had 'renounced the Turf for the Fathers' and taken to writing Unitarian tracts and catechisms.[7]

After horse-racing, the Duke's second passion was hunting. One reason why he spent so much of his time at his secondary seat at Wakefield Lodge in Northamptonshire was that here he could indulge in both these pursuits. This was where he kept the pack of hounds which he had inherited from his grandfather, the Grafton Hunt, of which he was Master. For twenty years, from 1768 to 1788, he also organized his own horse races on the 'Lawn' at Wakefield Lodge, a 250-acre stretch of smooth parkland below the Lodge, races which 'were generally attended by the élite of the sporting world'.[8] At Wakefield Lodge Duke Henry was also within easy reach of Newmarket, where he also kept a house for greater convenience during his regular visits to the races.[9] To accommodate his sporting guests Henry extended the house at Wakefield Lodge, and was presumably also responsible for building the huge stable block which could accommodate fifty horses.

The Duke's third and most notorious passion was for women. During the first few years of marriage with Anne Liddell, from 1756 to 1760, matters seem to have gone quite well, and the couple produced three children, two sons and a daughter. But by the early 1760s those in the know regarded him as a man of gallantry, and in 1762 he fathered on a Miss Scudamore an illegitimate son, Charles Fitzroy Scudamore, who died in 1782.[10] After 1760 the Duke became increasingly immersed in the tedious business of politics, while Anne became an inveterate party-giver and a passionate addict of the card table, at which she lost sums so large that even the Duke could ill afford them.[11] A footman later described how at this time, night after night, the Duke would

come home at eleven or twelve o'clock in the evening, and seeing a great many servants in the hall, he hath enquired of the porter, and finding a great deal of company, and that they were at card parties . . . hath turned back and went out of the house; and at other times . . . he would call his valet de chambre, and take candles and go into the library and never used to be seen afterwards.

This was the sort of behaviour which led Horace Walpole to describe him as 'one of the best bred men alive'.[12]

---

[7] *Walpole's Correspondence*, 31: 322.
[8] G. Baker, *History and Antiquities of the County of Northamptonshire* (London, 1822–41), ii. 230.
[9] Suffolk RO, HA 513/4/121–30.   [10] Ibid. 513/4/36.
[11] *Walpole's Correspondence*, 38: 66, 71; 34: 172.
[12] *Trials for Adultery at Doctors Commons*, iv. 120.

In 1764 the Duke and Duchess had a final tremendous quarrel, and the former decided that the only solution for his own peace of mind lay in a private separation. All accounts seem to agree that the Grafton separation closely followed in real life that of Lord and Lady Wronglove in Cibber's play, *The Wife's Resentment*, in which the husband declared to his wife: 'Your temper is at last intolerable, and now 'tis mutual ease to part with you.'[13]

The most detailed account of the marital break-up comes from a clearly well-informed, but somewhat suspect, source, the anonymous author of a series of scandalous but very detailed stories about notable persons and their mistresses, published in the 1770s and 1780s by the *Town and Country Magazine*. Discussing the Duke and Duchess of Grafton, the author observed that

home had no charms for her—quadrille and hombre engrossed her sole attention, so they scarce met for successive weeks. This, however, he passed over for some time, as the effects of giddiness and youth, and hoped maturer years would convince her of her error. Notwithstanding this prudent resolution, chagrin at her conduct had so far preyed upon his spirits that he was seized with a violent fever, which brought him to the brink of the grave.

Upon his first coming down, by the permission of his physicians, the lady was sitting in the parlour with the windows up, though in the depth of winter. He ordered them to be pulled down, but this she countermanded, and to avoid contention he returned to his chamber . . . Such repeated behaviour, joined with her prodigality and extravagance, with her losses at play, soon afterwards produced the rupture which ended in total separation.[14]

These precise details cannot be confirmed from other sources, but the Duchess's letters after the separation make it clear that in the passion of a flaming row she had said she hated her husband. This he regarded as unpardonable, and used it as a reason for turning her out of the house. She later admitted that 'I know I offended by repeated offensive things in my conduct (although no criminal ones)', and expressed her deep regret over 'those unfortunate words, which I do not mean to justify'.[15]

Relations continued to deteriorate throughout the summer and autumn of 1764, both during and after the time when Anne gave birth to their third child. Henry hardly came near her during her lying-in, and in November he ordered her out of the house at Euston, having irrevocably decided upon a formal private separation.[16]

---

[13] C. Cibber, *The Wife's Resentment* (1736).

[14] *T & C Mag.* I (Mar. 1769), 114–15.

[15] Suffolk RO, HA 513/4/53, 55; *NCC Trials for Adultery* (1780), ii. 11; *Trials for Adultery at Doctors Commons*, iv. 2.

[16] *Walpole's Correspondence*, 38: 429, 435–6, 441, 458, 462, 472, 481.

Grafton v. Grafton

Explanations differed about why Duchess Anne had behaved so badly and blindly. Lady Holland blamed the company she kept, in particular 'her good friends the Bedford clique', who according to her 'she may thank for having contributed to make her bring things to this *éclat*. Had she fallen into better company, I do believe she would have behaved more wisely.'[17]

Horace Walpole, who knew them well and liked them both, described more profound psychological causes that underlay the breakdown of the marriage:

The Duchess, a woman of commanding figure, though no regular beauty, graceful, full of dignity and of art too, passionate for admiration, unheeding of the Duke's temper, which, had she tried, it had been difficult to please, had yet thought to govern him by spirit, and had lost him before she was aware.[18]

By the time she realized what was happening, her husband had reached the point where he positively hated his wife. Belatedly she realized, as she told him, that 'I became first indifferent and then odious to you'.[19] All through the autumn of 1764, after she had been turned out of Euston, the Duchess did everything in her power to remedy the situation. She wrote letter after letter to her estranged husband, expressing her sorrow about her previous behaviour towards him, and about the unfortunate outburst of temper when she had said she hated him. She told him that 'we do not part by mutual consent, and . . . I am very willing to live with you and do my best'. Her mother, Lady Ravensworth, added to the pressure by writing that Duchess Anne was now desperately anxious to try to earn 'a return of your affections'. The Duchess also used the additional argument that a separation would upset the children. She admitted that it might not affect the eldest boy, now 4 years old, but it would certainly disturb little Georgiana, who would be 'laid open to all the suspicions this separation must naturally create in her when she comes to be a little older', and thus 'obliged to think ill either of her father or her mother'. She referred, of course, to the suspicion that the father of her baby sister might be someone other than Duke Henry.

Anne promised Henry that, 'if I come home once more I shall no longer be a woman of the world, but employ my whole thoughts at home'. She told him that 'I have the happiness of seeing you every night in my sleep', asked for pity on 'a wretched being who has no desire to live if her banishment is meant for life', and described herself as 'the tender mother of three loving children'. She excused her bad behaviour on the grounds of her

---

[17] *Leinster Correspondence*, i. 423 (quoted in *Walpole's Correspondence*, 38: 436 n. 48).
[18] *Walpole's Correspondence*, 34: 234–35.   [19] Suffolk RO, HA 513/4/53.

upbringing: 'an only daughter and consequently spoilt, though not by my parents, by having great court paid to me by others; married to a man I loved with passion . . . which made the change harder to bear. Then came a lying-in, when I suffered worse than the rack and went through more than I can express.'[20]

Despite these emotional appeals from Anne, the Duke declared that he could no longer endure 'the life that I have passed', and reiterated his determination to put into execution his plans for a formal private separation. But he had nothing with which to accuse his wife except extravagance, rude words, and offensive behaviour, and his own sense of propriety led him to arrange the separation 'with the utmost decency and politeness on his part'.[21]

Duke Henry did indeed behave like a perfect gentleman. Instead of using lawyers, family friends were appointed to settle the terms of separation. H. S. Conway, the brother of the Earl of Hertford, was the negotiator for the Duke, General Ellison, Lord Ravensworth's first cousin, for the Duchess, and they soon reached agreement on the financial terms, as well as on the custody of the children. Conway readily agreed that the Duchess's separation allowance was to be the same as her jointure in the marriage settlement, namely a princely £3,000 a year. He admitted to the Duke that 'it is a great proportion of your Grace's income', but insisted that it had to be done. He told the Duke bluntly that the Duchess had been very generous and accommodating, and that 'anything less, unless any charge had been laid against her Grace, would not be for her honour, nor I think for yours'. The Duke accepted the proposal without complaint, and freely gave the Duchess all her jewels. He also offered £150 a year, later raised to £190, for the maintenance of Georgiana and the baby, which was generous. But he jibbed at paying £1,000 in cash to furnish a home for her, on the grounds that he simply did not have the ready money. He also ordered that the eldest boy, his 4-year-old son and heir, Lord Euston, be sent to Anne's mother, Lady Ravensworth. This greatly upset Anne, who expressed her unwillingness 'to part with such a dearly beloved son unless you insist upon it'.

Even while these negotiations about the terms of separation continued, Anne did not give up all hope, but continued to use moral blackmail to persuade her husband to accept a reconciliation. She told Henry how little Georgiana had said to her: 'Indeed papa will love you again. Don't fret yourself to death.' When she confessed to Georgiana the mistakes she had made, the child replied, 'Mamma, you must not do so again, and then he

[20] Ibid., HA 513/4/51–3, 55, 56, 63.   [21] *T & C Mag.* 1 (1769), 115.

will live with you again.' Anne commented that 'it almost broke my heart'. Her final, more objective, conclusion about the collapse of the marriage was that 'I was much to blame on many occasions, but if I had had kindness from you instead of such a distance, we might have been happy.'[22]

On 3 December 1764 Horace Walpole reported that the separation was imminent. 'The Duke takes all on himself and assigns no reason but disagreement of tempers. He leaves Lady Georgiana with her mother, whom he says is the properest person to educate her, and Lord Charles till he is old enough to be taken from the women. This behaviour is noble and generous.' It also seems that in the end the Duke indeed relented and also agreed to leave the eldest son, Lord Euston, with Anne, at least for a short while.[23] As we shall see, he had good practical reasons not to want any children around the house. Even so, in view of the fact that by law the father had total control of all the children, and the mother no rights over them at all, regardless of their ages or her own innocence, his conduct was indeed generous by the standards of the times. By mid-December, when negotiations were almost complete, Anne was still writing letters full of remorse about herself and admiration for Henry: 'I own myself and only myself to blame . . . You don't know the happy feel it gives me to think you are the great noble character I always thought you.'[24] Conway also was full of praise for the way the Duke 'treats this matter in the noblest and handsomest way'.[25]

A few days later, however, the scales fell from Duchess Anne's eyes, and her mood changed abruptly to one of passionate indignation. This was because she had received an anonymous letter informing her that for at least a year the Duke had been carrying on an adulterous liaison with a notorious high-class courtesan, Nancy Parsons, and that, as soon as he had parted with Anne, back in August, he had openly set up house with her, and exhibited her in public with him at the Ascot races. Rumours of the liaison had reached Anne some time before, but she had refused to believe them. In August Walpole had reported that the Duke for some months now had been keeping Nancy Parsons, whom he described as 'one of the commonest creatures in London, once much liked, but out of date'.[26] Promiscuous she undoubtedly was, but hardly out of date (Plate 10).

She was born in 1735, and apparently started her career as an opera-singer, but was picked up by a wealthy nabob, Mr Horton, who carried her

[22] Suffolk RO, HA 513/4/61, 63, 65, 69, 74; *Walpole's Correspondence*, 38: 472 n. 14, 473.
[23] *Walpole's Correspondence*, 38: 472-3; *Trials for Adultery at Doctors Commons*, iv. 156.
[24] Suffolk RO, HA 513/4/71, 73.
[25] *Walpole's Correspondence*, 38: 473 n. 15.
[26] Ibid. 38: 435; 23: 344.

off to the West Indies, and allegedly married her. She later returned to London, and embarked on a long career as a mistress of men of title. She passed from hand to hand, being kept for a while by Lord Villiers, who introduced her to Duke Henry in 1764.

Nancy Parsons stayed with Henry for five years, and, when he finally pensioned her off in 1769 on account of her repeated infidelities, she was taken on by the Duke of Dorset for three years. Then at last, at the age of 37, she finally succeeded in cajoling her latest lover, the 23-year-old Charles, Lord Maynard, into marrying her. In 1771 Horace Walpole referred to her as 'the Duke of Grafton's Mrs Horton, the Duke of Dorset's Mrs Horton, everybody's Mrs Horton'.[27] She was clearly a woman of extraordinary sexual attraction and insinuating graces which enabled her to captivate, over a period of nearly twenty years, a succession of men of wealth, rank and, cultivation. She lived to the ripe old age of 80, dying in 1815.

Nancy was one of a small group of such women who acted as courtesans of the élite in the middle of the eighteenth century, serving to oil the wheels of matrimony in a society still tolerant of male infidelity. There was a story told of how one day Mr Montagu, the brother of the dissolute Lord Sandwich, was showing Lord Chancellor Hardwicke his picture collection. When they came to the full-length painting of two luscious female nudes, Montagu remarked 'these ladies you must certainly know, for they are most striking likenesses'. When Lord Hardwicke confessed his ignorance of them, Montagu replied: 'Why, where the devil have you led your life, or what company have you kept, not to know Fanny Murray and Kitty Fisher, with whose persons I thought no fashionable man like yourself could be unacquainted?'[28]

On learning that the rumours of her husband's liaison with Nancy Parsons were true, Duchess Anne exploded with rage:

Can it be that I have been thus deceived; that Lord Villiers's business and yours was what I ever feared; that you have [for] a year and a half (the very time the Duke of York first told me was at Ranelagh and which you solemnly denied) had this person as mistress in constant keeping; that Lord Villiers introduced you to her, she having formerly lived with him . . . that your whispers with Mr Jeffries was known to the whole Club at Arthur's; that you have fitted up her house in the richest way; that her extravagance is without end; that you was confined in town with a bad distemper this summer incog. with a groom; that this person vulgar in her manner has acquired such an ascendancy as to try to make you break with all your family, and prevailed? I find this, I am sorry to say, on undoubted authority.

---

[27] W. S. Lewis (ed.), *Notes by Lady Louis Stuart on George Selwyn* (New York, 1928), 14–15.
[28] R. Cooksey, *Essay on the Life of . . . Philip Earl of Hardwicke* (Worcester, 1791), 101.

To add insult to injury, the Duchess learnt that 'the Duke of York said as a piece of news at Court last Sunday that I had such a very bad temper you would not live with me'. Now, she is told, her husband had fitted up her old rooms in their London house to Nancy Parsons's liking, and wits were advising herself not to take lodgings too close 'for fear you should mistake the door'.

Though still bursting with anger and injured pride, Duchess Anne none the less expressed her satisfaction in knowing that her husband had been 'meditating my downfall, and that what I said last year did not occasion it'. On the other hand, she found it bitter to think that 'you hated me nine months before my poor last child was born, and maintained another woman', so that it was a child conceived without love. It was the timing that most mortified Duchess Anne, who up till then had believed that the sequence of events had been the quarrel; the separation; the Duke telling his friend Lord Villiers that he hated the Duchess; and Lord Villiers introducing him to Nancy Parsons to cheer him up in his loneliness. Now it seemed 'such a plot so deeply laid and so carried out by you two against one poor defenceless woman [as] is frightful to think of; who can be safe? I heard it said, justly, if every husband whose wife becomes indifferent to him is to put her away, what is to become of half the world?'[29]

Duchess Anne's anger was all too justified, since she had, as the letter makes clear, ignored several previous warnings about what was going on. In early November, her father, Lord Ravensworth, had violently reproached her, saying 'you have freed the Duke of Grafton to turn you out of his house and to live with a woman of the Town'. Even more galling was the fact that rumours were flying about that the Duke suspected that he was not the father of her last child—an accusation she indignantly rejected, and which in fact he never made publicly.[30]

The Duke's answer to this onslaught about his long-standing liaison with Nancy Parsons was dignified and calm, as befitted his reputation as a man of perfect manners. But it was not entirely candid. 'I shall not, as to what regards myself, say any more than that I am most grossly injured by anyone who can imagine that for any attachment of what nature soever I should have dissolved a family union of the kind ours ought to have been.' The sentence expresses the typical belief of upper-class males in the eighteenth century that the social and economic arrangements of a marriage and a family were one thing, and the sensual pleasures to be derived from a mistress were another; and that the two were not at all incompatible so long as the wife did not make domestic life intolerable as a result. But

[29] Suffolk RO, HA 513/4/68.   [30] Ibid. 513/4/54, 64.

the key phrase in the sentence is 'a family union of the kind ours *ought* to have been'. The Duke here conjured up a vision of a companionate marriage which had not been fulfilled in his turbulent party-giving life with Duchess Anne. The first draft of the letter contained a sentence which read: 'Whatever may be or may not have been my feelings, I never would have been so unjust to any one, as I find I am represented by you and others.' This, however, he deleted from the final version, presumably because he realized that it was not strictly true.[31]

The Duke's parting words to his estranged wife did not lack dignity and perhaps also sincerity:

You know, if you really think objectively, that this [separation] is not nor ever could be affected by a reason of the sort you have lately insinuated. Recollect the life we have led, which nothing but the hurry and dissipation of living in constant bustling company could ever have drove me so long to have endured. That, like the rest, was to end, my eyes were opened on my situation early, and it was [not] till repeated trials and expectations of a change that I was drove to seek this last method of redress. That you should not suffer in the opinion of the world has been my endeavour, whatever my private sensations.[32]

In fact, however, if Horace Walpole is to be believed, from 1764 or earlier 'hatred to his wife had been the motive of much of the Duke's conduct'— a statement supported by the fact that, whenever the two met by accident in the street, the Duke deliberately averted his face from her chair.[33]

(ii) *From Adulteries to Divorce, 1765–1769*

On 11 January 1765 the separation deed was signed and formal obligations of cohabitation by the Duke and Duchess of Grafton were ended. This left the former free to set up house with Nancy Parsons and to undertake, with little success, the burden of serving as Prime Minister of England. It left the Duchess to live quietly as a social recluse for at least a year, devoting herself to her children. Such correspondence as passed between the two over the first year of their separation was entirely confined to matters of child custody and visitation rights. In March 1765, a month after the signing of the private separation deed, Anne reported that Georgiana and the baby were well and she was glad of a visit from 'my dearest son, soon to part', that is, Lord Euston. She added, with prescience, 'I have a strong foreboding that from that time he will be dead to me.' She repeated that 'your continued dislike of me is a melancholy thing to me and my daughter', and

---

[31] Ibid. 513/4/70.   [32] Ibid.
[33] *Walpole's Correspondence*, 34: 241; NCC *Trials for Adultery* (1780), ii. 16.

expressed the hope that she might see her eldest son again. In December she wrote to express her relief to know that 'I may hope for my dear son's company during the holidays'. She explained that 'the thoughts of giving him entirely up . . . had got the better of me', so that she was often in tears.[34]

Between 1764 and 1769 the Duke was both Prime Minister and openly cohabitating with Nancy Parsons, and it is hardly surprising that ugly rumours soon began to fly. The anonymous author of the article in the *Town and Country Magazine* of 1769 described Nancy during these years as

attached to the most amiable man of his age, whose rank and influence raise her, in point of power, beyond many Queens on earth, caressed by the highest, courted and adulated by all . . . She presides constantly at his sumptuous table . . . The voice of calumny, however, is not silent upon her account . . . The mistress of a prime minister must have an interest at court, and it is natural for every candidate for preferment to make applications where success wears the face of plausibility . . . A scandal accumulates as it flows, the cupidity of gain is always considered as the first cause of her intercession . . . Many thousands she hath been supposed to receive by these imaginary means.[35]

This charge that the Duke's sexual infatuation with Nancy Parsons allowed her to use her influence on patronage appointments to her advantage does not stand alone. It seems to have been common gossip, for when Cornwallis was appointed Archbishop of Canterbury in 1768, Horace Walpole commented that it would be amusing to insert in the newspapers an article saying that 'three bishops had supped with Nancy Parsons at Vauxhall in their way to Lambeth'.[36]

Junius attacked the liaison from another angle, complaining that during the Wilkite riots in London in 1768 'the prime minister of Great Britain, in a rural retreat, and in the arms of faded beauty, had lost memory of his Sovereign, his country, or himself'. It was only in 1769, as the Duke was in the process of discarding Nancy Parsons (and divorcing Duchess Anne), that Junius finally stepped up the attack. He observed that he

marries to be divorced—he keeps a mistress to remind him of conjugal endearments. . . . Did not the Duke of Grafton frequently lead his mistress into public, and even place her at the head of his table, as if he had pulled down the temple of Venus and could bury all decency and shame under the ruins. . . . It is not the private indulgence but the public insult of which I complain.

---

[34] Suffolk RO, HA 513/4/76, 79, 80.
[35] *T & C Mag.* 1 (Mar. 1769), 115.
[36] *Walpole's Correspondence*, 38: 105; Lambeth Palace is the seat of the Archbishop of Canterbury.

But when the Duke finally parted with Nancy Parsons, Junius observed that 'his baseness to this woman is beyond description'.[37]

Junius's most mortal blow came in the form of a poem:

An Elegy in the Manner of Tibullus

Can Apollo resist, or a Poet refuse,
When Harry and Nancy solicit the Muse;
A statesman, who makes a whole Nation his care,
And a Nymph, who is almost as chaste as she's fair.

Dear Spousy had led such a damnable life,
He determin'd to keep any whore but his wife.
So Harry's Affairs, like those of the State,
Have been pretty well handled and tickled of late.

From Fourteen to forty our provident *Nan*
Had devoted her life to the Study of Man;
And thought it a natural change of her station,
From riding St George,[38] to ride over the nation.

Secret service had wasted the national wealth,
But now—'tis the price of the Minister's health;
An expense which the Treasury may well afford,
She who served him in bed should be paid at the board.

So lucky was Harry, that nothing could mend
His choice of a mistress, but that of a friend;—
A Friend so obliging, and yet so sincere,
With pleasure in one eye, in t'other a tear.

My Friend holds the Candle—the Lovers debate,
And among them, God knows how they settle the State.
Was there ever a Nation so govern'd before,
By a Jockey and Gambler, a Pimp[39] and a whore![40]

As for Duchess Anne, it was not to be expected that so handsome and ambitious a young woman (Horace Walpole said that she closely resembled Marie-Antoinette), of such high rank and fortune, so well known in London society, and before 1765 so inveterate a party-goer, would continue indefinitely to lead a life of monastic seclusion. The Duke had gone out of his way to cast no public blame on her for the break-up of his marriage, and

---

[37] Cannon, *Letters of Junius*, 63, 67–70, 75, 77–9, 250.

[38] An eighteenth-century expression for making love in the position with the woman on top.

[39] The 'pimp' may have been the Duke's intimate adviser, Thomas Bradshaw of the Treasury.   [40] Cannon, *Letters of Junius*, 454.

expressly 'desired his family and intimate friends to treat her with the same respect as before'.[41]

It is hardly surprising, therefore, that in the summer of 1767, when she met the 22-year-old Earl of Upper Ossory at Brighton, they should have fallen in love.[42] Indeed, Horace Walpole, who was a close friend of the Duchess, believed that she was almost driven to adultery:

Finding all solicitations ineffectual, and provoked by his affronting her in public places whither he openly attended his mistress, a girl distinguished by an uncommon degree of prostitution, one Nancy Parsons, the Duchess, whose passions had never been warm, had of late relaxed her reserve, had encouraged a lover, and undoubtedly was desirous of procuring a divorce even at the expense of her character.

It seems certain that Horace Walpole was wrong in thinking that the Duchess had been deliberately seeking to bring about a divorce. Her efforts to conceal her pregnancy, and later her extreme reluctance to give up the title and coronet of a duchess (Plate 8), both indicate that for a while she had been hoping to preserve both her reputation and her marriage.[43]

Walpole may have been right, however, in believing that Nancy Parsons was hoping for a divorce, in order to free Duke Henry to marry her. 'She had caused the Duchess to be watched, and the mistress of a first minister could not want sycophants to flatter her with hopes, as soon as the Duchess's frailty was discovered.'[44]

The liaison of Duchess Anne with Ossory continued all the winter in her London house, and by late January or early February she realized to her dismay that she was pregnant. Just at this critical juncture she made a move which in retrospect was open to a sinister interpretation. Her version of what happened was that young Lord Euston, who was still in her custody, had fallen ill. Since the Duke was worried about him, the Duchess kindly said that he could visit her house to see the child if he wished. The Duke's later interpretation of this invitation was that it was a plot to lure him into her company alone, so that she could later claim that he was the father of the child she was carrying. It is impossible to tell which version of this affair is the most plausible, but it cannot be denied that, if the Duke had come alone into the Duchess's company at that moment, it might well have wrecked his chances of later claiming that the pregnancy was proof of his wife's adultery.[45]

---

[41] *Walpole's Correspondence*, 4: 122 n. 7; 34: 172.
[42] *NCC Trials for Adultery* (1780), ii. 14, 39.
[43] Suffolk RO, HA 513/4/92; *NCC Trials for Adultery* (1780), ii. 12.
[44] *Walpole's Correspondence*, 34: 241; see also 23: 344 n. 66.
[45] *Trials for Adultery at Doctors Commons*, iv. 25–40, 156, 162–5.

There is certainly no doubt that Duchess Anne did everything she could to arrange for a secret delivery. But a person as prominent as she was could not possibly conceal a pregnancy, and by May, when she was five months pregnant, the secret leaked out and came to the ears of the Duke.[46] In his letter to her father, Lord Ravensworth, announcing the news, the Duke claimed that he had suspected the attachment with Ossory for years, and that this suspicion had been the real but hidden cause of the separation four years before. In fact, it is almost certain that this was a flagrant lie. But the Duchess's pregnancy certainly gave the Duke the opportunity of using it to obtain a Parliamentary divorce. He could then remarry and set up a new peaceable and respectable household, a welcome change from the rackety family life he had led with the Duchess and the disreputable public liaison with Nancy Parsons, of which he was now heartily tired because of her infidelities.[47] In his reply Lord Ravensworth expressed his astonishment and mortification at 'the shocking situation our daughter has now brought herself into'. So morally outraged was he that he refused to speak to her again from that moment until his death in 1784.[48]

The Duke's next step was to inform Duchess Anne, in the harshest terms, that he was aware of her pregnancy, and was determined to prove it and expose her publicly. He had some trouble delivering the message, since his two closest friends, Lord Hertford and H. S. Conway, flatly refused to accept an office so unworthy of a gentleman. The Duke tried unsuccessfully to persuade his secretary, Mr Stonehouse (his former tutor at Peterhouse), into doing it, and finally was obliged to use a footman as his messenger. It was a shabby way of conveying an ugly message about a disreputable business. The Duke later defended his action by saying that the message was sent so that 'she may not be risking her life or health by trying methods of concealing her delivery, the detection of which cannot escape the Duke's vigilance'.[49] In fact he was warning her not to attempt an abortion—something which was not unknown at the time, by ingestion of the plant savin.

Having enlisted the services of the best male midwife in London, Dr Hunter, the Duchess had retired into deep seclusion at Coombe House near Kingston in Surrey, where she was preparing for her secret lying-in. In order to defeat her precautions and to obtain overwhelming proof of the expected birth, the Duke marshalled a small army of detectives and spies. On 30 July he received a coded message from his agent, John Nuttall,

[46] Ibid. iv. 8–9, 25–32, 40.
[47] *Walpole's Correspondence*, 23: 344; Suffolk RO, HA 513/4/81.
[48] Ibid.; *Walpole's Correspondence*, 32: 352 n. 8.
[49] Ibid. 39: 102 n. 31; NCC *Trials for Adultery* (1780), ii. 21.

evidently based on information from servants inside Coombe House. Nuttal reported that the Earl of Upper Ossory had visited the Duchess, and had then left for Ireland; that a doctor and a surgeon had been consulted; that the Duchess was feverish and had possibly miscarried. This turned out to be a false alarm.

A month later, on 25 August, the Duke's close assistant, Mr Thomas Bradshaw of the Treasury, reported that Nuttall was about to 'employ an additional watch at Coombe', as well as developing more contacts inside the house. Nuttall believed that the Duchess was not yet within a month of delivery, but there were reports from her French maid that she was ill, and that a premature delivery was feared. Mr Bradshaw commented uneasily: 'I own I am alarmed upon the subject, as a dead child would be very unfortunate from the ease with which it might be concealed. Hunter is watched, and I will take care to know every place Mrs Oakes goes to.'[50]

There was also a disturbing report that Nuttall had intercepted a letter from the French maid to her husband, telling him she did not want to see him for some days. The conclusion had to be that the Duchess 'either had come before her time, or she expects to be brought to bed immediately'. But Bradshaw concluded reassuringly, 'it is scarce possible that a doctor or midwife should have got into the house without the knowledge of Nuttall's man or Joe, or that there should be a live child in the house'. This conclusion was based on the fact that 'the persons who walk about the house are alert and will give intelligence of every person that goes in or out', while both the French maid and the housemaid were being pumped for information.[51] Unbeknown to her, the noose was tightening about Duchess Anne.

She did in fact give birth on 23 August, so quickly that the child had arrived before Dr Hunter could reach the house. The child was immediately removed, without the Duchess being allowed to see it clearly, and it was sent off to a wet-nurse in London, while hares' skins were applied to the mother's breasts to dry up the milk.[52] It must have been immediately after the delivery that the Duke had the last two younger children removed from the custody of their mother, for she saw her beloved little Georgiana for the last time while she was still in bed after giving birth.

The Duke's attention now shifted to setting in train the legal proceedings necessary for the divorce. This inevitably involved massive publicity, since

[50] William Hunter was physician extraordinary to the Queen and the leading surgeon-accoucheur in London for royalty and aristocracy; he had delivered the Duchess's earlier children. Other detectives were already watching Hunter's house in London and following his movements. Mrs Oakes was presumably expected to be the midwife.
[51] Suffolk RO, HA 513/4/86.
[52] *NCC Trials for Adultery* (1780), ii. 24–7, 36.

it was the first and last time in English history that a prime minister in office had divorced his wife for adultery. In November, Horace Walpole remarked that 'the town will not want even private amusement . . . I mean the Duke of Grafton's divorce'.[53]

The Duke first consulted his lawyer, James Wallace, on how to go about the business. There were clearly problems, not least because of the well-known fact of the Duke's liaison with Nancy Parsons. If she chose to do so, Duchess Anne could use the liaison in the ecclesiastical courts to 'recriminate' the charge of adultery. It was the legal convention in these courts that, if each party could prove the other guilty of adultery, the two marital offences were taken as cancelling one another out, and a legal separation from bed and board was denied. This would effectively deny the Duke any hope of a Parliamentary divorce. So the first question was whether a sentence of separation in the ecclesiastical courts was necessary in order to obtain a Parliamentary divorce. The Duke was told that there had been no precedent for a Parliamentary divorce without such a sentence since the first case of all, that of the Duke of Norfolk in 1699. Despite some doubts recently raised by Lord Chancellor Hardwicke in the House of Lords, it was evident that the normal procedure would have to be followed. But the lawyer pointed out that the Duchess had nothing to gain and everything to lose by opposing a divorce, since she must want to be free to marry the father of her child even more urgently than did the Duke to marry again. To make sure, he felt that it was desirable to find 'some way of sounding the Duchess upon the subject', before coming to a decision.[54] In fact, he was suggesting collusion over the divorce proceedings.

The Duke's agent, Nuttall, wrote to tell the Duke that 'I have been exploring the enemy's camp, I mean in a legal way, as far as I dare'. He reported that Anne found that the prospective 'loss of title is a heart-breaking circumstance', but that there were no plans to oppose a divorce, since she and her lover Lord Ossory wished to marry as soon as possible. The first step was therefore a collusive suit for damages by the Duke against the Earl in the Court of King's Bench for crim. con. with his wife the Duchess. This was pure ritual, for Anne was unrepresented in the action, since as a wife she had no legal standing, and it was agreed in advance that the damages would not be collected. As Nuttall remarked to the Duke, 'in the case of Lord Bolingbroke, there was a verdict at law for £500, which he was to take no advantage of'.[55] The Duke followed suit and

---

[53] *Walpole's Correspondence*, 23: 6.   [54] Suffolk RO, HA 513/4/83.
[55] *Frederic Viscount Bolingbroke* v. *Topham Beauclerk* (Private Acts of Parliament 8 Geo. III, cap. 7).

was awarded damages of an unknown amount. Whatever they were, it is certain that they were not paid.[56]

The next step was a suit for separation from bed and board in the ecclesiastical court, which to succeed had involved the suppression of all mention of the Duke's notorious liaison with Nancy Parsons. Armed with a favourable verdict in these two suits, the Duke could then introduce a bill of divorce in the House of Lords. The only subject of negotiation was therefore what compensation was to be paid to the Duchess for loss of her present maintenance and her future jointure on the death of the Duke, which was £3,000 a year. The Duke would be obliged either to settle an annuity upon her or to return her marriage portion, which it will be remembered was £40,000. Nuttall concluded that 'nothing, in my judgement, can retard or obstruct but the adjudication of this single article'.[57] A few days later he warned the Duke that, despite the substantial size of the current annuity, 'I think she and her friends will fight hard in order to retain it.' He advised the Duke to agree, for the sake of avoiding 'altercation and a thousand disagreable things'.[58]

A day or two later Nuttall was worried about the Duchess using as blackmail 'the article of recrimination', but was relieved to find that this tactic had not been used to block a separation in an ecclesiastical court for twenty five years, the last known case being that of Lady Dineley in 1737.[59] On further reflection, he now thought that, since over three-quarters of the Duchess's portion had been settled on her younger children by the Duke, and since she had committed adultery, it would be more reasonable for the proposed life annuity to be reduced to £2,000 a year from the present £3,000. He reminded the Duke that, in the case of Lady Bolingbroke, by the terms of the Divorce Act the latter had lost her jointure of £3,000 a year and pin-money of £500, and had only been granted an annuity of £800 in return. On the other hand, in the present case, Anne was entitled to some compensation for surrendering without a fight her title of Duchess, meaning she would never again be addressed as 'your Grace', a humiliation 'which is most grievous' for someone of her pride and ambition.[60]

In the end all the details were settled satisfactorily and the Duchess agreed to accept £2,000 a year for life. As a result, the uncontested suits moved quickly through the King's Bench and the Consistory Court of London. The grounds for the Parliamentary Bill of Divorce were the proof of adultery by the Duchess, demonstrated by the success of these two

---

[56] *JH Lords*, 32: 278b.   [57] Suffolk RO, HA 513/4/87.
[58] Ibid. 513/4/88.   [59] See the Dineley Case, above, Ch. 5.
[60] Suffolk RO, HA 513/4/89.

collusive suits. In consequence of this adultery, it was argued, the Duke 'now stands deprived of the comforts of matrimony, and is liable to have a spurious issue imposed on him to succeed to his titles, honours, estate and fortune, unless the marriage be declared void and annulled by Act of Parliament'. No opposition was offered, and the bill passed both houses and received the royal assent in March 1769. The terms were the usual ones: the marriage was dissolved, the Duke (and by extension the Duchess) were empowered to remarry; all children born since 29 September 1665 were declared bastards; the Duke promised to settle £2,000 a year on his ex-Duchess for life; she was barred from all claims to dower after his death; and he was barred from all claims on her real or personal estate.[61]

In March 1769, after the bill became law, the Duke and his former Duchess returned each other's pictures, and she took the opportunity to write a moving letter of farewell. She made no attempt to 'justify my own conduct in any degree, nor seek to condemn any part in your Grace's'. After explaining her miserable condition after her pregnancy became known, 'abandoned and very justly by parents, friends and all mankind', she returned to the problem that bothered her most. 'If it is not thought absolutely improper, I hope to be permitted some time to see my poor children, who are continually in my thoughts, and the loss of whom I can never forget; any other loss, God knows, is hardly felt in comparison.'[62]

At the same time she wrote another farewell letter addressed to her 8-year-old Georgiana. She apologized for not writing to her before, the explanation being her reluctance to 'make your little innocent heart a sharer of my woes'. She described herself as an 'unhappy mother who dotes on you', and reminded the child that she had always tried to 'cultivate your mind as much as lay in my power, and to instil precepts for your happiness and honour. *This is my only* consolation and no small one it is.' She enclosed a ring containing a lock of her hair, which she hoped Georgiana's father, the Duke, would allow her to wear in memory of her mother, and asked for 'a plain glass heart for the breast with yours and your two brothers' hair'. She concluded: 'I sincerely pray for your health, happiness and every other blessing of life, and am, with the most heartfelt affection, your loving mother and true well-wisher, Anne Grafton.'[63]

(iii) *The Last Years, 1769–1811*

The rest of the story is soon told. Two weeks after the divorce bill was passed the ex-Duchess Anne married the Earl of Upper Ossory, and so far as is known lived relatively happily with him until her death in 1803 (Plate

---

[61] Ibid. G 3194.   [62] Ibid. HA 513/4/94, 95.   [63] Ibid. 513/4/131.

11). She does not seem to have seen any of her children again until she was on her death-bed—thirty years after she had parted with them—when she asked her eldest son Lord Euston to visit her. He did so, and reported back to his father the Duke that the interview had been 'soothing to her mind'. The Duke replied that, when he first learnt that Lady Ossory lay dying, he had meant to write to her to say that 'much lay on me to answer as well as on herself, and that I wished to hear that she forgave my wrongs in me as frankly as I did any received from her'.[64] It was an appropriately fair epitaph upon a failed marriage, made by a perfect eighteenth-century gentleman.

No sooner had the Duke been released from his marriage with Anne, and had pensioned off his mistress, Nancy Parsons, than in June 1769 he took as his second wife the daughter of Sir Richard Wrottesley, baronet and Dean of Worcester, described by 'Junius' as 'a virgin in the house of Bloomsbury' (that is, a connection of the Duke of Bedford). The marriage gave rise to a vicious satirical print, entitled 'the Political Wedding', published in the *Oxford Magazine* (Plate 12). On the far left Nancy Parsons is shown sloping off in tears, saying: 'I retire on a pension of £300 per annum to make room for Mrs Wrottesley.' On the far right are the ex-Duchess Anne and her new husband, the Earl of Upper Ossory. Anne is saying: 'He made me a Duchess and I made a cuckold out of him,' while Ossory consoles her, arguing that 'Your ladyship has made a good exchange: an Irish peer or even an Irish Member is better than an emaciated English Duke.' At the feet of the bride and groom lie a pair of horns labelled 'New Horns for Grafton'.

Perhaps it was this libel which still further exasperated the Duke against his ex-wife. He carried his revenge to the extent of preventing Lord Ossory from obtaining the post of Ambassador to Spain, which would have allowed him and Anne to withdraw from London society into decent obscurity for a while, until the scandal had blown over.[65] Whether or not his second wife was faithful to him, the Duke retained his reputation for gallantry, so that as late as 1773 it was being said that 'Grafton loves his pimps'.[66] At all events, the Duke fathered upon his new bride at least ten children, which is known since in 1789 he could talk of 'my thirteen children attending a Christmas party'.[67]

As for Anne, by her divorce and remarriage she had lost her ducal title and coronet, of which she was so proud (Plate 9), and was now mere Countess of Upper Ossory. She settled down with her new husband in his comfortable country house at Ampthill in Bedfordshire, where she suffered miscarriage

[64] Ibid. 513/4/116, 117. [65] *Walpole's Correspondence*, 32: 210 n. 8.
[66] *Peerage*, 1: Appendix H, p. 498. [67] Suffolk RO, HA 513/4/unnumbered.

after miscarriage, producing only one living child. She seems to have shunned London society, being determined to quarrel with it, and kept in touch only through regular correspondence with her friend Horace Walpole.[68]

As time went on, the Duke's finances improved markedly, especially after 1774 when he inherited annuities worth £7,870 a year from the Duke of Cleveland.[69] But this merely increased his desire to make financially advantageous marriages for his children, much to the dismay of his ex-wife Anne. In 1777 she appealed for help from her old friend Horace Walpole to find out the facts about Georgiana. Walpole investigated and reported that Georgiana was being earnestly courted by an MP, Mr John Smyth, a young man of excellent character and possessor of a good estate, but not one good enough for the daughter of the Duke of Grafton. The Duke had consulted Georgiana's grandfather, Lord Ravensworth, who disapproved of the match, and he had therefore forbidden Georgiana and Smyth to continue the relationship, despite the fact that the couple were in love. Since Lord Ravensworth had broken off all relations with his daughter after her adultery, no help could be expected from that quarter, but Walpole suggested that Anne could usefully write to her mother: 'Would it not demonstrate, to your honour, that, though separated from your children, no new affection has estranged your heart from them?' He reiterated his long-held position that 'I am no friend to love-matches', but admitted that 'it is certainly most imprudent to leave a young woman in the jaws of temptation, after increasing it by a prohibition'. But in the end the lovers had their way and were married a year later in 1778, John Smyth rising eventually to become a Lord of the Admiralty and Treasury, no doubt thanks in some measure to the patronage of his father-in-law, the Duke of Grafton.[70]

Another similar row broke out in 1785 when the Duke quarrelled so bitterly with his son and heir, Lord Euston, over the choice of a bride that for a while all relations between them were severed. Eventually the Duke made things up, but he kept the young man and his new wife on an allowance of only £1,600 a year, at a time when he himself was enjoying £25,000 a year. This was a situation which merely drove the boy deeper into gambling, drink, and debts. Things became so bad that in 1792 Lord Euston owed many thousands of pounds and was asking his father plaintively whether he should go to prison or abroad to escape his creditors.[71] In the end he did neither, but waited impatiently for his father to die.

---

[68] *Walpole's Correspondence*, 32: 57–8, 136, 144, 157, 188.
[69] Suffolk RO, HA 513/4/47.   [70] *Walpole's Correspondence*, 32: 351–2.
[71] Suffolk RO, HA 513/4/110, 111, 114; *Walpole's Correspondence*, 31: 451, 453 n. 1, 457 n. 3, 508.

But Duke Henry lived on until 1811, when he finally died at the ripe old age of 76 (Plate 13). He had spent his latter years in writing Unitarian tracts—a far cry from his earlier avocations as a passionate pursuer of women and an equally passionate devotee of the turf and the hunting field.

(iv) *Conclusion*

Few if any break-ups of marriage in the eighteenth century are recorded in such intimate detail as the Grafton affair, based as it is upon a remarkable set of private correspondence between the husband and his wife, the mother and her children, and the husband and his lawyers and agents. In some ways, it is a highly atypical case, but in others it is representative of its time and of the majority of such break-ups. It is atypical in that the protagonists were highly prominent persons and members of the super-rich. In these circles, the wife could not, like a person less in the public eye, simply separate from her husband and either live in concubinage or go through a bigamous marriage. The Duchess was therefore sexually and emotionally trapped by the private separation agreement, even if the Duke was free to do anything except remarry. The story is also highly atypical, since the Duke was so rich and so powerful that the option of a Parliamentary divorce was open to him, provided that he could prove that the Duchess was guilty of adultery, and he could persuade her not to contest the action by raising the issue of his own notorious adulteries.

The story is, however, perfectly typical in that all the legal proceedings were collusive, based on considerations of mutual advantage, so that only some highly selective aspects of the full story emerged in open court. In uncontested suits, which were the vast majority, much evidence was suppressed in order to achieve a settlement behind the scenes, arrived at by mutual negotiation and consent before the legal drama began. This is one of the rare cases where the historian can obtain a window on to these secret negotiations.

The other significant advantage of access to the private correspondence is that it reveals the full tragedy of separation and divorce as experienced by mothers who were at a moment's notice deprived of all custody of, or even access to, their children. As the affection-bonded family developed in the eighteenth century, especially in middle- and upper-class circles, so the anguish caused by these mother–child separations grew more acute. As a result, the issue of custody and access began to loom as large or larger than that of financial maintenance in the negotiations surrounding a marital break-up. Duchess Anne fought hard for substantial financial support, but the issues she took most to heart were first the loss of custody of her two older children, and then the total loss even of access to any of them. On the other hand, the intimacy of parent–child relations gave Duchess Anne a blackmail weapon with which to try to save her marriage, a weapon she did not hesitate to use to the full, if without success.

Attitudes towards marital relations are also revealed both in the correspondence and in the comments of well-informed observers such as Horace Walpole. The marriage had apparently been a love-match. But it had also been a financial bargain for both parties, since Henry had obtained an immediate huge infusion of £40,000 in cash, and Anne had been assured a correspondingly huge jointure of £3,000 a year during her widowhood after Henry's death, if she outlived him. What Duke Henry seems to have expected from the marriage was affection, obedience, children, and a peaceful household to which to return after long days in Parliament or Downing Street. Instead he found himself confronted by a strong-willed, bad-tempered woman with a powerful urge to have her own way, a passion for heavy gambling which threatened even his ample resources, and a taste for endless parties that turned his house into a noisy bear-garden night after night. She also cultivated the Bedford faction of the Whigs, for whom the Duke at that time had little affection, whether political or social. One way or another, she was a great disappointment to him, and within a few years she succeeded in turning his early love first into indifference and then into positive dislike. By 1764 he was determined at all costs to be rid of her. He subscribed sufficiently to the ideal of the companionate marriage to declare that, thanks to her treatment of him, their marriage had not been what it *ought* to have been.

On the other hand, despite this apparently genuine attachment to the companionate marriage ideal, Duke Henry clearly did not feel himself in any way obliged to surrender the traditional prerogative of the upper-class male to indulge in sexual infidelity. He regarded this activity as perfectly compatible with a stable marriage, although he, like everyone in the eighteenth century, took an extremely grave view of sexual infidelity by a wife. His five- or six-year liaison with a woman as notoriously promiscuous as Nancy Parsons shocked society. This was not because there was anything morally objectionable in a married man keeping a mistress, provided that the relationship was kept private. What was offensive about the Duke's behaviour with Nancy Parsons was the way he took her about with him at public gatherings, installed her in his house, and let her preside over his table. Her allegedly corrupt interference in the political patronage system of the Prime Minister was merely the last straw. Half a century later, by the early nineteenth century, such open indiscretions would have been almost impossible to carry off for one in his elevated political position. This was something which Lord Melbourne discovered the hard way, when his equivocal relations with Mrs Caroline Norton nearly ruined him.

The Grafton case thus vividly illustrates the conflict of values during a period in which moral attitudes towards marital relations, parent–child relations, sexual fidelity, patriarchal authority, and legal divorce were all in a state of flux. The Graftons, and their friends, clients, and lawyers, were forward-looking in some respects, backward-looking in others, to degrees which varied from one person to another. Thus Duke Henry and Duchess Anne held very different views about the double standard of sexual fidelity, and the duties and attitudes expected of a wife, which was what caused much of the trouble between them. It was an age torn between the attitudes to life of Defoe and Fielding, and those of Richardson and Rousseau; teetering between the libertinism of the previous generation and the romanticism of the next; caught between the patriarchalism of the late seventeenth century and the greater egalitarianism of the late eighteenth.

8
Middleton v. *Middleton*
The lady and the groom, 1781–1796

(i) *The Background, 1781–1791*

The family

Stockeld Park was a country house in ample grounds, situated in the parish of Wetherby in the West Riding of Yorkshire. Despite its remoteness from London, it was within easy riding distance of York, and the Great North Road from London to the Scottish border actually went through the village. By the late eighteenth century, when this story occurred, there were numerous stage coaches running along the road, and the village had at least two inns to accommodate travellers.

Stockeld Park had been in the hands of the Middletons[1] since the sixteenth century, but during the eighteenth century it passed rapidly from one collateral branch of the family to another, owing to repeated failures in the male line. The Middletons were devout Catholics, and for centuries had married only Catholics. They had suffered for their loyalty, one being fined for supporting Charles I and another imprisoned in 1680 for refusing to take the Oath of Allegiance. These tribulations had done little to reduce their wealth, however, and by the late eighteenth century their net income from land and stocks was well over £4,000 a year.[2] This was not a princely revenue, but it was a very comfortable one, enabling its owner to live in the style of a baronet or minor peer. The Middletons had no money worries.

The last of the male line of Middletons had been William, who had died without children in 1763 (see Genealogy of the Middleton family). His sister, Elizabeth, married a wealthy Catholic magnate, Sir Carnaby Haggerston, 3rd baronet of Haggerston Castle, Northumberland, and their eldest son succeeded his father at Haggerston and died there in 1777. The

---

[1] The name is variously spelt at various times (e.g. Midelton, Middelton, Midleton) but the spelling adopted here is the one that figures in the documents of the Court of Arches on which the story is based.

[2] LPCA, D.1395: 1951–66, 1969–81. Mrs Middleton claimed that it was nearer £6,000 or more, but she was merely guessing. On the other hand, Mr Middleton's statement, which put it at £3,760, was almost certainly an underestimate, and probably omitted fines, sales of woods, and sales of coals.

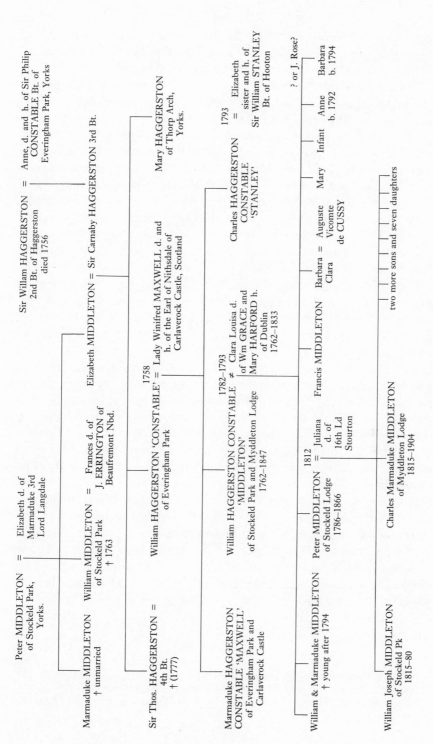

3. Genealogy of the Middleton family

second son, William, inherited the large estate of the Constables of Everingham, in the West Riding of Yorkshire. Because of this inheritance, William changed his name from Haggerston to Constable.

William Constable had three sons. The eldest, Marmaduke Haggerston Constable, inherited not only Everingham from his father, but also large estates in Scotland from his mother, *née* Maxwell, because of which he changed his name from Constable to Maxwell. The second son, William, who is the central male character in this story, had probably been named after his great-uncle William Middleton, from whom he inherited Stockeld Park in 1763, when he was only an infant. His father consequently changed the boy's surname to Middleton. The third son, Charles, married the heiress to the Stanley estate of Hooton, and therefore changed *his* name to Stanley in 1793. Thus the father, who was born Haggerston, changed his name to Constable, and his three sons changed theirs respectively to Maxwell, Middleton, and Stanley.[3]

From earliest childhood William Middleton, although born a younger son, had thus owned a large estate. How he was educated we do not know, but he was probably brought up by private Catholic tutors at home at Everingham Park. In late 1781 and early 1782 he courted and then married Clara Louisa, the daughter of a deceased Irish Catholic gentleman, William Grace. The Graces were a distinguished Anglo-Norman settler family in Kilkenny, Ireland, which could trace its lineage back twenty generations to the twelfth century. They had only occasionally risen to be knights, and they had survived the upheavals of seventeenth-century Ireland mostly by recouping political losses through marriage with heiresses. Clara Louisa's grandfather had made his peace with the government, and had inherited extensive estates in England. Her father was a third son, who married an heiress in Co. Dublin, but spent most of his life at Saint-Germain near Paris. They were deeply loyal Catholics, and Clara Louisa was presumably brought up in a Catholic nunnery in France. Her father died in 1777, and thereafter the family lived either in Dublin or in or near London.[4] Her elder brother, Richard, of Boley, Queen's Co., was an Irish MP and later, in 1795, became heir to a new baronetcy conferred on a cousin. Despite his religion, he was clearly a successful and influential man. Her second brother served in the Austrian army as captain of horse, and was killed in the siege of Belgrade in 1789. It is unlikely that she ever saw him after the family left France.

---

[3] T. D. Whitaker, *The History and Antiquities of the Deanery of Craven* (Leeds, 1878), 280; L. and J. C. F. Stone, *An Open Elite?: England, 1540–1880* (Oxford, 1968), 129–35.
[4] Sheffield Grace, *Memoirs of the Family of Grace* (London, 1823); LPCA, D.1395: 2896.

Middleton *v.* Middleton

When they met in 1781 both Clara Louisa and William were 19, and it seems likely that it was a love-match, the pair having met in Catholic circles in London. This supposition is strengthened by the fact that her marriage portion was only £1,000 down and some plate, together with a promise of a further £1,000 on the death of her mother. This was an unusually small portion for the wife of a man with a net income of over £4,000 a year. In return for the Graces' £1,000 down and £1,000 in reversion, William settled on Clara Louisa the substantial jointure after his death of £500 a year, as well as pin-money of £100 a year during his lifetime. It should be remembered that he was entirely his own master regarding the disposal of his fortune, and was therefore able to indulge in a remarkably generous marriage settlement, presumably inspired by his admiration for 'her beauty and social accomplishments'.[5]

In 1782 William took his young bride north to Stockeld Park. The main part of the house was almost new, having been built between 1758 and 1763 by the fashionable architect James Paine for William's childless great-uncle, William Middleton. As it stood, it corresponded to only part of Paine's design, which included two symmetrical service wings, linked to the main house by corridors on the well-known Palladian plan. These, however, had never been built, and the house in 1782 consisted of the new block, which served as the living quarters for the family and guests; and the old block, which still stood next to it. The latter building now housed most of the offices, including the kitchen, servants' hall, and bedrooms for the servants, and was linked to the new main block by a covered passage at the basement level, which was locked at eight o'clock every night (Fig. 1). About forty yards away were the stables, and further off again was the laundry. The whole had been well maintained during William's minority, having been let for nine years to a tenant, who had used it for the shooting.[6]

The new building where William and Clara Louisa were to take up their quarters was comfortable, but not extravagantly large. The main floor, which rested on a large above-ground basement floor with storage and servants' quarters, consisted of an entrance hall, drawing-room, dining-room, breakfast-room, and small study, as well as the balcony or 'tribune' looking down on the chapel, and William's dressing-room (Fig. 2). In the centre was a grand oval staircase that wound round up to the bedroom floor, and beyond to the smaller attic floor (Fig. 3). Because of this attic floor, containing four small bedrooms, which would later be used as nurseries for the children, the hall was dark even on the sunniest days, being lit only

---

[5] LPCA, D.1395: 260, 1983; *William Middleton* v. *John Rose* (London, 1795) (BL 518. 1 12 (6)) 2, 5n. [6] LPCA, D.1395: 4204.

BASEMENT PLAN

0   5   10 ft

1. Basement plan of Stockeld Park in 1794, by Thomas Atkinson

by two semi-circular windows high up at the top. This sombre appearance
was a source of considerable concern to William, who consulted several
architects, including Carr of York, on ways to improve the situation, but
with no success.[7] The bedroom floor contained the master bedroom and
Mrs Middleton's dressing-room, as well as four other bedrooms and attendant dressing-rooms for guests, and one bedroom—the Yellow Room—

[7] Ibid. 2628, 2719, 3041, 3841. The problem was solved in the nineteenth century by
putting in a glass roof.

Middleton *v.* Middleton

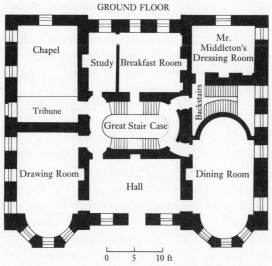

2. Ground-floor plan of Stockeld Park in 1794, by Thomas Atkinson

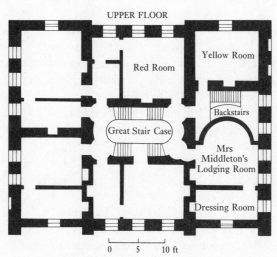

3. Upper-floor Plan of Stockeld Park in 1794, by Thomas Atkinson

accessible primarily from the back stairs and designed for 'tradesmen or any middling kind of company'. In order to support the cantilevered stone staircase, Paine had built the stone inner walls around the staircase no less than three feet thick, so that each bedroom was entered by two doors, one at either end of a short curving corridor (Fig. 3).[8] At the top of the house there were bedrooms for the children and their nurse.

In the basement floor, at the bottom of the back stairs, there were two cellars below ground, and above ground the butler's pantry, the shoe-room where the shoes were cleaned, the lower part of the chapel, the chaplain's room (later made into the steward's counting-room), and the door to the covered passage linking the main block to the old block containing the kitchen and servants' quarters (Fig. 1).[9] In addition, there was in the basement one important improvement to the house made by William and Clara Louisa: this was a water-closet, which was approached through an anteroom with a fireplace. This water-closet had a window opening on to the courtyard outside, and was supposed to be strictly reserved for the use of the family and their guests. The servants were expected to relieve themselves elsewhere, presumably in a latrine in the stable yard or outside the old block. In practice, however, the water-closet was so very convenient that it was impossible to stop some of them from using it from time to time, as the Middletons knew very well.[10]

The household set up by the young couple was soon enlarged by their rapidly growing brood of children. Although maternal breast-feeding was now coming increasingly into fashion, Clara Louisa stuck to the old ways. One nursemaid suckled her first child and brought the second up 'by hand' on a bottle; a second wet-nurse fed a third child; and other nurses presumably looked after the rest.[11] This may help to explain why Clara Louisa gave birth to no fewer than eight babies in eleven years between 1782 and early 1793, five of whom were still alive at the latter date.[12]

The only person who lived constantly with the family and ate with them was the resident Catholic chaplain. From 1789 this was a Mr Simpson, a nonentity despised by everyone in the household, but who kept William company after dinner over the port when the latter had no one else to talk to. So little was thought of Mr Simpson that, when serious domestic trouble broke out at Stockeld Park, he was neither informed nor consulted, since no one believed that his opinion was likely to influence anyone or his advice to be of any value. Whatever he may have heard in the confession

[8] LPCA, D.1395: 715, 1046, 2714.   [9] Ibid. 2475–6.
[10] Ibid. 1023, 1245, 1460, 2023, 2114, 2560, 2620, 3799, 4153.
[11] Ibid. 2601–2, 2811.
[12] Ibid. 1990, 2601, 2724, 3908, 2543, 3856–7, 2724, 2811, 3023.

box, he kept strictly to himself. William's maiden aunt, Mary Haggerston, lived only five miles away, and was constantly visiting the house for long periods at a stretch, so that she was almost one of the family. There is nothing to indicate whether it was William or Clara Louisa who was the keener upon having her in the house. So regular a visitor was she that she had a bedroom assigned to her, the Red Room, and she was said to have spent more time at Stockeld Park than at her own house at Thorp Arch. It seems likely that it was the pleasure of keeping company with the children while their mother was preoccupied with almost constant pregnancy which attracted this spinster to the house. This was certainly what brought Mrs Grace, Clara Louisa's widowed mother, on a protracted five-month stay from July to November in 1792. 'Being old and infirm', she spent most of her time in the nursery with the children.[13]

There can be little doubt that, for the first ten years of the marriage, the Middletons were an exceptionally devoted couple. Mutual friends were unanimous in declaring that, at least up to 1792, Clara Louisa was an affectionate, considerate, and faithful wife, a loving and conscientious mother, a pious and devout Catholic, and a charitable benefactor of the community. An impressive array of witnesses testified to all these qualities. Among them were aristocratic neighbours like Lord Loughborough, the Lord Chancellor, Lord and Lady Hawke, Jane, Lady Harewood, as well as Anglican clergymen and their wives in the vicinity, and respectable Catholic priests like the chaplain to the Spanish Ambassador in London. A land surveyor from York called John Bainbridge, who often dined at Stockeld Park, summed up the general opinion of the neighbourhood when he declared that Clara Louisa was 'a modest, prudent and affectionate wife, a tender and careful mother, and particularly attentive to the welfare of all her family and Mr Middleton's interests'.[14]

The servants generally agreed with this description, although they took a rather different view of her concern for her husband's interests. It is noticeable that Mr Bainbridge was careful not to apply the stock adjective 'obedient' to Clara Louisa's conduct as a wife, and the servants were of the opinion that it was she who dominated the household, including her husband. Everything we know about her suggests that she was an exceptionally strong-minded and self-willed woman and William an exceptionally docile husband. He was all that a loving husband should be, but he 'let his wife guide him in everything'. When he got involved in a protracted law-suit over changing the route of a road which ran near his house, a tenant who

---

[13] Ibid. 861, 1163, 4455, 4483.
[14] Ibid. 975, 2676–81, 3245, 3403; 3896, 3926, 3927, 3898, 4090, 3907.

got caught in the crossfire blamed Clara Louisa for egging him on to battle.[15] The butler, Henry Baldwin, whose duties led him to overhear a lot of their family conversation at mealtimes, was particularly disgusted at William's failure ever to stand up to his wife. He told his fellow servants that William was 'a fond indulgent husband . . . giving way so much to everything his wife said. . . . No man on earth would give their wife so much their own way as he did.'[16]

It should be pointed out that, although they themselves hardly ever seem to have stirred from Stockeld Park, its location just off the Great North Road made it very accessible to visitors, and the house was often full of guests. Moreover, mainly thanks to Clara Louisa, life at Stockeld Park was by no means without its lighter side. Thus one of the visitors to the house was a Roman Catholic priest, James Leslie, a slightly raffish character to find in this pious household. He was the chaplain to William's father, Mr Constable, at his house at Market Rasen in north Lincolnshire. His detractors said that earlier in his career he had served as assistant to the famous quack sexologist, Dr James Graham, participating in his 'lewd, indecent, and lascivious lectures' and helping him to run his sex therapy establishment at the Adelphi, called 'the Temple of the Goddess of Health'. His own account was that he had studied divinity at Pont-à-Mousson in Lorraine and then returned to London. There he had visited the Adelphi two or three times to see Dr Graham's 'performances on electricity', but, 'excepting the last time, Dr Graham's lectures were not, when I was present, lewd, indecent or lascivious, or unfit for the ears of a grave, sober priest'. He denied that he had ever heard Dr Graham's lecture on 'the effects of love and passion on the looks and countenance'. Less disingenuous observers recorded of Dr Graham that, 'among other exhibitions, a female was lectured upon who had no more clothes on than Venus when she rose from the sea'. Graham also owned 'The Celestial Bed', to the use of which 'by no very obscure innuendo, the barren and the impotent were invited'.[17]

Despite this rather dubious past, Father Leslie was invited to the Middletons at Stockeld Park in January 1793, and stayed for a couple of weeks. He later recalled how on two occasions he 'assumed the fictitious name of Captain Tempest and did dress in a hunting red coat of Mr Middleton, a stripe waistcoat of Mr Maxwell and a false tail; and I was so dressed at the desire of Mr and Mrs Middleton', the purpose being to see whether William Middleton's brother Charles Stanley would recognize

[15] Ibid. 3905, 448–9.   [16] Ibid. 701–2, 1027–8.
[17] Ibid. 582–3; for Dr Graham, see Stone, *FSM* 535–6; R. D. Altick, *The Shows of London* (Cambridge, 1978), 82; E. Jameson, *The Natural History of Quackery* (Springfield, 1961), ch. 6.

him in this secular get-up.[18] So as late as January 1793 William and Clara Louisa were still enjoying themselves together, and organizing rather puerile practical jokes.

There can be no doubt that both William and Clara Louisa were dutiful and observant members of the Roman Catholic Church. Her zealous piety was attested to by the chaplain to the Spanish Ambassador in London, Father Thomas Hussey, who had known her since she was 14 and had prepared her for confirmation. She was regular in her attendance at daily family prayers in the chapel morning and evening, and 'did abstain from riding out or taking amusement in Holy Week'.[19] She was, however, far from prim, and seems to have shown considerable interest in her maid's accounts of the goings-on below stairs: about who was courting whom, who was said to be pregnant by whom, who had quarrelled with whom, and so on. The servants all agreed that she was 'well acquainted with everything that passed in the kitchen'.

For example, they told her how the groom, John Rose, had wanted to marry a Miss Pick, but her parents would not give their permission, and how he had tried to get her with child, thinking this was the only way to force her parents to consent to the marriage. But, try as he might, he was unsuccessful in 'bairning her', as it was termed, and had thus lost all chance of the girl. The subject cropped up again one morning in the banter exchanged between Mrs Middleton's maid, as she dressed her mistress's hair, and the nursemaid Betty. When Clara Louisa enquired what they were giggling about, her maid answered, 'Betty's not at all afraid of John. He can't bairn a woman,' at which her mistress smiled and said, 'Never mind, Betty. If you have a child, I will indemnify the Parish' (for its upkeep).[20] These are surprisingly free and uncensorious remarks about extramarital sex coming from a pious Catholic lady. They also show her ability to get along with her inferiors, without becoming too familiar.

Several very detailed descriptions have survived of how the Middletons spent their time during their first ten years at Stockeld Park. Everyone agreed that they kept extremely regular hours, varying little from day to day. Clara Louisa was always awake by eight in the morning, when she would ring the bell for her maid. As soon as the fire was lit, if it was winter, 'the children used to run downstairs from the nursery into her room, and play about there while she was dressing'. Thus on one particular morning, 31 March 1793, Peter, Mary, and Anne were there, 'Peter and Mary at hide and seek in the bed, Mary being covered up with the bedclothes, and Peter

---

[18] LPCA, D.1395: 1898–1906.
[19] Ibid. 2896–7, 1436.   [20] Ibid. 1250, 2758–60.

upon the bed pulling them off of her'. Often they were joined by their favourite playmate, a large, patient old Newfoundland dog called Hector, who slept in the stables. He would 'jump upon the bed and the children would maul and pull him about on it'. Next door, in the closet, there was a birdcage with birds in it, which the children enjoyed looking at.[21]

Daily prayers were conducted by Mr Simpson at nine, when the whole family would troop into the tribune or balcony of the chapel, while the domestic servants, who, with the exception of the coachman William Greave, were all Roman Catholic, assembled below in the body of the chapel. Breakfast was served in the breakfast-room an hour later, at ten o'clock sharp, although Clara Louisa was often late since she lingered upstairs in her room with the children. Sometimes she did not come down to breakfast until eleven. After breakfast she would teach the children for an hour or two, or go out in the carriage with them or with William, or would walk or go for a ride on horseback. The whole family was very fond of horses, and a great deal of their time was spent in watching them being fed and groomed, as many as three or four visits to the stables each day being quite usual.[22]

Dinner was served at four o'clock, and, if there was company, as happened about three days a week, Clara Louisa would spend up to three hours dressing herself and doing her hair with the aid of her maid. On such occasions, the coachman and groom were enlisted to help as waiters, each taking up a position behind the chair of one of the diners. After dinner, Clara Louisa would often go out once again for an hour, either alone or with William and/or the children. They would walk in the grove or shrubbery nearby, or would visit the stables one last time. Sometimes Clara Louisa went alone, while William stayed in the dining-room talking to the guests or the chaplain, Mr Simpson, or else reading a book in his study. Whatever else she did, Clara Louisa never omitted to go upstairs to the nursery every evening to say good-night to the children. Indeed, in every respect (except breast-feeding) she was an exemplar in real life of the Rousseauesque ideal of the attentive and affectionate mother.

Clara Louisa was equally careful to attend to the wishes and needs of her husband. On his birthday she would give ribbons to the maids, and new gloves and neckcloths to the menservants, in order to create a festive air; and sometimes in the evening she would join William in his study 'and there sing or play music to him for a considerable time together'. At nine o'clock the family and servants assembled once again for evening prayers in

---

[21] Ibid. 653–4, 973–7, 1434, 1821, 2492–3, 2511–12, 2632, 2710, 2723–7.
[22] Ibid. 650, 837, 973–4, 1821.

the chapel, at ten o'clock supper was served, and by eleven o'clock the family had all retired to bed.[23]

As described by many witnesses, the life led by the Middletons during the 1780s was calm, contented, and regular. The couple appear to have been an almost archetypal model of the affection-bonded, child-oriented squirearchy family of the late eighteenth century, reinforced by zealous Catholic piety. They also represented the model of an Arcadia so beloved by the proponents of the 'country' ideal: a life of quiet rural living, devoted to horses, hunting, shooting, fishing, giving aid and comfort to their tenants and the villagers, and offering generous hospitality to their social equals. The guest list included most of the neighbouring nobility and gentry, together with the local Anglican clergy and their wives, for the difference of religion seems to have presented no obstacle whatsoever to harmonious social relations, even with the clergy. What is also striking, however, is that neither Clara Louisa nor William seems to have formed any really close friendships among the neighbours, so that, when there occurred a crisis in their marriage, neither of them had anyone nearby to whom to turn for advice. Clara Louisa had to write for help to her Jesuit father confessor in London, and William Middleton relied on rare visits from his elder brother, Marmaduke Maxwell.

Although life at Stockeld Park was punctuated by Clara Louisa's almost annual pregnancies, it otherwise consisted of this unchanging daily routine. What is so unusual about the Middletons' life is that they hardly ever went away, and during the first eleven years of the marriage Clara Louisa seems to have been almost entirely confined to the house. Because of his religion, William was excluded from all participation in the political or administrative affairs of the county, so that even this outside interest was lacking. Moreover, unlike most squires of his status and income, he neither possessed nor rented a London house for the season, no doubt because as a Catholic he was debarred from a seat in Parliament, which for many of his class provided the justification for such an establishment.

On the rare occasions when William did go away, he almost always took Clara Louisa along with him; until relations became strained in 1792, he had left her behind when he went on a trip only six times in as many years. Two of these occasions were brief excursions to a nearby hunting box called Myddleton Lodge, near Ilkley in Wharfedale, and another was a visit to York 'to have a tooth drawn'. Two other occasions were when he went to visit his father at Everingham, some thirty miles away. His leaving Clara Louisa behind and the lack of reciprocal visits suggest that his father may

[23] Ibid. 600, 655–6, 974, 2511–12, 4097, 2710.

have disapproved of the marriage, with its excessively generous financial provisions. Subsequent events support the hypothesis that the Constable family also disliked Clara Louisa personally, perhaps because they thought William was too much under her thumb.

It was not till 1792, as relations between them began to cool, that William began to go away alone, once to London on business for a week, and twice to Myddleton Lodge for a couple of nights, with the intention of 'riding, walking, fishing, shooting (grouse) or looking over his grounds in the neighbourhood'. The first time William seems openly to have resisted Clara Louisa's desire to accompany him was in November 1792, when he went to Myddleton Lodge to supervise a search for coal on the estate, and flatly refused to take her with him, leaving her in tears.[24]

Apart from the lack of really intimate friends, there was one other serious drawback to this peaceful and uneventful existence: it lacked variety or excitement, and was ultimately boring to such an energetic and active woman as Clara Louisa. This presumably explains why she spent so long dressing for dinner, and why she persisted in going riding despite her fears of falling off her horse. In 1792 even William, presumably prodded by his energetic wife, had reached the conclusion that they needed a change, and they were planning to shut up the house and go away on holiday together, first on a visit to the gaieties of Bath in the spring of 1793, and then on a long summer tour of the Continent, presumably giving a wide berth to revolutionary France. But by then it was already too late to save the marriage: he should have suggested such a trip at least two years earlier.

Further to add to Clara Louisa's vague sense of dissatisfaction was the fact that, although she was fond enough of her amiable husband, by her later admission he had never inspired in her either romantic love or sexual passion. Nor, according to the servants, did she show much respect or wifely obedience to William, to judge by the authoritarian tactics she employed to get her own way. One has a sense that William occupied himself primarily with his field sports and the management of the estate, and Clara Louisa with the breeding and educating of her children, and that they met together mainly on fairly formal occasions at the dinner-table and in chapel. But then such comment is true of most marriages, and it is only with hindsight that these possible flaws in the partnership become apparent.

There may also have been another, still latent, problem in the marriage. By 1791 Clara Louisa was over 30 years old and reaching the peak of her sexual potential. Although her all but constant state of pregnancy is a testimony to the quantity of her sexual relations with her husband, it may

[24] Ibid. 265, 662–3, 846, 985, 2017–18, 2699–704, 3403, 3785.

174

1. Benedict Leonard Calvert, 4th Lord Baltimore

2. Barbara Villiers, Duchess of Cleveland, after Sir Godfrey Kneller (1690)

The Hono:^{ble} Collonel Robert Fielding

G. Kneller pinx: E. Cooper ex: I. Beckett fe:

3. Robert "Beau" Fielding by Sir Godfrey Kneller; engraving by E. Cooper

TO THE

FAIR LADIES OF GREAT BRITAIN,

OLD, OR YOUNG.

Sir JOHN DINELY, Baronet, having it in his power to offer to any Lady who may be inclined to enter into the sacred and all-soothing state of Matrimony, not only the Title of LADY, but a FORTUNE of THREE HUNDRED THOUSAND POUNDS, besides the very great probability of succeeding to a CORONET,—condescends thus publicly to tender his hand to such Ladies as are qualified* to accept his MARRIAGE OFFER upon the terms stipulated in his Advertisement in the Morning Advertiser of the 12th of Jan. last.

Sir John is aware that some few, prejudiced by etiquette, may smile at his mode of address;—let them laugh:—he has once experienced its comfortable effects, and will not be dissuaded from giving it a decided preference to the tedious forms of fashionable routine.

All the objections that can possibly be urged against this maxim,—"*that it is equally incumbent on the Ladies, as on the Gentlemen, boldly to advance in a candid and liberal manner in matrimonial negociations,*" are merely chimerical: the advantages in favor of it, are great and many. By pursuing this principle, the sickly Damsel who has long pined in secret, may recover her health. The woe-begone Widow, whose weeds are an almost insupportable load, may be relieved from her burthen; and, the sweet blooming Miss of Sixteen, to whom the trammels of a boarding school are quite intolerable, may be raised to Liberty and Love!!! Let me entreat you, therefore, my angelic Fair, ingenuously to unbosom your sentiments.

nor trust to dangerous delay, for I am resolved to give her the Preference who is most explicit and most expeditious.

———

* Lest the Terms of Qualification alluded to should not be generally known, Sir JOHN conceives it expedient to declare, that previous to his entering on the Preliminaries of the sacred Contract with any Lady, he must be assured of her being possessed of such of the following Sums, as is required according to her age and condition; viz. Those under Twenty-one, only Three Hundred Pounds;—those from Twenty-one to Thirty, Five Hundred; and from Thirty to Forty, Six Hundred. All Spinsters turned of that age, must be treated with according to circumstances; and, probably few will be eligible with less than a Thousand. However, Widows under Forty-five will have such Abatement as personal Charms and accomplishments entitle them to expect.

These several sums, are mere trifles, compared with what Sir John might reasonably demand, on account of his high and noble Descent, which may be seen in Nash's History of Worcestershire; and his Claims to the vast family estates known, by a Reference to JOHN WATTS, Esq. No. 34, Queen Ann Street, East, London.

JOHN DINELY.

N. B. It has been maliciously reported, by those envious revilers, who would wish to deprive me of my approaching happiness, that I am turned of 52; but, let those that view my Portrait or my Person, believe it if they can.

P. S. Please to address your Letters, Post paid, to Sir John Dinely, Bart. Windsor Castle.

Pub⁴ Feb. 16 1799 by C Knight Windsor.

THE COURTEOUS BARONET
OR THE WINDSOR ADVERTISER

How happy will a Lady be,
To have a little Baronet, to dandle on her Knee.

———

I do hereby declare this New Edition of my last Address to the Ladies, to be a true Copy, and that Mr. C. Knight hath my Authority to publish the same as an Embellishment to my Portrait

Windsor Castle, October 23d, 1799.

John Dinely

ENTERED AT STATIONER'S HALL.

4. John Dinley's advertisement, 1799

5. Henry Somerset, 3rd Duke of Beaufort, attributed to John Wooton (1736)

7. William, 2nd Lord Talbot of Hensol,
by Daniel Gardner

6. Frances Scudamore, 3rd Duchess
of Beaufort

8. Augustus Henry Fitzroy, 3rd Duke of Grafton, by Joseph Wright of Derby

10. Anne Liddell, Countess of Upper Ossory, by Arthur Pond
(c.1755)

9. Anne Liddell, 3rd Duchess of Grafton,
by Sir Joshua Reynolds (1760)

11. Nancy Parsons by Thomas Gainsborough (*c.*1760)

12. Second Marriage of Augustus Henry Fitzroy, 3rd Duke of Grafton, with Elizabeth Wrottesley in 1769

A NOBLE DUKE.

taken on the STEYNE at BRIGHTON.

13. 3rd Duke of Grafton (*c.*1800)

14. Emily Cecil, 1st Marchioness of Westmeath (*c.* 1850)

also have contributed to reduce their quality. Thus it is a little odd to find on the house plan that William's dressing-room, containing a single bed, was on the ground floor, while the master bedroom was on the upper floor and specifically labelled 'Mrs Middleton's Lodging Room' (Figs. 2 and 3). In most country houses at that time the husband's dressing-room was located next to his wife's bedroom. It is also noticeable that all descriptions of Clara Louisa's early morning routine—the ringing of the bell, the maid coming in to light the fire, the children coming down to play on the bed— make no mention of William's presence in the room. This could mean that by 1792 William and Clara Louisa normally slept apart, on different floors, except when he visited her for the specific purpose of sexual relations.

We have no idea whether Clara Louisa's almost constant condition of pregnancy created an obstacle to regular intercourse and consequently left her sexually dissatisfied. There were theoretical objections in the eighteenth century in some quarters, both medical and lay, against sexual activity by a pregnant woman, but most couples about whom we have evidence seem to have ignored this advice. It is also possible that, after eight children, five of them still alive, William had decided that enough was enough, and was practising either abstention or *coitus interruptus*, which left his wife frustrated. Whatever the cause, the record suggests that her powerful libido was still unawakened. But these problems lay well below the surface, and all outside observers were unanimous in declaring that the Middletons seemed to be a model of conjugal harmony.

The servants

Below stairs there was a substantial staff to attend to the needs of William and Clara Louisa and their growing family. Apart from the land steward, who lived on a farm and managed the estates from his office in the main house, the indoor male staff consisted of a butler and an under-butler (who also served as footmen at dinner parties). The female domestic staff included Clara Louisa's personal maid, the upper nursery maid, the nursemaid, and sometimes a wet-nurse, all closely associated with the activities of the family. There was also a cook, first a female and then a male, a kitchen-maid, a laundry maid, and a dairy maid, all of whom lived in, and a washerwoman, who came in from the village as required. The outside staff, who also lived in the servants' quarters and ate in the kitchen, consisted of a coachman, a groom, and a postilion or stable boy. The grounds were looked after by people from the village: the gardener, the gamekeeper, and several labourers were all men, and the weeders were women. Repairs and services were carried out as needed by tradesmen from the village. A brewer came twice a year for six to eight weeks to make the beer, a local tailor made the servants' clothes, an upholsterer repaired the furniture, and a carpenter and cabinet-maker were constantly on call for odd jobs around the house.

To sum up, the living-in staff, who mostly slept in the old house, consisted of two to three indoor and three outdoor male servants, making five to six in all, and six to seven female indoor servants.[25] Apart from the butler and the coachman, the holders of the two most senior and responsible positions, who were in their late thirties, virtually all the living-in servants were in their twenties or early thirties. None of them was married, so that it is not difficult to imagine that life below stairs was full of sexual rumours, jealousies, and intrigues. There were also those clashes of personality and temperament that inevitably arise among a small group cooped up together in isolated conditions, interacting closely with one another every day, and competing for the favours of their superiors. These servants were to play crucial roles in the unfolding drama.

In 1791 the head of the domestic staff was the 40-year-old butler, Henry Baldwin, who had joined the household in early 1786. He was a sensible and level-headed man, who felt responsible for all that went on in the house, and was the first to have doubts about Clara Louisa's true feelings. He was loyal to William right through the long-drawn-out tragedy, did his best to discover the truth, but then decided to adopt a neutral stance and to remove himself at the earliest opportunity before the crash came. Through the influence of William's mother, Lady Winifred Constable, in early 1793 he was offered and accepted promotion to the position as butler to Lord Willoughby de Broke at the grand mansion of Compton Verney in Warwickshire.[26] This shrewd move enabled him to avoid becoming involved in the ruin of the Stockeld Park household.

The under-butler was an ambitious and lively young man called Robert Maltus, then aged 25. He had started his career nine years before in 1782 in the humble position of assistant tapster at Bluell's Inn at York. There he quickly made a reputation for himself, both with the master of the inn and the well-to-do clients, as 'a very steady man' of good character. His master described him as 'a fine sharp boy', and was disappointed when a local gentleman, Mr Thomas Stapleton of Carlton, took a fancy to the lad, and lured him away to be his under-butler. Robert stayed there for nineteen months until he was let go since his master was going to live in France and was shutting up the house. He then returned to his father while looking for a new position, and after three months was hired by William Middleton in 1784 to serve as under-butler and footman at Stockeld Park. William 'was

[25] Ibid. 3166, 3211, 3236.   [26] Ibid. 1690, 1784.

very particular having all his indoor servants Roman Catholics', and Robert was indeed one. He was obviously a young man with considerable charm and ability to please, but the crisis in the Middleton family was to prove too much for him to handle.[27]

Clara Louisa's personal lady's maid was a young Catholic widow of 30, called Hannah Canridge, who had been hired in January 1787. Before that she had lived in York with her husband, a bricklayer, and contributed to the family income by working as a mantua-maker. Although very poor, she had a very good reputation at York among her employers. She was engaged by a number of middle-class housewives to come to their houses and work for several days at a time as a mantua-maker, and all agreed that she was 'a cheerful, light-hearted, industrious, good sort of woman'. The woman who took her in as an apprentice and first taught her her trade described her warmly as 'the most pleasing and engaging imaginable, and the most affectionate creature to her and her children that ever was'. Others testified to her care and devotion to her father, who was sick and for whose surgical care she paid.[28]

If her employers thought very highly of her, her neighbours and acquaintances took a rather different view. One critic was a linen-weaver who had apparently once courted her but eventually thought better of it. He described her as 'a busy, inquisitive, talking woman, prying into everyone's concerns'. This judgement finds confirmation from another witness, who alleged that her neighbours regarded her as 'a light-behaved sort of woman, and not to be trusted in what she said'. This assessment by her social equals is by no means incompatible with the description of her by her employers as cheerful and lively. Indeed the two fit together very well. There was only one really serious allegation made against Hannah Canridge's reputation at York, which was that she was a friend of Suky Sutherland, the madam of 'a notorious bawdy house', and frequently visited the house. Hannah did not attempt to deny the connection, but explained it away by the fact that her husband had done some repairs to the brickwork of Suky's house, and that she was employed by Suky to make the clothes for some of the girls. She firmly denied that she had ever been before the York magistrates for 'riotous disorderly conduct', and no evidence was ever produced that she had. No evidence was provided for the accusation that she once 'did exhibit herself and dance on a mountebank's stage and perform mountebank's tricks in the service of a strolling mountebank'; it is certainly possible that dire poverty after her husband's death may have

---

[27] Ibid. 4415–21, 901, 953.
[28] Ibid. 600, 636, 4533, 4539, 4543, 4546, 4549, 4552, 4560, 4569, 4573, 4561, 4571.

driven her to such straits. Nor was any evidence produced to support the allegation that her loose behaviour had driven her husband to commit suicide by drowning, which sounds like mere fabricated slander.[29]

The general tenor of the evidence about Hannah suggests that, when Clara Louisa first hired her as her personal maid in 1787, she was no more than a cheerful, talkative, gossipy young widow. She immediately became a great favourite with Clara Louisa, whose rather drab life she must have brightened up with her lively chatter and indiscreet reports about the goings-on below stairs. We have already had occasion to quote an example of the racy dialogue and banter that went on between mistress and maid. As can easily be imagined, this penchant for telling tales soon made Hannah extremely unpopular among the other servants, who resented the way everything that they said or did was reported back to their mistress. She was 'very generally disliked among her fellow servants for telling tales back and forth' and 'was considered to stir up and raise a great deal of mischief among the servants by being too free with her tongue'. Others went further and called her 'a most notorious story-teller and maker of mischief with her tongue'. But Clara Louisa took pleasure in her scandalous gossip, and encouraged her to tell tales about her fellow servants. In return she was very generous with Hannah. Not only did she give her all her cast-off clothes, which was a normal perquisite for a lady's maid, but she also sometimes bought her a new gown. When Hannah's brother needed money to be indentured as an apprentice, she paid the two guineas, and she once gave 9s. to buy Hannah's sick father half a dozen bottles of red wine. As was common at that period, mistress and maid were on extremely intimate terms and spent a great deal of time in each other's company.[30] Apart from her children, and perhaps her husband, Clara Louisa seems to have been more closely bonded to her maidservant Hannah Canridge than to anyone else in the world.

It should be noted that Hannah Canridge had known Robert Maltus the under-butler for nearly twenty years, ever since they were both children. At some point, probably after they were thrown together at Stockeld Park in 1787, Maltus courted her in marriage, but nothing came of it except two rather scabrous stories, the second of which was widely spread by Clara Louisa. The first was that one night at Buckington's (apparently Suky's bawdy house), Suky Sutherland and Hannah were in bed together and tried to pull Robert in with them; the second was that once Robert and Hannah had been caught in bed together, apparently in the servants' quarters

---

[29] Ibid. 3778, 3791, 754, 1059–60, 4535–6.
[30] Ibid. 654, 1545, 1766, 3205, 3264, 3317, 3368, 3438.

at Stockeld. It is impossible to determine the truth of the two stories, but it is clear that the lady's maid and the under-butler had known each other for years, had certainly once been romantically linked, were widely rumoured to have been caught in bed together, and were still very good friends.[31]

Another important figure in the story in its early stages was a 52-year-old labourer and odd-job man, William Hodgson. He had lived in the village most of his life and was well known to the community. He had been for many years a gamekeeper, the first of his employers being Edward Constable of Burton Constable. He had also once been gamekeeper to Mr Wilson of Follifoot, 'who gave a very favourable character in writing of his qualifications and civility'. In the 1770s he had been gamekeeper to Sir Thomas Vavasour of the adjacent property of Sickling Hall, so that he had served two of the principal landowners in the area. But the villagers did not like him, accusing him of being an idle good-for-nothing who combined poaching at night with his official duties as gamekeeper by day, but no proof was offered of this.

Perhaps because of these rumours, by 1790 Hodgson had come down in the world, and by then was no more than a casual labourer about the Stockeld estate, kept on by William Middleton largely because three generations of Hodgsons had served the family. For example, he had worked as a building labourer during the conversion into the chapel of one end of the new block, and continued to do odd jobs about the grounds. He rented a cottage from William Middleton as tenant-at-will for a nominal rent of 1s. a year, and was usually permitted to eat in the kitchen along with the other servants. But there had been two occasions when William Middleton formally forbade his admittance into the house, once in about 1789–90, when Hodgson had quarrelled with the butler, Henry Baldwin, and once again in 1792.[32]

The legion of witnesses against Hodgson, many of whom had known him for thirty years or more, ranged from élite ex-employers such as Sir Thomas Vavasour, to knowledgeable members of the middling sort like the clerk to the local JP, to fellow labourers who had known him all their lives. The main burden of the accusations was that he had been 'a notorious liar ever since he was a child, so much so that it was a common by-word in the village to say: "Such a story is one of Hodgson's lies." ' One witness went so far as to call him 'the greatest liar in the whole country'.[33]

---

[31] Ibid. 1057, 1060, 1078, 1472, 1545, 1588, 1767, 4571; after her discharge from Stockeld Park in December 1792, Hannah went back to York and within 3 months had married a shoemaker, supplementing his income with her needle (ibid. 600, 635.).

[32] Ibid. 680, 781, 873–4, 4460–1, 3002, 3746, 3802, 3810, 3815, 3854, 4180–2.

[33] Ibid. 680, 1158, 3002, 3048, 3187, 3264, 3317, 3367, 3741, 3751, 3759, 3761, 3768, 3771, 3802, 3810, 3815, 3826, 3843, 3852, 3853, 3858, 3897, 4457, 4526.

As usual, however, there were two sides even to this question of William Hodgson's character. Some other witnesses took a more charitable view of him as a man who merely liked to embroider a story or make one up to entertain the company, but who basically meant no harm. He was, said one, 'addicted to lying or telling stories of the wonderful and marvellous kind without any foundation in truth'. Another merely charged him with 'romancing when in company', although 'he means no ill by it', and a third said much the same thing.[34]

There can be no doubt that many of the hostile witnesses had personal grievances and grudges to work off against Hodgson. A fairly disinterested witness remarked that 'many people speak worse of him than he deserves owing to his situation in life as gamekeeper for the gentlemen of the neighbourhood, having been very strict about their game'. He had been active in 'taking the guns of several unqualified persons and informing against others, and thereby injuring his character'. In a number of cases this process of paying off old scores by denigrating Hodgson's character can be shown to have been at work. One of his accusers admitted under cross-examination that his son and his servants had been caught by Hodgson stealing 'bundlings' from the woods in Stockeld Park. Another had been put in the Wakefield House of Correction by him for 'setting snares for rabbits' in a warren occupied by Hodgson's father. In the process of arrest, Hodgson had gone so far as to shoot him and wound him in the legs.

Another hostile witness, a labourer, had reasons for revenge for an injury done him some eighteen years before. He and his father had been out duck-shooting at Christmas, and on their return had taken a short cut home through Sir Walter Vavasour's woods at Sickling Hall. They were just about to emerge and climb over the hedge when Hodgson rose up before them and accused them of killing game on Sir Walter's property. They denied it, but Hodgson took them before the local JP, the Revd Collins of Knaresborough. With his usual taste for rhetorical exaggeration, Hodgson said that they had 'beat every bush in Lime Kiln Wood'. The Justice commented sceptically that 'it is a hard thing to beat every bush in the wood', but said that the law gave him no option but to fine them both £5 each. The older Hudson asked permission to appeal for mercy to Sir Walter Vavasour in person, which was allowed by the Justice, who was clearly hostile to Hodgson and doubted his veracity. After hearing their story, Sir Walter forgave them, ordering them merely to pay the cost of the summons. But Hodgson protested vigorously that he deserved some recompense for his time and trouble over the detection and prosecution,

[34] Ibid. 4183, 4394, 4409.

and, despite Sir Walter's objections, obliged Hudson Senior to pay him a guinea. Eighteen years later the memory of this episode was clearly still vivid in Stephen Hudson's mind, as well as in that of his father. In view of stories such as this, it is small wonder that the villagers hated William Hodgson.[35]

It should be borne in mind that Hodgson had come down in the world from gamekeeper for several of the leading gentry to a mere casual labourer and odd-job man, living largely on the charity of the Middletons in a rent-free house, with access to free meals in the kitchen. The charity of the Middletons went further, however, since Clara Louisa took a personal interest in the welfare of him and his family. She often visited their cottage and had been 'very charitable and bountiful' to the Hodgson children for several years, providing them with clothes and extra food. When Hodgson's daughter Dorothy developed a 'sore breast' in August 1792 and was ill for six months, Clara Louisa saw to it that she was put under the care of the doctors of the Leeds Infirmary. Thus Hodgson had long-standing reasons for gratitude for favours rendered by Clara Louisa.[36]

Mention should also be made of two other servants who were to play a minor role in later developments of the story. The first is the cook appointed by William in May 1792. He was a 30-year-old Frenchman, Jean Bouvier, an exotic figure to find in an isolated country house in remote Yorkshire, although perhaps Clara Louisa's childhood in France had given her a taste for French cooking. He had begun his career at the age of 14, serving as undercook to the Governor of Pondicherry, with whom he spent six years, mostly travelling with his master about the East Indies. On the death of the Governor, he returned to Paris, where he was cook to the Maréchal de Richelieu and the Duc de Laval, with whom he stayed for four years. After the Revolution broke out he decided in 1790 to seek his fortune in England. He must have carried with him some laudatory letters of recommendation from the Duke, for he was immediately taken on by the well-known and wealthy MP, Wellbore Ellis, for whom he cooked for fifteen months until he was discharged, since 'I did not please my mistress Mrs Ellis.' It was then that he was discovered by William Middleton, probably through one of his brothers or perhaps his mother, Lady Winifred Constable, and was hired as cook at Stockeld Park. He stayed there for ten months from May 1792 to March 1793, when he gave notice 'under pretence of being ill'. He obviously regarded himself as socially far superior to the other servants, and was not popular among them, if only because he

---

[35] Ibid. 4459–60, 3815, 3852, 3858–67, 3901–4.
[36] Ibid. 685–7, 858–9.

was a foreigner, and a Frenchman at that. He was quite out of place at Stockeld Park, and no doubt was only too happy to get back to the civilization of London.[37]

Another newcomer who played only a minor role in the story was the 27-year-old Margaret Burnet, who arrived at Stockeld as kitchen-maid in September 1790. For the previous nine years she had had the usual chequered career of eighteenth-century domestic servants, never staying in any place for more than a couple of years. If she is to be believed, in most cases the decision to quit her job had been hers. In the next two-and-a-half years she rose rapidly from kitchen-maid to laundry maid to housemaid, despite her very shaky past, and despite the story, certainly true, that the groom at Stockeld Park, John Rose, had courted her, and the rumour, apparently false, that she was pregnant by him.[38]

(ii) *Trouble, 1791–1792*

The event which was to trigger off the unravelling of the tightly knit community at Stockeld Park was the sudden death in the early summer of 1791 of Thomas Price, who had been groom of the hunting stable for the last seven years. In July, William Middleton appointed as his successor a young man called John Rose. He had previously lived with his mother at Black Hambleton near Thirsk, 'where he kept a public house which was resorted to as a place for training running horses'. His social background was mainly in the liquor retail trade, with an uncle who kept a public house at York and a brother-in-law who kept another at Northallerton. He must have learnt to look after horses at his mother's pub, and the position at Stockeld Park was his first in domestic service. He was probably not more than 20 years old, with his way to make in the world and nothing to help him but a handsome face, a winning way with women, and some experience at grooming and training race-horses.[39]

Since William, Clara Louisa, and the children were such regular and frequent visitors to the stables—sometimes three or four times a day— Rose soon became acquainted with the family. Clara Louisa's first kindness to John Rose was to help him to spruce himself up, since it will be remembered that one of the jobs of the groom at Stockeld Park was to help wait at table whenever there were guests for dinner. At least at first he seems to have resented this extra duty, grumbling that 'it is none of my business to do so'. Among the horses, Clara Louisa had a particular favourite, an old hunter called Top, who had been given to her by William when they were

[37] Ibid. 1205, 1219–22, 1226, 1258.
[38] Ibid. 1418–21.   [39] Ibid. 782, 2971, 2980, 3197.

married, and whom she loved to feed herself and to watch being rubbed down, either by the groom or the stable boy. She would linger in the stables with Top for up to an hour at a time, and would sometimes stand at the front door of the house, call him to her, and feed him bread out of her hand. So fond of Top was she that she had two pictures of him painted, hanging one in her bedroom and the other in the breakfast-room. She was also fond of a grey horse, bought for her by William at Newcastle in the summer of 1788, and which she rode now that Top was too old and lame and had been put out to grass.[40]

Although she was devoted to her horses, and regularly rode for exercise, except during the last three months of her many pregnancies, Clara Louisa was a very poor rider, being 'quite a coward on horse-back', and quite incapable of managing a restive animal. She had fallen off once, and her horse had bolted several times, once running full tilt into a gate an experience which had left her very nervous, and fearful of another fall, especially when she was pregnant. As a result, instead of following along 'at a respectful distance behind her' in the normal eighteenth-century deferential manner, any servant who accompanied her was under orders from William to ride abreast of his mistress, ready to grab the bridle at a moment's notice.[41]

The butler, Henry Baldwin, seems to have been the first to realize that Clara Louisa was becoming attracted to the new young groom. As early as November 1791 he observed that, when Rose was waiting at table, standing directly behind William's chair, Clara Louisa, who was sitting opposite, could not keep her eyes off him. A local chaplain who came to dinner in November also noticed Clara Louisa eyeing John as he waited at table, and John smiling back at her—behaviour which he regarded as 'highly improper'. Some six months later, at Whitsun 1792, the footman behind a dinner guest from York noticed the same thing, and afterwards said to Baldwin and Maltus in the butler's pantry, 'Surely your mistress must be in love with him, as she never had her eyes off him the whole time of dinner'—a remark that was met by an embarrassed silence. Certainly by April 1792 the suspicion that Clara Louisa was in love with John Rose was familiar to Henry Baldwin, to the under-butler, Robert Maltus, and to her personal maid, Hannah Canridge. In April Hannah mentioned the matter to the servant of a visitor, who told her mistress. The latter kept her eye on Clara Louisa throughout the dinner, and soon detected her ogling John across the table. So absent-minded or so confident in his wife was William that he never even noticed whether or not she 'had directed her eyes to John Rose

[40] Ibid. 605, 665, 849, 2471, 2684, 3168, 3252, 3262, 4039.
[41] Ibid. 2448–50, 2468, 2604–5, 2684, 3000, 3018, 3168, 3298, 3732, 3823.

in an amorous lascivious manner'.[42] On the other hand, three other visitors also declared that they noticed nothing.[43]

By the spring of 1792 two other things had aroused the suspicions of the other servants. The first was John Rose's sudden affluence. He had arrived in July 1791 badly dressed in 'coarse linen with a coloured handkerchief round his neck', and 'in a very low distressed circumstance', having borrowed a guinea off his uncle just to get him to Stockeld Park. By early 1792, however, he was as well dressed as his master, 'having fine shirts and neck clothes', 'stockings of fine cotton or silk', and 'plain handsome silver shoe-buckles'. On one occasion a year later, in March 1793, he was wearing 'a duck-coloured coat and a red waistcoat faced with silk at the breast'. He was by now clearly quite a dandy. His fellow servants also noticed with envy that he seemed to have plenty of money 'when giving change or playing at cards', and Robert Maltus said he always had £15 or £20 in his pocket.[44] It did not take long for some of the servants to conclude that Clara Louisa must be supplying him with money on a generous scale.

Their suspicions were further aroused by the fact that she was spending more-and-more time alone in the stable watching John tend the horses. She was also more and more frequently going for rides on horseback accompanied by him, when they were often seen talking and laughing together as they rode abreast. Although the stable yard was paved with stone, and it was therefore not easy silently to creep up on them, several servants reported opening the stable door and finding them standing or sitting very close to one another. In May the unreliable Thomas Hodgson alleged that he timed a visit by Clara Louisa to the stable with his watch, and found that it lasted two hours. He then crept up and threw open the door, allegedly finding Clara Louisa sitting on the corn bin, and John standing beside her with an arm round her shoulders. A much more reliable witness, the butler Baldwin, also discovered them once in the stable 'with their faces within two or three inches of each other's'.[45]

It was alleged that it was indeed at just this time, in April 1792, that Clara Louisa first openly made overtures to John—no one ever imagined that *he* would have dared to make the first move. According to Robert Maltus, one day when she was out riding in the lane leading to Sickling Hall with John and her two elder boys, she sent the children on ahead, took John by the hand, 'and expressed great love and affection for him'. Maltus said that she admitted it when he confronted her, but it is difficult to see where he obtained this detailed information about time and place, unless it

[42] Ibid. 691, 701, 835, 919–20, 1102, 1703, 1400, 1426, 1932–41.
[43] Ibid. 3908, 3928, 4097.   [44] Ibid. 269, 602–3, 782–3, 902–3, 1696, 3881.
[45] Ibid. 272, 785–9, 904–6, 1696.

was from some indiscreet boastful talk by John Rose himself. In late April the two elder boys were sent off to boarding school, to 'an academy for young gentlemen' at Tudhoe in far-off Co. Durham. This loss must have increased their mother's sense of loneliness, and further stimulated her growing emotional infatuation with John Rose.[46]

For the next few months after this alleged declaration of love, that is from mid-April to mid-August 1792, nothing much happened, since Clara Louisa was now in an advanced state of pregnancy, giving birth to her eighth child on 15 July. Up to that time there was no evidence that any-thing improper had occurred between her and John, although three or four servants had seen enough to convince them that she was in love with him. They were, therefore, on the watch, particularly when William went off for a few days to his small secondary house, Myddleton Lodge near Ilkley, for the opening of the grouse season on 12 August, by which time Clara Louisa had just recovered from her confinement. At four o'clock in the afternoon of 15 August 1792 the butler Henry Baldwin noticed Clara Louisa walking rapidly along the path leading to the 'bathing well' and he told William Hodgson to follow her at a distance and observe her movements. Later in the day Hodgson told Baldwin that he had merely 'seen her reading a book under a tree'.[47]

A few days later, however, he told a very different story. The bathing well, traces of which can still be seen, was about a quarter of a mile from the house, and was used as a swimming pool in the summer by the family, and also, it seems, occasionally by the servants. It was a pool surrounded by a high stone wall, inside which was a stone dressing-room, the only opening being a glazed door that opened on to the pool. Hodgson alleged that he followed Clara Louisa to the bathing well, and heard voices inside the dressing-room and chairs being moved about. He had a key to the outer door and tried to unlock it, but found that it was bolted on the inside. John Rose came up from inside and said to him through the keyhole: 'Why can't you get away?' So Hodgson withdrew about a hundred yards up a meadow, and lay down in a place where he was concealed by long grass but could still observe the outer door. After half an hour he saw John open the door and look around to see if anyone was watching. He then went in again, and a few minutes later came out with Clara Louisa, who ran off towards the house as fast as she could go, leaving John to lock the door behind her.[48] If Hodgson was for once telling the truth, the clear presumption of the story

---

[46] Ibid. 267–8, 904, 1893, 2087, 3833, 4033, 4414; for the boarding school, see ibid. 2087, 2543, 3856–7.
[47] Ibid. 280, 283, 1699, 2087, 3023.   [48] Ibid. 280–3, 792–6.

was that adultery, or some form of sexual activity, had taken place between the mistress of the house and her groom.

There were, however, so many obstacles to accepting Hodgson's story that for many months after he first heard about it William Middleton refused to believe it. It was not merely the fact that Hodgson had a general reputation as a man who made up or embroidered stories, but that the account, as he told it, was simply not credible. The first objection was the extreme risk Clara Louisa was taking in making a daylight assignation in a place to which many servants had access, since the same key fitted the bath-house, the stables, the gate of the ice-house, and other outbuildings. There were, therefore, at least five or six keys available which would open the bath-house door, which makes Clara Louisa's alleged behaviour look like an act of reckless folly. Secondly, it was extremely doubtful whether it was possible for Hodgson, standing outside the wall of the bath-house, to have heard any talking or moving of chairs inside the dressing-room, seeing that the wall was solid stone, over a foot thick, and windowless.[49]

The last and most disputed question was whether there was anywhere in the meadow whence Hodgson could have observed Clara Louisa and John while remaining undetected. Some witnesses were certain that the meadow had been cropped bare by cattle, leaving no place for Hodgson to hide. One man who had cut the field in the autumn declared at first that 'the pasture near the bathing-house well was eat so bare that I could have taken a half-crown and thrown it a hundred yeards from me, and gone and picked it up again without difficulty in looking for it'. But on further reflection he changed his mind, and agreed with others that there had been clumps of 'windle grass' still standing, which might possibly have provided conceal-ment. But Hodgson's story was in the end destroyed by two practical experiments made to test his evidence. In the first, he lay down in a position which left him easily visible from the door. In the second, he lay down in a different position altogether. He was certainly now concealed, but he could not see the door of the bathing-house at all since he was over the brow of the hill, although if he had got up on his knees he could perhaps have seen people coming along the path away from the door. The dispassionate and careful testimony of the architect Thomas Atkinson, who performed the two tests, ruined Hodgson's credibility.[50]

Nor were matters helped by Hodgson's many changes of his story. As we have seen, on the afternoon of the incident he merely told Baldwin that Clara Louisa had been sitting under a tree reading a book. According to

[49] Ibid. 675–6, 2556, 2615, 3034–6.
[50] Ibid. 3034, 3306–7, 3830, 4046, 4143, 4378–9, 4383, 4398, 4404–5, 4414, 4426, 4579–80, 4607–10.

him he realized the gravity of what he had seen, and wished to try to protect her reputation. In fact, however, he seems to have been practising a little quiet blackmail. The next day, immediately after the servants' breakfast in the kitchen, he went by the stables to talk to John Rose. They went off together towards the bathing well 'to see whether everything was ready for the children to bathe on the following morning'. Hodgson said that in the dressing-room he confronted John with his alleged discovery, and advised him to leave the house at once. Later on, as he was standing by the hall door charging an air-gun for his master when he returned, Clara Louisa saw him and called him to her. She said that what he had seen was entirely innocent, to which he retorted that 'no one could imagine you went there for any good purpose'. Clara Louisa then said, 'I have a very great respect for John.' According to him, Hodgson replied sternly, 'you ought to be ashamed of acknowledging an attachment for him who is only a stable boy. You ought to get rid of him.' If she refused, he threatened to tell her husband, William. Clara Louisa then agreed that John should go, and promised that, if Hogson kept silent, 'I will always be a friend to you and your family,' as indeed she had already been for years.[51] Eight or nine days later, that is on about 24 August, Clara Louisa sent for Hodgson late in the afternoon and, so he alleged, said she would walk home with him to see his daughter, whom she had for several years been supplying with clothes and other necessaries. As they walked to his cottage, he noticed that John was following them at a distance. On the way Clara Louisa again assured him that John would soon be leaving the house for good.

On arrival at the cottage, she gave Hodgson's wife and daughter some clothes, and then left. As she returned, Hodgson watched her, and saw her meet John 'at a rock in the warren, and stay there talking with him alone for about half an hour'. Hodgson then came up and escorted her back to the house. As he returned through the stables, John took him aside, asked if Clara Louisa had given him any money, and, hearing that she had not, pressed a guinea into his hands, at the same time promising to leave in a few days.[52]

But John still did not leave, and some time in late August Hodgson went to Baldwin and Robert Maltus and told them what he now claimed to have seen at the bathing well. Some days later Baldwin and Maltus told Clara Louisa about Hodgson's accusation, which she flatly denied. By then the story was spreading, reaching her maid, Hannah Canridge, not only from Robert Maltus but also from the wife of a tenant. On 31 August, while William and a friend of his, Colonel Taylor, rode out to look for partridges

---

[51] Ibid. 285–6, 797–803.   [52] Ibid. 803–8.

in order to show their wives how to catch them in nets the next day, Clara Louisa paid a visit to the stables at eleven o'clock in the morning and stayed there. Robert Maltus was watching closely, and after two hours crept up and suddenly opened the door, to find her and John sitting side by side on the corn bin holding hands and Clara Louisa 'crying very much'. But she soon rallied to her own defence, for she was an active and resourceful woman, and a desperate one.

Some days later Hodgson was working on the haystacks when he received a message that Clara Louisa wanted to see him in the hunters' stable, where John worked. When he arrived, they were both there, but what was said between them we do not know. All that is certain is that this was about the time when Clara Louisa saw to it that Hodgson's daughter obtained treatment for her sore breast at the Leeds Infirmary. Hodgson's story is that Clara Louisa said that, if he would retract his accusation, John would leave at once, and that he agreed for the sake of peace in a family which he and his father had served for so many years. But this is implausible, since he kept his mouth shut for another six months, although John still did not leave. At all events, John went off to fetch Henry Baldwin and Robert Maltus, and when they arrived, Hodgson duly retracted his story, saying that he had made it up and it was false. Baldwin and Maltus were furious, and said, reasonably enough, that he 'must be a great liar'. According to Maltus, the retraction was obviously a bare-faced lie, and Hodgson made it 'in a strange, uncommon, stammering, silly manner'. But for the moment Clara Louisa was safe, at least so long as Hodgson did not change his story once again. As Baldwin left the stable in disgust, she said to him reproachfully: 'I think you are very envious in watching me.'[53]

After this crisis, things quieted down at Stockeld Park, although John remained in the household. On the other hand, it was one day in the next month of September, as it was later discovered, that Clara Louisa rode into York and went to the shop of Prince and Hampson, the leading jeweller and silversmith in the city, and indeed the county. There she bought a gold watch chain, paying cash for it out of her pin-money, despite the fact that the Middletons had 'a running account open' at the shop. A week or two later John Rose came into the shop with the same gold watch chain, and asked for it to be exchanged for a set of silver buttons with the letters 'JR' on them, an exchange of which Clara Louisa had approved. Here was incontrovertible evidence that she was making John expensive presents, although this may have been intended to be a farewell gift.[54]

---

[53] Ibid. 289, 689, 809–13, 909–10, 915, 1701–2.
[54] Ibid. 270–1, 1372–84, 1879, 3719.

Middleton v. Middleton

So things went on throughout October and November, with Baldwin and Maltus and Hannah Canridge on the watch, and Clara Louisa doing everything she could to conceal her movements from them. She was in the habit of walking out alone after dinner in the dark, even on the coldest and foggiest of Yorkshire autumn nights, coming back some time later with her shoes and stockings so wet that they had to be changed immediately. Once Canridge followed her, and caught her lurking with John in the grove or shrubbery, a two-acre area of dense trees and undergrowth quite near the house. Meanwhile, William was innocently reading in his study. Rumours of the goings-on were spreading steadily among the servants, and came to the ears of old Mrs Mead, the personal maid of Clara Louisa's mother, Mrs Grace, who had come to Stockeld for a long stay to see the children. Mrs Mead was said to have been so furious when Hannah Canridge came back indoors with her story that 'she would have stabbed her [Clara Louisa] at the time'.

Meanwhile Robert Maltus, besides watching Clara Louisa closely, kept imploring her to discharge John so as to save the family from the disaster which he saw approaching—a disaster which would not only destroy the happiness of the Middleton family but would also expose many of the servants to dismissal, if the house were shut up. They therefore all had every incentive to try to break up the liaison before it was too late. At this time, Robert Maltus seems to have been genuinely disinterested. He urged Clara Louisa to discharge John at once, to go off either to Bath or to visit friends for an extended period, and to discharge all the servants who had any knowledge of what was going on—including himself. In early October he also went to John Rose, and strongly advised him to leave before William Middleton got wind of the affair.[55]

One morning Clara Louisa thought it prudent to tell William that false accusations were being made against her by some of the servants, a statement that William apparently accepted at its face value, without making any effort to check its truth. He merely replied 'turn all the servants away, for we shall go abroad in the spring'—a reference to the European tour which they were planning. That afternoon she called to her dressing-room Mrs Mary Warwick, a 74-year-old widow and the mother of one of the leading tenants. She said she assumed that Mrs Warwick had heard 'the scandalous report in circulation concerning me and Jack Rose', declared she was 'as innocent as the child unborn', and burst into tears. She told Mrs Warwick about her conversation with her husband, and said that she intended to dismiss all the servants except Robert Maltus.[56]

[55] Ibid. 693, 698, 739, 852.   [56] Ibid. 904, 921–4, 4149, 4465–6.

(iii) *The First Crisis, November–December 1792*

But October dragged into November, and things went from bad to worse. First Robert Maltus, ever on the watch, caught Clara Louisa and John in the stables, standing close together with John's hands on her hips. On an-other occasion he hid in the bushes and saw them kissing in the shrubbery. A few days later, when William was away at Myddleton Lodge, Hannah Canridge followed Clara Louisa on one of her evening walks in the shrubbery. It was a dark foggy night as she stumbled through the undergrowth, but it was light enough for her to surprise John and Clara Louisa standing together with his arm around her waist. Canridge screamed loudly, seized John, and started pummelling him with her fists. Clara Louisa in alarm said: 'For God's sake be pacified. If you love me or my family, don't make such a noise.' Hannah Canridge threatened to tell William, and demanded that 'that villain should go away'. John agreed, saying: 'I will go now, madam. I would have gone before but you would not let me. I will take no person's advice, for I am determined to go.' He evidently realized that things had gone too far, and that both he and Clara Louisa were threatened with ruin if he stayed. But Clara Louisa clutched him, saying: 'John, you shall not go. If you go, I shall go too.' Finally, they all three calmed down a little, and Hannah and Clara Louisa returned to the house. When they got there, Hannah noticed that her mistress's dress was wet and dirty all up the back, from which she concluded that she had been lying on her back on the wet leaves in the fog, presumably being embraced or made love to by John Rose. Later that evening Clara Louisa confessed to Hannah: 'I love him above all others. I never knew what love was until I knew him.'[57]

Hannah told her story to her fellow servant Robert Maltus, who put such intense pressure on John that two days later, on 20 November, he gave notice to quit his job. That afternoon, when Robert Maltus brought Clara Louisa the mail, she begged him to let John stay. When he told her that John had already given notice, she refused to believe it, and demanded to see him at once. So Robert went down to the servants' hall, and fetched John up to William's dressing-room. They found their mis-tress half-collapsed, lying face down over a chest of drawers. When John came in, she jumped up and ran to him, crying and saying: 'My dear John, why will you leave me? What have I done to you, my dear, dear John?' When she declared that she could not part with him, Robert said that in that case he would have to tell her husband, William. Clara Louisa went down on her knees and begged for mercy, saying, 'Let him stay another

[57] Ibid. 293–6, 608–15, 910–12.

month, and I will try to get the better of my love for him,' at the same time threatening that, if William were informed, 'I have that in my pocket which will do for me.' She assured Robert that 'it cannot be said that even my last child was by him' (i.e. John), and added sadly: 'I have everything that heart could wish but one, which is to marry John, which I never can.'[58] Faced with this irresistible combination of anguished pleas for more time, dark threats of suicide, and pathetic laments about her tragic situation, Robert Maltus, who was a young man, too young to carry such a burden of decision over other people's lives, inevitably gave way. He appears to have been a decent man, anxious only to save his mistress and her family from inevitable disgrace. Once more Clara Louisa had gained a temporary reprieve.

Immediately after this alarm, Clara Louisa wrote to her Catholic adviser and friend in London, Father Hussey, the Spanish Ambassador's chaplain, and to her mother, seeking their advice and vigorously protesting her complete innocence 'of all the charges against me'. They took her word for it, and advised her, firstly, not to tell her husband any more, so as not to run the risk of arousing his jealousy and suspicion on the grounds of baseless rumours; and, secondly, to dismiss all the servants who were spreading the accusations. But, on the grounds that the Middletons were anyway planning to close up the house and leave for Bath early in the new year, and then to go abroad all the summer, Clara Louisa postponed doing anything at all.[59]

On 11 December, however, Marmaduke Maxwell, William's elder brother, arrived at the house for a visit. He found a letter lying on a table in his room, addressed to himself, which ran as follows:

Sir,
Your humble petitioner hopes your goodness will read this with the strictest silence and fly to the flirtation [*recte* protection] of the most virtuous man breathing. My heart is ready to break and my hand tremble to relate to you the destructive tale. My once valuablest and best of mistresses has taken an unfortunate affection for the groom. I fear will be the ruin of this good family, that dear good man, and their dear children. On our knees Mrs Mead and me has begged her to part with him. On our knees we have begged the young man to go, but he will not. She said to us she will go with him if ever we tell our master, or she will put an end to her life is what we are afraid of. We wish to conceal it, if she would have parted with him, but she will not. Every servant in the house knows it and is constantly watching her. . . . She has walked out with him every night, be it ever so dark, as soon as that good man get set down in his dressing room, and left poor Mrs Grace with the dear children.

---

[58] Ibid. 302–5, 618–19, 926–31.   [59] Ibid. 2017, 2899–901.

The last time my good master was at the Lodge, it was a very bitter night. She took off at 7 o'clock. Robert begged Mrs Mead to make the watch. I went to the stable, neither of them was there. The moment I was gone, being very dark, the boy set a whistling 3 times. I flew into the breakfast room. Mrs Grace, crying, said Mrs M. would get her death of cold. I flew round the grove without my shoes. In the far shrubbery I see them. I run so fast and screamed so loud that he could not get away. I beat him, I tore him almost to pieces, I was almost out of my senses. . . .

I am sure it will be the death of poor Mrs Grace. Good dear sir, think of some speedy remedy to quit that villain. She must not know or I fear what will be the consequence. . . . I cannot bear it no longer. If anything should happen [to] this good family, I hope your goodness will think I have done my duty. I mean to quit this place. I told her I would not stay for all the world. Dear sir, if you can put a stop to this shocking affair without wounding that good man will be the last prayer of all his servants for your goodness.

With the greatest affection to your good worthy family, and gratitude to you, dear sir, for so gracious an action.

H. Canridge

As you are a gentleman, I hope you will not tell of this letter, as there is none in the house will inform you better than I, who has watched this half year.[60]

It is difficult to decide whether to be more nauseated by the betrayal and sycophancy or startled by the high romantic style of this remarkable epistle. Hannah had clearly been reading too many trashy novels. Maxwell, however, took the allegation seriously, and when she came to his room later that night was ready to interrogate her at length about what she knew. The next evening he grilled Robert Maltus. Whatever Canridge may have told Maxwell, Maltus was always careful to stress that, although Clara Louisa had frequently admitted she loved John, she had never admitted that she had committed adultery with him. Indeed, she once told him that 'he has behaved remarkably well to me, considering the very great liberties I have permitted him to take with me'. Maxwell finally decided that the accusations were true, that Clara Louisa was certainly in love with her groom, and might possibly have committed adultery with him, and that to avoid family disgrace it was essential to get John Rose out of the house at once. He therefore ordered him to leave that night. John replied, via Canridge, that he 'objected to going without money to support himself until he could get another place', aspecially since 'it was not his fault', presumably meaning that Clara Louisa had first encouraged him rather than vice versa, which was almost certainly true. Maxwell promptly sent down a £10 banknote, remarking that it was worth it to save the family from ruin. Half an hour later John changed his mind, returned the £10 note, and determined to

---

[60] Ibid. 1594–9.

bluff it out. It was not until two in the morning that he could be persuaded to leave, and Maxwell once more sent him down his £10 note.[61]

And so John finally left the house on foot soon after 2 a.m. on 13 December 1792, accompanied as far as the nearby village of Wetherby by Robert Maltus. Why Maltus went with him is obscure, but he spent the rest of the night, from three till eight or nine in the morning, sitting drinking with John in the Blue Boar public house. He later indignantly denied implausible accusations that he had been trying to persuade John to return. The next morning, on learning what had happened, Clara Louisa was enraged, and promptly dismissed Canridge, who had so long been her friend, confidante, and personal maid, telling her that she would get John back despite her and 'he will live here when you are starving for a morsel of bread'. Canridge had certainly broken the bonds of loyalty to her mistress, which her previous role of confidante should have imposed upon her. Clara Louisa blamed Canridge for accusing her to Maxwell, and for listening at the door on 20 November when there had been that agonizing scene between herself, Robert Maltus, and John.[62]

Exasperated at finding herself taking the full brunt of Clara Louisa's anger, Canridge sent another letter to Maxwell, who was now back in London. In it she described in lurid terms the scene that morning and her own consequent predicament:

She [Clara Louisa] flew to the stable, they told her he was gone. She came in distracted. Our good master was gone off hunting. She rang the bell for Robert. 'Shut the door you villain.' She knelt down on her knees to curse us. She wished Hell to open and swallow us up, she wished us so tortured too with all sorts of plagues all the days of eternity. 'Damned villain and that eternal bitch, you have banished him, you has banished, you and that eternal bitch. I never must see him more, you villain. Where have you sent him to, you villain?'

When Robert Maltus told her that he had left John at Wetherby, she took horse and galloped to the village, only to find that he had already left for Northallerton. On her return, she again threatened that she had something in her pocket 'that would do for her very soon'. Since it was discovered that she had visited the doctor at Wetherby, 'we was sure she would poison herself'. Canridge and Robert Maltus stayed up all night on watch, for 'If she murders herself we shall never be happy.'

Canridge then turned to her own plight:

It has all fallen upon unfortunate I. She sent me word to get out of her house directly . . . for I had ruined her and her family for ever. I will not go without

---

[61] Ibid. 305–6, 620, 932–5, 1572–83.   [62] Ibid. 620, 746, 936, 1065–8, 2743.

Robert. I thought it very hard upon me as he had me into it. I thought he had a right to go at the same, or I shall be entirely ruined, for all the weight to fall on me. . . . It is a cold time of the year to be turned out of doors. I fear I shall have a cold Christmas.

It is a letter full of whining self-pity and malicious desire to drag Maltus down with her. Canridge had no first-hand knowledge of what had passed between Clara Louisa and Robert Maltus, who later said nothing publicly about all these histrionics. Moreover, there is credible evidence that, when she was dismissed, Canridge demanded a month's wages in recompense, and on being refused both that and a reference left swearing that she would be revenged on Clara Louisa.[63] It is a measure of the latter's desperation, or possibly innocence, that she did not stop to assess the possible consequences of making a mortal enemy of one who already knew too much.

Canridge also wrote to Clara Louisa, implicating Robert Maltus in the revelations to Marmaduke Maxwell about her conduct. As a result, on 22 December, a week after the departure of John, Clara Louisa approached William and told him what had happened: how Canridge and Maltus had falsely accused her to his brother Maxwell of misconduct with John Rose, how Maxwell had believed them and had fired Rose, and how she had fired Canridge. She also apparently told him of Hodgson's story about the assignation in the bathing house the previous August, and how he had later publicly retracted it. Clara Louisa had had great difficulty in bringing herself to make this confession to William. She had been advised by letter from her London confessor, Father Hussey, to say nothing, and advised by a Catholic priest visiting Stockeld Park for a while, Father Timothy Ryan, to tell William at once. The night before, she had been in tears at dinner at the thought of what she had to do. But she must have put her case skilfully, for William believed every word she said and was persuaded that she was a much-maligned woman, persecuted by a handful of dishonest and slanderous servants. Father Ryan reported that the couple were particularly affectionate towards each other the two days following the confession.[64]

Within hours of hearing his wife's account of events, William summoned Robert Maltus to his dressing-room and dismissed him on the spot, ignominiously ordering him to be out of the house in two hours. Maltus offered to tell William all he knew, but the latter refused to listen to him. Another servant saw Robert a little later 'crying and packing up his things'. His career as an upper servant was in ruins, with the prospects of a new job negligible since he now could not get a reference from his first and only

[63] Ibid. 761, 1600–5.   [64] Ibid. 307, 2017, 2107, 4091–6.

employer, William Middleton. Maltus had for months been under intense strain, as he sought vainly to avert or postpone catastrophe, both to the family and to himself. Thomas Horner, the steward, once remarked 'poor Bob is so much affected with the affair that is going on between his mistress and John Rose that he can get no sleep at night, and has drunk at different times great quantities of liquor to obtain sleep, without effect'.[65] After this long-drawn-out ordeal, dismissal must have come almost as a relief to him. The fact remains, however, that Clara Louisa had destroyed the careers of two servants in order to protect her reputation. It was an act that was to come back to haunt her.

Three days later, on Christmas Day, William sent a message to John Rose and reinstated him in his old position of groom, as public proof that he did not believe a word of the accusations of Hannah Canridge and Robert Maltus against his wife. Clara Louisa later claimed that John Rose was brought back on William's insistence and against her own wishes. Indeed, it may well have been the case that she was seriously trying to cure herself of her infatuation, but did not trust herself if John were once more installed in the house. Marmaduke Maxwell certainly later said that he had received a letter from Clara Louisa, complaining that William had recalled John against her wishes, to which he had replied, advising her to get him dismissed again as soon as possible. So it seems to be true that the recall of John Rose was indeed at William's insistence, and not at that of his wife.[66]

In the last days of December, soon after all these upheavals at Stockeld Park, Marmaduke Maxwell, now back in London, called on Father Thomas Hussey, Clara Louisa's friend and confessor. He told him what he had done, and produced two letters from Canridge and Robert Maltus as supporting evidence. Hussey read them and refused to believe them, not unreasonably in the light of what we know of Canridge's letter. Maxwell admitted that he had kept in touch by letter with Canridge and Maltus after their dismissal, presumably supplying them with money and advice. Hussey told Maxwell firmly that he had been duped by slanderous tales of deceitful servants, and strongly advised him to go at once up to Yorkshire, recover his letters from Canridge and Maltus, and try to make his peace with his brother William. Maxwell was sufficiently disturbed by this advice to set off at once for Yorkshire, where he managed, either by persuasion or money, to recover his letters. But he did not have the courage to call in at Stockeld Park to see his brother.[67]

---

[65] Ibid. 308, 865, 937–8, 4523.
[66] Ibid. 308, 2030, 2107, 2920–1, 2567, 4104.   [67] Ibid. 2916–19.

(iv) *The Second Crisis, February–March 1793*

By the time the next stage of the drama at Stockeld Park began in February 1793, there was a new set of servants below stairs. After Christmas, the household lacked an under-butler/footman for William and a personal maid for Clara Louisa. Then in February, the butler, Henry Baldwin, who had managed to steer clear of the crisis of late 1792, handed in his notice in order to accept another more prestigious and less insecure and psychologically unsettling job. One reason why Baldwin had kept out of the crisis in December may have been his suspicion that Canridge and Maltus were plotting against him. It will be remembered that the latter had formerly courted the former, and that there was a widespread story that they had once been caught in bed together. One rumour in circulation in late 1792 was that Canridge had been intriguing with Clara Louisa to have Baldwin discharged, in order to get her lover, Maltus, promoted to the position of butler.[68] Whatever the truth of this story, Baldwin left, so that by February there were three key servants to be replaced.

Of the new servants who came in February 1793, by far the most important was William Davis, who succeeded Henry Baldwin as butler. He was 41 years old when he arrived at Stockeld Park, and had been a butler for at least ten years. He had had a chequered career working his way up through the ranks of the servant hierarchy to reach this position at the head of it. He earned the approbation of one employer as 'a good and faithful servant' by the courage he displayed in defending his master's London property at the time of the Gordon Riots in 1780—by which one may reasonably conclude that both Davis and his employer were probably Roman Catholics, like the Middletons and most of their other servants. But he had a morose, suspicious, and sometimes brutally violent disposition, which in the past had got him into trouble. In about 1779 he was clapped into Slapton gaol for a week on a charge of breach of the peace, though he denied ever having been gaoled elsewhere. Nor did it help his reputation that in 1778 he had worked in Bath for seven or eight months as a servant out of livery to the notorious Dr Graham, the charlatan sexologist who has, oddly enough, already turned up once in this story.[69]

By about 1780, however, Davis had secured his first job as a butler to G. W. Hanson Esq., a merchant and dry salter at London Bridge. It was clearly not a very distinguished or large household to rule over, but it was a start. Davis left after four years, since he fell ill of a fever—a sick servant had no job protection in the eighteenth century. He lived off his savings for four to five months until the fever left him, and then became butler and

---

[68] Ibid. 1690, 759.   [69] See above, p. 170.

footman to Thomas Wright Esq. of Henrietta Street, Covent Garden. This was no better than his previous job, and he left after ten months, due to a characteristic petty quarrel with his master about the distribution of the latter's cast-off clothes, all of which he claimed for himself as part of his rightful perquisites in the job. Mr Wright said he also let him go 'because he was not sufficiently active for his service'.

His next position was a major promotion, as butler to the large and aristocratic household of a cousin of William Middleton, Constantia Lady Langdale, widow of Lord Langdale, serving both at her town house in Welbeck Street and her country seat near Richmond in Yorkshire. It must have been his Catholic faith which got him the job. He stayed there five years, until he was dismissed by Lady Langdale for 'insolent and insulting language offered to her ladyship'. He then became butler to another Catholic family, that of Lord Clifford at New Park near Stourton in Wiltshire. But he stayed there for only five months before leaving after an angry row with his employer, who had accused him—falsely according to him—of joining with other servants in making a noise in the hall at two o'clock in the morning. He stayed in the area for two years working as a farmer, but when he was hired by William Middleton in February 1793 he had been living unemployed on his savings for five months.[70]

In view of this chequered career, Davis was an odd choice for a butler, but, if William Middleton had wanted someone to spy on Clara Louisa, he could not have picked a better man. William Davis had a record as a servant of scrupulous honesty, but also of sullenness, truculence, occasional violence, extreme obstinacy, and a pathological suspicion of the chastity of everyone, especially women. As an example of his morose and obstinate temper, he had once lived for six months in the house of his sister without ever once speaking to her. By 1793 he was a bachelor of 41, and was tormented by sexual frustration, which took the form of eager courting of female fellow servants, whose affections he soon alienated by unfounded suspicions that they had other lovers. He 'seemed to have a bad opinion of all women'. Fellow servants, both at Lady Langdale's and at Stockeld Park, testified that 'his general conduct was full of jealousy, malevolence and distrust of all persons about him'. Lady Langdale called him 'a sulky fellow', while her maid, Phoebe Roberts, whom Davis had courted and then spied on, was particularly harsh about him, not without reason. Others all agreed that, although 'faithful and just' to his master or mistress, he was 'a suspicious, malicious person, in the habit of making and circulating reports against the characters of women'.

[70] LPCA, D. 1395: 1309–12, 1347–51, 4188–94, 4169–72, 4214–16A.

There are several concrete examples of his obsession with the sexual frailty of women. When he courted Phoebe Roberts, he falsely accused her of being pregnant by the coachman, and, in order to catch her out, he would creep out on the leads in all weathers and spend hours on the roof peering down through the skylight into the kitchen. He behaved in an identical manner at Stockeld Park, first courting Clara Louisa's new maid, Hester Swinburne, and then recklessly accusing her, on the flimsiest evidence, of sleeping with John Rose, who, he alleged, infected her with venereal disease. He also accused, equally falsely, another servant of Lady Langdale's of taking a male visitor up to her bedroom and keeping him there all night. His suspicions were not confined to women, and, when in service with Lord Clifford, he accused—falsely, it seems—a fellow servant of breaking open his box and stealing things.[71] All in all, William Davis was clearly a perennial trouble-maker, and a dangerous man to have in an already very unstable household, rife with rumours and intrigues.

The second new servant to arrive in February 1793 was Daniel McAnulty, the 30-year-old replacement of Robert Maltus as under-butler and footman. He had had almost as chequered a career as Davis, and had displayed almost as much truculent independence and shortness of temper. The son of a farmer in Newry in Ireland, his first position was as a footboy to a Mr Maitland there, staying two years until his master left to go abroad. He then became footboy to another Newry gentleman, but left 'on account of a horse falling with me'. After this he got his first promotion, to butler and valet to a third Newry gentleman. After three years, however, with the encouragement of his master's sister-in-law, he left his native town in order to try to better himself, and became butler and valet to a gentleman at Carlingford. After a year there he left because 'they would not perform their agreement to his having his master's clothes'—the identical grievance which had caused Davis to quit a similar post. There followed a two-month stint as butler to a Major back at Newry, which he quit 'because my wages were not raised'.

He then went to Dublin to look for a better job and was taken on as valet by a Mr Scott. It was Mr Scott who first brought McAnulty to England, taking him with him to Bath and Bristol Hot Wells. But Mr Scott let him go after five months, since he had 'no further occasion for a valet'. He was unemployed for six weeks before being taken on as footman to Sir Edward Williams, Bt., of Clifton Hall, Bristol. This was a definite step up in the world, even if he was only a footman. But he quit that service after a row

---

[71] Ibid. 27, 1201, 1350, 1545, 2498, 2518, 2781–91, 2799, 2954–5, 2963, 2988, 3266, 3368, 4129, 4174–7, 4189–90, 4193–4, 4197–201.

with Sir Edward, who had accused him of speaking disrespectfully to his mother. There followed a series of temporary jobs as substitute footman or butler, after which he drifted to London, where after some more temporary positions he was finally taken on as footman by Dr Street in Sloan Street, Knightsbridge, where he stayed for eight months—quite a record for him. But eventually his obstinacy once again got the better of his good sense, and he quit because Dr Street wanted him to serve as both footman and butler combined. It was at this point that, thanks to a letter of recommendation from the tolerant Dr Street to Clara Louisa's mother, Mrs Grace, he was hired for Stockeld Park by the Catholic chaplain, Thomas Hussey. He thus owed his job to the patronage network of the Grace family, not to that of the Middletons. He took the stage coach from London and arrived at Stockeld Park on 19 February, travelling with William Davis and Hester Swinburne, Hannah Canridge's successor as Clara Louisa's personal maid.[72]

Like William Davis, Hester Swinburne was recruited to the household through the Middleton family network, stretching back to William's cousin Lady Langdale. She was a 28-year-old spinster, probably from the Durham area, since both her brothers lived there. Her first post as domestic servant had been at Sutton Place near Guildford, the huge Tudor pile that then belonged to John Webb Weston. She had left Sutton Place for a better position with Lady Langdale, where she had spent two years and therefore knew William Davis quite well.[73]

The circumstance which was to trigger off the next domestic crisis at Stockeld Park was that Davis fell in love with Swinburne, but that she scorned him, preferring the younger and more handsome and dashing John Rose. Clara Louisa's evident devotion to John does not seem in any way to have interfered with the latter's pursuit of love-affairs and seductions below stairs. Gossip connected him with the flighty laundry maid, Margaret Burnet, who was said to have fallen in love with him soon after her arrival at Stockeld Park, and even to have been made pregnant by him—a rumour alleged by Hannah Canridge to have been spread by Clara Louisa herself. Margaret herself hotly denied the pregnancy, apparently truthfully, but admitted that John had courted her 'as a sweetheart' and made her presents of ribbons, a pair of scissors, and a pair of garters. She freely accepted all these presents, but later alleged that she never liked John. He also made overtures to another maidservant, Anne Boothby, and we have seen how he wanted to marry a Miss Pick, trying in vain to make her pregnant in order to force the hand of her parents. Hannah Canridge also insinuated that John Rose had tried to seduce the nursemaid, Elizabeth Aspinall. In addition

[72] Ibid. 1100, 1128–204.   [73] Ibid. 2516–18, 2522.

to all these sexual adventures, John was said to have been reported in the newspapers—falsely it seems—to be married to 'Nanny Skelton', a local girl. To conclude the list of John's rumoured or actual amours, in early 1793 he openly admitted that he 'was actually affected with a venereal complaint', presumably contracted from yet another of his conquests.[74] Clara Louisa undoubtedly loved John Rose to distraction, and part of his attraction for her may have been that he was such a successful and promiscuous womanizer. But it is also possible that these many other low amours may have caused Rose not to press her too hard for full sexual relations.

So far as the pathologically suspicious William Davis was concerned, John Rose was now his rival for the favours of Hester Swinburne—and he naturally won, much to Davis's fury. The latter was said to have beaten Hester for going out with John, and he finally accused her of committing fornication with him in the chapel tribune—rather a public place for such activity—and of being poxed by him (i.e. infected with venereal disease). Whether or not his suspicions were well founded, the fact remains that Davis's jealousy was wrought up to a high pitch, and his desire to be revenged upon John Rose was acute.

From the moment he arrived, the attention of Davis, and indeed of all the servants, was also focused on the relationship between John and Clara Louisa. Now that the former was reinstated as groom in the hunters' stable and his accusers had all been ignominiously dismissed, Clara Louisa may have thought that she was safe. In the dark cold nights of February she resumed her nightly walks, returning once more 'with her gown often dirtied at back, and handkerchief and sash much rumpled', and also with marks of dirty hands around her waist. These signs that she was secretly meeting and hugging John during these nocturnal rambles were carefully observed by several witnesses, when she and the rest of the family assembled at nine o'clock every evening in the breakfast-room to go to prayers in the chapel.

By now, Clara Louisa had won to her side not only the nursemaid, Elizabeth Aspinall, but also the coachman, William Greave, and the 14-year-old stable boy, Thomas Birkenshaw. Whether by kindness, gifts, bribes, or threats, or merely as a result of the lesson to be drawn by the sudden ruin which had befallen Robert Maltus and Hannah Canridge, Clara Louisa had now acquired the complicity of three of the four servants most able either to expose her or to cover up for her. The servants' hall was thus divided into two factions, the spies and the accomplices, set apart by

[74] Ibid. 742–4, 1170, 1201, 1259–60, 1497, 2499, 2747, 2758–60, 4120.

different hopes of gain and fears of ruin, and by complex personal jealousies and loyalties. This situation had its dangers for Clara Louisa, for suspicious observers like the French cook, Bouvier, who wrote everything
down in a notebook for future reference, observed that she was frequently
seen whispering and laughing with the three stable servants, John Rose,
William Greave, and Thomas Birkenshaw. It was this unnatural social
mixing of Upstairs and Downstairs, as much as the suspicion of a sexual
intrigue, which seems to have been most shocking to the servants, just as
it was to Clara Louisa's social equals. Bouvier, for example, was morally
outraged to observe Greave and Rose 'in their stable waistcoats, talking to
Clara Louisa Middleton with their hats on'. This reaction to social egalitarianism is what one could expect from a nobleman's cook who had run
away from the French Revolution. But, when combined with her infatuation
with the groom, John Rose, this open neglect of hat deference by Clara
Louisa may perhaps indicate that she had been somehow affected by the
egalitarian ideas of the French Revolution.

In February and March 1793 Clara Louisa had still to win the support
of her new maid, Hester Swinburne, who was busy telling the other servants
that she had seen her mistress and John walking in the shrubbery, laughing
and talking, with his arm about her waist. She also told them that she had
noticed that Clara Louisa's white muslin robe was 'all down the back
stained with green'—the obvious conclusion being that she had been lying
on her back on wet grass. It was not until April that Clara Louisa at last
managed to win Swinburne over to her side, and caused her to stop spreading
this dangerous gossip about her.[75] Clara Louisa now had four allies of
critical importance to her.

During February Davis alleged that he often spotted John Rose climbing
in the water-closet window, and Clara Louisa coming downstairs to go in
the water-closet door. He claimed that once he hurried to the door and
tried to open it, but it was slammed and locked in his face. His conclusion
was that John Rose and Clara Louisa were using this unsavoury and highly
visible spot as a place for adulterous assignations. The only support for this
implausible allegation comes from the dubious source of the dairymaid,
Margaret Burnet, who testified that she once saw John climbing out of
the water-closet window at ten o'clock at night. On balance, this story is
scarcely credible, if only because either John or Clara Louisa were almost
bound to be observed. The water-closet window was visible from two
windows in the kitchen, while the passage near the door to the water-closet
was constantly being used by servants coming and going about their business

---

[75] Ibid. 911, 1030, 1209, 1212, 1226, 1233.

(Fig. 1). Besides, it was generally admitted that, despite strict orders, some of the servants made use of the water-closet from time to time. Altogether, a more unsatisfactory and dangerous place for an adulterous assignation could hardly be imagined. Even the grove or shrubbery on a cold wet Yorkshire night would have been preferable.[76]

As might be expected, these rumours generated a great deal of gossip in the neighbourhood, which eventually spread as far as York, where they reached the ears of Mr William Carr, a friend and attorney of William Middleton. After some hesitation, Carr discreetly offered his services to William, in case he could be of any help. William was now in great psychological torment. He still fully believed in his wife's innocence, but was increasingly troubled by the persistent and spreading rumours. It was he who had summoned John Rose back to Stockeld Park in December, as a proof of his confidence in Clara Louisa's innocence, but he now realized that John's continued presence merely fed the flames of gossip and further damaged his wife's reputation. On 26 March, when Clara Louisa's brother, Richard Grace, was staying in the house for a few days on a journey north, William summoned Mr Carr urgently to Stockeld Park. On his arrival, Carr was shown into the breakfast-room, where he found a family council, consisting of William, Clara Louisa, and Richard Grace.

The three men took little time in deciding that John Rose must immediately be given one month's notice and dismissed. Their argument was that, true or false, the rumours would continue to spread so long as he remained in the house. But now Clara Louisa 'warmly opposed the same', on the grounds that the dismissal would be interpreted as meaning that William at last believed her to be guilty. She argued strongly for an hour, before giving way to the unanimous opinion of the other three. William wanted her to dismiss John herself, but this she flatly refused to do, on the reasonable grounds that it was William, not she, who had rehired him in December. The quarrel was heated and Clara Louisa 'flew into such a rage that her brother, Mr Grace, who had just been writing a letter to Mr Maxwell upon the subject, threw it into the fire, saying: "I wash my hands of the business."' After this threat of abandonment by her own brother, Clara Louisa calmed down and reluctantly gave way, but only on condition that John 'first sign a declaration of his innocence', in order to clear her reputation. So John was summoned by Mr Carr and Richard Grace, and was offered the declaration to sign, which he did upon the Bible. He was then given a month's notice to quit.[77]

---

[76] Ibid. 398, 1279–82, 3036–40, 3312, 3885, 4427–9, 4504, 4581–4, 4606, 310–11, 1622, 1794.　　　　[77] Ibid. 311–12, 1079–81, 2037–8, 2123–32, 4106–10.

Middleton v. Middleton

The second decision taken at the meeting was that William should leave at once for London to talk to his brother, Marmaduke Maxwell, and persuade him that his conclusion that Clara Louisa was probably guilty of adultery was baseless. William left the next day, 27 March, and on arrival in London summoned his brother Marmaduke to meet him at their father's house in Portman Square. Present at the meeting was their father, old Mr Constable, his two sons, Marmaduke Maxwell and William Middleton, and Father Thomas Hussey as a friend of the Grace family. Marmaduke gave William the two letters from Hannah Canridge, which have already been quoted at some length. William read them, and—with good reason— 'commented with warmth on their malice and falsehood'. He called them 'all lies', and denounced his brother for taking them seriously. Turning to his father he said: 'This Canridge, my wife's maid, has been turned out of my house for her bad conduct, and is an infamous bitch; and so is Robert a worthless dog; and he and she were caught in bed with one another. And it is very hard my wife's honour shall depend upon such wretches. My wife is as virtuous as any of your daughters.' As for the other witnesses against her, they were 'scandalous characters themselves or low dirty people' like Hodgson, who 'is the most cursed lying scoundrel alive'.

Finally, to confirm his belief in Clara Louisa's innocence, he sent for his ex-butler, Henry Baldwin, who, it will be remembered, had discreetly retired into the background of the affair, no doubt foreseeing the disaster ahead, and had obtained for himself a good new job with Lord Willoughby de Broke. When he arrived, William did not ask Baldwin what he suspected or had been told by others, but merely if he had himself ever seen Clara Louisa and John Rose in an improper situation. Baldwin replied truthfully that he had not, and signed a paper to this effect. On 2 April William returned from London to Stockeld Park after a week's absence, now fully confirmed in his belief in his wife's entire innocence, and in the worthlessness of the evidence against her.[78] More objective observers would conclude that there was very strong evidence of Clara Louisa's romantic infatuation with John Rose, but so far no proof of adultery.

(v) *The Final Crisis, March–April 1793*

While William had been away, however, some strange things had been happening at home. On 28 March, the day after he left for London, Clara Louisa had been shut up alone with John Rose for an hour or more in the breakfast-room, as observed by the ever-watchful William Davis. John had

---

[78] Ibid. 1583–8, 1705, 2903–6. William's outburst had been written down at the time by Father Hussey, in case there was a lawsuit later.

then left to prepare for a trip to his relatives in Northallerton in order to look for another job, not proposing to be back at Stockeld before the evening of Easter Sunday, 31 March. At two in the afternoon of the 28th, John was drinking at his usual haunt, the Blue Boar Inn at Wetherby, where he met his friend Thomas West, 'gentleman' of Sickling Hall. Since West was to play a central part in the events of the next few days, we must here pause to describe his dismal career and feckless character.

West's father had been an apothecary at Bath for twenty years, and had clearly made a good living, as might be expected, considering that Bath in the eighteenth century was the place of last resort of almost every sick person in Britain who could afford it. When the son was about 15 or 16, his father bought him a seven-year apprenticeship with an apothecary at Salisbury, clearly intending that the boy should take over his own business in Bath when he retired. But after five years and nine months of his time was out, he, or rather his father for him, 'bought out the remainder of my time, not liking my situation'. He stayed with his father for six months doing nothing, until the latter persuaded him to go to work again for a London apothecary in Somerset Street, Portman Square, a most fashion-able and expensive district. But he stayed there for only a year before he finally confessed to his father that he disliked the profession and would not pursue it. Very generously, his father accepted this announcement and gave the boy a life annuity of £80 a year, leaving him free to do whatever he wished. The trouble was that he did not very much want to do any-thing. He got a job as a Tide Waiter in the Board of Excise for two years, but then threw it up, and had been unemployed ever since. He married a widow, Anne Taylor, who must have had some money. But she was sickly —perhaps tubercular—and on medical advice he moved her out of the polluted air of London, first to Hull and then in February 1793 to Sickling Hall, just outside Stockeld Park. The house they rented was owned by his wife's uncle, William Kendall, the tailor and upholsterer to the Middleton family. He stayed there with his wife until after she died in the middle of 1793.

Later that year, however, he was to have a drunken quarrel with Kendall, who threw him out of the house on suspicion of having seduced his daughter Fanny. Kendall had good reason for doubting Fanny's virtue. She was a 27-year-old ex-kitchen-maid at Stockeld Park, who admitted in court that two years before: 'I was called upon to swear a child, and did swear it to Robert Wigglesworth. I never have been married.' What this means is that Fanny had got herself pregnant and had confessed under oath the name of the father to the parish officers. When not pursuing Fanny, Thomas West haunted the inns and alehouses of Wetherby, since he had little else to do, and it was there that he met and made friends with the hard-drinking and free-spending John Rose. They had much in common, from their lowly social origins to their aspirations to gentility to their taste for women and the bottle. The best account that West could make of how he spent his time was that 'I have at times performed in plays with companies of players at Wetherby and at Spofforth, but I did not perform for pay but for my own amusement, and at the desire of ladies and gentlemen who knew me.' This down-at-heel loafer and son of an apothecary was desperately anxious to cling to his self-appointed status as a gentleman interested in amateur theatricals.[79]

When asked by John Rose to go with him to Northallerton, West readily agreed to come 'for the jaunt, having nothing to do at the time'. He went home to tell his wife and fetch his greatcoat, and the next morning, which was Good Friday, they took the stage coach to Northallerton. There they stayed at the Sign of the Tickle Toby, a public house kept by John's brother-in-law. John was hoping for a job which he had heard was vacant with Squire Pierce at Thimbleby, but discovered on arrival that he was too late and the place was filled.[80]

The next morning, Saturday, 30 March, they learnt of an opportunity for a free ride home on two horses being taken to Wetherby by a groom of Sir Thomas Gascoigne. So they hitched a ride on the two horses, arriving at Wetherby at about five in the afternoon. There they stopped at the Swan and Talbot Inn and gave the groom a drink in recompense for his kindness. John then suggested that they go on another five or six miles to Tadcaster to visit Anne Boothby, the ex-servant at Stockeld Park whom he had courted some months before. They tried to hire a one-horse chaise but found it was not available. When John suggested that they walk to Tadcaster, West put his foot down and refused to go. So instead they went back to their usual haunt of the Blue Boar public house, where they spent the evening drinking fairly heavily. According to the publican they drank four beakers of spirits and water, until they got 'quite drowsy'. At about mid-night John announced that he intended to return the two miles to Stockeld Park for the night, and persuaded West to go with him by offering him half his bed when they got there. So off they went into the night, arriving at Stockeld Park at one o'clock in the morning.[81]

What happened next is not entirely clear. According to West, who was evidently fuddled with drink, they saw a light still shining in the maids' bedroom over the servants' hall in the old wing. So they slunk past into the

[79] Ibid. 318, 2841–5, 3076–8, 3158.   [80] Ibid. 2849–51, 2826, 2971.
[81] Ibid. 2826–30, 3064–7, 3114–17, 3200.

stable, where John pulled off his boots and took off his greatcoat, and said he would go to see if he could get the maids to let him and West into the house. Ten minutes later he returned, saying: 'Damn them, they won't let us in.' West was, not unreasonably, 'a good deal out of temper at being so treated, after having been induced to leave Wetherby against his inclination', and talked angrily of leaving John and going home to Sickling Hall a mile away. John was equally cross and snapped: 'Damn it, can't you be easy where you are?' But after further argument he went back to the house to see if he could get in, while West wrapped himself in his greatcoat and fell into a drunken sleep in the hay.[82]

At this point we must turn to what was going on inside the house. After William had left, the only members of the family were Clara Louisa, who slept in her usual bedroom, and Miss Mary Haggerston, who was visiting to keep her company and slept in the Red Room, probably with her maid, Lavinia (Fig. 2). Also upstairs were the three children and their nursemaid, Elizabeth Aspinall, who slept on the attic floor, and Clara Louisa's personal maid, Hester Swinburne, who would have slept close to her mistress. The only other people in the main block of the house were the butler, William Davis, who was in his pantry in the basement, and the under-butler and footman, McAnulty, who slept in the shoe-room. The rest of the servants were in the old wing, which was cut off from the main block at night by two locked doors, the keys being kept by McAnulty.

Clara Louisa stayed up late that evening, long after Miss Haggerston had gone to bed, and did not retire from the drawing-room to her own bedroom until after midnight. Hester Swinburne stayed up later still, until about one o'clock in the morning, talking to Davis in the basement store-room. After Swinburne had gone to bed, Davis checked the house to see if all the windows were secure. He discovered that the window into the chapel tribune, which the maid had locked at nine o'clock, was now open, although the curtain was drawn to conceal this fact (Fig. 2). One witness asserted that often 'the maids used to have their sweethearts come into the house at night to see them by means of the window in the tribune of the chapel'— in other words to practise the standard eighteenth-century courting procedure of 'bundling'.

If this story is correct, it certainly was not known to Davis, whose suspicions were immediately aroused by the open window. He retreated to the doorway of the breakfast-room, from which he could see the window, and waited in the darkness to see what happened. After a long while he heard some tapping at an upstairs window and a sash window being opened,

[82] Ibid. 2831–2, 2047–56, 2136–40, 3083.

and later vaguely saw two women talking at the top of the stairs, whom he took to be Hester Swinburne and the nursemaid, Elizabeth Aspinall.[83] At about half past one Davis saw a man, whom he could not identify in the dark, climb in the chapel tribune window and disappear up the back stairs. He heard a door open upstairs, and later swore that he saw the man step out on to the upstairs gallery, and enter one of the main bedrooms. His belief at the time was that the man was John Rose, and that he had been admitted to Hester Swinburne's bedroom.[84]

After waiting for a while in the darkness and silence of the night, Davis went down to the shoe-room, woke McAnulty, told him that he had seen a man enter the house and go into one of the bedrooms, and ordered him to dress and join him in the watch for the man to come out again. For about three and a half hours Davis and McAnulty stayed quietly in the door-way to the breakfast-room, waiting for something to happen. At about 5.30 McAnulty distinctly heard the click of a door-lock upstairs. Shortly after-wards John Rose came out of the back stairs and went past the door. As he did so, Davis jumped out and grabbed him by the arm. After talking to him for a while, Davis let him go, and John proceeded to climb back out of the chapel tribune window and return to the stables. There the sleepy Thomas West woke up sufficiently to ask if he had 'been with some of the girls in the house', which he denied. They then both went to sleep in the hay, to be found a few hours later by the stable boy, Thomas Birkenshaw.[85]

The critical question was where had John Rose been between his entry into the house at about 1.30 a.m. and his departure at 5.30? John's own story was that he had found the tribune window open and had climbed in—not without difficulty for it was over five feet above the ground. He went down the back stairs to find McAnulty in order to get him to unlock the kitchen door, but found the pantry locked. He then went back to the ground floor, remembered that the Yellow Room at the top of the back stairs was unoccupied, and so went up the back stairs to it, lay down on some chairs, and went to sleep. The Yellow Room, it should be noted, was not easily accessible from the main staircase and was not a principal bed-room used by the family and their guests. On his return, he was intercepted by William Davis, who accused him of spending the night in the bedroom of Hester Swinburne, which he flatly denied. As can be seen on the plan (Fig. 3) the Yellow Room had direct access from the back stairs, and was cut off from the main staircase by double doors. If Rose had gone in there, he would have been unheard and invisible from the breakfast-room door

[83] Ibid. 318–26, 712–14, 871, 1107, 1289–93, 1501, 2713.
[84] Ibid. 1108, 1294–5.   [85] Ibid. 327, 1109, 2863–4, 3083–6, 4690.

except when entering or emerging from the back stairs on the ground level. But McAnulty later confided to a friend that 'I heard a door opened and locked again, as plain as ever I heard anything in my life'. Unlike his formal testimony in court that he actually saw John Rose emerging from Clara Louisa's bedroom, there is no reason to doubt the truth of this private statement.

If Rose's story was false, and he was not in the Yellow Room, then in which room was he? There is overwhelming evidence that at the time neither Davis nor McAnulty were certain whether it was the bedroom of Clara Louisa or that of Hester Swinburne. The former's later testimony in court is demonstrably false. He alleged that at 1.30 he had seen and heard John knock on Clara Louisa's door, heard her jump out of bed and come to the door saying 'Is that you, John?' and heard him reply, 'Yes, ma'am,' saw the door unlocked and John go in. He also declared that he had seen and heard John emerge from that same bedroom.[86] Later tests and measurements showed that it was impossible to see from the breakfast-room door more than the top six-inches of one corner of Clara Louisa's 6' 6" high outer door, much less to see or hear anything at the inner door (Fig. 4). One witness declared flatly that one 'cannot possibly see any person go in or come out of the outer door of the bedchamber', a statement the truth of which can be demonstrated by a visitor today.[87] The conversation described by Davis must also be pure fiction, since the walls of the bedrooms were 2' 8" thick, as was the gap between the inner and outer doors.

The final proof that Davis and McAnulty had no idea in which bedroom John had spent the night is provided by the fact that, when the former first confronted John at 5.30 in the morning as he was leaving the house, he accused him of having spent the night with Hester Swinburne. So convinced was he of this that he had a noisy confrontation with Hester two and a half hours later that morning in the butler's pantry, a row overheard by several witnesses, in which he again accused Hester of sleeping with John. He also summoned John, and a servant overheard the following dialogue:

WILLIAM DAVIS. Why John, you are a pretty fellow.
JOHN ROSE. On what account?
DAVIS. You was in Swinburne's room last night.

[86] Ibid. 1294–7, 2714, 2056–60, 3085–6, 4690.
[87] Many witnesses had views about this, but the key scientific tests and measurements were made by the surveyor John Bainbridge and the architect Thomas Atkinson (ibid. 3044–5, 3104, 3315, 3329, 3349, 3364–7, 3911, 4160, 4367–70, 4585–8, 4598–606, 4626–31, 4652–7, 4662–5, 4677–82).

Middleton v. Middleton

VERTICAL SECTION

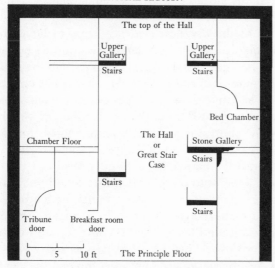

The top of the Hall

Upper Gallery | Upper Gallery

Stairs | Stairs

Bed Chamber

Chamber Floor | The Hall or Great Stair Case | Stone Gallery

Stairs

Stairs

Stairs

Tribune door | Breakfast room door

0   5   10 ft   The Principle Floor

4. Vertical section through the Staircase Hall of Stockeld Park in 1794, by John Bainbridge

ROSE. Probably you might be mistaken, but you may have your own way, as I will not satisfy you by saying where I was.

DAVIS. I will have it my own way, for I know you was in Swinburne's room and nowhere else, and I will take my oath of it.

Swinburne indignantly and tearfully denied the whole story, and called Davis a liar.[88]

Most of the rest of the morning was taken up with communal attendance at lengthy Easter Sunday services in the chapel, which lasted until 1 p.m. Meanwhile, reports of Davis's accusations against Swinburne spread below stairs, and led to a furious quarrel in the kitchen between the latter and the French cook, Jean Bouvier. He suggested that she was carrying on an affair with John Rose, and asked why she sent for him every day if she was as innocent as she claimed. Hester Swinburne, who was already in a semi-hysterical state after the confrontation with Davis, lost her temper completely, and shouted, 'You are a rascal, villain, abominable man, and so is every Frenchman,' picked up two or three cups of tea and their saucers, and hurled them at him. Bouvier leapt to his feet and called her 'you whore' twice. Hester then rushed at him and beat him with her fists, screaming 'he has called me a whore'. Bouvier was just about to strike her back, when

[88] Ibid. 1099, 1359, 1862, 2059–60, 2482–3, 2572–3, 2714–17, 2836, 3433–4, 3887–9.

Davis and McAnulty intervened and restrained him by grabbing him by the collar.[89]

In the course of the day new evidence came to light to suggest the possibility that John had in fact been not in Swinburne's bed at all but that of Clara Louisa. Because of the long chapel service in the morning, which included mass, confession, and communion, it was not until after midday that the servants had time to go into Clara Louisa's room to make her bed. The maids were Margaret Burnet, the 27-year-old girl who had formerly been in love with John Rose, and had been promoted from kitchen-maid to housemaid over the last two and a half years; and Margaret Wilkins, who had only just joined the household as laundry maid and therefore had no motive for lying. They both reported that they found the bed 'remarkably tumbled, particularly about the middle towards the bottom'. There were also signs of two bodies having slept in it, although, unlike most other married women earlier in the eighteenth century, Clara Louisa never took her maid to bed with her when her husband was away. Very occasionally she would get Swinburne to sleep on a mattress on the floor, but on 30 March she had slept alone. The two maids soon told what they had seen, and the news spread rapidly among the servants. The only objection to the story was that they had not come to make the bed until so late in the day, and the fact that the little children Peter and Mary had been playing about on it early in the morning while their mother was dressing, perhaps also with the dog Hector. Clara Louisa's maid said they had been playing hide-and-seek under the bedclothes. Even so, the report was enough to cause tongues to wag, although well into the evening Davis was still accusing John Rose of sleeping with Hester Swinburne.[90]

It was not until the next morning that Davis finally decided that, in the light of the evidence about the state of the bed, his accusations against Swinburne were unfounded, and that she had merely been acting as an accomplice of her mistress, Clara Louisa. He rounded on John, who was still not saying where he had spent the night, and said, 'if you was not in Swinburne's bedroom, then you was in your mistress's bedroom'. He commented openly in the servants' hall that John 'would hardly sleep with the maid when he could get the mistress'. Davis apologized to Swinburne, and set about collecting information, rearranging the evidence in his mind—and inventing some more to make it sound more plausible—in order to be in a position to prove that Clara Louisa had committed adultery with John Rose.[91]

[89] Ibid. 1256–60, 1351–2, 2495.
[90] Ibid. 329, 1404–12, 1418, 1489–92, 1503–6, 2067, 2724, 2743.
[91] Ibid. 1359, 2502, 3087.

Middleton *v.* Middleton

Davis had an ulterior motive in destroying John Rose, quite apart from his jealousy of him over the favours of Hester Swinburne, for they had had a bitter quarrel about John's use of the store-room. He had told John, 'If I ever see you there again I will break your neck,' to which John had retorted, 'I will go there whenever my business requires it.' Now Davis saw his chance for revenge and told John, 'Young man, you think you have a long lease here, but when your master returns I will take care to shorten it,' adding, 'you are a fine fellow to be in Mrs Middleton's bedroom for several hours in the course of last night.'[92]

By now Davis had decided that the truth of the matter was that there had been a pre-arranged assignation between John and Clara Louisa; that both Hester Swinburne and the nursemaid, Elizabeth Aspinall, had been active participants in the plot; that the tribune window had been deliberately opened by one of them; and that Clara Louisa had been lying in bed awake, expecting John to come to her bedroom that night. This elaborate conspiracy theory, however, is clearly unsupported by the facts. After all, John's first intention had been to go off to Tadcaster for the night to see his old girlfriend, Ann Boothby. Next he had sat drinking from five in the afternoon until midnight; next he had persuaded a male friend to accompany him back to Stockeld Park and share his bed; and finally he had done all he could to wake the household. This is hardly the behaviour of a man with a secret late-night assignation with a married woman in her bedroom.

But John Rose's story that he spent the night on chairs in the Yellow Room is almost equally implausible, since McAnulty said privately that he clearly heard a lock click, which meant it had to come from a door to one of the main bedrooms. His story is made even more implausible by the attested fact that, although 'apt to get in liquor', John had an excellent head, so that, although there were rumours that he 'did occasionally get overcome with liquor', no one testified that he had ever seen him 'so much in liquor as to be intoxicated'.[93] Since he was sober enough to climb in at a window five foot off the ground, it is unlikely that he had stumbled drunkenly up to the Yellow Room and passed out there, as his friend Thomas West had already done in the hay in the stable. The most plausible solutions are either that he slept with Hester Swinburne, or that, when the opportunity unexpectly offered itself, he slipped into Clara Louisa's bedroom and spent an energetic night of love with her, tumbling the bedclothes in the process. The only objections to either of these possible scenarios are the angry denials of both women, which were only to be expected, and John's wholly unsupported claim that at the time he was suffering from

---

[92] Ibid. 1354–8.   [93] Ibid. 712, 870, 1167, 3093.

venereal disease and therefore unfit to sleep with any woman. The plausibility of this particular defence is badly undermined by his abortive plans
to visit Ann Boothby for the night. The one thing which is certain is that
John spent the night in one of the main upstairs bedrooms inside the
house, either alone in the Yellow Room, or in bed with Swinburne or her
mistress, Clara Louisa.

The final stage of the drama began when William Middleton returned to
Stockeld Park from London on the night of Tuesday, 2 April, two days
after all these events. He was flushed with his victory over Clara Louisa's
detractors in London, full of affection for her, and sure in his own mind of
her total innocence of all charges against her. He slept in her bed instead
of in his dressing-room, both that night and the next.[94] On the morning of
4 April, however, William Davis approached his master in his dressing-
room and informed him that he had seen John Rose enter and leave his
wife's bedchamber in the middle of the night, and that McAnulty would
bear him out. William went into psychological shock, his doting affection
for his wife turning in an instant to intense hatred of her for what he took
to be her gross betrayal of his trust. In an instant he changed from her most
loyal friend to her most implacable enemy.

William's immediate reaction to the news was to ride off to York to fetch
his two lawyers, Mr Townsend and his friend William Carr. On their
arrival back at Stockeld Park, they established themselves in the breakfast-
room and proceeded to interrogate all the servants one by one. Robert
Maltus, the under-butler who had been dismissed so ignominiously in
December, was hastily recalled. He later told a friend that, on receiving the
summons, he 'was afraid he might be shot before he got home'—presumably
by John Rose. When he arrived, William said to him before Townsend and
Carr: 'I wish, Robert, you would be so good as to repeat to Mr Townsend
what you was going to tell me when you was dismissed my service.'[95]

The next day, as the interrogations were still in full progress, William
sent a message to Clara Louisa through William Carr, ordering her to leave
the house at first light the next morning, despite her indignant denunci-
ations of 'the most infamous falsehoods'. She was told that the coach would
be put at her disposal to take her wherever she wanted to go, but that all
her five surviving children, including the baby not yet nine months old,
would stay behind, and her clothes would be sent on later. Several witnesses
said that 'it would have turned a heart of stone to see the manner in which
Mrs Middleton parted from her daughters.'[96]

---

[94] Ibid. 1477.   [95] Ibid. 944–5, 1299, 1363, 3070.
[96] Ibid. 338, 1192, 4704.

Middleton v. Middleton

As she rumbled away from Stockeld Park on that early April morning in 1793, accompanied by no one but the coachman, Greave, and her maid, Hester Swinburne, Clara Louisa's situation was truly lamentable. It looks very much as though, like Lady Teazle,[97] she had allowed 'the consciousness of [her] own innocence' in the matter of her connection with John Rose to lead her into so many indiscretions as to leave her temporarily defenceless when accused of committing adultery with her groom in her husband's own bed. If she was in fact innocent, as seems at least possible, the moral as well as the social degradation of finding herself now publicly accused of such a crime must at last have opened her eyes to the folly of her infatuation with John Rose. On his account, she had forfeited the all-forgiving affection of a devoted and compliant husband, and as a result now found herself separated from all her children, including her baby; uprooted from the home which had been the centre of her universe for the last twelve years; degraded from her position in society; and exposed to all the scandal and malicious gossip associated with an accusation of adultery. The prospect of confronting her mother and her brother in such circumstances must have been grim indeed, as the coach driven by William Greave headed down the Great North Road towards her mother's house in London. It was lucky for her peace of mind that she was unaware that she was pregnant.

At Stevenage, within a day's drive of the City, Clara Louisa's courage for once failed her, and she wrote a desperate letter to her confessor, the Revd Thomas Hussey, begging him to come to her immediately to help her in her distress, 'cast off from all which is dear to me in life'. When Father Hussey replied, regretting that prior commitments would keep him from going to her that moment, he received a still more hysterical letter accusing him—'the only friend I have in the world'—of abandoning her like everyone else. Father Hussey immediately came to meet her and escorted her to her mother's house in Weymouth Street.[98]

As soon as Clara Louisa had left Stockeld Park, William's new hatred of her took a macabre turn. If he could not kill her in person, he could at least kill everything she loved best. He ordered Hodgson at once 'to knock out the brains of her horse Top with a hatchet and hang her dog Hector'. Hodgson obeyed, although he claimed he actually shot Top—and in his characteristic way made a private profit of 5s. from the hide. William also packed the four elder children off to boarding school, keeping only the baby, and dismissed the nursemaid, Elizabeth Aspinall, because she refused

[97] R. B. Sheridan, *The School for Scandal*, Act IV, Sc. iii.
[98] LPCA, D.1395: 2923–6, 2943–9.

to give damaging information against Clara Louisa. A few months later he set about closing down the house altogether, for he could not bear to live in it any more, with all its fond and terrible memories.[99] He determined to discharge all the servants, shut up the house with a caretaker in charge, and go to live a lonely life of reclusive retirement at Myddleton Lodge out on the moors near Ilkley, attended by no more than a skeleton staff of servants. By the summer of 1794 he was gone and the house was closed. He was clearly a broken man, who now lived only for revenge. As the steward, Horner, remarked in an unguarded moment, he 'is so set against Mrs Middleton that he hates everyone who offers to speak well of her or in her favour'.[100]

(vi) *The Litigation, 1793–1796*

The battle for the servants

Their mistress's abrupt expulsion polarized the servants in the house into two camps. There were those who had taken an active part in prosecuting her, and who recognized that their careers were now at stake in making sure that her ejection was permanent; and there were those who had helped to cover things up for her, and who rightly feared that they would lose their jobs because of her. Proof of how deep feelings ran is the fact that, on the night before her departure, Davis, Horner, the steward, McAnulty, the under-butler, and William Hodgson, the odd-job man (who had now re-emerged with his old story of what he had seen at the bathing-well house back in August) sat up together all night drinking to celebrate her expulsion. Hodgson publicly boasted that, so clever was Clara Louisa's defence, that 'she would have beaten them all, had it not been for me and Davis'.[101] They now had their master's ear, were certain to be the key witnesses in the forthcoming lawsuits, and expected to profit from their depositions. They also realized, of course, that, if Clara Louisa were to be vindicated, and William took her back, they would be turned out of the house at a moment's notice without a reference, and their careers would be ruined, as had happened to Robert Maltus. They had now burnt their boats, but had reason to celebrate this initial victory.

Meanwhile, the lawyers Townsend and Carr proceeded with three separate interrogations of all the servants, taking signed depositions from them, while the leading accusers did everything they could to put pressure on their fellow servants. Davis in particular bullied those he suspected were

---

[99] Ibid. 466, 683, 893, 3381, 4456.

[100] Ibid. 4523; for Myddleton Lodge, see N. Pevsner, *Buildings of England: Yorkshire, West Riding* (London, 1959), 278.

[101] LPCA, D.1395: 892, 1201, 1368, 3266.

witholding information to make a full revelation of all they knew, or perhaps more than they knew. He had already perjured himself by saying that he had seen John Rose going in and out of Clara Louisa's bedroom door, whereas it is certain that he could have seen no such thing from where he stood, and that in fact he thought for a day that John had gone into Swinburne's bedroom door. He had also invented a conversation between John and Clara Louisa which he could not possibly have heard. His fellow witness, Daniel McAnulty, who admitted privately that he had seen nothing and had merely heard the click of a lock in the darkness, was persuaded to testify falsely that he too had seen John coming out of Clara Louisa's room.[102]

Davis concentrated his attention on the 14-year-old stable boy, Thomas Birkenshaw, whom he strongly suspected, probably rightly, of knowing a good deal about the meetings between Clara Louisa and John in the stable and in the shrubbery. On 9 April Birkenshaw signed a harmless affidavit that he had often seen Clara Louisa and John talking together in the stable, but nothing more. Davis took the boy into his pantry and coaxed him for a long time, insinuating that 'you must have seen some fine sport about the corn bin' in the stable, and finally in exasperation beat him savagely to try to make him talk. Thomas went home crying to his grandmother, exhibiting bruises all over his arms and shoulders. Davis also pressed the nursemaid, Elizabeth Aspinall, to admit her complicity with Clara Louisa, telling her that 'it would be better for her to confess that she did know of such a connection', and told another potential witness that she 'had nothing to be afraid of, since Clara Louisa would never warm her bottom again at Stockeld'.[103]

Thomas Horner the steward also did his best to pressure the servants into testifying against Clara Louisa, if only because as a tenant at will of Stockeld farm, held from William, he had every incentive to keep in the good graces of his landlord.[104] Robert Maltus, whose career had been blasted and then revived because of his leadership in the earlier charges against Clara Louisa, was naturally particularly active in drumming up support in the village. He reproached old William Kendall, the tailor, for having 'anything to say to any person who was not in Mr Middleton's interest', adding, 'damn you, if you had the value which I have for Mr Middleton, you would stand in the pillory for him'—a fairly plain hint that he was now ready to risk the penalty for perjury in order to advance his

---

[102] Ibid. 4689, 4702–4, 4717–19.
[103] Ibid. 817, 944–7, 1093, 1820, 2506, 2731, 3054, 3189, 3267, 3269, 4032–3, 4046, 4702–4, 4710, 4719.   [104] Ibid. 4500, 4524, 4531.

master's lawsuits against his wife and her alleged lover. When another villager, old William Greave senior, denied he could offer any evidence against Clara Louisa, Robert Maltus came up to him in the street and 'struck him in the breast'.[105]

Since William Hodgson was so universally distrusted, he was not much use in drumming up evidence in the village against Clara Louisa. He was reinstated in Mr Middleton's good graces on 8 April, three days after Clara Louisa had left, but the best he could do was to spread scandalous stories about her in the local public house. Again and again he told his tale of the assignation of Clara Louisa with John Rose at the bathing-well house in August, adding the embellishment that 'damn her, she was full of bairn at the time'. This was untrue, for she had in fact given birth a bare month before. Emboldened by this lie, and fortified by the rumours that John Rose suffered from venereal disease, he went still further and in the various bars in Wetherby told everyone within earshot that 'Mrs Middleton was poxed and Dr Cooper of Wetherby knew it and had cured her'. This was so egregious and slanderous a falsehood that the doctor threatened to sue him for libel. He then compounded the two stories, saying 'she must be a damned bitch as well as a whore, for that she was big with child at the time I saw her and John Rose come out of the bathing well, and she was poxed by John Rose'.[106] These wild accusations did not go down at all well with the villagers, the great majority of whom were convinced that Clara Louisa was innocent.

Indeed, if one surveys objectively the evidence available at that time, in March to April 1793, it appears that William had solid grounds for believing that Clara Louisa had long been infatuated with John Rose, but nothing but disputed circumstantial evidence and some evident lies to sustain a charge of adultery committed in the marriage bed, which is what turned him so violently against her. Despite this uncertainty, he immediately began to sue her for separation on grounds of adultery in the ecclesiastical courts. The paucity of hard evidence is probably what worried Mr Townsend, William's first attorney, who as a result was soon fired. It also caused a disinterested spectator like the surveyor John Bainbridge to develop doubts, after being shown the staircase hall at Stockeld Park by William on 13 April. He had the courage to tell William that Davis's story of what he saw in the hall could not be true and that Hodgson, Canridge, and Maltus were not to be trusted. William reluctantly agreed that they were 'not much to be relied on'. As a result Bainbridge became fascinated by the

---

[105] Ibid. 3056–7, 3191.
[106] Ibid. 864, 3051, 4325, 4484, 4620, 4647, 4676–7.

case, and 'took a great deal of pains to investigate the affair to my own satisfaction'.[107]

There were only four pieces of evidence that pointed directly to adultery: the bathing-well episode, about which Hodgson had already given four different versions, and some of the details of which were quite impossible to believe; the allegation that sometimes on her return from her evening walks Clara Louisa had green stains all down the back of her dress, indicating that she had been lying down on her back on wet grass; the very implausible and poorly documented story of secret assignations in the water-closet in the evenings; and Davis's claim to have seen John Rose enter and leave Clara Louisa's bedroom on the night of 30 March, which was physically impossible from where he stood and was in contradiction to his own original conclusion that John had been sleeping with Swinburne.

Although the evidence of Clara Louisa's indiscretion and love for John Rose was overwhelming, the evidence of her actual adultery was thus sufficiently shaky to induce the Grace family, headed by her brother Richard, to rally round Clara Louisa, and to throw themselves vigorously into organizing her legal defence. Their first step was to get hold of John Rose, who after a month with his relatives in Northallerton was moved down to London by stage coach under the care of his friend, Thomas West. Once there, he handed over identifying articles like his watch and his silver coat-buttons to his friend West, and simply vanished. This disappearance baffled and infuriated William Middleton's lawyers and agents, who were desperately seeking to arrest him and sue him for damages in a common-law court on a charge of crim. con. with Clara Louisa. There were rumours that John was dead, or in the army, or in Ireland; but no one really knew. There were other rumours that he had been pressed as a sailor, had gone abroad, or was hiding in London near Clara Louisa.

What in fact had happened was that Richard Grace had whisked him off to Ireland and hidden him in Baltimore, Co. Cork, where he lived unemployed on an allowance from the Graces. The same disappearing act was also performed by the Graces with the young stable boy, Thomas Birkenshaw, whom William Davis had beaten so cruelly. Threatened with discharge by William Middleton for his refusal to talk, he went to London to seek the help of Clara Louisa. She supported him for ten days in London, where he lived with her in Mrs Grace's house, and then sent him off to Dublin as a servant in the household of her brother Richard in Great George Street.[108]

---

[107] Ibid. 3908–14.
[108] Ibid. 2875, 2983, 4037, 4060–1, 4058–67, 4122, 4133, 4177–8.

Another loyal supporter of Clara Louisa was the nursemaid, Elizabeth Aspinall, who must have known what really happened during the night of 30–1 March. But repeated interrogations could not make her speak, despite an offer by William to keep her on as nursemaid to the last child left at home if only she would tell what she knew. But talk she would not, and ten days later William dismissed her. She thereupon took the next coach south to London and was at once taken on by Clara Louisa in Weymouth Street as her personal maid; later, after the birth of the new baby, she would revert to her position as nursemaid. Another mouth had been effectively shut.

To ensure her discretion, Clara Louisa had earlier made her a gift of clothes, which Elizabeth noted 'would have been Hannah Canridge's if she had held her tongue'. Her enemies' view of this transaction was that she 'was bribed by a parcel of damned nasty gowns and petticoats to infamy and meanness'. The seriousness of the polarization of loyalties among the servants is shown by the fact that her siding with Clara Louisa apparently destroyed her last chance of marriage. Already 42, she was being courted by the 60-year-old tailor, William Kendall, the owner of Sickling Hall, who was a widower. But Kendall was visited by Robert Maltus, who told him that, if he married so active a supporter of Clara Louisa, it would be the ruin of him, 'for you will never more set foot within Stockeld Park'. Since Kendall made the liveries for the Middleton servants, this was work he could not afford to forgo. He therefore wrote to Elizabeth to break off the match, to which she replied scornfully: 'I do not value you and can do without you.'[109]

Other servants wavered in their choice of loyalties. The coachman, William Greave, had long been an ally of Clara Louisa, allegedly covering up her meetings with John Rose in the stable and the shrubbery. On her expulsion on 5 April he was ordered to take her wherever she wanted to go, and then to return to Stockeld Park. Instead, he stayed on in London for a whole month, until, presumably homesick for his brother and friends in Wetherby, he went back to Stockeld and asked 'if he might take charge of the horses again'. But his request was denied and he was formally discharged. So he returned to London and became Clara Louisa's footman and coachman at her mother's house in Weymouth Street, and consequently a loyal and discreet—not to say lying—witness on her behalf.[110]

Another potential witness who sat on the fence to see which way it would pay him to jump was John Robinson, William Middleton's postilion and

[109] Ibid. 1056, 1071, 1138, 1501, 2775–8, 3056–7, 4486.
[110] Ibid. 2537, 2594, 2598, 3206–7.

groom of the coach horses between 1784 and 1791. He was a drunken and quarrelsome character who could not be relied on. He and John Rose had both been given notice on the same day, 9 November 1791, since William was angry with them for going to the Spofforth village feast, staying out all night, and getting drunk. When they both refused to stay 'to be so abused', William replied, 'You are all welcome to go', but pardoned John Rose, whom he said he would keep. Robinson then obtained a job at Leeds, but soon found himself in exactly the same trouble. One Sunday night he got drunk and stayed out late without permission. When he returned, his employer 'struck me on the head with a stick', at which he gave notice that he would leave. On the following Tuesday his employer offered to keep him on if he apologized, but he refused and left. His next employer, also at Leeds, soon dismissed him for staying out too long when sent to get some ale. But William Middleton must have thought he might know something about the early stages of the affair between his fellow groom John Rose and Clara Louisa, for he took him on again in June 1793, after extracting a promise from him to avoid getting drunk and abusing the other servants. But he did not behave well, on his own admission staying out late and getting drunk again at the Sickling Hall feast. But still William kept him on, even after he had moved with a skeleton staff to Myddleton Lodge, and only got rid of him in early 1794, when it became clear that he had nothing to disclose. Given the fierce hunt for witnesses, it is hardly susprising that later that same year he turned up in court to testify on behalf of Clara Louisa![111]

Other servants followed more clear-cut patterns of loyalty and reward. Hester Swinburne left Stockeld Park with her mistress on 5 April and came with her to London, stayed in her service, and six weeks later married one Joseph Meynell of Weymouth Street, possibly another servant of the Graces who had been courting her before she left to take the post with the Middletons. This patronage by the Graces, cemented by a marriage, meant that she could be relied upon to say the right things in court. It also explains why Betty Aspinall was able to step into her shoes as lady's maid, shortly after her arrival in London towards the end of April.[112]

Within a few months after her ejection from Stockeld Park, Clara Louisa, with the help of her brother Richard Grace, had thus succeeded in patronizing and controlling many of the key witnesses. John Rose himself and the stable boy, Thomas Birkenshaw, were safely hidden in Ireland; William Greave, who must have known a lot about what had gone on in the stables, and Elizabeth Aspinall, one of two possible witnesses of what had really

---

[111] Ibid. 3373–81.   [112] Ibid. 2465, 2516, 2529.

taken place upstairs on the night of 30–1 March, were in her employment, and the other, Hester Swinburne, was married to a dependent. She was thus well protected against her accusers.

For his part, William Middleton was equally active in securing the loyalty and co-operation of other important witnesses. Hannah Canridge, who had been dismissed without reference by Clara Louisa, was waiting for her revenge. An apparently reliable witness reported meeting her in a London street in July 1793, when she had been summoned to make a deposition in court. She said openly that it was Clara Louisa's own fault that she was a witness against her, because she had refused to give her a character and thus blocked her from getting another job as a domestic servant. By 1794 she was in York, remarried to a shoemaker, and once more making a precarious living as a mantua-maker. William may have given her some money, but if so there is no record of it.[113]

William Hodgson, the witness of the alleged bathing-well house assignation, was perhaps the most untrustworthy of all the accusers of Clara Louisa, having changed his story no fewer than four times in the space of eight months. William Middleton was taking no chances with him, and assured his loyalty by granting him an annuity of £20 a year, the gift of a cow, and the promise of the use of a field in which to keep it. After the great house had been shut up and William had moved to Myddleton Lodge in the summer of 1794, he hired Hodgson to act as gamekeeper of the deserted park and caretaker of the empty house.[114] In return for all these favours, Hodgson in court told the most damaging version of what he claimed to have seen and heard at the bathing well.

Robert Maltus, who had been abruptly dismissed in December 1792, and equally abruptly recalled by William Middleton in April 1793 to make his deposition, was still unemployed and living with his mother on his savings in late 1793. However, eventually he too had his reward, being hired as butler by William Middleton's younger brother, Charles Constable. David McAnulty, the under-butler, was kept on in that position and so had everything to gain from giving testimony that tended to incriminate Clara Louisa, even if some of it was false, as it almost certainly was when he said on oath that he had seen John Rose emerge from Clara Louisa's bedroom in the early hours of 21 March. As for Jean Bouvier, the cook, thanks to a strong letter of recommendation from William Middleton he had been hired at double his Stockeld Park wages as cook for the Comte de Firey in London.[115]

---

[113] Ibid. 578, 635, 1889, 2653–4.
[114] Ibid. 4347, 4388, 4402, 4438, 4498–9, 4509.   [115] Ibid. 1219–20, 1370.

Middleton *v*. Middleton

William Davis, the butler, was fully committed to his story about the night of 30–1 March, despite the fact that parts of it were clearly false. In the first week of April he 'wrote down on paper the particulars of the transactions of that night'. He also wrote letters about it to six friends, the butler to the Hon. Mrs Molyneux, the steward of Sir Michael Hoare of Stourhead, a Francis Sheppard at Stourhead, his brother James Davis, and his former employers, Mr and Mrs John Hanson. He had handed his memorandum over to William's lawyer, Mr Townsend, and by his letters ensured that his version of the story would spread rapidly all over the country. He was Clara Louisa's most implacable enemy, inspired partly by his personal jealousy of John Rose as his rival for Hester Swinburne, and partly by his loyalty to William Middleton, which was reinforced not only by his continued employment by him as butler, but also by a life annuity from him of £20 a year.[116]

Other rewards were doled out to servant witnesses as prudence or circumstances might dictate. When the house was closed, the steward Horner was given all the surplus wines and liquors from the Stockeld Park cellar, as a reward for his efforts to collect evidence against Clara Louisa.[117] Margaret Burnet was immediately rewarded by promotion from kitchen-maid through the lower ranks of the Stockeld Park staff up to housemaid, by having her wages raised immediately after Clara Louisa's departure, and being given some of the latter's childbed linen, which had been removed from her trunk before it was sent on to her, as well as some of William's old sheets. When Stockeld Park was closed up, she was provided with a position as laundry maid to Mr Langdale, a Middleton cousin, thanks to a favourable letter of reference from William Middleton.[118]

Much the same treatment was given to Molly Swearbuck, an illiterate and allegedly pregnant laundry maid, who gave useful testimony about seeing Clara Louisa in the shrubbery as dusk fell, waving a white handkerchief to attract the attention of John Rose. Her father rented a farm from William Middleton, and she too had her wages raised when Clara Louisa left, and was given a share of the latter's linen and William's old shirts. Another witness, Thomas Shelton, was given four cart-horses three weeks before he was summoned to give evidence for William. Merely in order to keep her out of the way and shut her up, Nanny Dickinson was taken into the household at Stockeld Park during the week when Clara Louisa was at Wetherby nearby collecting evidence. Another servant, Anne Dighton, was told that, if she would give evidence against Clara Louisa,

---

[116] Ibid. 1268, 1317–18, 4178, 4347.
[117] Ibid. 4478.   [118] Ibid. 1418, 4453, 4480, 4486.

'she or her family would never want a good home'. William Brainthwaite was given a brand new suit of clothes in which to go to London to give his deposition. Little rewards helped to keep little people in line.[119]

Thus, as the marriage dissolved, the normal horizontal layers of social deference were shattered, to be replaced by two vertical columns of warring factions and their clients. Both principals in the marital dispute used patronage, employment, influence, and money to produce or silence potential witnesses for the coming litigation. These witnesses were nearly all poor servants, tenants, or other dependents—who were easily persuaded by small gifts, jobs, or the granting or withholding of letters of recommendation. In any case, only a few of them—at any rate among the servants—were in a position to be purely detached and objective; many had some personal axe to grind. With many it was their desire to please that led them to embroider on the truth, and to allege that they saw things they could not in fact have seen but only suspected. Rumour tended to become fact—Nanny Dickinson admitted she had been persuaded to turn hearsay into personal testimony[120]—suspicion to harden into certainty, and half-truths to be elevated into truths. In any case, ambiguities and uncertainties were liable to get lost in the adversarial procedures of the courtroom, particularly since the signed depositions were made only after coaching by skilful proctors.

In this particular case the pressures were especially fierce since two determined and wealthy families were pitted against one another in legal combat, the one out to destroy and the other out to vindicate the honour of a woman. As a result, no marital dispute in the whole of the eighteenth century produced so staggering a mountain of documentation—well over half a million words and five thousand pages in all—and none sucked into the battle so many people, not only servants and friends, but also villagers, tradesmen, lawyers, and mere bystanders.

The early litigation, 1793–1794

The battle was so fierce and so long drawn for three reasons. The first was because Clara Louisa and the Grace family fought so stubborn a rearguard action, using every trick in the legal book. Her mother and brother knew very well that Clara Louisa had been guilty of a long, imprudent, and degrading infatuation with the groom, John Rose. But they must have been convinced by her denials of actual adultery, a conviction which was certainly not challenged or questioned by her confessor, Father Hussey, who was,

---

[119] Ibid. 1786, 1794, 1807, 4455, 4459, 4482, 4488, 4527–8.
[120] Ibid. 4480.

admittedly, bound by a vow of silence. The second reason for the length and ferocity of the litigation was that the evidence about her adultery was suggestive but not conclusive; and the third was that for a long while John Rose could not be found.

During the summer of 1793 Clara Louisa lived in her mother's house and kept a very low profile. She attended mass daily at the Spanish Ambassador's chapel, where Father Hussey officiated. She also went for lonely walks in the fields early in the morning before the quality were up, or later during the fashionable dinner hour, so as to avoid meeting any of her acquaintances. Everywhere she went she was accompanied by William Greave, and sometimes, it would seem, dogged by a detective hired by William's lawyers in hopes of a lead to John Rose. In the late summer, when her pregnancy was about mid-term, she went to stay by the sea at Littlehampton with her mother.

Once William tried to trap her by writing an unsigned letter offering that, if she would acknowledge her guilt of adultery and go abroad, 'you might recover my affection'. On the advice of Father Hussey, she rejected this offer as a transparent device designed by William's lawyers to trick her into admitting to adultery. Although William's lawyer, Mr Carr, denied ever having told her that 'the separation was to be effected in a friendly way and without carrying it to a court of justice', others seem to have done so. Thus the French cook, Jean Bouvier, was once used by William to pass on a verbal offer of pardon in return for a confession of guilt, but Clara Louisa once again refused to fall into the trap.[121]

In June 1793, after William Middleton's proctor had presented his 'libel' before the London Consistory Court, and just as the testimony of witnesses was beginning to be collected and as both sides were girding for the legal fight ahead, the waters were muddied by the publication in the *Bon Ton Magazine* of an anonymous story entitled 'The Wanton Wife, or the Lady in the Straw'—which gave a lurid but apocryphal description of how Clara Louisa had been caught *in flagrante delicto* in the stable with John Rose. Clara Louisa's lawyers wanted William to join her in suing for libel, but he refused, although he admitted that parts of the article were untrue. Clara Louisa therefore sued for libel in the King's Bench the bookseller and printer, who were wise enough not to contest the case after the puritanical Lord Chief Justice Kenyon had told the jury that 'this is a double offence, since it tends to debauch the morals of young people'. The case was therefore settled out of court. But, then as now, a scandal sheet does not give up easily, and, when the second edition of the June 1793 issue of the

---

[121] Ibid. 1093, 1260–5, 2529–33, 2926–8.

Bon Ton Magazine came out, the offending article was omitted but the readers were encouraged to think that there were even juicier items to come. An editorial note explained:

We have expunged an article inserted in the first edition of this number called 'Stable Duty etc.', it having been deemed a libel by the Court of King's Bench, the suit against the lady being yet depending in Doctors Commons. When the cause shall be determined there, our readers may expect some extracts from the depositions of the witnesses.[122]

What made this episode particularly unsavoury was that the authorship was traced to one Simons, an intimate in the house of William Middleton's mother, Lady Winifred Constable, 'where he was employed to read plays'. The sprawling Constable–Haggerston–Middleton clan was clearly prepared to stop at nothing to bring public discredit upon Clara Louisa, and Father Hussey may have been right when he said he believed that William was 'a dupe of some of his relations, whom I know to be weak, credulous people'.[123]

So long as the trials lasted, Clara Louisa was able to live in considerable comfort, since her husband was obliged to pay her assessed legal costs, while in addition she had been awarded by the ecclesiastical court temporary alimony of £600 a year until the case was finally decided. She thus had no interest in bringing the suits to a speedy conclusion, and was obstinately determined to fight to the bitter end. There is also one piece of evidence of the deliberate use of delaying tactics by her lawyers. William exhibited his 'libel' against her in the London Consistory Court in the early summer of 1793, and in the Michaelmas Term Clara Louisa's proctors put in her 'responsive allegation'. But so lengthy and full of irrelevancies was the document that the judge, Sir William Scott, was driven to protest publicly that 'this allegation is in such a form as will never enable me to get at the material parts of the case; and it appears to me, if I suffered it, I should bequeath a legacy to unborn judges'. He went on to admit that he did not have the legal authority to reject it, but added: 'on my own account, I shall much regret the drudgery of reading through these cart-loads of trash with which it is at present loaded'.

This unusual outburst caused Clara Louisa's proctor to withdraw the allegation and her counsel to rewrite it in an acceptable form. Even so, Clara Louisa summoned no fewer than fifty-nine witnesses in her defence, while William summoned another fifty-one against her, the examination

---

[122] *London Chronicle*, 1 (1794), 197; *Bon Ton Mag.* 3 (June 1793), preface (second edition; neither the Library of Congress nor the Bodleian Library possesses the first edition). I owe this reference to Dr J. J. Looney.

[123] LPCA, D.1395: 1592–3, 2929–34.

and cross-examination of whom, in London, Yorkshire, and Ireland, naturally lasted well into 1794. During the summer vacation of 1794 the documentation was 'published', that is to say that 'this unprecedented mass of evidence was copied out for the contending parties on both sides' —a job which occupied the whole summer.

The trial resumed in the autumn of 1794, but before Christmas Clara Louisa's lawyers submitted an 'exceptive allegation', claiming that some of William's witnesses had testified 'corruptly and falsely'. This was standard procedure, but it meant that many old and new witnesses had to be examined all over again.[124]

Meanwhile, Clara Louisa had not been idle. On 4 January 1794 she had given birth to a baby girl, her ninth (and sixth living) child. The paternity of the child was in some doubt, since it was born just nine calendar months after the two nights when William had slept with her following his return from London, which was three days after the controversial night when Clara Louisa was accused of taking John Rose into her bed. Despite this uncertainty, it is a measure of the influence exerted by the Grace family that the godparents at the christening of the child were the Irish Earl of Fingall and the English Countess of Shrewsbury.[125] Belief in Clara Louisa's innocence was clearly still widespread in high society in London and Ireland.[126]

Nor was it any less strong among the villagers in the neighbourhood of Stockeld Park up in Yorkshire. Clara Louisa was a courageous and determined woman, and, after she had recovered from childbirth and as soon as the roads became passable in April 1794, she travelled north to see her children at school, and to stop at Wetherby to collect more testimony in her defence. She was accompanied by her mother, Mrs Grace, her maid, Elizabeth Aspinall, and her new baby, all in the family coach driven by William Greave. The reception she met with at Wetherby cannot have been wholly spontaneous, but, even if carefully orchestrated, probably by William Greave's brother, the innkeeper, it must have represented a genuine outburst of support for her and her cause. Half a mile out of town they were met by a large crowd of townspeople, who unhitched the horses and themselves drew the coach up to the Black Swan and Talbot Inn, where they were to spend the next two nights. That evening and the next there were tumultuous street demonstrations in Clara Louisa's favour. Stuffed effigies of her leading accusers—the butler, William Davis, the maid, Hannah Canridge, the under-butler, Robert Maltus, and above all the detested

---

[124] *William Middleton* v. *John Rose* (BL 518 1 12 (6)), 4–5.
[125] Barbara, wife of the 2nd earl.   [126] *Middleton* v. *Rose*, 2 n.

gamekeeper, William Hodgson—were paraded around the town. The effigies were then taken to a huge bonfire and thrown upon it, while free beer was distributed to the cheering crowds. It was probably on one of those evenings that Hodgson found himself 'hissed and hooted at, and at one time pelted with rotten eggs, dung and other filthy things by the townspeople of Wetherby'.[127]

All the features of these extraordinary demonstrations—the dragging of the coach in triumph by a crowd, the parading and burning on a bonfire of the effigies of the enemy, the distribution of free beer to the crowd, and the pelting of notorious supporters of the foe—were taken from the standard riotous repertoire of English eighteenth-century electoral practice, here taken over wholesale for use in a domestic marital dispute. But this was no mere charade of a hired mob—the townspeople were strong supporters of Clara Louisa, if only because she had done her charitable duty by them. Moreover, since many of them had previously worked or still worked in the house or grounds of Stockeld Park, the whole community stood to suffer economically by the shutting-up of the house and the withdrawal of William Middleton to Myddleton Lodge, which by then must have been imminent. They therefore all had a stake in proving Clara Louisa innocent. Moreover, John Rose was a popular young man in the town, a hard drinker who passed much time in the public houses but virtually never became intoxicated, who spent his money freely, and who chased the girls, not without success but mostly without getting them pregnant. Hodgson, on the other hand, was the most hated and distrusted man in town. All the same, these violent mass demonstrations in Clara Louisa's favour can have done little to soothe her husband's feelings, especially since one uncorroborated story had it that the villagers also burnt an effigy of William himself—if true, a gross breach of the normal pattern of village deference to the local squire.

The later litigation, 1795–1796

Up to the spring of 1795 Clara Louisa stood an excellent chance of acquittal in the lawsuit, since the Middleton and Constable family still had produced no credible eyewitness for any proven act of adultery, and some of their key witnesses were clearly lying. As for the night when John Rose was supposed to have been seen entering Clara Louisa's bedroom, careful measurements and inspection of the stairwell by the surveyor, William Bainbridge, proved conclusively that it was impossible to see the outer door to her bedroom from the position taken up by the witnesses (Fig. 4). The two

---

[127] LPCA, D.1395: 898, 3283–90, 335–6, 3389–91.

witnesses, Davis and McAnulty, therefore had to have been lying about what they saw.

There is little doubt that by the spring of 1795, when the London Consistory Court was about to issue the sentence, the judge, Sir William Scott (later Lord Stowell), was preparing to pass sentence in her favour. In a public statement a little later, he openly referred to 'the defects of the proof of the former pleas', and 'the extreme obscurity which appeared in the original case', despite 'the quantity of evidence produced'.[128] If only Clara Louisa had exercised a little patience and discretion, it seems certain that she would have won.

She had spent June and July 1794 by the sea at Littlehampton with her mother and a Mr and Mrs Dorset. Mr Dorset was a Bond Street banker with whom the Graces had made friends the previous summer, when both families had also been together at Littlehampton. The Grace party consisted of Clara Louisa, her mother, her baby, her maid, Elizabeth Aspinall, another maid for her mother, and William Greave, now serving as her footman. During her stay there she was seen by locals meeting secretly with 'a strange person who passed by the name of John Richards or Richardson, a person of low condition known only to the servants of Clara Louisa'.[129]

On 18 August the Graces followed their friends the Dorsets to Lowestoft, another seaside resort, where they moved into lodgings upstairs in the house of one Allen, who kept a china shop and circulating library. Later research by Mr Dorset into the Yarmouth coach reservation book showed that on 20 August a man calling himself 'John Richardson' took a place in the coach and got off at Lowestoft, where he first stayed for a couple of weeks at a public house, The Fishing Boat, and then moved to another one called The Sign of the Compasses. Immediately on arrival in Lowestoft, 'Richardson' was visited by William Greave, and they had a long and friendly talk. Thereafter Greave took the man's dirty boots and dirty linen back to Clara Louisa's lodgings to have them cleaned. The linen was reported by the washerwoman to be very fine and marked 'J.R.'. 'Richardson' seemed to have had plenty of money, and was very free in treating to wine or punch everyone at Lowestoft who came by. William Greave visited him every day and became his habitual—and heavy—drinking companion.

'Richardson' had various ways of meeting secretly with Clara Louisa. At first she would go out for a ride, and go slowly past The Fishing Boat, allowing time for 'Richardson' to slip out and join her further along the road. Later they would meet by appointment, and he was observed walking

---

[128] *Eng. Rep.* 162: 1039.   [129] LPCA, D.1395: 4728–9, 4741; Eee. 17, fo. 42.

by her horse's side, talking and laughing with her. Sometimes he kissed her and put his hand on her knees, sometimes she dismounted and they walked together hand in hand. On other occasions she would hire a curricle or one-horse pleasure cart and drive out of town, to be met by 'Richardson' at a predetermined place. 'Richardson' would then climb in, put his arms round her, and kiss her. The most common site of assignations, however, was 'a place called the Deanes among the rope walks and fishing houses, a place very retired and very little frequented by genteel people'. Clara Louisa would hurry down there from the back door of Mr Allen's house between six and seven o'clock every morning, and she and 'Richardson' would walk about hand in hand or arm in arm. They would meet again at noon in the same place, and a third time after dinner. The moment she caught sight of 'Richardson' she 'ran with apparent transport to meet him', and kissed him. Then they 'withdrew out of sight among the rocks and in the most retired and unfrequented places by the sea side'. It was assumed by the prosecution that hidden behind the rocks by the shore the pair lay down and made love, but it is striking that no one ever actually saw them doing so.[130] The final visual proof of adultery thus continued to elude Clara Louisa's pursuers.

Rumours about these frequent assignations with 'Richardson' soon began to circulate in Lowestoft. The owners of the two public houses where he stayed observed his friendship with Clara Louisa's footman, and his free-spending ways. The rope-makers in the rope-walks could not help seeing the two of them walking arm in arm or kissing in the Deanes, just beside their front doors. Clara Louisa's story was apparently known to the locals, and soon it was reported all over Lowestoft in the public houses that 'Mrs Middleton had brought her stallion with her to Lowestoft'. Inevitably these rumours were picked up by a servant of Mr Dorset, but it was only after three months, in early October, that he reported them to his master. Alerted by her husband, Mrs Dorset made some preliminary enquiries, found plenty of evidence to support the allegations, and was told by her husband to confront her friend Clara Louisa in person. She asked her about it, but the latter flatly denied any truth to the story. She said she had merely once taken a walk with an attorney's clerk who came to Lowestoft to see her about her legal business.

Two or three days later Mr and Mrs Dorset, accompanied by three witnesses, went to Mr Allen's house and were shown up to Clara Louisa's room, where an embarrassing exchange took place:

[130] LPCA, D.1395: 4742–58; Eee. 17, fos. 43–9.

Middleton *v.* Middleton

MR DORSET. Madam, you deny ever having been seen walking with any man whatsoever since you have been in Lowestoft.

CLARA LOUISA (in a low voice). I told you, Mr Dorset, that I have not been seen walking with John Rose.

Mr Dorset then produced his three witnesses, who testified that they had frequently seen her with 'Richardson'. Clara Louisa was confused and agitated by these detailed accusations. She leant her arm on the chimney-piece and retorted defiantly: 'I am not accountable to anyone in Lowestoft for my conduct, for I pay for what I have here.' Mr Dorset then upbraided her about the impropriety of her behaviour, 'speaking in a loud and angry tone of voice'. Clara Louisa urgently begged him to lower his voice, saying: 'I would not for the world that my mother should know anything about the matter.' She then collapsed, and exclaimed despairingly: 'My God, if this man should be taken up by Mr Middleton, I cannot defray the expense of defending him. I shall be ruined both in character and fortune.' So the interview ended, and that same afternoon 'Richardson' was seen with his trunk on a cart, on the way to Yarmouth to catch the coach to London and to disappear once more into hiding.[131]

Soon afterwards, Clara Louisa and her mother and baby returned to London, but the Dorsets, despite their indignation, did not betray her secret either to her mother or to her vengeful husband, who still did not know the whereabouts of John Rose. William's intention was to launch a civil lawsuit for damages for crim. con. against Rose, but he could do this only if he could serve a warrant on him in person. He does not seem to have kept a round-the-clock watch on Clara Louisa's comings and goings at her mother's house on Weymouth Street. He was, therefore, totally unaware that during the winter of 1794–5 she was regularly visiting John Rose, hidden away in obscure lodgings in a back room upstairs above a tailor's shop in Chapel Street off the Tottenham Court Road, and now calling himself John Robinson.

Clara Louisa, who passed herself off to the landlord as Robinson's sister and a lady's maid, would visit him three or four times a week for about an hour, usually early in the morning, often before he was up and dressed. If he was not ready, she whiled away the time chatting with the landlady in the kitchen, or went into another room and played a chamber organ. The 'brother' and 'sister' seemed very affectionate towards each other, but the landlord and landlady, Mr and Mrs Smith, suspected nothing amiss, much less saw any signs of sexual relations. The landlord was present at one revealing conversation between them. John came into the room, put his

[131] LPCA, D.1395: 4759–66; Eee. 17, fos. 42, 44, 51, 54.

arm round Clara Louisa's waist, pointed to some silk for breeches lying on the table and said: 'My dear, if you will treat me with a new pair of breeches, I will treat you with a kiss.' When he said the breeches would cost two guineas, she promptly produced the money, saying: 'There, Mr Smith, is the money.' At which John quickly picked up the money and put it in his pocket, saying: 'Thank you, my dear.' When Clara Louisa told him to give the money to the tailor, he retorted: 'It is time enough to pay when the breeches are made.'[132]

It was only by sheer luck that in the end the Middletons picked up the trail of John Rose, although it is likely that Clara Louisa's imprudence would eventually have revealed his whereabouts. On 2 January 1795 there happened to be in London a shoemaker from Spofforth in Yorkshire, whose master had for years made all the shoes for the Stockeld Park household. Quite by chance, he spotted John Rose going into the tailor's house in Chapel Street. Knowing that William Middleton was extremely anxious to lay hands on Rose, and no doubt anticipating a handsome reward, he hurried off to William's brother, Marmaduke Maxwell, to tell him of his discovery. Maxwell had a writ all prepared, and at once sent him off to Chapel Street with a process-server. The shoemaker entered the house, took one look at 'Robinson', said, 'He is John Rose, and I am ready to swear to his person,' and watched the legal proceeding of serving the writ take its course. Only trying to be helpful, Mr Smith suggested to 'Robinson': 'Had you not better send for your sister?' He replied in a whisper: 'Hold your tongue. Don't mention anything of my having a sister come to see me. She is not my sister. It is about her that they are making all this bustle.' But 'Robinson' was later identified by other witnesses brought down from Yorkshire as John Rose, and his 'sister' was identified as Clara Louisa by Mrs Smith the tailor's wife, who was taken to see her at her mother's house. After this serendipitous discovery, the jig was up. William Middleton immediately brought an action for £10,000 damages for crim. con. against John Rose in the Court of King's Bench, and the latter was imprisoned in the Marshalsea to await trial.[133]

It will be remembered that the publicity had been blocked hitherto by the suppression of the article in the *Bon Ton Magazine*. As his counsel explained: 'Mr Middleton had spent so much time and money in the Spiritual Court without any immediate prospect of a final issue to his suit, he was advised to bring his action for damages against John Rose in the Court of King's Bench in order that some eclaircissement might be given

---

[132] Ibid., fo. 41.
[133] LPCA, D.1395: 4767–73; Eee. 17, fos. 41, 54; E.48/26.

to the public upon the case.'[134] But in the Court of King's Bench Rose did not even enter a plea, and the verdict of guilty was therefore made by the Judge in default, without the presentation of the case or the calling of any witnesses. As a result, the assessment of the size of the damages was referred to a jury presided over by the Deputy-Sheriff of Middlesex.

It seems more than likely that the decision not to defend the suit against Rose in the King's Bench was a shrewd legal move, rather than one dictated by financial necessity. The Lord Chief Justice at the time was Lord Kenyon, who was in the habit of instructing the jury that a secret withdrawal to a secluded spot by two adults of the opposite sex was sufficient evidence that adultery had taken place. When it came to awarding damages, he told them that they had a duty not merely adequately to compensate the injured husband, but also to make the amount large enough to act as a severe deterrent to future adulterers, and so to strengthen the moral tone of the nation. He also instructed them to ignore the financial circumstances of the defendant, coining the slogan 'he who cannot pay with his purse must pay with his person', meaning that a man unable to pay the damages must be left to rot indefinitely in a debtor's prison.[135] Clara Louisa's legal advisers no doubt rightly thought that, since a conviction was inevitable, they stood a better chance of getting an award of only moderate damages from a Sheriff's jury than from one subjected to such a lecture from Chief Justice Kenyon.

During the jury trial for the assessment of damages on 28 February 1795 Rose was again undefended by a barrister, his only legal adviser being Clara Louisa's solicitor Mr Allen, who had acted for her previously in suppressing the *Bon Ton Magazine* article. William Middleton's counsel opened the case by describing in detail the whole story, supported by the oral testimony of the key witnesses. He asked for the huge sum of £10,000 damages on a variety of grounds. First, he pointed out that William Middleton was a man 'of considerable fortune and family', and that, when he married her, Clara Louisa had shown 'every personal accomplishment, every mental endowment, every grace and trait of virtuous conduct', of the enjoyment of all of which he was now deprived. Secondly, there were many children to the marriage, and for a decade the couple had lived 'in a state of perfect conjugal felicity'. From the time of his discovery of the adultery, however, he had been 'deprived of . . . the affection, society and comfort of his wife continually from thence hitherto'. William was entitled to large damages in compensation for the loss of his 'conjugal felicity' with such a paragon of a wife.

[134] *Middleton* v. *Rose*, 5–6.
[135] NC *Trials for Adultery* (1797) *passim*; *Crim. Con. Gaz.*, 1 (1839), 4.

The only possible flaw in William Middleton's case was that, by deliberately reinstating John Rose at Stockeld Park after the first warning about the love-affair, he had laid himself open to the suspicion of collusion, or possibly even of entrapment. To meet this possible objection, it was argued that in fact William had acted out of quixotic blind faith in his wife's integrity, and had wanted publicly to show his confidence in her innocence by reinstating John Rose into the household. As his counsel put it, William thought that, if he did not take Rose back,

the meddling world will say that, however I may pretend to be satisfied, yet if I discharge this man, who has been made out as the object of suspicion, the world will say 'it is mighty well . . . he puts his horns in his pocket; for he would not have discharged the man unless there had been something in it!

When it came to assessing the amount of the damages, William Middleton's counsel stressed that the fact that Rose was a servant exacerbated his crime, since he had broken the bond of confidence and trust between man and master. Worse still was the evidence that 'to this very hour their criminal intercourse is continuing'. And worst of all was the evidence that on one occasion Rose 'contrived . . . to violate his master's honour in his own conjugal bed whilst he is absent'. Middleton's lawyer went on to ram this point home. He put it to the jurymen:

let me ask you, if such a misfortune was necessarily to happen to you, where was the last place you would chose to have the scene enacted? Every man will say his conjugal bed is the last. So I say, if there can be anything more to violate the feelings of every man of sentiment, or every man of honour, of every man with the smallest affection for his wife, it would be to have such a scene transacted in the place which had afforded him confort and happiness for the space of ten or eleven years.

William Middleton's counsel also referred to the pain and suffering of his client who would never know for certain whether he or John Rose was the father of the baby to which Clara Louisa had given birth on 4 January 1794. He also made the point that even if, as was likely, it was Clara Louisa who first seduced John Rose, rather than vice versa, the latter's continuing connection with her 'marks such a callous and depraved mind as will not, in my opinion, admit of the slightest excuse'. He admitted that no money could compensate a cuckolded husband for 'the total destruction of his honour, which he has lost', but argued that large damages were needed in this case, in order to clear William Middleton of any suspicion of collusion or entrapment.

Finally, William's counsel admitted that John Rose was poor, and in no position to pay heavy damages, but he argued that poverty should not be a bar to punishment: 'The law will not suffer the honour and happiness of the husband to be violated because a person can say "I am poor and therefore cannot pay any damages."' In any case, if Rose was poor, Clara Louisa for the time being was not, thanks to her £600-a-year temporary alimony from William. Moreover, Rose's elegant appearance in court showed that he still 'riots and wallows in luxury' at Clara Louisa's expense. 'Up to this very hour . . . this man is living in a state of gross and infamous adultery, supported by her means, and rioting in the wealth she is taking from her husband's pocket.'[136] It was a very able speech, which was followed by lengthy depositions of witnesses about the known facts of the adulterous connection.

For the defence, Mr Allen, the solicitor, began by denying—somewhat implausibly—that Clara Louisa had 'the smallest interest in the event of this suit', and that his client was John Rose and no one else. He explained that the failure to defend the suit was due to Rose's inability to raise the 'many hundred pounds' needed to collect, transport, house, and prepare his witnesses from Yorkshire. He then turned to easier questions, the first being the possible motive of William Middleton in bringing the suit. It could not be to bolster his case in the ecclesiastical court, since the latter did not accept a common-law verdict as evidence. It could not be to clear the way for a Parliamentary Act of Divorce, since the Middletons were Catholics and regarded marriage as an indissoluble sacrament. It could hardly be to get money, since Rose had none, and anyway Middleton was too honourable a man to act on such sordid motives. The only possible conclusion, therefore, was that William's motive had to be revenge, to win an award of punitive damages far beyond Rose's capacity to pay, which would effectively condemn him to a debtors' prison for the rest of his life, and 'deprive him totally of his liberty'. If not revenge, then the motive must be to score a moral victory, 'to carry this verdict in his pocket as a matter of triumph', without attempting to execute it.

He reminded the jury that there was still no indubitable proof that adultery had actually taken place, and that there was not a shred of evidence that Rose 'made any advances to her'. Such advances as may have been made must have been on the part of Clara Louisa, and Rose could have been no more than a passive partner in the connection, whatever it was. This being the case, Mr Allen pleaded that, in view of Rose's 'circumstances and situation . . . a small measure of damages will suffice'.

The Sheriff then gave his directions to the jury. He told them that the

[136] LPCA, Eee.17, fo. 55; *Middleton* v. *Rose*, 8–20.

adultery was admitted, since no defence had been offered. He said that, in his opinion, Mr Middleton had not been guilty of giving 'the slightest encouragement to the least indecorum', and therefore was free of any suspicion of collusion in his wife's guilt. He denied that poverty was a valid justification for small damages, since, if they were small, they 'would throw an imputation upon the plaintiff's case'. This added up to an instruction for moderate damages, and the jury complied with a verdict of £500 plus costs, which the sheriff assessed at £154. John Rose was therefore faced with a bill for £654 before he could obtain his freedom.[137] This was one of several examples of juries awarding substantial damages in a crim. con. case against a lower-class man, although it was self-evident that the wife must have been the seducer and the man could not pay. The point was made in another case in 1807, citing this case as an example.[138]

That the prime purpose of the suit was to bring William Middleton's side of the story before the public as soon as possible was proved by the rapid publication of a full transcript of the legal speeches and depositions of witnesses, especially those for the prosecution, accompanied by an explanatory introduction and overtly partisan footnotes. Unlike similar published reports about particular legal cases, this pamphlet was openly stated to be 'more immediately intended for the public at large than for Gentlemen of the Long Robe, for whose use reports are usually published'.[139]

Meanwhile, the gigantic lawsuit in the London Consistory Court was slowly grinding on. It will be remembered that the suit had started in the summer of 1793, and that by the summer of 1794 the publication of the huge mass of documentation had been decreed. This was an end to the admission of evidence, which thereafter could be neither retracted nor added to without the express permission of the court. But at the last minute, in January 1795, William's proctor brought in an affidavit of William Middleton and himself, stating 'that since the publication of the depositions, evidence of certain facts of adultery had come to their knowledge' and therefore asked permission formally to add the new evidence to that already before the court. This put the judge, Sir William Scott, in a very difficult legal position. By tradition, nothing could be added on either side after the publication of the depositions. The reason for this rule was fear of subornation of witnesses to induce them to retract or alter previous depositions, and the near-certainty of the further prolongation and cost of the suit. On the other hand, if he allowed the production of the new evidence of recent

---

[137] *Middleton* v. *Rose*, 63–8; LPCA, E.48/26.
[138] *Fowler* v. *Hodgson* (1807); *Crim. Con. Gaz.* 1 (1830), 93.
[139] *Middleton* v. *Rose*, 1.

adultery taking place while the suit was under litigation, this would 'throw great light on the real state of the facts, and will . . . materially serve the interest of truth'. He therefore allowed the new evidence to be brought before the court.

Sir William Scott pointed out that Clara Louisa, if innocent, had nothing to lose from the admission of the new evidence for, 'if these new facts cannot be proved, her character will be vindicated'. He therefore urged her not to block the admission of the new evidence, by appealing up to the Court of Arches his decision to allow it. But, knowing well how damaging to her defence would be the evidence of her recent association with John Rose in Littlehampton, Lowestoft, and London, Clara Louisa instructed her proctor to object to the admission of this new evidence. Her argument was that 'the cause should not have been commenced if the husband had not evidence enough, and that he ought to get sentence on the facts alleged in the former part of the case'. When she was overruled, she appealed the decision of Sir William Scott to the Court of Arches on this technical procedural issue, despite the publicly stated opinion of Sir William that 'he thought her very ill-advised'. The Court of Arches took its time: it agreed to accept the appeal of Clara Louisa only in November 1795, and published the final sentence dismissing it only in May 1796.[140] The London Consistory Court heard the new evidence and declared the Middletons separated from bed and board, on the grounds of the adultery of Clara Louisa. As a result she lost her alimony, as well as all rights of access to her children. Just over three years after her ignominious expulsion from Stockeld Park, the legal battle was at last at an end.

It is possible to make some rough estimate of what all this litigation cost, bearing in mind the fact that her husband William had to pay for the assessed costs in the ecclesiastical courts of Clara Louisa as well as his own. It was reported that he had spent 'immense sums' on the suit, and this must certainly be true. For her total legal and other expenses must have come to well over £1,000. How she managed to pay this huge sum is unknown, unless her family came to her rescue or she had some private money of her own. After 1796 all she received from William was her pin-money of £100 a year.[141] Her mother and brother must have been infuriated when they learnt that, at the very time that they were making every effort to support her and her legal defence, she had been secretly continuing her intimate relations with John Rose. It made them look like

[140] *Eng. Rep.* 162: 1038–41; LPCA, D.1395: 4906; B.19/92; E.48/22, 26; E.11/75; E.17, fos. 41–55, G.155/45, 56–8, 64–5; *Middleton v. Rose,* 5 n.*.
[141] LPCA, D.1395: 4900; J.23/23.

gullible fools, and may well have induced them to wash their hands of her.

(vii) *Conclusion*

The society

The story of the Middleton affair is more than merely a familiar, banal, tale of female adultery and its aftermath. The evidence thrown up by it exposes a microcosm of life in an eighteenth-century large village or small town and a small country house which is unsurpassed in the intimacy of its detail concerning the thoughts and behaviour of all classes from the squire to the labourer.

In the first place, it demonstrates how the domestic affairs of a great landlord directly impinged upon the lives and economic welfare of a large circle of dependents, including most of the inhabitants of the village next to the country seat. Although Wetherby was primarily a busy coaching halt on the Great North Road, many of its inhabitants were servants of the Middletons, or at one time or another had worked or still worked in and around the great house. They had a direct stake in its continued occupancy, and its abandonment must have hit the local economy hard. No longer would the women find casual work wet-nursing children, sewing clothes, washing laundry, or weeding in the garden. No longer would the men be employed to mend the furniture, renew the upholstery, fix the plumbing, maintain the carpentry, make the clothes and shoes, attend the horses, or brew the beer. No longer would the local shops supply at least some of the necessities for the household and its guests. No longer would the alehouses do a roaring trade with lively, hard-drinking menservants of an evening. No longer would the lads of the village be able to slip up to the house at dead of night, climb in through the chapel tribune window, and 'bundle' with the maids. No longer would the young menservants climb out to go roving about the village looking for likely girls to woo. No longer would those villagers who were Roman Catholic be able to come up to the Chapel every Sunday to attend mass, and to confess their sins at Easter. No longer would Clara Louisa be available to provide medicines and necessaries for the needy and to arrange medical treatment for the sick. The social, economic, medical, sexual, and even religious aspects of life in the village were thus deeply affected by the mere presence of the Middletons at Stockeld Park. Their departure was severely felt, as was shown by the tumultuous reception accorded to Clara Louisa in 1794. The villagers not only wanted to see her honour vindicated; they wanted her back and the house kept open.

Middleton *v*. Middleton

If the villagers were drawn into the fray, even more so were the domestic servants. In size and functional organization, the Stockeld Park household was an intermediate one. Composed of ten to twelve servants, fairly equally divided between men and women, it was not like those of the great mansions with their staffs of thirty to fifty persons, mostly men, arranged in strict hierarchy of rank and each with a highly specialized function. Nor was it like the small establishments of two or three servants attendant upon someone of middle-class rank and income. There was only one servant's hall at Stockeld, and most of the servants performed varied functions, the coachman and groom acting as footmen at table when there were guests for dinner, and the kitchen-maid helping to make the beds. Hierarchy of rank was obscure, competition and jealousy were rife, and in consequence the internal tensions in the servants' hall ran very high. These tensions rose higher still as the domestic crisis upstairs came to a head, especially since one of themselves, the outside servant John Rose, was personally involved. It is hardly surprising that downstairs finally exploded in angry quarrels and even physical violence.

Since the servants consisted of equal numbers of young men and young women, all unmarried, the kitchen and servants' hall inevitably became arenas where were played out scenes of sexual flirtation, indiscretion, intrigue, frustration, and jealousy. Drink was unlimited, and drinking to excess a common failing among the servants. But life for them was far from free, for they were expected to be back at the house by ten or eleven o'clock at night, and no visitors were allowed thereafter. As one might expect, they found ways around these regulations. They not only disobeyed orders never to use the only water-closet in the house, but they sometimes kept the Chapel tribune window open at night for easy ingress and egress for themselves and their suitors. Who was courting whom, who was in love with whom, who was sleeping with whom, who was pregnant by whom, who was secretly married to whom were standard staples of gossip below stairs, passed on by her lady's maid to the eager ears of Clara Louisa above stairs.

Every now and then the servants would all kick over the traces, especially at the regular annual feast-days in the neighbouring villages. Indeed these feasts and fairs, relics of an ancient communal past, emerge as bacchanalian orgies that punctuated the eighteenth-century rural year. It was all-night drunken attendance at the Spofforth feast in November 1791 which led to a general tongue-lashing of several male servants by William Middleton the next day, causing two or three of them to give notice in protest. It was the Sickling Hall feast which would have been the undoing of the groom John Robinson, had he not had the prudence to apologize for his late-night revelling before being reprimanded. Another servant got leave to go to St Wilfred's feast at Ripon, this time apparently without any untoward consequences. But it was on fair day at Wetherby that Hodgson got so excited that he told everyone in the crowded bar at the Blue Boar that Clara Louisa had been given venereal disease by John Rose.

And it was the drunken goings-on at the fair at Thorp Arch which cost Lawrence Thorp his job as personal servant to Miss Haggerston. He and his mistress had gone for the night to Mr Fox's house at Bramham Park nearby. He and all the servants were given leave to go to the fair, 'where Mr Fox's servants got too much in liquor, and they went with him home to Miss Haggerston's house in Thorp Arch, where they behaved riotously and made a great disturbance'. When Miss Haggerston got to hear of it, she discharged Thorp on the spot, notwithstanding seven and a half years of faithful service.[142]

One of the features of the Stockeld Park household was the casually exploitative attitude of both master and servants. No servant lasted very long; indeed in 1791 not one of the domestic staff had been at Stockeld longer than five years. Servants themselves did not hesitate to give notice if affronted or annoyed, and the master and mistress dismissed servants on minor provocation and without compunction. If an individual servant fell sick and was unable to perform his or her duties, he or she was discharged. If the master closed down the house and went abroad for a while, as William Middleton proposed to do in early 1793 when he planned an extensive trip first to Bath and then to the Continent, the servants would be dismissed, only a skeleton staff being left on board wages. When the Middletons moved to Stockeld Park after getting married, they found no established body of servants waiting for them, since the house had been indirectly inherited some time before and then rented. In consequence, when the crisis broke, there was no responsible old retainer with long service in the family to whom to turn for comfort and advice.

Under these circumstances, when the time of testing came, fidelity and loyalty turned out to be commodities in rather short supply. Servants could be bought for money, but could not be relied upon. Suspicion of adultery committed by the mistress of the house with one of themselves instantly converted some of the servants into spies—there were never less than four in the house at any one time. All were thrown into turmoil as they tried to calculate how best to profit by their knowledge, and how to save themselves from being caught in the possible dissolution of the household. The first decision was whether or not to get involved. Some, particularly the senior

---

[142] LPCA, D.1395: 3373–6, 3380–1, 3446–8, 4498, 4621, 4647.

servants and the lady's maid, had little choice. They could either take sides, or leave as the butler Baldwin did: neutrality for them was impossible. Other servants in less prominent positions found it easier to watch and wait, spying assiduously, and sometimes taking written notes of what they saw or heard. After the crash came, they were usually ready to sell their information or their silence to the highest bidder. Not a few were prepared to embroider on the truth, if they were paid enough to do so.

The next decision was whether to side with the master or the mistress. The former had more to offer, but female solidarity and friendship often induced the lady's maid actively to collude with her mistress, at any rate for a while. In the end, however, a sense of what was morally right, or a fear of the consequences, usually led to betrayal. Before the court Hannah Canridge stated her sense of what was expected of her: 'I conceive it to be every servant's duty, upon discovering a formal intrigue of his mistress, to make the same known directly or indirectly to his master, unless he can without such information prevent the same from being carried on.' Later she elaborated a little, saying: 'I profess I was bound to reveal to my master any conspiracy against his fortune, his honour or life that I might happen to know as soon as I did know it.' On the other hand, she explained that she had refrained from telling William Middleton of his wife's infidelity for many months since she knew he would not believe her (as indeed he did not); since she did not want to spoil the happiness of the family (meaning more likely that the ejection of her mistress would put her out of a job); and that she hoped to be able to persuade John Rose to leave the house and so put a stop to the intrigue.[143] This last was the policy advocated not only by her but also by the under-butler Robert Maltus and by William Middleton's elder brother, Marmaduke Maxwell. An alternative tactic was that employed by Elizabeth Aspinall, who followed the principle that 'those that say the least about it are the best off'. As she discovered, this brought immediate rewards, but it also ran the risk of alienating one or both parties in the dispute.[144]

There was also the more activist option of out-and-out commitment to one side or the other. This was adopted by William Davis, who acted more like a private detective and enforcer than a butler; on the other side there was the young stable boy, Thomas Birkenshaw, who resolutely but implausibly denied that he had ever seen anything improper, despite both cajoling and a severe beating. Finally, there were a few unscrupulous turncoats, such as William Hodgson, who kept trying to maximize his blackmail leverage or economic advantage by first concealing, then revealing,

---

[143] Ibid. 671, 744.　　　[144] Ibid. 2775.

then retracting, and then restating his story, some of the details of which were in any case patently false. One way or another, the attitude of the servants to the domestic crisis was mostly a mixture of prurient curiosity and a keen eye to the main chance. Only Robert Maltus seems to have been at first genuinely concerned about the human tragedy that was developing, so much so that he developed insomnia from worrying about how to put a stop to it.

Thanks to the unique richness of the documentation, it is possible to expose all the details of the moral, psychological, and financial inducements of reward and the threats of punishment proferred by both sides in order to persuade the servants to give, manufacture, or conceal evidence as their interests might dictate. Perjury, subornation, and concealment of witnesses were common, even normal, features of these cases, and go far to explain the directly contradictory evidence so often offered in court. An intense struggle, not so much for the hearts and minds as for the voices of the servants, began the day the marriage broke up, and would continue until the final judgment in the subsequent lawsuits. The servants were at the same time confidants and spies, advisers and manipulators, protectors and blackmailers, accomplices and betrayers. There was a built-in ambiguity in all such relationships.

There were a number of signs of modernity in the little world of Stockeld Park and the nearby village of Wetherby. There were new technological devices, such as the fast stage coaches rumbling up and down the Great North Road, or the brand new water-closet installed by the Middletons for their personal use. There are also one or two changes in fashion, for example, the trend to bathing. The bathing well in the park, used by both family and servants during the summer, was surely a novelty. And there was the new habit, apparently well established with old Mrs Grace, of spending the summer by the seaside. Finally, Clara Louisa's romantic infatuation with a groom may well have owed something, perhaps a lot, to her reading of the trashy novels of the day, which certainly served as exemplars for Hannah Canridge's arch and stilted prose. It is also possible that William's policy of allowing the servants to use the bathing pool, and turning a blind eye to their use of the one water-closet, and Clara Louisa's habit of allowing the menial servants to talk with her with their hats on, are all signs of the influence of more socially egalitarian ideas derived ultimately from the French Revolution.

Another relative novelty was the high level of literacy. All the servants could read and write, with the exception of the dairymaid and the wet-nurse, and both Davis, the butler, and Bouvier, the cook, kept notes in memorandum books of suspicious events they witnessed (Father Thomas

Hussey in London did the same). It was a letter from the lady's maid Hannah Canridge to William's brother which first alerted the Constable family to what was going on. Publicity about the affair was spread by correspondence by the servants: the butler Davis sent letters to his friends in service elsewhere, and Margaret Wilkins, the laundry maid, sent a letter to her sister.[145] By 1790 Stockeld Park was an almost entirely literate universe, a factor which had important effects on how matters developed.

Even the London press, with its relatively new taste for scandalmongering, became involved in the struggle. Before the suit came to trial, the Constables tried to use the press to publicize their side of the story, by planting a scurrilous account of the adultery in the *Bon Ton Magazine*. After their victory in the crim. con. case, they took care to have a stenographic record of the trial published as a pamphlet. The scandal was clearly the talk of London, and, having won the battle, the Middleton–Constable family used the printing press to make its victory as widely known as possible.

The extreme hatred felt for the local gamekeeper was a feature peculiar to the eighteenth and early nineteenth centuries. So also, perhaps, was the easy ecumenical religious atmosphere of Yorkshire, which was a world away from the anti-Popish passions of the seventeenth century, which were still simmering just below the surface in London, as shown in the Gordon Riots of 1780, in which the butler Davis apparently played a courageous part. The Middletons were devout Catholics, and their indoor servants were virtually exclusively Catholic, and yet they were on the most friendly social terms with the local Anglican parsons and their wives, and with the local Anglican nobility and gentry.

The marital breakdown

In its basic features, the story of the breakdown of the marriage seems like a straightforward but tragic case. Clara Louisa was an energetic and strong-willed woman, married to a wealthy aristocratic rural landowner who was completely under her thumb and gave in to her every wish. She was a dutiful wife and a loving mother, but in 1791, after ten years of marriage and seven children, she was bored. She was bored with living year in and year out in the country house isolated in its park; bored with the endless dinner parties with the neighbouring gentry and parsons; bored with her amiable but dull husband. She was uninterested in country sports, and frightened of riding; contemptuous of the spineless domestic chaplain; and perhaps sexually deprived as well as tired of the stress of almost annual pregnancies. She had formed no really close female friendships, and her

[145] Ibid. 1226, 1229, 1317–18, 1519, 1594–605.

affections were focused on her children, an old horse, and an old dog. But these were not enough to satisfy her longing for romantic love, about which she must have been constantly reading in the novels and poems of the day, but which she once admitted that she had never experienced before she met John Rose.

At that juncture there joined the household a handsome, debonair Don Juan of a groom of the hunting stable, with a taste for elegant clothes as well as a winning way with the ladies. His reputation as a sexual athlete aroused the interest of his mistress, who began to haunt the stables, fell in love with him, and gave him money and clothes to spruce himself up. There were more frequent meetings and secret assignations, and more lavish gifts of money and jewellery—much of these signs of infatuation occurring at a time when she herself was in an advanced stage of pregnancy. Finally she directly declared her affection for him, and they exchanged embraces and kisses. Whether there was more still remains not entirely certain. The doubt about guilt or innocence of adultery of Clara Louisa was genuine, and it was the fact that each side was supported by wealthy and well-connected families which generated what seems to have been the largest, the most expensive, and the most long-drawn-out marital lawsuit of the century. When the domestic crisis burst open, and Clara Louisa was expelled, it is remarkable how quickly the two families of origin broke apart again and became two warring factions. There is reason to suppose that the Constable family had never been very enthusiastic about the financially rather disadvantageous marriage of William to the daughter of a cadet branch of an ancient but not very distinguished Dublin family. But, as long as the marriage held, the brothers of the two protagonists, Marmaduke Maxwell and Richard Grace, did their best to keep it intact. After the break, however, the Constables formed a solid front, and the Graces rallied loyally around Clara Louisa, despite their certain knowledge of her romantic infatuation with a groom. No expense was spared on either side to hire lawyers and detectives and to muster a formidable array of witnesses, while the Graces actually spirited away and hid the key actor in the drama, John Rose himself.

Clara Louisa was amazingly successful over a very long period of time in convincing her friends and relatives of her innocence of actual adultery, despite the weight of circumstantial evidence against her. The reason for this unwillingness to believe in her guilt lay in the system of values of the century. Élite opinion on the whole was tolerant of adultery by the male, especially with women of inferior social status such as maidservants, kept mistresses, or prostitutes. Outside the highest court circles, however, it had always been severely critical of female adultery, even with persons of the same social status.

Middleton v. Middleton

But the one sexual relationship that was totally outside the bounds of the moral order in eighteenth-century England was adultery between an upper-class woman and a lower-class male, especially a mere domestic servant. Such a liaison represented the gravest of social inversions, as well as a breach of the theoretical bond of fidelity between servant and master. It also involved the risk that a great estate might pass to a child of lower-class paternity. There was, therefore, something peculiarly repugnant to the patriarchal ideology of the time for an upper-class woman to choose as a lover a servant in preference to a gentleman. It was a shocking example of the world turned upside down. Even the domestic servants shared both the double sexual standard and the highly deferential ideology of their masters above stairs. They had clear ideas about norms of behaviour suitable to each rank, even if in practice their daily duties threw them into the most intimate relationship with their superiors.

This was why so many people, including all of Clara Louisa's relatives, her friends, and the villagers themselves, persisted so long in their conviction of her innocence of the accusation against her. They could not believe that this devoted wife and mother, this pious Catholic chapel-goer, this kindly patroness of the village, this model of female propriety, this elegant, well-born, and well-educated lady, should have sullied herself and humiliated her husband by copulating with her groom in the grass or the hay, much less in the marital bed.

This lawsuit took place at a time when the ideal of the affection-bonded child-oriented nuclear family was quite common in the very topmost levels of high society. The cosy and intimate domestic atmosphere at Stockeld Park before the crash, with Clara Louisa devoting so much time and affection to her children, letting them romp about in her bedroom before breakfast, teaching them herself, and tucking them into bed every night, was characteristic of the late eighteenth century. So, too, was the psychological involvement of William with his young wife, which had begun when he first selected her, apparently against the wishes of his family.

Clara Louisa's sudden overwhelming passion for the dashing young stable boy may well have been inspired by a reading of contemporary romantic novels, which aroused in her a longing for an all-consuming love that her amiable but plodding husband had never satisfied. In that sense, her socially abhorrent infatuation with a stable boy was a reflection of the current idealization of romantic love, and was therefore peculiar to the period. But so also was the deep melancholia induced in William Middleton by news of the infidelity of his wife in the marital bed, and the tenacious thirst for revenge which drove him in his relentless legal pursuit of his wife and her lover, as well as in the brutal execution of her favourite dog and

horse. It was thwarted romantic love which filled him with an overwhelming desire to destroy both Clara Louisa and John Rose, even if in the
process he should destroy his own happiness.

The protagonists in the case

What are we to make of John Rose, the seducer of girls, the elegant dresser,
the penniless low-born groom of the hunting stables, who in the end was
passing for a gentleman in fine clothes supplied by his mistress and lady
friend? Clara Louisa evidently loved him to distraction, and for his sake in
the end lost her reputation, her husband, her children, her money, and her
comfortable life. But what did he think of her? Was he merely selling her
his company and his body like a gigolo? On the one hand, the long periods
they spent in each other's company without sex, but merely laughing and
chattering together, suggest genuine affection on his part as well as hers.
On the other hand, some observations rather doubtfully attributed to him
cast his attitude in a more cynical light. It was reported—and denied—that
he once remarked that: 'I am almost master of the place, and if I stay in
my place I will have a sufficiency to live upon. I damn working.' At other
times, he was said to have boasted that, 'I am kind to my mistress' or 'she
is kind with me', a highly imprudent piece of sexual braggadocio, if indeed
it was made.[146] The story of how he wheedled money out of Clara Louisa
in London to pay for some new breeches certainly proves that he was
trading kisses for cash.

Today, two hundred years later, despite three judicial decisions in three
different courts of law, all of which went against her, and despite over half
a million words of argument and testimony, it is still not certain beyond the
possibility of doubt that Clara Louisa was technically guilty of adultery.
There is no question whatever that at the age of 30 she became totally
infatuated with the stable groom John Rose, to the extent that she was
prepared to run the risk of sacrificing husband, children, home, fortune,
and reputation to keep company with him. She was even prepared to
deceive her mother, her brother, and perhaps her father confessor over a
period of years in order to continue to meet John in secret while the trial
was still in progress. The most likely explanation of her conduct is therefore
that she was a woman in the prime of her sexual powers, who found herself
suddenly overwhelmed by uncontrollable physical passion. Her slumbering
libido was at last awakened by a man with wide experience in the ways of

---

[146] Ibid. 3463, 3833.

giving sexual pleasure to women. The probability is that the contemporary courts were right, and that the connection between Clara Louisa and John Rose was not only romantic but also sexual.

There is, however, a shadow of uncertainty about the truth of this scenario. In the first place, despite the fact that her every movement was constantly being spied upon by many observers over a period of several years, no one ever testified that he or she had seen anything take place between them more serious than holding hands, hugging, kissing, or walking arm in arm. Secondly, so pious a woman as Clara Louisa would surely have revealed her adultery in the confession box if she had been guilty, and yet her confessor Father Hussey stood by her to the end, as was his duty. Thirdly, there is her remark that John had treated her remarkably well, considering all the liberties she had allowed him. Fourthly, there is the fact that John was apparently afflicted with venereal disease during at least some part of their association. Fifthly, there is the evidence of his landlady that, when John was living in secret in London in 1795, Clara Louisa never entered his bedroom, but always waited for him to get dressed and come into another room. Finally, it has to be remembered that, during the whole period of their association, John was constantly pursuing and sleeping with other women, at least some of which seductions were well known to Clara Louisa. As for the episode of the night of 30–1 March, John was certainly either in her maid's bedroom or hers, but it is impossible to prove that it was definitely the latter. Moreover, why did he take a drunken companion along with him to a lovers' all-night meeting? Furthermore, in 1792 Clara Louisa was clearly trying to break herself of her infatuation with Rose. She opposed his return to the household after his first dismissal in 1792, and was acquiescent in, and may actually have proposed, the plan to shut up the house and go abroad for an extended period in 1793. Taken all together, the evidence certainly proves that Clara Louisa loved John Rose to distraction, but leaves it uncertain whether or not she ever actually slept with him. If she had not, this would go far to explain why she put up so strenuous a defence against the accusation of adultery, fighting desperately, recklessly, and expensively in the courts for a period of three years.

By the time if was all over, however, public opinion had turned strongly against her. In a discussion of a bill against adultery in the House of Lords in 1800 the Earl of Carlisle referred to the motives behind Clara Louisa Middleton's long legal battle in the following harsh terms:

knowing that at length she must be divorced [i.e. separated] and irrecoverably driven from society, she would at least protract the time, and interpose five years between her detection and ultimate disgrace; which she would be the better able to do as all the proceedings would be at the expense of her husband.[147]

This view of the Middleton case was shared by members of the legal profession, who regarded this prolonged litigation as a classic example of how a guilty woman could use her husband's money and the complexities of the law to defer a final sentence.

The consequences

Whichever interpretation of Clara Louisa's motives and actions is correct, the consequences of her stubborn defence were ironically a tragedy for all parties involved. By the time William Middleton had completed his fanatical vendetta in 1796, he was a broken-hearted recluse. He had killed his wife's favourite dog and horse, destroyed her reputation by publicly exposing her as an adulteress with a stable boy, closed up his country seat, discharged most of his servants, and sent his children off to boarding school. He had withdrawn in melancholy and lonely isolation to a very small hunting lodge on the moors of Yorkshire, where he continued to live almost alone until he died half a century later in 1847. His only addition to the house was a private chapel, so perhaps he found some consolation for the ruin of his life in the comforts of the Roman Catholic Church. During all this while, Stockeld Park remained shuttered and empty.

As for Clara Louisa, she had correctly prophesied at Lowestoft that she was 'ruined in both character and fortune'. All of her elder children were almost certainly never allowed to see their mother again until they had reached majority and were free to decide for themselves. Moreover, her new baby would forever be suspected of being the bastard of a stable boy. As for John Rose, it is to be presumed that Clara Louisa somehow scraped together the £654 to pay the court-assessed costs and damages and so to keep him out of gaol. But, unless she had inherited money of her own, which is possible, she was now almost entirely dependent financially on the good will of her relations, her old mother in London and her brother Richard in Dublin. She had grossly deceived and shamed them by secretly consorting with John Rose at Littlehampton and Lowestoft, at the same time as she was making vigorous assertions of injured innocence under oath in court. They may therefore have washed their hands of her. It seems very unlikely that her infatuation for John Rose survived the revelation of his venereal disease and his concurrent amours (only some of which she had known about at the time). If they did stay together, however, the pair would have had to withdraw abroad or to some remote part of Great

[147] W. Cobbett, *Parliamentary History of England* (London, 1806–20), 35: 380.

Britain in order to escape from the public obloquy which now surrounded them. Clara Louisa lived on after the end of the trial for another thirty-eight years, only dying in 1833, but in what circumstances we do not know. Like Samson, William Middleton obtained his revenge for the terrible injury that he believed had been done to him, but in so doing he brought down the temple. Between them he and Clara Louisa created a desert of broken lives around them, all because of an attachment which was universally regarded as socially unacceptable.

It is generally agreed that one of the mainsprings of the novel since the eighteenth century has been adultery. In the Middleton case, reality has imitated art, even to the extent of leaving the truth still full of ambiguities.

9
Loveden v. Loveden
The lady and the don, 1794–1811

Born in 1750, Edward Loveden Townsend inherited his father's fortune in 1767, which enabled him to complete his studies at Winchester and enter Trinity College, Oxford, as a Gentleman Commoner. In 1772 his maternal uncle Edward Loveden died without children, leaving him his whole estate (see Genealogy of the Loveden family). Edward Loveden Townsend consequently took by royal licence his uncle's name and arms, thus becoming Edward Loveden Loveden, and inherited Buscot Park near Faringdon in Berkshire, where the Lovedens had been seated for three centuries. Later, between 1780 and 1783, he rebuilt and enlarged the old family seat in the latest fashion, making it one of the finest houses in the county.

Edward Loveden Loveden was a man of considerable culture, if not refinement. He was an accomplished classical scholar who built up a fine library at Buscot Park, and he took an amateur interest in a variety of intellectual pursuits. He was given an LLD degree by Oxford University and elected a Fellow of the Royal Society and of the Society of Antiquaries. When young 'he was remarkably handsome' and 'delighted in keeping what is called a good house' at Buscot Park. He sat for several decades in the House of Commons as a member for the 'country' interest, voting in a non-party manner and distinguished only for his somewhat naïve insistence that 'an unblemished moral character was a *sine qua non* in a minister'. This emphasis of his on moral integrity was to play its part in the closing stages of his third marriage. Wraxall, who knew him from the early 1780s, observed that 'his figure, manners and address all bespoke a substantial yeoman rather than a person of education and condition, but he did not lack common sense, nor language in which to clothe his ideas'.[1]

In 1773 he married Margaret Pryse, a Welsh heiress with property worth over £1,000 a year, a life interest in which came to Edward on her death in 1784. She left one surviving son, Pryse Loveden, who changed his name to

[1] L. B. Namier and J. Brooke, *History of Parliament, The House of Commons, 1754–1790* (London, 1964), s.n. Loveden; *Gent's Mag.* 1 (1822), 88–9; N. W. Wraxall, *Memoirs, 1772–84*, ed. H. B. Wheatley (London, 1884), v. 251.

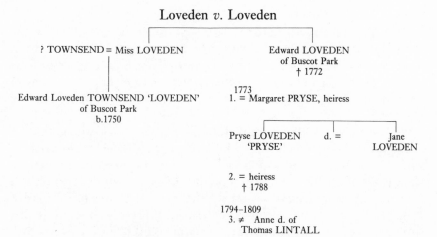

Loveden *v.* Loveden

? TOWNSEND = Miss LOVEDEN

Edward Loveden TOWNSEND 'LOVEDEN'
of Buscot Park
b.1750

Edward LOVEDEN
of Buscot Park
† 1772

1773
1. = Margaret PRYSE, heiress

Pryse LOVEDEN   d. =   Jane
'PRYSE'   LOVEDEN

2. = heiress
† 1788

1794–1809
3. ≠ Anne d. of
Thomas LINTALL

4. Genealogy of the Loveden family

Pryse Pryse when he later acquired her inheritance. There were also two surviving daughters, one married to a clergyman and the other a cripple who lived at Buscot Park with her father, confined to the ground floor by her disability. Soon after his first wife's death, Edward Loveden married yet another and even richer heiress (her father was a wealthy London hop-merchant), whose childless death in 1788 left him with a life interest in her property in the Midlands, worth £4,500 a year. The third time around he again sought a wealthy bride, this time settling for one with a large cash portion. She was Anne, daughter of Thomas Lintall of Norbiton Hall, Kingston, in Surrey, who brought with her a marriage portion of £13,000 in 3 per cent bank annuities, which provided Edward with another £400 a year. Edward Loveden Loveden's very large fortune was thus entirely built upon inheritances from an uncle and three wives.[2] In 1809 he declared under oath that he enjoyed a gross income of £8,667 a year, encumbered with debts of £54,000, probably caused by the expense of building Buscot Park in the 1780s. After deduction of interest and mortgage payments, his net income was still a very comfortable £5,100 a year.[3]

When she married Edward in 1794 Anne Lintall was 21 and Edward was 43, so that she was younger than her husband by over twenty years. It may well have been her mother who promoted so socially advantageous a marriage, and in 1807–8 Mrs Lintall came on a lengthy year-long visit to her daughter and son-in-law at Buscot Park, not much to the satisfaction of

[2] Namier and Brooke, s.n. Loveden; *Gent's Mag.* 1 (1822), 88–9; *The Four Visitations of Berkshire, 1532, 1566, 1623, 1666, Harleian Soc.*, 56 (1908), i. 242; 57 (1908), ii. 172; N. Pevsner, *Berkshire* (The Buildings of England, 30; London, 1966), s.n. Buscot.
[3] LPCA, D.1312: 395–411.

Anne, who found her a bore.[4] There was also living in the house the
crippled daughter of Edward Loveden by his first wife, who by 1809 was
about 25 years old, a shadowy figure who played little part in the unfolding drama. This enlarged family resided for eight to nine months of
every year in Buscot Park, and spent the rest of the time in rented housing
in London.

We know very little about how Edward and his young wife got along.
It was said, without much supporting evidence, that 'she was to her husband a most affectionate and amiable wife; and in the estimation of the
whole circle of her friends, a lady of peculiar domestic habits, accomplished
manners, and unspotted virtue. At the dissipated fopperies of fashionable
men, Mr Loveden had no cause for alarm.' What we do know is that
Edward was often away from home, performing his official duties as MP,
first for Abingdon and later for Shaftesbury, as well as fulfilling his considerable obligations as Colonel of the Berkshire Militia during this period
of the Napoleonic Wars, when the county militia was permanently under
arms as defence against a French invasion. Attendance at the meetings of
the numerous societies of which he was a member must also have taken
him away a good deal, and, even when he was at Buscot Park, he spent
much of the time out coursing and hunting with his friends. Anne had a
stillborn child soon after the marriage, and thereafter was childless.[5] Judging
by a letter of hers, written in 1808, she felt neglected and lonely in the
great house, cut off from the world by its gardens, shrubbery, plantations,
and park. She found her daily routine profoundly boring. At that time
her mornings were usually spent in attending to the needs and wishes of
her husband, and her afternoons and evenings in acting as companion
to her elderly mother. But Edward was very hospitable, and the tedium was
somewhat relieved by the coming and going of a stream of visitors, including
many of his old friends, and by a month-long house party every Christmas.[6]

One of the more frequent guests from 1804 onwards was a young lay
Fellow of Merton College, Oxford, Thomas Raymond Barker.[7] He was a
younger son in a large landed family of eight or nine children, and therefore

---

[4] Ibid. 113; *Trial of an Action by Edward Loveden, Esq. against Thomas Raymond Barker,
Esq. for criminal conversation* (London, 1810), 13; I am greatly indebted to Mr Jordan D.
Luttrell of Meyer Boswell Books Inc. for lending me a copy of this very rare trial pamphlet,
and drawing my attention to yet another copy.

[5] *Trial*, x. 114.

[6] Ibid. 215–16; LPCA, D.1312: 80, 40; *JH Lords*, 48 (1810–12), 254a; Wraxall, *Memoirs*,
v. 251; *Gent's Mag.* 1 (1822), 88–9.

[7] Barker had matriculated at Oriel College in 1795 and taken his BA in 1799; he had been
elected Fellow of Merton in 1802 and had taken his MA a year later (I owe this information
to the kindness of Dr Roger Highfield).

had to make his own way in the world. His father was a close friend of Edward, and lived at Fairford Park, a big house nine miles away just over the border in Gloucestershire. Buscot Park was a convenient stopping place for the night during Thomas's many trips on horseback between Oxford and Fairford, and it also became something of a second home for him after his father had remarried in the early 1800s. Tom Barker, therefore, was 'received into the family of Mr Loveden in the most familiar state of hospitality and friendship'. Indeed Edward Loveden supported him financially while he was at Oxford.[8]

In 1805 family, friends, and servants at Buscot first began to notice and gossip about the growing intimacy between the bored and childless Anne and the young bachelor don. The pair took every opportunity to be alone together, and showed overt signs of falling in love. The housekeeper, Hannah Calcutt, later testified that she already suspected that the couple had 'conceived a criminal passion for each other'. One old family friend took it upon himself to warn Anne of the gossip, merely to have her snap back at him: 'Since Mr Barker behaves so well to me, I cannot behave otherwise than I do.' At this stage the old gentleman only suspected 'partiality', and so held his peace. But the love-affair continued through 1806 and 1807, during which time the servants observed how Anne and Thomas often walked arm in arm about the grounds of the house, and how in Edward's absence they would remain shut up for long periods together in Anne's upstairs dressing-room, which she used as her private drawing-room and to which gentlemen were not normally admitted. It was also known that, when Thomas was away, he and Anne contrived secretly to exchange letters. The upper groom testified that: 'I heard my fellow servants remark on the particular behaviour of Mr Barker and Mrs Loveden to each other, which was frequently the subject of conversation among them.'[9]

During the year 1806 more and more evidence accumulated that the relationship between Thomas and Anne was more than that of a platonic friendship. Whenever Thomas came to visit, Anne ordered the servants to tell visitors that she was not at home, and in July of that year the butler first saw something to suggest that there was physical intimacy between them. Early one morning, when Edward was away presiding over a meeting of the local Agricultural Society, he noticed first Anne and then Thomas go into her private dressing-room before she had even rung the bell to announce she was awake. They stayed there for some forty minutes before coming down for breakfast. He also noticed that they ate sitting close together, with

[8] LPCA, D.1312: 21, 114–15; *Trial*, 6, 77, 80, 114–15.
[9] LPCA, D.1312: 79, 83, 98, 115, 123, 145, 189, 328, 353–4; *Trial*, 42–3, 288.

the tablecloth hanging down to conceal whatever was happening underneath. But standing as he was behind Anne's chair, he could see that they
'were almost constantly mixing their legs or feet together in a very peculiar
and indecent fashion'.[10]

In December 1806 Edward Loveden first began to suspect that something was wrong, when one morning he found Barker and Anne in her
dressing-room, with the door partly closed. He asked the advice of an old
friend, Francis Knight, the Inspector General of Army Hospitals. Edward
was 'very warm and indignant' about the episode, and expressed a determination to expel Anne and send her back to her mother. Knight expostu-
lated with him, pointing out that he had no evidence that any sexual
impropriety had taken place. Edward admitted that this was true, and
commented that the situation 'arose out of mere vanity in the man, who
was flirting with every woman he came near'. Knight strongly advised
Edward to carry on with the marriage, at least until he had some solid
evidence of Anne's adultery. He also took the precaution of talking to Tom
Barker, telling him of Edward's suspicions, and advising him 'to be as
sparing of his visits to Buscot Park as possible'. Barker naturally protested
his innocence, and so for a while the affair blew over.

Nine months later, however, in September 1807, Knight was urgently
summoned by Anne to Buscot Park. When he arrived he found that,
during her husband's absence, she and Tom had spent two nights at the
Barker family house at Fairford, contrary to Edward's express wishes.
Edward was furious with her, but once again Knight told him that, since he
had no evidence of any misconduct, there was no justification for a formal
separation. So, once again, the marriage was patched up. Edward still
believed in his wife's innocence, having made no attempt to find out from
the servants what, if anything, they knew.[11]

The Lovedens spent the first six months of 1807 in a rented house in
Knightsbridge in London, and the outdoor servants soon noticed that
when Anne went out in her carriage she often picked up Tom Barker in the
street. One warm and sultry day in May she made the coachman put up the
hood of the landau barouche, while they drove around the crowded West
End of London for a long time 'with the sun blinds drawn down'. When
they got out, Anne 'appeared much heated and very red', with her hair
disordered. It was difficult to avoid the conclusion that sexual relations of
some kind had taken place in the coach.[12] On another occasion the groom
saw Barker standing for a long time with his hands on her shoulders, and

[10] LPCA, D.1312: 96, 220–4, 355.   [11] *Trial*, 211–13.
[12] LPCA, D.1312: 28–9, 102–5, 183, 197–200; *Trial*, vi. 14–15, 27, 32–4, 119–21.

once 'clap his hand upon her rump' in an affectionate sexual gesture. All this was suggestive of adultery, but not conclusive, so the servants continued to do nothing but wait and watch.

After the family returned to Buscot Park in the summer of 1807 things became easier for the presumed lovers, since Thomas could stay in the house, even in Edward's absence, without arousing too much suspicion— or so he thought. In November, however, they had a narrow escape from detection. They were together upstairs in Anne's dressing-room when Edward unexpectedly returned. Hearing the front doorbell, Anne rushed out of her room and cried, 'I am not at home to anybody', only to be told by Edward's manservant, 'It's my master.' She just had time to return to her bedroom, and for Thomas to slip down to the library, while her husband and a friend were still talking in the conservatory.

Other encounters were equally fraught with danger of discovery. One day around Christmas 1807, when all the other guests were out coursing, the cook looked all over the house for Anne to ask her how to cook some fine fish. She searched high and low, but could not find her. Finally Anne emerged from the dining-room, followed shortly after by Tom. The cook noticed that she was 'very red in the face and extremely confused, and held her riding habit half-way up her legs as if she did not know what she did for the confusion she was in'.[13] By now more rumours of an improper liaison began to reach Edward Loveden and his son, Pryse Pryse. The latter reproached Tom Barker with his behaviour, and his father ordered him never to set foot in the house or grounds again.[14]

Despite these injunctions, during the first half of 1808 the pair were several times seen kissing in the rose garden or in the plantations. One Sunday, while the others were in church, they were almost detected making hurried love in the greenhouse when they thought no one was observing them.[15] Each time they managed to get a few minutes together it was a frantic and frightening occasion, and a letter later produced at the trial gives a sense of their predicament. Their sexual passion for each other was now overwhelming, but the dangers surrounding its fulfilment were enormous.

It was frustration at these rare, uncomfortable, brief, and unsatisfactory encounters that led them to risk planning to spend the night together in Anne's bed on 8 August 1808, when Edward was to be away for the night to attend the annual Lord Mayor's feast at Abingdon. Anne made the most careful plans to slip Thomas into the house and up to her bedroom. But

[13] LPCA, D.1312: 119–21, 240.   [14] Ibid. 225–9; *Trial*, 63.
[15] *Trial*, 21–4, 148–50; LPCA, D.1312: 30, 119–211, 141, 144, 150–3, 311–15.

she had to work alone, since she did not trust her lady's maid to help her. Nor did she realize how much the servants already knew, and how closely they were monitoring all her actions. On 30 July she sent for a carpenter from Faringdon to plane down the top of the billiard-room door 'to make it go easy'. On 6 August, two days before the event, she asked a servant for some oil. This request immediately aroused the suspicions of the butler, Warren Hastings, who as head of the household felt a particular responsibility. When the footman came to him with the request for oil, he handed it out in a tablespoon, remarking, 'I know what she wants the oil for. She has some mischief in her head.' He shared his suspicions with the four other upper servants, the elderly housekeeper, Mrs Calcutt, Anne's personal maid, Elizabeth Haynes, the personal attendant of the crippled Miss Loveden, Anne Strange, and Edward's manservant, Thomas Hooper. He also inspected the locks and hinges in the house and found that all the connecting doors between the conservatory downstairs and Anne's bedroom upstairs had been oiled, presumably while the servants were at dinner. The next day, the 7th, Anne asked for more oil, and on later inspection Hastings found that two more doors had been oiled. At breakfast, Anne also made the odd request for a whole wax candle, explaining vaguely, 'I want to try an experiment.'

Now thoroughly suspicious, Hastings and the manservant Hooper stayed on watch all night on the 6th and 7th, but observed nothing. On the 8th Edward duly set off to spend the night near Abingdon, and Anne's maid reported that her mistress had 'made rather unusual preparations in her bedroom by getting lavender, hyacinth roots, roses and other flowers which Mr Barker was very fond of'. Hastings concluded that this was to be the night on which Tom Barker would be smuggled into the house, and he, the housekeeper, and Anne's personal maid began their vigil in his bedroom at six in the evening. At nine o'clock they heard Anne go into the billiard-room and then come back. When they investigated, they found that she had freed the latch of the door leading from the conservatory into the house. At eleven Anne rang the bell for the supper things to be taken away, and went up to her bedroom.

Hastings kept watch in his pantry to observe Tom Barker enter the house, while the two women stood or sat on the stairs above, where they could see down into the passage leading to Anne's bedroom. There was a full moon and it was a clear night, so that visibility was good. At half-past eleven Anne came out of her bedroom into the stairway. In their eagerness the two women servants leaned over the banister rail above and were seen by Anne, who asked them what they were doing. They said they thought they had seen a man on the staircase—having mistaken Anne for a man

—and went down to tell Hastings. The latter locked the outside door to prevent Thomas slipping in, and went up to search the house. He passed Anne on the stairs, 'in her bed-gown and night-cap, and leaning with her face in her hands over the baluster by her sitting-room'.

The search revealed no trace of an intruder, but Hastings did observe the candle half-burned in a room, which he suspected had been used as a signal to Thomas outside. He then told the women servants to lock the door behind him while he searched outside the house. He walked around, found nothing, and returned to report to Anne that 'it was a false alarm. There's no one here, ma'am.' Having told the women servants to lock the door behind him, he quietly let himself out of the house again, and tiptoed along the colonnade so that Anne could not hear him go. He took up a position under some elm trees thirty yards from the north front of the house, and waited. Forty-five minutes went by and he saw nothing, although he noticed Anne looking out from a window. After another forty-five minutes he heard the sound of someone jumping down from the roof of the outside privy, having already climbed over the paling into the park. He took a loaded pistol from his pocket and confronted the intruder, who turned out to be Tom Barker. Hastings said, 'You are the man I am in search of,' and angrily ordered him off the premises. Thomas asked him not to speak so loudly, and declared that he merely wanted to talk to Mrs Loveden. Realizing that other servants might be watching, he asked to speak to Hastings privately.

The two men went together under the trees, where they spent three-quarters of an hour in conversation, for which we only have Hastings's uncorroborated testimony. He began by reproaching Tom Barker for his ingratitude to Mr Loveden 'in coming to disturb his peace of mind and the peace of his family, who has always treated you in the most friendly manner'. He warned him that his relations with Mrs Loveden were well known, both inside the house and in the neighbourhood. They had, for instance, been seen kissing in the plantation by the underkeeper, who had spread the story all over the countryside, so much so that Miller the horse-dealer had mentioned it in the public market at Fairford. He reminded Thomas that both Edward Loveden and his own father had ordered him not to visit Buscot Park any more and that Pryse Pryse had reproached him for his ill-conduct, because of the persistent rumours of his liaison with Anne. He told Tom Barker that, so far as he knew, neither Edward Loveden nor Anne's mother, Mrs Lintall, knew the full story about the affair, but that behaviour such as this, attempting to enter the house at night in Edward's absence, would immediately become public knowledge and create a major scandal. He accused Thomas of planning to get into

Anne's bedroom that night, and pointed out that, if the female servants had not spoilt the plan, he would have been caught red-handed.

Thomas admitted that this was all true, but begged Hastings not to expose him. Hastings finally said that he was willing to give him one more chance. If he would promise never to visit the house again, he would refrain this time from informing anybody, including his master, Edward Loveden, of this attempt at adultery with Anne. Tom gave his promise, they shook hands on it, and went their separate ways. Hastings kept his word and said nothing about his finding Tom in the park, not even to his fellow servants on watch inside the house.

Hastings had not had much sleep for three nights and was still in bed at nine the next morning when Anne summoned him to her dressing-room. When he arrived, she came close, holding out her hands to him and crying: 'Oh! Hastings, what a miserable night I have passed. I am a ruined woman forever.' Hastings commented that her behaviour was most imprudent and that he knew all about her aborted plans for the night. She admitted them, but promised never to see Tom again or correspond with him in any way, if Hastings would conceal his knowledge from her husband. He then told her of his conversation with Tom and of his promise, and made her also promise never to see him again. Anne was overcome with joy, and called him 'the greatest friend I ever had'. Later she pressed into his hand a five-guinea note which he admitted that he accepted, although under protest.[16]

Alas, however, for promises, and perhaps also for good intentions. After this traumatic crisis in August 1808, Anne was again in secret communication with Tom at least by November and possibly before. On 29 November, as James Hooper, Edward's manservant, was taking the locked bag of out-letters from Buscot Park to the Faringdon Post Office, he was warned by Anne's maid that 'she knew there were letters therein for Tom Barker', for Anne had been seen writing for several hours while her husband was out riding a few days before. Moreover, Anne had insisted that the bag be locked and removed before Edward came home. Hooper, therefore, bent open the leather pouch, shook out the letters, found an envelope addressed to Tom, and removed it.[17]

That night in the privacy of his bedroom Hooper opened the envelope to find that it contained three letters. One was an old one from Tom dating back to May 1804, probably the first he ever wrote to her; another was a passionate love-letter from her, written three days before on 26 November 1808, describing her dreary life with her unloved husband and her boring

---

[16] LPCA, D.1312: 243–64, 214, 320–6, 358–67; *Trial*, 59–63.
[17] LPCA, D.1312: 125–33, 174.

old mother, and lamenting the obstacles to their meeting during the coming winter.

It was the letter of a woman head over heels in love, and consumed by sexual and romantic passion. She described how she kept in a secret place a miniature portrait of him (the work of James Green in London) along with the most recent of his letters. Every morning and every evening, 'I repair to my little Treasury, where I indulge myself with contemplating your image, caressing it, and telling you how anxiously I covet your presence.' Anne rhapsodized about the safe receipt of his last letter: 'Oh, beloved creature! How shall I describe the various emotions of joy which seized my every nerve, and filled me with the most extravagant rapture. Never, never, sure, was mortal half so happy, half so gratified, or half so thankful for such a tribute. It was a masterpiece of perfection.' Despite the danger of discovery, she wrote that she was determined to keep the letter. She went on to say that 'what may at present be essential for you to know ... the other envelope will speak for itself. I doubt not your caution and prudence in making use of it.'

This third letter, in a sealed envelope and folded very small, was the final conclusive evidence of adultery which the servants had been seeking for years. In this extraordinary memorandum Anne provided Thomas, at his request, with full details of her projected menstrual cycle over the coming winter months, so that he would know the days when it was not worth the risk of trying to arrange a meeting. She had been keeping careful note of the dates in previous months and promised, 'if you wish, I will even for a greater security regularly mark as you direct the period of its appearance, from whence you can always compute without difficulty'. She recommended avoidance of intercourse, and therefore of attempts to arrange a meeting, for six days afterwards. Anne found this disclosure extremely embarrassing and made it only because of the acute danger of discovery every time they met. She concluded: 'Now, love, you cannot but consider me most indulgent. I flatter myself too, most explicit, but I am so much ashamed of what I have said that I shall instantly seal it up and expect that you as readily and immediately commit it to the flames.'[18] Hooper later stated that he did not immediately turn this highly incriminating evidence over to his master, Edward, but kept it for three-and-a-half months, until March 1809. But he took good care not to destroy it.

As 1808 drew to a close, Anne was in despair at ever getting together with Tom. 'An attempt would be madness,' she lamented. As the leaves fell, so cover disappeared in the grounds, while workmen were everywhere,

---

[18] Ibid. 54–6; *Trial*, 214–19; *JH Lords*, 48 (1810–12), 254b.

cutting trees and clearing shrubbery. She concluded gloomily 'in daytime I see no possibility of escaping detection, and weather and ways are so bad and uncertain that I know not how to invite you to nightly attempts'.[19]

The correspondence between the two lovers continued throughout the winter, and by March 1809 Anne had decided on the reckless step of again attempting to hide Thomas in the house for a night or two. She chose a week when her husband was away on a visit to his son, Pryse, a trip on which she had declined to accompany him. He left on 8 March and the next day Anne aroused the suspicions of the servants by dressing in 'much gayer clothes than she had been accustomed to wear at home without she expected company'. She told her maid: 'I will bedizen myself when I go to dress.' The servants concluded that she was unlikely to get herself up like that just to have dinner with her lame stepdaughter. Next day, 10 March, she had the bedroom 'put in nice order'.

All these preparations aroused the suspicions of her maid, Elizabeth Haynes, who warned the housekeeper, Mrs Calcutt and the butler, Warren Hastings, who decided once more to set a trap for Tom Barker. Hastings took it as a personal affront that Barker should be planning to break his solemn promise of the previous August, and was determined this time to catch him. He kept watch from his pantry that evening from six till nine, when he saw Anne come down the vestibule stairs and open a window in the hall. He heard, but did not see, someone jump in through the window and walk through the breakfast-room into what sounded like the study. As he usually did when he went away, Edward Loveden had locked his study, taking the key with him. In order to check his suspicions, Hastings went into his own bedroom, which was in the basement directly underneath the study, and stood on a table the better to hear. There was the sound of someone (presumably Anne) going out of the room and locking the door, and also of someone (presumably Tom) moving about inside it. Hastings immediately went up to the other door to the study and tried to look through the keyhole, only to find it plugged with paper, and the gap below the door blocked by a rug placed against it, so that no light whatever was visible.

Hastings went back downstairs to the housekeeper's room and told his allies, Mrs Calcutt, Elizabeth Haynes, and Anne Strange, 'I have got Mr Barker safe in my master's study'. But at first they would not believe him, since everyone in the house knew that only Edward Loveden had a key to his study. The idea that Anne had taken the trouble, and been clever enough, to have had a copy of the key made for the purpose of hiding Tom

[19] LPCA, D.1312: 59–62; *JH Lords*, 48 (1810–12), 255.

was more than they could credit. Hastings also told them that, as often as he opened the mahogany door from the hall to the stairs, someone shut it again, thus preventing anyone from seeing Tom slip out of the study and up the stairs into Anne's bedroom. By 10 p.m., when Anne rang her bell for supper, the mahogany door was open once more and there was no sound to be heard coming from the study, so Hastings concluded that Barker had already moved into Anne's bedroom. At 11 p.m. Anne rang for her maid and went to bed. Hastings sat up on watch till 2 a.m., heard and saw nothing, and finally went to bed.

When Anne rang the bell for her maid the next morning, the latter noticed that one half of the bed was extremely tumbled, but that the feather mattress showed no sign of the usual two depressions made by two bodies instead of one. After Anne had gone down to breakfast, the maid and housekeeper also carefully inspected the sheets, but found no stains upon them, or on Anne's bed-shift, although both were extraordinarily crumpled.[20] They were convinced that the 'tumbling' of the bedclothes and shift indicated sexual intercourse, but admitted that there were no tell-tale signs of two depressions on the mattress and stains on the sheets.

At quarter to nine the next morning they reported all this to Hastings, who concluded that Tom Barker must still be somewhere in the house. Hastings went to his bedroom to listen, and heard someone moving about overhead in the study. Since it was a cold morning, he went outside to see if there was smoke coming from the study chimney, which indeed there was. Anne Strange further reported that she had seen Anne carrying breakfast into the study. Hastings and the other servants were at last absolutely certain of their facts, and therefore felt free to take drastic action to expose Tom Barker.

Hastings laid his plans carefully. He posted one male servant outside to watch the north front of the house, and another to watch the stairs. Meeting Anne outside the study, the following exchange took place:

HASTINGS: Ma'am, I should be glad to have the key of my master's study.
ANNE: What, the key to your master's study?
HASTINGS: Yes, Ma'am, the key.
ANNE: I have not got the key. You know Mr Loveden never leaves the key.
HASTINGS: Ma'am, you must have got the key.
ANNE: I have no key at all. It is surprising conduct in you, Hastings. What can you think?
HASTINGS: Ma'am, there is a fire in the room and a person in the room too.
ANNE: There is no fire; there is no person; I have no key.

[20] *JH Lords*, 48 (1810–12), 332–7; *Trial*, 67–9, 73–5.

HASTINGS: Ma'am, you have the key.

ANNE: I have no key.

HASTINGS: Here is the very man Thomas Barker, who shook me by the right hand and gave me his word of honour last August that he would never come here again, now in this room, and I heard you let him in through the hall window at five past nine last night, and if you refuse to give me the key I will force the door open with my shoulders.

At this point, Mrs Calcutt appeared, and suggested that, instead of breaking down the door, they should get the carpenters at work on the house to put up their ladder outside the study, pull down the upper sash window, and open the shutter. Hastings went outside, where he met the under-butler, Robert Major, to whom he said: 'That rascal Barker is in the house and we will have him out.' He then ordered the two carpenters to do the work, despite repeated orders from Anne that he should stop. They pulled down the top window and broke open the shutter, but could not see fully into the room since the sash window was too high. So Robert Major got a stool, put it on the window-sill, stood on it to peer in, and saw Thomas pressed flat against the outside wall, trying to hide himself. He reported: 'Here he is sure enough, and all ready for starting'—meaning that he was in his riding boots and with his horsewhip in his hand. The game was up.

Soon after the discovery, Hastings went into the breakfast-room to remove the things on the table, followed by Anne in floods of tears. 'You have ruined me forever,' she sobbed; 'Oh! Hastings, how could you have employed those men, as by your employing them it will be known all over the country.' Turning to sarcasm, she continued: 'I am much obliged to you for your officiousness. You have undone me for the rest of my life.' To this he replied coldly: 'You should have delivered up the key, then.' Fifteen minutes later he was summoned to the library, where he found Anne crying on the sofa and Tom Barker with her. The latter received him truculently, exclaiming: 'A pretty piece of work you have been making, and do you know the consequences of it?' Hastings retorted by reminding him of his broken promise of last August. Tom tried to argue that he had only just been let into the house that morning, but Hastings brushed all that aside. Tom said defiantly: 'Well, you can make nothing of this.' 'What?', replied Hastings indignantly, 'not when you have been caught in the very sanctuary of my master's house?'—meaning the locked study full of private papers.

At this point Tom gave in, and asked the butler what he proposed to do. Hastings answered that he and the housekeeper had already sent a letter to their master telling him the whole story, and urged Barker to leave the house immediately. But Barker still had some fight in him and replied: 'I did not come into the house like a thief, and I will not go out like one.' But at three in the afternoon he finally went away, while Anne continued in floods of tears. The next day she asked Hastings not to mention the episode of the previous August, but he explained that it was impossible to conceal it, since it was now known to several of the servants.[21]

Meanwhile at Woodstock, where Edward Loveden was staying with his son, Pryse Pryse, his manservant Hooper received the letter from Mrs Calcutt telling all. He took the letter, along with the packet of letters he had been keeping ever since he had intercepted them in November, and handed them all over to Pryse, so that he could break the news to his father. His explanation of why he had not passed on the letters sooner was the lame one that, whenever the opportunity had arisen, Pryse had been out hunting, and he had not had a chance to talk to him privately. Next day Pryse told his father, who, he claimed, went into shock and burst into tears. Finally Edward Loveden pulled himself together, sent for his attorney, and instructed Pryse to go straight to Buscot Park and demand that Anne hand over all the keys of the house. Anne meekly surrendered three or four, and when asked for her duplicate key to the study reluctantly pulled open a drawer and handed it over to her stepson. The next day, 13 March, Pryse rode over once again to Buscot Park, and, in the presence of his crippled sister Jane, ordered his stepmother to leave the house forever, which she did two days later.[22] The stately eighteenth-century formalities for the expulsion of an adulterous wife from the marital home were thus scrupulously complied with.

The various steps taken by the injured husband in such cases were a civil suit against the wife's lover in King's Bench for damages for crim. con.; a suit in the London Consistory Court for separation from his wife, without alimony, on grounds of adultery; and finally a bill in the House of Lords for full divorce. Despite the very strong circumstantial evidence, no one had actually seen Barker and Anne Loveden committing adultery, so Anne, who had nothing to lose since her husband had to pay most of her legal costs, fought every step of the way.

In her husband's crim. con. suit against Thomas Barker, claiming damages of £10,000, the latter's lawyer, Sergeant Best, argued that the jury should acquit him of charges of adultery. This was a plausible case to argue, since the really incriminating evidence had to be withheld on technical grounds.

---

[21] LPCA, D.1312: 110–12, 269–89, 337–40, 373–86; *Trial*, 52–8, 110, 209; *JH Lords*, 48 (1810–12), 171a, 171b. [22] LPCA, D.1312: 88–90, 133, 387.

Edward Loveden was unable to introduce into a common-law court his wife's letter about her menstrual cycle, since it had not been delivered to the intended recipient, whoever he was.[23] Even so the evidence against Tom Barker was still strong.

The prosecuting counsel pressed for a verdict of guilty and for very large damages to compensate Edward Loveden for the gross betrayal of his friendship and hospitality. If all that was alleged in the preface of the pamphlet about the trial was true, Tom Barker had certainly behaved abominably. It was claimed that Edward Loveden had acted like a father to the young Merton Fellow, paying personally for the furniture for his room at Oxford, and for his clothes. He had also lent him 'a very valuable horse', which Tom Barker only returned under threat of a lawsuit. In addition to these gifts, there were unknown sums lavished on Tom Barker by Anne Loveden, to discover and recover which Edward Loveden later launched a somewhat futile suit in Chancery, which Barker did his best to delay.[24]

But these were minor issues. The key question which faced the jury was whether or not the evidence laid before them about adultery was sufficient to justify a verdict of guilty. The defence lawyer insisted that, although Tom Barker might have been guilty of an attempt at adultery at Buscot Park on 10–11 March, there was no evidence that he had succeeded. He argued that, according to the common law, 'it is incumbent upon the plaintiff to make out the fact of a carnal connection having taken place, by evidence that can leave no doubt in your mind that it has taken place'. He admitted that this charge might be made out by presumptive evidence. 'But what is presumptive evidence? It is that which arises out from circumstances instead of ocular demonstration. But they must be circumstances which shew the existence of the fact to be proved as clearly, and satisfactorily, as if it had come under the eye of the witness.'

Given this premiss, the defence lawyer made much of the fact that the two women who inspected the bed could not find either of the two clear signs of sexual activity: the impression of two bodies on the soft feather bed, or stains on the sheets and on the lady's shift. The plaintiff's lawyer argued that, in view of the publicity given to these incriminating pieces of evidence in recent trials for crim. con., it would be only too easy and natural for clever adulterers to take the trouble to cover their tracks.

Even so, the defence lawyer hardly expected to win, and therefore spent a good deal of time producing reasons why, if the verdict were guilty, the damages should be moderate in size in view of Tom Barker's lack of an estate and his inevitable expulsion from his Fellowship. He also observed

---

[23] *JH Lords*, 48 (1810–12), 155b.   [24] *Trial*, pp. ix–x.

that Edward Loveden was 'in an advanced period of life', insinuating that he was perhaps no longer capable of giving his third young wife the sexual satisfaction to which she was entitled. He also made the point that the court had been offered 'very slight evidence of the degree of felicity in which these parties lived together'.[25]

In his summing up to the jury, Lord Ellenborough ran through eight different episodes over a period of some three years, which the prosecution had suggested might be regarded as evidence that adultery had taken place. Most of these he dismissed out of hand, including the hot day in May 1808 when Anne Loveden and Tom Barker had shut themselves up in a coach with the blinds drawn, all the way from Bond Street to Fleet Street to Hyde Park Corner, where Anne emerged red-faced and with her hair in disarray. He could not believe that 'the last act of carnality then took place there, for that would be outraging all sense of decency'. He could only conceive of 'very great and very indecent personal familiarity' possibly taking place in a coach. This flat rejection as unthinkable of a happening which appears to have been commonplace at the time is in striking contrast to the definition of proof of adultery offered by his predecessor as Lord Chief Justice. In 1796 Lord Kenyon had instructed a jury that, 'where the parties have been traced to a place of privacy and closeted for a given time . . . the parties must have so retired for the indulgence of an illicit passion'.[26]

Lord Ellenborough found the greenhouse episode suggestive but inconclusive. As for the discovery of Tom Barker in the study at Buscot Park on 11 March 1809, he suggested that even that evidence was not entirely convincing. He interpreted Anne's bitter remark to the butler Hastings: 'I thank you for that, Hastings, and you have ruined me,' either as an admission of guilt of adultery, or as pointing out that the publicity given to the episode would destroy her reputation regardless of her criminality. He reminded the jury that the evidence of the state of the bed was ambiguous, lacking as it did the impression of two bodies or stains on the sheets. He took the line that Tom Barker had certainly intended to sleep that night with Anne but that it was uncertain whether or not he actually did so. He ended by recommending that, if the jury found Tom Barker guilty, as he hinted that he expected they would, they should give 'such temperate but adequate compensation as the party complaining has a right to ask at your hands'.

The special jury consisted of four esquires living at smart addresses in the West End of London, and eight substantial craftsmen and retailers

---

[25] Ibid., p. xv n. *, 9–10, 80, 90–2, 94–5.   [26] Stone, *Road to Divorce*, 279.

(a coal merchant, two victuallers, a stationer, a carpenter, a plumber, a broker, and one 'gentleman'). They deliberated for the unusually long time of forty minutes, before bringing in a verdict of not guilty.[27]

The acquittal by the jury took everyone by surprise, including Lord Justice Ellenborough and the defence lawyers, and even Tom Barker himself, who had already resigned his Fellowship in order to anticipate expulsion from the College. One reason behind the acquittal was the abnormally high standards of proof which had been set by Lord Ellenborough. Another possible explanation is that the jury may have interpreted the absence of Edward on a visit to his son as a trap deliberately laid to catch her. After all, the liaison had been going on for over four years, and most of the indoor and outdoor servants and many of the neighbours and even relatives had long known about it.

Stunned by the verdict, the prosecution moved for a retrial, citing previous cases where similar circumstantial evidence had been sufficient to entitle the plaintiff to 'exemplary damages'. This motion was rejected by Lord Ellenborough and the other judges on two grounds. The first was that, although they themselves might disagree with the verdict, as it appears that they did, it was a question of fact not law, and so a matter to be determined solely by the jury. And, secondly, it was not so blatantly in contradiction with the evidence as to justify overturning it.[28]

In the London Consistory Court Edward Loveden fared much better. Anne freely admitted 'an improper attachment' and 'indelicate acts' such as walking arm in arm and kissing, but still firmly denied adultery. She also claimed that she had been 'living among spies, and that they all seem to have acted with unfavourably conceived impressions'. By thus challenging the evidence, most of which was highly circumstantial but not conclusive, she turned what should have been a routine trial into a lengthy legal battle which became a test case for the rules of evidence in the ecclesiastical courts. It forced the judge of the London Consistory Court, Sir William Scott, to restate at length the standards of proof which were customarily required in canon law in cases of adultery.[29]

To clear the ground he restated the traditional view that a common-law verdict carried little weight in an ecclesiastical court. The defeat of Mr Loveden's suit in King's Bench 'is a matter entirely out of the view of this Court'. He described it as 'not direct proof, but merely a circumstance'. This scepticism about a jury verdict in a crim. con. case was based on the

[27] *Trial*, 96–104.   [28] Ibid. 105–11.
[29] *Eng. Rep.* 161: 651; *The Judgement pronounced by Sir William Scott in the Trial of Loveden* v. *Loveden* (London, 1911) (BM 1509/696 (5)).

inability of the wife to defend herself. As Sir William Scott put it, 'how can that be evidence against the party, which has passed in a suit to which she was not party?' Secondly, the jury might have knowledge which had not been presented to the ecclesiastical court.[30] In fact, of course, it was professional jealousy between the practitioners of two different systems of law which lay behind this attitude of contempt for a verdict at common law.

Sir William Scott also argued that Lord Ellenborough had set the standards of proof too high: 'it is a fundamental rule that it is not necessary to prove the direct fact of adultery; because if it were otherwise there is not one case in a hundred in which that proof would be attainable: it is very rarely indeed that the parties are surprised in the direct act of adultery.' In canon law, all that was demanded for a separation from bed and board on grounds of adultery was 'that the circumstances must be such as would lead the guarded discretion of a reasonable and just man to the conclusion' that adultery had taken place.[31]

Sir William Scott then went out of his way to stress that this was not a case of entrapment. What

occurred in this case, though certainly in an uncommon degree . . . happens in many others—that the husband is the last person who entertains a suspicion of his misfortune. There is, I think, no reason whatever to presume any kind of connivance on his part or any other forbearance than what arose from the most profound ignorance of the dishonour that was being practised on him.[32]

So much for the lurking suspicion that Edward Loveden may have either deliberately turned a blind eye on his wife's adultery or set a trap for her. It was an argument somewhat undermined by the later evidence of Mr Knight before the Court of Arches that Edward Loveden had suspected Anne's fidelity for years, and had actually banned Tom from the house.

Turning to the evidence, Sir William Scott laid great stress not only on the final episode when Barker was discovered in the house, but also on Anne's letter about her menstrual cycle and the times when intercourse should be avoided—a letter which he would not allow to be read out in open court in the interests of public decency. He observed, reasonably enough, that the letter was the work of 'a woman who had made a sur-render of her body, her mind, and everything which belonged to either the one or the other, to the person to whom this letter was addressed'. Sir William therefore declared himself satisfied that an adulterous connection

---

[30] *Eng. Rep.* 161: 556 n.; Shelford, 414.
[31] *Eng. Rep.* 161: 648–50; Shelford, 406.   [32] Shelford, 652.

had subsisted between Anne Loveden and Tom Barker for a very considerable length of time, and that 'Mr Loveden is most unquestionably entitled
to the sentence which he prays, of separation'.[33]

Despite this ringing condemnation in the Consistory Court, Anne appealed the sentence to the Court of Arches, but wisely dropped her suit
there before it came to sentence. She had nothing to lose by thus prolonging
the case, since, as long as it was not finally settled, her husband was obliged
to continue paying her the £800-a-year temporary alimony assigned to her
by the Court—a large amount, but one which was equal to the jointure
assured her by Edward in their marriage contract. In addition, of course,
Edward had to pay for all her taxed legal costs.[34]

Such was the animosity between the couple that the continued payment
of this alimony during the trial was also the subject of litigation, which
again became a test case. The sentence in the Consistory Court was issued
on the last day of Trinity Term, and Anne's appeal to the Court of Arches
was entered on the first day of the following Michaelmas Term, three
months later. She asked for the alimony to be renewed from the date of
the sentence, he from the date of the appeal. The judge declared that, since
she had appealed on the first possible day, she should not be left without
alimony for three months merely because the court was not in session.[35]

The legal set-back in King's Bench was thus no hindrance to a favourable
verdict for Edward Loveden in the ecclesiastical courts. Nor did it do
anything to hinder his subsequent bill in the House of Lords in 1811, for
full divorce from Anne on grounds of adultery, with permission to remarry.
But in this respect the bill made legal history, since it was the only occasion
for many decades in which the House of Lords was prepared to pass a
divorce bill with the support of a sentence by an ecclesiastical court, but
against the verdict of a common-law jury.[36]

But if, after the passage of the bill through the House of Lords, Edward
Loveden was counting on total victory, he was in for a rude surprise. The
House of Commons, which always took special care to look after the right
of a divorced wife for adequate maintenance, awarded Anne an allowance
after divorce of £400 a year, the exact income Edward enjoyed from her
marriage portion. Enraged at this generosity, Edward asked the House of
Lords to drop the bill altogether, rather than pass it in this amended form.
He claimed that his wife was now openly living with her lover, Thomas
Barker. He argued that the stipulated allowance 'has a manifest tendency

---

[33] *Eng. Rep.* 161: 665.
[34] LPCA, H.134/8; for taxed costs, see Stone, *Road to Divorce*, 187–90.
[35] *Eng. Rep.* 161: 962–4.   [36] MacQueen, *House of Lords*, 491–2.

Loveden *v.* Loveden

to loosen the bonds of conjugal fidelity, by holding out a premium to the
wife for the commission of adultery', and therefore would 'endanger the
best and dearest interests of society'. He described himself as 'alarmed at
the pernicious consequences which might flow from such an example in
domestic life, and greatly deprecating the idea that any legislative measure
would in the remotest degree cherish a relaxation of public morals'. For
these reasons of high principle, for which he was well known, he asked the
Lords not to pass the amended bill, a request with which they complied. As
a result, the bill made legal history, since, in order to avoid such a fiasco in
future, Parliamentary procedure was altered. From now on a husband had
to have agreed to provide satisfactorily for the maintenance of his wife
before his bill could be introduced.[37]

Edward Loveden's real motives were probably not as exclusively high-
minded as he claimed. He now had little to lose and much to gain by
having the amended bill defeated. At his age he presumably had no intention
of marrying a fourth time, but by dropping the bill he deprived Anne not
only of a substantial maintenance, but also of the freedom to marry her
lover, Tom Barker. Instead of having to pay her the £400 a year allowed by
the House of Commons, Edward, by abandoning the bill, would now be
obliged as long as he lived to pay Anne only her pin-money under the
marriage contract, which was probably no more than £100 a year. He had
thus almost ruined her financially; he had publicly disgraced her in the eyes
of society, especially by the revelation of her letter to her lover describing
in detail her menstrual cycle; and he had driven her from his house into
rented lodgings in London. On the other hand, Anne was certainly now
free to live openly with Tom Barker as his mistress, and she may well have
had some private family income of her own after the death of her mother.

As for Tom Barker, he prudently resigned his Fellowship at Merton
in order to anticipate inevitable deprivation under the College Statutes,
and his academic career was ruined.[38] Moreover, his behaviour in de-
ceiving his father's friend and his personal patron, and in breaking his
word of honour to the butler, Warren Hastings, was enough to blast his
reputation as a gentleman, while it must still further have exacerbated
his already strained relations with his father and family. It seems unlikely
that the latter would have rallied to his rescue after this betrayal of the

[37] *JH Lords*, 48 (1810–12), 448A; MacQueen, *House of Lords*, 147; *Thoughts on the dangerous tendency of introducing into Bills of Divorce a Provision for the Adulteress, as was recently
done in the bill for the divorcing of Edward Loveden Loveden Esq., by his wife* (London, 1810).
This pamphlet is known only by an advertisement of it, inserted in one of the pamphlets
about the case. I owe this reference of Mr Jordan D. Luttrell of Meyer Boswell Books, Inc.
[38] Merton College records; I am indebted to Dr Roger Highfield for this information.

long-standing family friendship with Edward Loveden. It is not known how long Tom Barker and Anne Loveden continued to live together. Nor is it known whether she married him after the death of her husband, at which time she would have come into her jointure of £800 a year.

As the injured husband, Edward Loveden had been privately wounded and publicly ridiculed by having the world believe that he had been cuckolded in his own bed by a man half his age. His honour was also impugned by the perverse verdict of the King's Bench jury, which laid him open to suspicion of entrapment. Although there is no sign that he was anything more than the rather indifferent and neglectful elderly husband of a young and lonely wife, he presumably also suffered from the loss of his wife's company and the break-up of his household routine.

In human terms, this is a somewhat banal story of a bored, neglected, and childless young wife falling in love with a lively and attractive young man, who had free access to the house. What marks it as peculiar to the first decade of the nineteenth century is the artificial atmosphere of high romanticism with which Anne enveloped what was at bottom an overwhelming sexual passion. To satisfy that passion she and her lover took absurd risks, the result of which was the ruin of them both.

The most interesting feature of this story is the critical role played by the servants, first in concealing from their master their suspicions about the adultery for four long years; then in watching for evidence with such intense curiosity; and finally in revealing all they knew or suspected, thereby precipitating the family crisis. By the early nineteenth century, servants were neither as submissive to their superiors, nor as protective of adulterous wives, as they had once been. Their loyalty now lay primarily in the cash-nexus that bound them to their paymaster, the head of the household. Moreover, the rise of the ideal of family domesticity and the moral force of evangelical religion caused adultery, especially female adultery, to be regarded with greater public disapproval in lower-middle-class circles than it had been in earlier times. As a result, not even a lady's personal maid was now as willing as she had been in the past actively to promote and protect an adulterous connection by her mistress. Unlike the great majority of eighteenth-century adulteresses in high society, Anne was all alone, unable to rely on the loyalty even of her lady's maid. As a result, her two attempts to smuggle Tom Barker into her bedroom were inevitably discovered.

On the one hand, the strong sense of shame felt by the servants, and their desire somehow to hold the family together, induced them to conceal what they knew or strongly suspected for the exceptionally long period of four years. On the other hand, they clearly had strong moral feelings, not only about wifely adultery, but also about the betrayal of the hospitality and friendship offered to Tom Barker by Edward Loveden, thanks to which he for a long time enjoyed free access to the house whenever he wanted. Even when the butler caught Tom red-handed, as he did on the night of 8 August 1808, he merely made Tom promise upon his word of honour that he would come to the house no more. Like his upper-class betters, he felt that the preferable course of action was to stop the affair and hush the matter up, rather than to destroy the marriage and expose the family's dirty linen in open court; and he was genuinely and rightly angry with both Anne and Tom when he discovered that they had broken their word to him and had continued to plot a second night of love together. Tom Barker also violated the eighteenth-century code of domestic honour in two ways which shocked the upper servants. The first was by allegedly committing adultery in the marital bed, and the second was by gaining entry to the locked study where the master of the house kept all his private papers.

From a legal point of view, the importance of this case is that it set a series of precedents in canon law of sufficient importance to be publicly reported for future citation. These precedents were set by the sentence of Sir William Scott, in which he redefined the degree of proof necessary in an ecclesiastical court to obtain a verdict of separation for adultery. He also reinforced the standard doctine that a jury verdict of acquittal in a crim. con. case was irrelevant as evidence for the defence in a separation suit in an ecclesiastical court. Nor in this exceptional case did it block divorce proceedings in Parliament. The passage through Parliament of the Loveden divorce bill also settled once and for all that the husband had to comply with the wishes of the Commons over the settlement of adequate maintenance upon his wife before such a bill could be returned to the Lords.[39] Thus in several ways the Loveden divorce litigation made legal history.

[39] MacQueen, *House of Lords*, 147.

10

Cadogan v. Cadogan
The lady and the parson, 1777–1794

Charles Sloane, 3rd Lord Cadogan, was the grandson and heir of one of Marlborough's leading generals. He was a wealthy nobleman with two seats, one at Caversham near Reading, and another at Sandford Downham in Suffolk, as well as a town house in Grosvenor Street, in London, and a small seaside beach-house at Lowestoft.[1] His first wife was the daughter of Lord Montfort, who brought him the very large portion of £20,000, the interest of which he continued to enjoy as long as she lived.

After her death, which occurred in 1768, after twenty-one years of marriage and the birth of twelve children, Lord Cadogan made up for the loss of the interest on her portion by obtaining the not very demanding office of Master of the Mint. In 1776 he at last inherited his father's title and estates, and began looking for a new wife. His eye fell on Mary Churchill, the daughter of a good but impoverished family. She was a young woman some twenty years his junior, and when they married in 1777 she was 28 and he was nearly 50. Her lack of a marriage portion had presumably hitherto barred her from the marriage market, but this was no great deterrent to Cadogan. He now had plenty of money, and was seeking—according to Mary—an entertaining and agreable companion to share his pleasures, and presumably also a younger sexual partner. For nearly a decade the marriage went very well, and Mary produced seven children. The Cadogans seem to have been a genuinely cheerful and affectionate couple, and attentive and loving parents.

Things only began to go wrong after nine years of marriage, in 1786, when one of their daughters died. Mary was extremely upset by this, her first and only loss of a child, and went into a deep depression. This psychosomatic illness was exacerbated by the growing irritation and indifference of her husband. He lacked the patience to support the burden of an invalid wife, when what he wanted was a cheerful companion and hostess for his life of pleasure. His increasingly negligent attitude towards her merely made Mary's condition worse, and before long she had turned

[1] LPCA, D.350, 351.

into a chronic invalid, who spent most of her life in bed, and never got up and dressed until two or three in the afternoon. She also suffered from frequent muscular cramps in the stomach, and occasional fits, during which she had to be restrained by force to prevent her from doing herself an injury.[2]

In about 1790—witnesses disagreed as to just when the event took place —Mary's fits induced Lord Cadogan to remove himself from her bedroom, and in future Mary slept with her personal maid, Farley Bull, upon whom she became more and more dependent as her husband grew increasingly remote from her. But sexual relations did not cease altogether when Cadogan moved to a separate bedroom, for in June 1793 Mary gave birth to her seventh and last child.[3]

In about 1791 Mary's depression was greatly increased by a bitter quarrel between her husband and her own close relatives, with whom he had previously been very intimate. For some unknown reason Cadogan turned against her father, Charles Churchill, as well as her mother and brothers, and relations between the two families were totally broken off. Now that she was physically isolated from her parents and siblings, who were forbidden access to the house, Mary's condition perceptibly worsened.[4]

The Cadogans had long been friends with Sir Grey Cooper, Bt., and his family, who were their neighbours in Suffolk, and Mary became especially intimate with Sir Grey's daughter, with whom she shared a passion for music. Both she and Lord Cadogan were also close friends of one of the younger sons, William Henry Cooper. He had begun a career as an officer in a Guards regiment, but, presumably because his father would not or could not put up the money to buy him his promotion, had abandoned the army and had taken holy orders instead. In 1790 he was about 25, had recently married, and already possessed a young and growing family.

The Revd Cooper held both a rectory and a prebend at Rochester, which provided him with a gross income of about £500 a year. He also earned some money as the legal custodian of his mother-in-law, Mrs Franks, who was insane, and he had expectations from his father-in-law, Mr Franks, reputedly 'a man of immense fortune'. But when Mr Franks died in 1791 he turned out to be insolvent, so that, instead of inheriting vast riches, the Revd Cooper suddenly found himself entangled in bankruptcy litigation, and faced with the prospect of spending the rest of his life in modest retirement in the country. In this crisis Lord Cadogan generously offered the Revd Cooper and his family indefinite use of free apartments both in

---

[2] Ibid. 252, 256–9, 832, 842.   [3] Ibid. 210, 261, 312, 695.   [4] Ibid. 256, 832.

his London house in Grosvenor Street and in his Suffolk seat at Sandford Downham, an offer which was gratefully accepted.[5]

The two families were thus brought into close physical propinquity, with disastrous results. In 1792 the Revd Cooper fell in love with Mary, the invalid wife of the benefactor in whose house he was residing and upon whom he was largely dependent for survival. And Mary, still in deep depression because of the death of her child and the neglect of her husband, responded with equal passion. From its start, a key role in the affair was played by Mary's personal maid, Farley Murray Bull. She was a 40-year-old spinster who had served Mary for eighteen years, almost the whole of her married life, first as nursemaid to the children and then as personal lady's maid. She was fiercely loyal to her mistress, and it was she who smuggled Cooper in and out of Mary's bedroom, concealed him when necessary in the water-closet attached to it, and on occasion prevented Lord Cadogan from paying an unwanted visit to Mary's bedroom by claiming that her mistress had a violent headache that day.[6]

After the discovery of the love-affair, Mary blamed her adulterous behaviour on her husband's callous treatment of her during her illness. She claimed that she had suffered severely from emotional and physical neglect by her husband in recent years, when he seemed 'more angry or hurt at the bustle which his wife's illness occasioned than concerned for her sufferings'. She once told her surgeon that the disease had been brought on by Cadogan's neglect of her and by his quarrel with her parents and relatives, which 'preyed much upon her spirits'. Proof that her illness was psychosomatic, and that it was prolonged by her husband's indifference, is provided by the fact that her depression seems to have lifted altogether as soon as her love-affair with Cooper began.[7]

The first really incriminating episode in the affair took place in May 1793, a month before Mary gave birth to her last child. Farley Bull brought Cooper into the house and up to Mary's bedroom at three in the afternoon, when the other servants were still at dinner, and he stayed there until ten or eleven that night behind locked doors. Farley Bull was vigilant in keeping the other servants away and in finally smuggling Cooper out of the house again.[8]

In July of the same year, only a month after Mary had given birth, Cooper stayed in the house for a couple of weeks, during which time on several occasions he spent the night with Mary, while Farley Bull, who was her usual bedfellow, slept on a sofa downstairs. When in August the

[5] Ibid. 337–52, 922, 1371.   [6] Ibid. 2336.
[7] Ibid. 220–2.   [8] Ibid. 199–202, 442.

Cadogan v. Cadogan

Cadogans moved to their seaside house at Lowestoft, adultery again seems to have taken place. One day when the whole family except for Mary and Farley Bull had gone off to a Field Day—presumably an exercise by the local militia held at the nearby seat of Hopton Court—Cooper came to the house, was admitted by Farley Bull, and spent several hours in Mary's bedroom. Early the next year, 1794, the lovers became even more infatuated with each other, and consequently even more reckless. On 24 February Cooper again slipped into Mary's bedroom in Grosvenor Street for many hours. Farley Bull stopped the maids from entering the room to bring in more coals for the fire, and later on the footman, James Chapman, smuggled him out. A month later, on 20 March, Cooper spent all night in Mary's bed, while Farley Bull slept on the sofa downstairs.

Despite Farley Bull's efforts, it was impossible that all this activity should have escaped the notice of at least some of the other servants, and even relatives of the family. Already by the spring of 1793, the servants, as well as a woman friend of Mary's, Mrs Bates, had their suspicions. The leading activists in discovering the truth were the coachman's wife, Mrs Meaross, who acted as housemaid and had been with the family five years, and Betty Russell, a housemaid who had served for six. It was the old-established servants who deliberately turned a blind eye to what was going on, and the more recent ones who determined to investigate, presumably hoping to profit by their discoveries.

On the very first occasion in 1793 when Cooper was secretly admitted to Mary's apartment, Betty Russell's suspicions were aroused when she found that the door to Mary's bedroom was locked. She therefore kept watch in the darkness of the dining-room to see if Cooper emerged from the bedroom, which he did at about 11 p.m. She had told her friend Mrs Meaross that she 'would lay anything Cooper was there' and the latter had also hidden at the top of the stairs, waiting for Cooper to come out.

Betty Russell was genuinely upset by her discovery, and cried; but Mrs Meaross was made of sterner stuff. After Cooper had left, she and Betty Russell were summoned by Mary to remake the bed. Mrs Meaross examined it carefully, finding the bed still warm and that the sheets had 'marks or stains . . . as are made when two persons have been in the act of carnal copulation', to use the bowdlerized language of the courtroom. She continued with her espionage, and often observed such stains on the sheets after secret visits by Cooper. She destroyed Farley Bull's explanation that the stains were caused by Mary spilling some chicken broth while eating in bed, by pointing out that the stains always occurred lower down, in the middle of the bed.

After the family returned from Lowestoft in late 1793, the liaison became the subject of common gossip in the servants' hall, and Mrs Meaross learnt that the other servants at Lowestoft reported things 'very prejudicial' to Mary. For the moment, however, none of the servants took any steps to warn Lord Cadogan. Either they were indifferent; or possibly they sympathized with Mary, since her husband had not slept with her regularly for a long while; or they were afraid that the household would be broken up and they would lose their jobs.

Despite this silence of the servants, which kept Lord Cadogan unaware of his wife's adultery, relations deteriorated between him and Mary to such a point that, on 9 February 1794, he formally separated from her and moved out of the Grosvenor Street house. Although it was hotly denied at the trial, a possible alternative explanation of the separation is that Lord Cadogan already knew about the adultery, and had moved out of the house as a deliberate plan to encourage Mary into some act which would provide him with certain proof of her guilt.[9]

The gossip from the servants had long before been passed on to the butler of the Revd W. B. Cadogan, Lord Cadogan's second son by his first marriage, and it was probably this butler who conveyed it to his mistress, the Hon. Lady Jane Cadogan. At all events, as early as March 1793 Lady Jane had become suspicious, and had alerted her husband. But he refused to say anything to Lord Cadogan without proof, although his wife was fully convinced that Cooper and Mary were 'strongly attached to each other'. She had observed them closely while staying at Lowestoft that summer, and had noticed that when one day Mary was in her warm sea-bath, which was kept indoors for therapeutic treatment, she had accidentally exposed her breast, the sight of which had evidently greatly excited Cooper. But this could be the reaction of any man to any woman, and was hardly the sort of evidence to support a charge of adultery.[10]

In March 1794, after Lord Cadogan had formally separated from Mary, she clearly felt more free to indulge her passion for Cooper. First she forbade the maids ever to enter her bedroom to make the beds or carry coals or any other business unless they were previously rung for. She then began to allow Cooper to spend all night in her bedroom, while the faithful Farley Bull slept on the sofa downstairs. After an all-night session in March, the Revd W. B. Cadogan's butler was immediately informed of it by the servants. He passed the message on to his master, who in turn informed his father, Lord Cadogan, who now had all the proof he needed.[11]

---

[9] Ibid. 337–52, 442–61, 720–49, 1082.
[10] Ibid. 940–1076. [11] Ibid. 442 (1853).

Cadogan v. Cadogan

Thereafter Cadogan acted with the swift purposefulness of a man determined both to get rid of his wife and to destroy her lover. Five days later, on 26 March, Mary was formally ejected from the house in Grosvenor Street, and took refuge temporarily in her father's house, still protesting her innocence. He then launched a civil suit against the Revd Cooper for crim. con. in the Court of King's Bench, hiring the great advocate Thomas Erskine to make his case. In his address to the jury, Erskine stressed the exceptional degree of injury done to the plaintiff, Cadogan, and the exceptional treachery of the defendant, Cooper. He brushed aside the twenty-year age difference between the spouses, on the grounds that 'that disparity of years is often lessened by the different constitutions', so that the jury would be wrong to infer that Lady Cadogan had been tempted into adultery because of sexual deprivation. He passed very rapidly over the fact that the Cadogans had for years slept in separate bedrooms due to her ladyship's illness.

To enhance the enormity of the offence, Erskine laid great stress on the very close ties of friendship and comradeship in arms which had bound Lord Cadogan to the father of the Revd Cooper, and the generous way the former had saved Cooper from obscure retirement into the countryside when his father-in-law died insolvent. This magnified the ingratitude shown by Cooper in seducing his benefactor's wife.

He ended with a typical rhetorical flourish, urging the jury not merely to recompense Lord Cadogan for his injury, but also 'to give stability and security to domestic life'. He alluded to Lord Howe's recent victory at sea over the French, and claimed—somewhat implausibly—that military valour is dependent on 'habits of virtuous life'. 'This', he declared 'is the foundation of all that is good, of all that is great, of all that distinguishes the most Christian nations.' He tried to persuade the jury that the poverty of the Revd Cooper was no reason for giving modest damages, and quoted the favourite dictum of the moralistic Lord Chief Justice Kenyon, who was presiding over the trial: 'It is a maxim of the law that he who cannot pay with his purse must pay with his person. Justice must be satisfied.' He therefore asked the jury to award exemplary damages, even if they would result in the Revd Cooper being confined to gaol for an indefinite period because of his inability to pay them.

In the face of Erskine's onslaught, there was not much that the counsel for the defence could say. He challenged the proof of the crime, asking whether it was likely that a woman who had married at 28, been faithful to her husband for eighteen years and produced seven children, should suddenly turn to adultery with a man who was also married and had four children. He reminded the jury that Lady Cadogan was now 49 and in perpetual ill-health, while the Revd Cooper was 27 and very healthy, thereby insinuating that, if seduction had indeed occurred, it was unlikely to have originated from him since she was sexually not at all attractive. Finally, he suggested that the whole affair would have been avoided if Lord Cadogan had treated his wife more kindly during her sickness and had attended upon her personally at night when she had her fits. This was his strongest argument for a mitigation of damages, and a valid one.

In his summing up, Lord Justice Kenyon in his usual manner demolished the case for the defence. He told the jury that 'circumstances more or less pregnant', not 'positive proof', was all that was necessary to determine the facts in cases of adultery. He pointedly asked why the defence had not put Farley Bull on the witness stand, if they thought Lady Cadogan was innocent. As for damages, he told the jury it was their duty to assess the degree of injury to Lord Cadogan due to the loss of the affection of a wife, and the care of a mother over her six living children. He emphasized the gross breach of friendship and hospitality by Cooper, and dwelt upon the betrayal of his religion by a man of the cloth. The jury took an unusually long time for the period—half an hour—before bringing in a verdict of £2,000 damages plus costs, a sum which was far beyond the capacity of the Revd Cooper to pay.[12]

After the verdict, Mary and Cooper seem completely to have lost their heads, a development which Lord Cadogan and his lawyers may well have anticipated. It must be remembered that Cooper had a wife and several young children, was very impoverished because of the financial failure of his father-in-law, and was now faced with a debt of £2,000 to Lord Cadogan, which could well put him in a debtors' prison for life unless the latter chose to take pity on him. As for Mary, she was now entirely dependent on the support of her parents, who were unlikely to look favourably on any continuation of her adulterous connection with a married clergyman. Moreover, the trial for separation in the ecclesiastical courts had still to take place, and the evidence for her adultery was good but still not completely watertight. There was still a chance, even if not a large one, that her husband's separation suit might fail for lack of overwhelming proof, and out of sympathy for her because of her husband's neglect during her long period of serious illness. Every counsel of prudence pointed to a careful avoidance for the time being of any further contact between Mary and Cooper.

They proceeded, however, to do the exact opposite. The day after the verdict was handed down in the Court of King's Bench, and no doubt after a violent family row over her behaviour as revealed at the one-day

[12] *NC Trials for Adultery* (1797), 1.

trial, she left her father's house and moved into rented lodgings in the Edgeware Road. Meanwhile Cadogan had ordered his estate steward, Thomas Bigelstone, to keep a careful watch on the movements of both Mary and Cooper. He was especially anxious first to get more conclusive evidence of adultery between them, and secondly to put Cooper safely behind bars to prevent his fleeing abroad to avoid arrest for the debt.

Bigelstone's detectives soon located Mary in her rented house, and Cooper at a friend's house in Great Cumberland Street. He was living there, since his wife and family had presumably now separated themselves from him because of his adultery. The detectives maintained their watch, and on 24 August observed Mary and Cooper climb into a chaise together and flee towards the West Country. The pair were not hard to follow, since Mary cut an unusual figure, carrying a birdcage with two bullfinches in it, and they were soon tracked down to the Angel Inn in Abergavenny. They were attended by Mary's two faithful servants from the Cadogan household, her maid, Farley Bull, and her manservant, James Chapman, who had covered up the adulterous meetings in the Grosvenor Street and Lowestoft houses.

The pair rented a house in the suburbs of Abergavenny for a while, and Bigelstone himself secretly observed them walking arm in arm in the garden. For the lovers it was a brief period of sunshine before the storm broke. The only precaution they took against detection was that Cooper always spent at least part of each night at the Angel Inn. During her escape from London to Abergavenny, and her stay there for about six weeks from late August to early October, Mary showed no signs whatever of being the weak, sickly, neurasthenic woman that she had formerly been, subject to muscle cramps and fits, who could only get herself out of bed in the mid-afternoon. The awakening of her libido in her late forties entirely cured these symptoms. The subsequent vigour with which she defended herself in her inevitably losing legal battle in the ecclesiastical courts against separation from her husband on grounds of adultery suggests that the cure lasted for at least a year or two.

While Mary and Cooper enjoyed their brief idyll in what they believed to be their secret hideaway in the Welsh hills at Abergavenny, Lord Cadogan in London kept them under observation, and made his preparations to move in for the kill. First he struck at Cooper. He ordered his London solicitor to send down to Abergavenny a writ for Cooper's arrest for non-payment of the £2,000 damages. The writ was presented to the under-sheriff, who issued a warrant for the arrest, as a result of which Cooper was seized and locked up in Monmouth gaol, where he was to languish until he could either produce satisfactory sureties or pay the debt.

Cadogan's lawyers then turned their attention to Mary. They interrogated the servants and assembled a battery of witnesses who would testify in the ecclesiastical courts, not only to the adultery in Cadogan's houses in the previous year, but also that Mary and Cooper had recently slept in the same bed at an inn at Hay and at the Angel Inn in Abergavenny. Farley Bull and James Chapman remained loyal, however, and nothing could be wrung out of them on the witness stand about what had happened in the rented house at Abergavenny.[13]

The lawsuit in the ecclesiastical courts in 1795–6 was bitterly fought, but the outcome was inevitable. Lord Cadogan won his case, thus gaining three victories: the first in the Court of King's Bench against Cooper; the next against his wife in the London Consistory Court, where Sir William Scott delivered a 'long and elaborate judgment';[14] and the third in the Court of Arches, to which she vainly appealed the verdict.

He then used these three sentences to support a successful private bill in the House of Lords for full divorce from Mary, with freedom to remarry. As a result of the Act of Divorce, Mary lost her husband, any right of access to her children, and any claim to dower or jointure after Lord Cadogan's death, which occurred in 1807, for, since the marriage was annulled, so was any settlement for her widowhood that went with it. Her only consolation was that, as it usually did, the House of Commons saw to it that a clause providing for an appropriate provision for the divorced wife was inserted into the Act.[15] She would not starve.

One can only speculate about what happened next. At the end of the affair Mary was a woman ruined in reputation, cut off from her six living children, most of whom were now adolescents, and at the very best in reduced financial circumstances. She may well have been abandoned by her parents and siblings because of her flagrant adultery, and, unless she could find the money to pay his debt of damages to her ex-husband, she would have to face the prospect of her lover languishing indefinitely in Monmouth gaol. Even if he got out of prison, the Revd Cooper's prospects of advancement in the church were now virtually nil, while it seems unlikely that he could or would try to effect a reconciliation with his own abandoned and financially burdensome wife. The lives of both Mary and the Revd Cooper must have been irretrievably shattered.

Lord Cadogan had got free from marriage with a sickly and boring wife, but the vindictive way he hunted down the guilty couple indicates that he was deeply wounded by the infidelity of his wife Mary and the betrayal of

---

[13] LPCA, D.350: 256–61, 832–42.   [14] *Eng. Rep.* 61: 649 n. a.
[15] House of Lords RO: Private Acts of Parliament 37 Geo. III, cap. 58.

his hospitality by his young friend Cooper. It was said that he was so shattered by 'some unhappy connubial events' that he abandoned his seat at Caversham on a sudden despairing impulse. He sold 'house, furniture, wine in the cellar, and, if we are to credit report, the very roast beef on the spit, to Major Marsac for a sum of money one day before dinner'.[16]

[16] *Biographical Index of the House of Lords* (London, 1808), quoted in *Peerage*, ii. 462 n. c.

11

Otway v. Otway
Private and public separation, 1790–1811

Sarah Cave was the sister and heiress of a childless baronet, Sir Thomas Cave, the last in the male line of the Caves of Stanford Hall, on the Leicestershire–Northamptonshire border. The Caves were a very old family, one of the richest in Leicestershire, and Stanford Hall was one of the finest seats in the county, built by Sir Roger Cave in 1697–1700. Sarah had inherited from her father a marriage portion of £15,000, and stood to inherit property worth £8,000 a year on her brother's death, and £1,400 a year more on that of her mother. She was, therefore, a very great financial and social catch.

The husband she chose was an Irish landowner, Henry Otway of Otway Castle, Co. Tipperary. She married him in 1790, at the age of 22, and when, two years later, her brother died, the couple inherited the great Cave estate and mansion. It was a marriage of personal choice and attraction between two people who had known each other for a long time, and Sarah later admitted that she believed Henry 'to be much attracted to me for several years'. A year after the marriage there developed friction between Henry and Sarah's mother, to whom he was soon sending abusive letters. But this does not seem to have affected the marriage, and in the next fourteen years the couple had nine children, six of whom survived infancy.

But according to Sarah the marriage was turning sour by 1804 or earlier, when Henry's drinking became so bad that it made him 'appear mad at times'. In his drunken fits, he accused her of being 'an incestuous whore' who was sleeping with his brother, and treated her and the children with torrents of frenzied verbal abuse and threats of physical brutality. To make matters worse, between 1804 and 1809 Henry attempted to seduce or rape many of the female servants in the great house, beginning with all six of the successive governesses of his eldest daughter, and running down to a nurse and a laundry maid, two of whom he made pregnant.

As a result, the couple parted beds in 1809 and serious discussions of a private separation began in that year, always centred, as usual, around the two issues of the wife's maintenance allowance, and her custody of the children. His first proposal was that Sarah should go to her mother with the three children, but without any maintenance, a proposal which Sarah refused—very reasonably in view of the huge portion and estate which she had brought to the marriage, and which Henry now enjoyed. She demanded maintenance proportionate to this gigantic contribution to Henry's income and assets.

In 1811 the end finally came, when Henry in a rage ordered Sarah out of the house, but refused to let her take even her 2-year-old daughter with her. Sarah left the house and put the negotiations for separation into the hands of her cousin,[1] William Fremantle, MP, supported by a squadron of lawyers. Her stated objective was to secure 'a separate and ample maintenance and, regardless of her marital offences, communication with her children'. This presumably meant that she wanted to retain her maintenance and her right of access to the children, even if she started living with someone else. By law, Henry retained full custody of all the children until they were 21, and the most that Sarah was now seeking was custody of the three daughters for most of the year. She realized that her three sons, who were by now away at school at Eton, were beyond her grasp.

The main lever she and her lawyers used in trying to extract agreement out of Henry was his fear of scandal. If she were to sue him before an ecclesiastical court for separation from bed and board, on grounds of adultery and cruelty, it would not make a pretty story. All the sordid details, about Henry's drunkenness, his many attacks on the chastity of the maidservants, and his cruel and abusive behaviour to his wife and children would come out in court, and be printed in the newspapers. The other lever was the expense of litigation, and Henry was reminded that he would have to 'pay the expenses of the suit on both sides, and also alimony during its dependence, and be compelled to set forth the property upon oath'. The twin fears of public disgrace and high legal costs were strong inducements to make him settle out of court.

Sarah told her cousin and legal adviser that she was most anxious about 'my future maintenance, and obtaining possession of my poor children (whose situation is very deplorable)'. She insisted on having her daughters with her, since she was convinced that the two head servants at Stanford Hall were 'most improper persons for them to be with: the butler acted as a pimp in procuring women for his master; and the housekeeper not only connived at what went on, but also herself acted indecently'. Sarah's proctor threatened Henry with 'the most public exposure of all the transactions which have occurred since your marriage', beginning with the circulation

---

[1] The file of correspondance between Sarah Cave and her lawyer cousin survives in Bucks. RO, Fremantle Papers D/FR/48/1.

of Sarah's bill of particulars to all his family. On the other hand, her lawyers advised Sarah that she should not ask too much for maintenance, in view of the fact that Henry would be responsible for the upkeep of Stanford Hall, as well as the education of the six children.

Henry resisted this pressure, denying the charges of cruelty, expressing willingness to come to 'an amicable arrangement', and stressing 'the heart-rending grievances of which I have to complain'. One of Henry's letters to Fremantle shows something of his paranoid sexual suspicions of his wife. He charged Fremantle with 'false and base' menaces and went on: 'not that I mean to insinuate that you have any amorous propensity to my wife—No, sir, No. I quite acquit you of this.' In response, Sarah's lawyer again urged upon Henry's solicitor the desirability of making a private separation agreement, arguing that it was good for 'the character and reputation of a most respectable family, and for the happiness of all parties, that the separation should take place without resorting to legal steps'.

The sticking-point, however, was the custody of the three girls. The compromise Henry offered was that they should divide their time between him and Sarah, but in return he demanded a reduction in the size of her maintenance. But the most Sarah was willing to concede was that she should have custody of her daughters but that they could visit their father 'at stated periods' for six to eight weeks a year—'but only attended by a governess chosen by me'. Sarah knew that the Court of Chancery could and did intervene to settle custody of heirs to great estates, and was prepared to start a Chancery suit to obtain custody of her daughters.

While she was fighting for the custody of her three daughters, Sarah was careful to avoid stating exactly what she was demanding as maintenance. It seems clear that she was leaving this open, being prepared to sacrifice some income in return for child custody. However, this message was lost on Henry, and the negotiations reached breaking-point over the child–custody issue before a figure for maintenance was even mentioned on either side.

The fear of scandal continued to weigh heavily, especially on the Otway family, and at the last minute a family friend offered himself as a mediator in order to save 'the peace, honour, reputation, and happiness of the ancient and respectable family at Stanford Hall'. But it came too late. The wheels of the law had already been set in motion, in a suit begun by Sarah for separation from bed and board on grounds of adultery and cruelty. Sarah lost in the Consistory Court, presumably because Henry had never actually struck her, and male adultery with serving maids was a commonplace event, which sensible wives were expected to ignore. But Sarah appealed her case to the Court of Arches, where she won. Since there had been no actual blows struck, the Court hedged as to whether or not, if it had stood

alone, the charge of cruelty would have been sufficient to justify a separation. But, taken together with the repeated acts of adultery, the Court
decided to grant a separation, a decision which marked something of a legal
landmark.[2] Who finally obtained custody of the three girls is not known.
Sarah threatened to appeal for help from the Lord Chancellor, but it is
very doubtful whether she would have won her case.

What this story brings out so vividly is the intense concern by family
friends and legal advisers to avoid the shame and disgrace of airing domestic
grievances in open court. On the other hand, such was the obstinacy of
Henry Otway that the two critical issues upon which the resolution of the
separation negotiations depended were unable to be resolved. These two
were, first, a substantial maintenance allowance for Sarah, bearing in mind
that the bulk of the fortune of Henry Otway had come from her; and,
secondly, some compromise over the custody of the children. Sarah insisted
on having full custody of the three girls, with arrangements for visits to
their father, conceding to her husband custody of the three boys, but
demanding visiting rights to them. But Henry was unwilling to yield on
either of these points, as a result of which litigation and the attendant
publicity became inevitable.

[2] *Otway* v. *Otway* (1811), LPCA, H.170/1–22; *Eng. Rep.* 161: 1088–90.

12

Westmeath v. Westmeath
The wars between the Westmeaths, 1812–1857

(i) The Failure of the Marriage, 1812–1818

In the early months of 1812 George Nugent Lord Delvin, the 26-year-old son and heir of the Irish 7th Earl of Westmeath, and a half-pay captain in the army, was paying court to the 23-year-old Lady Emily Cecil, second daughter of the 1st Marquis of Salisbury (see Genealogy of the Nugent (Westmeath) family).[1] An Anglo-Irish acquaintance noted in her diary in April: 'Lady Emily Cecil is going to be married to Lord Delvin, Lord Westmeath's son. He is very poor, and I think it is a wretched match for her, but they have been long in love.'[2] Apart from his poverty, other drawbacks to George as a prospective husband were that his mother had been divorced for adultery, so that in strict circles he was regarded as coming from a scandalous family, and that he was already the father of a child by a mistress in Ireland. Emily knew about the liaison, having been told about it by her brother, Lord Cranborne. The latter had explained to her that, when young and with the regiment—that is before 1805 when he was only 19—George 'had been saddled with a child by a woman he had seen a few times', and he advised his sister to ignore the matter. Assuming that the affair was long since over, Emily saw no reason to reject George's courtship, and they were married in her father's private chapel at Hatfield House in May 1812.[3] It has to be assumed that so apparently unsuitable an alliance between a Cecil daughter and the heir to a raffish and impoverished Irish peerage must indeed have been a love-match on both sides. On the other hand, her mother may have favoured the marriage, since she was the

---

[1] The materials for this story are drawn partly from private correspondence in the Stowe MSS in the Huntington Library and the Westmeath Papers at Hatfield House. The bulk of the evidence, however, comes from numerous lawsuits over the case. They are drawn from LPCA, D.2240; and many printed records in *Eng. Rep.*, especially vols. 5, 6, 162; RIA/HP 1342; BL 1609/4162; *British Trials, 1660–1900*, published in microfilm by Chadwick Healey (1992); and two personal pamphlets: *Narrative of the Case, and Reply to the Narrative*.

[2] Calvert Diary, 11: 21 Apr. 1812; I owe references to this document to my wife, Jeanne C. Fawtier Stone.　　　　　　　　　　　　[3] LPCA, D.2240: 107–9, 491, 1021.

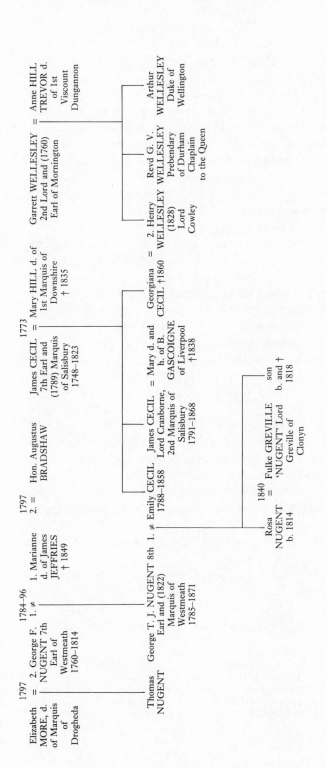

5. Genealogy of the Nugent (Westmeath) family

daughter of an Irish peer, Lord Hillsborough, later Marquis of Downshire, and liked to regard herself as an Irishwoman.[4]

This marriage into the Cecil family was in financial and political terms a distinct step up for the Nugents. They were an old Norman baronial family which had been settled in Ireland since the twelfth century, but it was only quite recently, in the middle of the eighteenth century, that they had abjured Catholicism and become firm Protestants. The marriage settlement reflected the financial disparity between them. The Marquis of Salibury provided Emily with a portion of £15,000, but it was strictly settled on any future younger children of the marriage. Only £5,000 of it was supposed to be in cash, contributed by her mother, the Marchioness of Salisbury, but in fact even this was not paid, since the money was still owing to the latter. The remaining £10,000, contributed by the Marquis, took the form of an annuity of £500 a year at 5 per cent interest.[5] This arrangement continued until the Marquis's death in 1823, soon after which his son and heir, flush with the fruits of his own marriage with the great mercantile Gascoigne heiress, paid off the £10,000 in cash.

In return, Emily was guaranteed pin-money of £500 a year out of her marriage portion annuity, which was for her exclusive use so long as George lived; and a jointure of £3,000 a year as a widow after his death, out of the Nugent estates. As George was to complain, decades later in 1857, 'nothing was paid down to me upon my marriage'.[6] By this socially ambitious marriage, George and his father had taken on a much larger financial burden than their family estates could support. As a result, George discovered in 1824 that 'the heavy jointure settled on this lady [Emily] on her marriage . . . compromised my security, so that I could not then raise money on my property'.[7] To make matters worse, the Nugent family estate was burdened with debt, much of which went back to 1796, when George had been 11 years old and his father had divorced his mother for adultery; while much of the estate was let out on old three-life leases dating back to 1736.

For the first year after their marriage George and Emily alternated between his residence at Black Rock near Dublin, and long stays with her family at Hatfield House. In May 1813, however, George took Emily away to the Nugent family seat at Clonyn Castle in Co. Westmeath, Ireland,

---

[4] C. Colvin (ed.), *Maria Edgeworth: Letters from England, 1813–44* (Oxford, 1971), 327.
[5] *Eng. Rep.* 5: 367; LPCA, D.2240: 189, 378; H.365/10; *Reply to the Narrative*, 7.
[6] LPCA, H.365/1, 10, 20; 2; other estimates were as low as £1,200 net and as high as £6,600 (H.365/20) or £10,000 when the long leases expired, which is what George allegedly told Emily's family before the marriage (*Narrative of the Case*, 90, 111, 170, 205, 207, 209, 210 n.).   [7] *Reply to the Narrative*, 20.

where they lived until September 1815.[8] When they returned to London it was partly at the insistence of Emily, and partly because of some signs of violence in the Irish countryside. A friend wrote to Emily that he was 'delighted that you are out of the way of such horrors'.[9] But, even if it had been safe from violence, residence in a tumbledown old castle lost in the woods in the remote Irish countryside represented a traumatic and most unwelcome change for Emily. Hitherto she had lived a life of luxury and frenetic gaiety amid the highest circles of English society, whether at Court, where her father had been Lord Chamberlain until 1804, or in London during the season, or amid the splendours of Hatfield House. Marital friction was held at bay, however, by Emily's pregnancy, and in May 1814 she gave birth to a daughter, who was baptized Rosa—'quite a novel name' in those days.[10]

Meanwhile both Emily and George inherited money. In 1813 Emily's aunt, Lady Anne Cecil died, leaving her all her plate, jewellery, and furniture, as well as the reversion of £12,500 on the death of her father, the Marquis of Salisbury. In 1814 the old Earl of Westmeath died at his town house in Dublin, leaving George in full possession of the family seat of Clonyn and the much encumbered and still unsettled Nugent estates. In 1819 George was boasting to Emily that he was free to do as he pleased with them, and he did not finally settle the estates until 1822.[11]

By early 1814, less than two years after their marriage, and immediately after the birth of Rosa, the couple were already quarrelling bitterly. The disputes arose mainly because of Emily's jealousy of George's mistress in Ireland. She resented the fact that George not only still saw the woman, but had recently fathered another bastard child on her. She also resented the financial support he was still giving this second family, particularly in view of the penurious conditions to which she was condemned at Clonyn, where George left her for weeks at a time without a penny for housekeeping.

In 1815 marital relations became so bad that the situation had to be patched up by a formal meeting of reconciliation orchestrated by a close mutual family friend, Henry Widman Wood, who owned a seat a mile and a half from Clonyn.[12] Under the terms of the agreement, George solemnly undertook never to see his mistress or their children again; to give them no

[8] *Eng. Rep.* 162: 1018, 1024 (*Westmeath* v. *Westmeath*, 1826).
[9] Hatfield House, Westmeath Papers.
[10] Calvert Diary, 20: 9 Feb. 1819.   [11] *Narrative of the Case*, 79, 80.
[12] LPCA, D.2240: 127, 357–9; RIA/HP 1342: *Reports of Some Cases in which the Marquis and Marchioness of Westmeath have been Litigant Parties* (1825); *Eng. Rep.* 162: 1004, 1018, 1020 (*Westmeath* v. *Westmeath*, 1826).

more than a fixed and limited amount of money, transmitted solely through Emily's trusted personal maid, Sarah Mackenzie; and never to write to or receive letters from them. In return, Emily promised never to mention them again. But even then she was afraid that George would break his promise, and that 'it would come at last to her being driven to apply for a divorce'. To prepare her documentation for such an eventuality, she told George, 'I plainly tell you I expect you to give me a written paper' about the terms of the agreement.[13]

In order to remove George physically from his Irish mistress and his children by her, the reunited couple left for a nine-month stay in France, mostly in Paris, Emily being accompanied by her friend Miss Wood, the daughter of the peacemaker. In Paris George suffered an attack of ophthalmia, and was confined to his hotel for three weeks. During this time Emily 'was out hunting constantly, and riding hard', while 'in the evenings she was frequently at parties from home'. In short, she threw herself into 'a perpetual round of gaiety'. Not only did she neglect her husband while he was incapacitated, she also spent much more money than he could afford.[14] As a result, early in 1817 the Cecil trustees had to be persuaded by Emily to advance £3,600 from Lady Anne Cecil's legacy as a loan to help her and George pay off debts accumulated during their trip to France, and to finance the setting-up of a house and establishment in London, all of which allowed Emily to avoid having to return to Clonyn.[15]

Emily disingenuously told her trustees that 'Lord Westmeath has been so uniformly kind to me that I cannot bear to see him unhappy'. This was a double lie; first, because it was she, not George, who was determined to set up house in London; and, secondly, because, both in France and later in London, a good deal of quarrelling had gone on and they had already separated beds. The main cause of the rupture was Emily's discovery that George had broken his word and had continued to keep in touch with his mistress and bastard children.[16]

There had also been one recent act of impulsive physical violence by George, which illustrates not only his hair-trigger temper, but also Emily's petulant and prudish nature. The party was travelling from Calais to Paris on Christmas Eve 1815, just as the whole British army was withdrawing to the coast, after the battle of Waterloo and the occupation of the French capital. As a result, all the hotels on the road were already crammed with

---

[13] LPCA, D.2240: 378, 411–13; *Reply to the Narrative*, 76–7.
[14] *Sketch*, 25; LPCA, D.2240: 347, 1175, 1191, 1203.
[15] LPCA, D.2240: 1045, 1132–4, 1167–9, 1723; H.365/10; *Eng. Rep.* 162: 1010 (*Westmeath v. Westmeath*, 1826); *Reply to the Narrative*, 18.
[16] LPCA, D.2240: 130, 240, 333–7, 411, 425; H.365/10.

carousing soldiers, and there was not a bed to be had. It was midnight and snowing when, tired, wet, and cold, the party reached Grandvilliers, having been unable to find any accommodation at all at the previous town. Their postilion somehow managed to find them a room in the best hotel, the Hotel de la Poste. It was full of drunken and noisy officers and their women, as were all the hotels from Calais to Paris. George expected gratitude for finding them a room at all, but instead Emily turned on him and demanded to know why 'have you brought me to a brothel?' It was under these trying circumstances that he lost his temper and hit her, shouting: 'Go to Hell. I wish I had never seen you.'[17]

In the summer of 1817 Emily finally left George, taking with her little Rosa, and decided to sue him for legal separation on grounds of cruelty.[18] George was heart-broken, and in the months after they were separated wrote Emily a series of agonized letters. In them he repeatedly expressed his passionate love for Emily, his acute misery at being separated from her, and his sincere repentance for his previous behaviour towards her. The letters express an extreme agony of mind, bordering on suicidal despair:

I know well I brought everything on myself by a bad outset . . . All I dare hope for, and what I only value in the world, is your regard, that the person who had the heart to be the most disinterested being on earth to me, whose soul was given over to be the loving friend of wretched, wretched me, should not fling me from her mind . . . You say I only live in your recollection to be detested. I cannot go on in life under such a conviction. Tell me you do not hate me, Emily . . . Poor little Rosa, her mother deserved to have had an husband of whom she could have spoken to her as I fear you can never do of me, but it is bad for her, poor little thing, that the best she can know of her unhappy father is not to have known him at all. May God bless you, and comfort you, for the blast I have made of your happiness. I have not now an object on earth, and I only wish and pray to die. I have gone through my repentance, but bitterly, bitterly have I suffered. At one time I fully determined to go with the child, and never see you again; at another, to leave everything with you, but go; at a third, to destroy myself; but it is evident that I can do nothing. Oh, pardon and forgive me, Emily; what a comfort it would be to my very great wretchedness to think that I was dear to you in any degree.

Pardon for so much brutality. I was an Hell to you. I do still cling to the hope, however, that when I am gone, you will try to forget your wrongs from me, and to forgive them here: I have not now an object on earth, and only wish and pray to die when I have secured my impoverished estate in the way you wished it to little Rosa, your flesh and blood. It is my intention to do for her what her mother's heart to me calls for and deserves; tell me you do not doubt it. Indeed I am

---

[17] LPCA, D.2240: 237, 335, 423; *Reply to the Narrative*, 81.
[18] LPCA, H.365/10.

crumbling fast, and only wish to live for that. Don't say you wish her dead; she will be a comfort to you, though I never was, but the reverse; pray tell me this, for I am very, very wretched. Tell me you do not hate me, Emily. Do support me until I can, for I really do think that in the state I have been for a month past, I shall not hold it out. I only wish and pray to die.

Amidst these hysterical lamentations, George admitted that he had treated Emily abominably: he had abused and struck her; and he had threatened to turn her out of doors and disinherit Rosa. He had also falsely assured her that on his father's death he would be worth £10,000 a year, whereas rents had now fallen by half; he had omitted to disclose that the property was saddled with heavy mortgages for debt; and, worst of all, he had continued to supply his mistress and her family with money.[19]

Once again, matters were patched up between them, thanks to the renewed mediation of Mr Henry Wood, the abject contrition of George, and the determined opposition of Emily's parents, the Salisburys, even to a private separation, much less to the public scandal of a suit for separation in the ecclesiastical courts. The Marchioness of Salisbury went down on her aged knees and begged her daughter 'not to make themselves the talk of the town'.[20]

By resisting these desperate pleas for forgiveness from October to December 1817, Emily slowly wore George down until he was at her mercy. When she at last agreed to a reconciliation, it was strictly on her own terms. She wrote: 'Let us say no more about it, mon cher ami. . . . I hope we may yet pass many happy years of comfort, as if nothing had happened. On my part, I assure you I forgive you and will sincerely try to forget; and on yours I hope you will excuse any violence of words on my part.' George was overjoyed to hear that he was forgiven, and replied ecstatically: 'I am sure, my dearest Emily, my dear little soul, you will not expect me to describe my feelings at your last letter. After your feelings had been so much wounded, I confess I did not expect so great a blessing. I cannot be too thankful.' He accepted her terms unconditionally, and was willing to sign anything: 'I cannot bear to lose a day in expressing my gratitude to you. I shall be anxious to make arrangements such as you must naturally desire to secure yourself in case of any unfortunate recurrence. . . . I wish your will to be my law.'[21]

The key to the reconciliation was a new financial settlement, worked out

[19] LPCA, D.2240: 171–85; H.365/15; RIA/HP 1342: 60–9 (*Westmeath* v. *Westmeath, Cranborne et al.*, 1821).
[20] *Reply to the Narrative*, 75; *Sketch*, 15.
[21] RIA/HP 1342: 60–7 (*Westmeath* v. *Westmeath, Cranborne et al.*, 1821); LPCA, D.2240: 151–85; H.365/16; *Eng. Rep.* 162: 1021–3, 1027–9 (*Westmeath* v. *Westmeath*, 1826).

in December 1817 and embodied in a written indenture. In it Emily drove a very hard bargain indeed. In return for her withdrawal of the threat to sue George for legal separation on grounds of cruelty, and her agreement to renew cohabitation and sexual relations, George now agreed to settle on Rosa, not only the reversion of her mother's portion of £15,000, but also the reversion of much of his own Nugent estates, if he and Emily failed to produce a surviving male heir. This was a very unusual arrangement, since it potentially separated the descent of the property from that of the title, and cut out of the inheritance George's half-brother by his father's second marriage.

At the same time George also signed a separation indenture conditional upon possible marital breakdown in the future—something known at the time as a 'prospective deed'. If Emily should at any time decide to separate herself from him, George promised to make her an allowance—the amount of which was to be settled by the Cecil family lawyer and other family friends; to pay for the maintenance and education of Rosa; and to concede to Emily full custody and control of the child.[22] This was a remarkably one-sided document, later described by an ecclesiastical court judge as 'rather an extraordinary specimen of matrimonial law'.[23] Even 'the confidential legal adviser of the Cecil family', William Sheldon, a Bencher of Gray's Inn, was shocked by it. He told George that, if he were in his shoes, 'he would rather cut off his right hand than put it to such a deed'.[24]

For about three months after the signing of the indenture in December 1817 the couple stayed at Hatfield House, and the reconciliation held. George was sufficiently alarmed by his financial situation, and sufficiently respectful of his wife's abilities, to agree that Emily should take over the management of his estates, paying him £500 a year as pocket money, spending £2,000 a year to maintain the two of them, and using the rest of the income to pay off debts. This arrangement pleased Emily very much since it greatly increased her power, and her mother reported that 'she seemed in high spirits at it'. By March 1818 she was pregnant again.

But soon after the pregnancy was confirmed, fresh violent marital quarrels erupted, and in May 1818 George and Emily again parted beds—as it turned out, for ever.[25] Three days later George was summoned and asked to sign yet another indenture, which contained the details of the separation, while the pregnant Emily waited in the next room. He signed it, but at the

---

[22] LPCA, D.2240: 131–5, 189–207, 245, 495, 1041, 1124.
[23] *Eng. Rep.* 162: 1006 (*Westmeath* v. *Westmeath*, 1826).
[24] RIA/HP 1342: 45 (*H. W. Wood* v. *Westmeath*, 1822); LPCA, D.2240: 359.
[25] LPCA, D.2240: 457, 810, 1126, 1132, 1175; *Eng. Rep.* 152: 1008 (*Westmeath* v. *Westmeath*, 1826).

same time wrote a letter, stating that he only did it because, 'considering the known violence of her temper, had I refused, the worst consequences, perhaps her death and the miscarriage of the child of which she was pregnant, would probably have ensured'. George also complained that, as soon as she knew she was pregnant, Emily had broken the terms of the earlier indenture of 1817 by refusing to continue to sleep with him. He added that 'even my child Rosa has been encouraged by my wife to open disobedience and rebellion to me'. George gave copies of this curious protest to Emily's two legal advisers, Sheldon and Wood. The latter interpreted the document as a way of preparing the ground for a later evasion of the terms of the deed. In consequence, 'considering it as an intended fraud, I treated it with indignity'.[26]

What seems to have happened was this. Emily's first inclination after they had parted again had been to revive her plan publicly to sue George in the ecclesiastical courts for separation on grounds of cruelty, but she had been persuaded by her mother and legal advisers to accept a private deed of separation instead, being assured that 'the end would be answered by a deed, and would be less irksome to Lord Westmeath', who like the Saliburys was most anxious to avoid a public scandal. So in May 1818 a second separation indenture was prepared for signing, which assured Emily her pin-money of £500 a year, a very generous separation allowance of £1,300 a year, and full custody of both Rosa and the unborn child. George also promised to leave Emily in peace to live where and with whom she pleased, and not to sue her in the ecclesiastical courts for 'restitution of conjugal rights', a legal device by which he could force her to return under his roof and control.

Just as George was about to sign this one-sided document, Emily put her victory in jeopardy by boasting to a friend: 'I now have George completely in my power.' On hearing this, George lost his temper, rushed off to the stationer's office where the indenture had been sent for copying, snatched it up, tore it into shreds, and immediately left for Ireland. It was not until August that he had calmed down sufficiently to allow himself to be persuaded to sign another copy.[27]

After the separation, Emily let the Nugent town house in London and rented a smaller one, where in November 1818 she gave birth to a baby boy. But George requested permission to occupy in the house a bedroom, a sitting-room, and a room for his servant, so as 'to conceal from the world

---

[26] *Reply to the Narrative*, 51–3; LPCA, D.2240: 274.
[27] LPCA, D.2240: 139, 211, 253, 361, 372–4, 810, 1047, 1126; RIA/HP 1342: 9–10 (*Westmeath* v. *Westmeath, Cranborne, et al.*, 1821); 46–9 (*H. W. Wood* v. *Westmeath*, 1822).

as much as possible their domestic differences'. Because of his earnest pleas, strongly supported by her mother, the Marchioness of Salisbury, the family friend, Mr Wood, and the Cecil family solicitor, Mr Sheldon, Emily very reluctantly allowed George to take up residence in her house, but only as a lodger and without any authority whatever over the household or the servants. She always slept behind locked doors, while her maid slept in the anteroom, the communicating door of which was always left open so that she could protect her mistress from any attempted marital intrusion. Emily was assured by Mr Sheldon that by such an arrangement she ran no legal risks of appearing to condone George's previous marital faults of physical cruelty to her and continued adultery with his old mistress.[28]

For nearly a year the couple continued to live in the same house, but met only at the dinner-table. Emily systematically spurned all George's overtures, for example refusing to be handed into her carriage by him. When they quarrelled, as they often did, they spoke in French so as to conceal what they said from the servants, so that we do not know the subjects in dispute. During a Christmas visit to Hatfield, they slept in the same apartment they had always occupied, but in separate beds. Appearances were thus kept up, both before friends and before the family, and a visitor to the house in February 1819 merely remarked in her diary: 'We got in at Lady Westmeath's. She is a dear little woman, and has got the nicest little girl of nearly four years old.'[29] The visitor was clearly entirely unaware, not only that the couple were not sleeping together, but that they were barely on speaking terms.

(ii) *The Causes of the Failure*

The time has now come to try to disentangle the many causes of the breakdown of the marriage. Both George and Emily were difficult people. George was exceptionally quick-tempered, and liable to fly into uncontrollable rages on the slightest provocation. As his housekeeper testified, 'he is a most violent passionate man'. In the heat of anger he occasionally struck Emily, several times quite brutally, and he was constantly shouting at her. A companion on the French trip said: 'his temper appeared to be ungovernable.' On one occasion he was described as 'in a most violent and extraordinary passion, amounting to almost fury, though apparently in a degree exhausted; was pale as a sheet of writing paper, his hands quivered, his whole frame shook with rage'. The best that anyone could say about this

---

[28] LPCA, D.2240: 141–3, 457, 1047, 1127, 1153, 1157, 1207–211; *Eng. Rep.* 108: 429 (*Hindley* v. *Westmeath*, 1827); 6: 619, 623 (*Westmeath* v. *Westmeath*, 1830); 5: 353 (*Westmeath* v. *Westmeath*, 1832). [29] Calvert Diary, 10 Feb. 1819.

trait was that he 'is apt to be violent so far as hasty talk goes, when irritated. He is excitable, but his passion is soon over.'[30]

A good example of George's hair-trigger temper is provided by his relations with Henry Wood, the close family friend who negotiated the marital reconciliation of 1817 and the private separation of 1818. By early 1819 George had somehow convinced himself that Wood, along with his daughter, who was a great friend of Emily, had been conspiring against him, a suspicion for which there was not a shred of evidence. On Good Friday 1819 George burst into Wood's London house, shaking his fist and shouting at him, accusing him of hiding some of his property which had been removed by Emily. Wood retorted calmly, 'I am not afraid of you,' and explained that Emily had indeed deposited some of her property with him. George snapped, 'I am answered,' and stormed out of the house as suddenly as he had appeared. The next day there was a fresh exchange between them about the incident. George, who was clearly in a very agitated state of mind, claimed that he had apologized, explaining that his outbreak was caused by his 'nervousness'. Two years later, however, after Wood, in his capacity as Emily's trustee, had sued him in Chancery for payment of her maintenance allowance, George sent him 'a very indecent and offensive message', in which he called him 'a liar, a hypocrite, a coward, and one of the greatest rascals that ever pretended to be an honest man'. This was clearly intended to provoke Wood (who was in his sixties) to a duel. But, instead of taking up the challenge, Wood sued George in King's Bench for 'provoking him to fight' and therefore making himself 'guilty of a breach of the peace'. The case gave Wood's barrister, the arch Tory Charles Wetherell, the opportunity to make a ringing declaration of that favourite English paradigm of the total equality before the law of nobleman and commoner. George hired both the Solicitor-General and Brougham to defend him, but it was no use. The jury found him guilty, and the Chief Justice condemned him to prison in the Marshalsea for three months.[31] He bitterly resented the fact that, on the eve of his imprisonment, Emily went to the Duchess of Londonderry's ball. While he was in prison Emily arranged to have him watched, in hopes of catching him in adultery, as George later discovered.[32]

The violent temperament that landed George in the Marshalsea is clearly exposed in a bundle of letters written to his estate agent in Ireland in 1821,

[30] LPCA, D.2240: 121–30, 137, 335–7, 357–8, 381, 443, 1032, 1179, 1239; *Greville Memoirs*, iii. 69–70.
[31] LPCA, D.2240: 375–7; RIA/HP 1342: 31–59 (*H. W. Wood* v. *Westmeath*, 1822); Hatfield House, Newspaper Clippings, 1821.
[32] *Sketch*, 38; *Reply to the Narrative*, 70–1.

when bailiffs working on a court order obtained by Emily were busy trying to distrain his land and personal property for non-payment of her separation allowance. How these letters found their way into Emily's hands is a mystery, but she seems to have bought them after the death of George's agent. It should be remembered that, at the time, George was Governor of the County of Westmeath, Colonel of the County Militia, and about to be raised to the rank of Marquis by a Tory government. And yet, not only did he resort to every legal trick in the book to protect his property, but he also openly incited his tenants to resist distraint by physical force.

He ordered his agent to keep the house at Clonyn 'well secured', and added: 'If they [the bailiffs] break in they may be shot.' He repeatedly referred to the bailiffs as 'villains, robbers, wretches who are a disgrace to humanity, devils, trespassers', and promised that 'the devil will claim his own and have them at last'. He told his agent that his friend the Duke of Buckingham 'has always said that force ought to be always opposed to any attempt to make distraints on my property'. In accordance with this advice, he ordered his agent to urge his tenants to 'resist them by force . . . and beat them off and treat them like robbers'. These were the language and tactics of a gangster rather than of a nobleman, a great landowner, and a leading public figure in the county.[33]

Years later, in 1834, when his endless litigation with Emily was before the Judicial Committee of the Privy Council, George almost got into a fight in the House of Lords with Brougham, now Lord Chancellor, and had to be physically restrained by a peer sitting beside him. Friends urged the Lord Chancellor 'not to exasperate that madman, who would say or do something violent'.[34] Further evidence of George's hasty verbal temper was that he was once sued for libel in Ireland, and had to pay large damages.[35]

George did not suffer merely from habitual shortness of temper. He was also a passionate advocate of extreme views upon a wide variety of issues, including marriage, politics, and religion. For example, he was not merely a staunch Protestant, but a fanatical anti-Catholic, as is shown by some of his surviving correspondence. After 1815 he was a candidate to be elected to a seat in the British House of Lords as one of the twenty-eight Representative Peers of Ireland. As vacancies occurred, new Representatives were in theory elected by the Irish peerage as a whole, but up to 1825 the victor was in practice nominated by the current Lord-Lieutenant, who represented the British government. George was defeated in 1825, when he rested his claim on his long residence in Ireland 'and the antiquity of his

---

[33] *Narrative of the Case*, 141–6, 150, 160, 162.
[34] *Greville Memoirs*, iii. 69–70.   [35] *Reply to the Narrative*, 91–2.

peerage'.[36] When he tried again in 1830, his electoral platform was based on diehard opposition to the recent Catholic Emancipation Bill. He assured his backers that he shared with

the Protestant party the apprehensions they entertain of a projected dismemberment of the church. I will never aid in that. Besides a public feeling on that subject, I have a considerable property in tithes myself, and I never will assist in robbing myself of I know not what. My object is the good of Ireland, my determination is to support the British connection and to discourage all agitation which can weaken it. These are my principles, and as a public man I hope they may entitle me to the honour of your support.

They did, and in 1831 he was duly elected Representative Peer for Ireland for life.

In 1828 he was outraged that the Duke of Wellington should be supporting Catholic Emancipation, and told his friends: 'I abhor the Duke of Wellington and will denounce him while I live.'[37] As the years went by, George never wavered in his contempt and hatred of Roman Catholics. In 1834 he flatly refused to give a site for the first National School in the parish of Delvin, which he owned.[38] In 1836 he complained to his friend the Duke of Buckingham about the growth of immorality, caused, he claimed, by the feeble policies of the Whig government. Religion 'enters into every dealing between man and man when a Roman Catholic is a party. That class are so ignorant that they have run wild, and systematically they are employed in *worrying* the Protestants whenever and wherever they can.'[39]

Old age did nothing to mellow George, and nearly thirty years later he was even more vitriolic on the subject of Catholics. In 1865 he wrote an angry letter denouncing the electoral address of his more liberal grandson Greville, who was standing for the County of Westmeath:

I take leave to say, that I consider the two words 'Tenant Right' (adopted by the priests as their catch-word for mischief) as rank nonsense. I am sure no member of my family would ever propose at a public meeting 'Three cheers for the priests'—animals who, although nurtured upon the public stirabout and buttermilk of Maynooth, have in many places in Ireland and, as we know in the county of Westmeath, in the interests of the Church of Rome, assumed to themselves, *by means peculiarly their own*, to be the patrons of the county representation.'[40]

[36] Public Record Office of Northern Ireland, Farnham Papers, letter of 5 Oct. 1825 (I owe this reference to Dr A. P. W. Malcomson).

[37] Ibid. letter of 9 Dec. 1830.

[38] H. Fitzsimmons, *The Great Delvin* (Dublin, 1975) 99 (I owe this reference to Dr A. P. W. Malcomson).

[39] Huntington Library, Stowe MSS, Box 82 (29), letter of 22 Oct. 1836.

[40] Public Record Office of Northern Ireland, Longford/Westmeath Library, Howard Bury Papers, T3069, K6, letter of 10 Aug. (1865 (I owe this reference to Dr A. P. W. Malcomson).

Given the shortness of George's temper, the intransigence of his views, and his total inability to curb either his tongue or his pen, he cannot have been an easy man to live with. He was always close to boiling-point on some subject or other, whether private or public. On the other hand, George's letters of 1817 leave no doubt whatever about his passionate love for Emily, however badly he might momentarily treat her when in a rage. The two separation deeds he meekly signed were by the standards of the day very humiliating for a husband.

If George was in many ways impossible to live with, Emily had an equal share in responsibility for the breakdown of the marriage. She evidently possessed an iron will, was extremely obstinate, and never forgot or forgave an injury. Again and again it was her dogged refusal to compromise, her cold and sullen resistance, and her occasional bursts of anger, which stimulated George to fly into one of his uncontrollable rages. Even her father and mother admitted these defects of character.[41] Though very small and slightly built, when she was young she was generally regarded as very pretty (Plate 14).

In 1809 a Persian diplomat in London, who tended to gush about all women, called her 'this lovely jewel', declared that at first setting eyes on her 'my heart skipped a beat', and described her conversation as 'flirtatious'. In a lawsuit in 1825 her lawyer described her to the court as 'young, beautiful, accomplished, gay and high-spirited'.[42]

As time went on, more discriminating observers noticed a harder streak underneath the surface prettiness. Maria Edgeworth remarked that Emily's elder sister was 'not handsome, but I like her countenance better than Lady Westmeath's', and a favourable witness conceded that, despite her charm and vivacity, she was 'a quick-tempered woman, and, when irritated, would show it, but she was never inclined to quarrel'. Henry Fox was more brief and to the point, describing her as 'a lively pretty little vixen, which I believe she is'.[43]

In 1857 Emily published her *Narrative of the Case*, recounting all the wrongs done to her in the long years of litigation. In it she comes out as obstinate, petty, vindictive, and fanatical about the injustices done to married women under existing English law. She admits that she rejected no fewer than five attempts at arbitration of the many issues involved in her marriage

---

[41] LPCA, D.2240: 240–3, 349, 416, 489, 1126, 1133, 1138, 1667.

[42] *A Persian at the Court of King George* (London, 1988) (I owe this reference to the kindness of Mr Robin Harcourt-Williams); RIA/HP 1342; 5–6 (*Westmeath v. Anne Connell, et al.*, 1825).

[43] *Eng. Rep.* 162: 1017 (*Westmeath v. Westmeath*, 1826); Colvin (ed.), *Maria Edgeworth: Letters*, 327; *Journal of Henry Fox* (London, 1923), 133.

and separation. At the same time her self-righteousness is almost unendurable. She told the world that 'I have the approbation of my own conscience'; she complained of losing in twenty-five years of litigation 'such a large portion of my just rights'; she objected to 'the want of common courtesy, which I always show to others and therefore expect to receive'; and she boasted that 'I pique myself upon being fair and above-board in my dealings.' In mitigation, it should be said that her endless legal troubles had ruined her health, so that she had been forced to spend many years abroad, in order to avoid the English winters; and there can also be no doubt that married women in her situation were abominably treated under current English law.[44]

According to her, she published her *Narrative* in order to help support the proposed laws about divorce and married women's property law. In the dedication of her pamphlet she states that she was publishing the account of her legal experiences to help 'to obtain justice for a suffering class'. She allied herself with Mrs Caroline Norton in this cause, claiming that her own story 'has few parallels in the sad history of the wrongs of women'. She was outraged by Lord Chancellor Cranworth's airy dismissal of casual male adultery as merely 'a little profligate' and thus not a cause for breaking up a marriage, and concluded that 'an English wife is absolutely nothing but a slave, and a most helpless and oppressed one'. Because of the laws about married women's property, 'a pauper every wife is in this country'. She angrily denied that 'woman was made or intended to be, only a plaything or a slave'. She concluded ominously that, as long as natural justice is not granted to women, 'the very foundations of society are sapped and an empire sinks into decay, like a vicious man from the very consequence of his own misdoings'. For 1857, this was strong language indeed.[45]

When the marriage broke down, there were two pieces of evidence which told against Emily. The first was the fact that not one of her own family supported her in her desire for public separation from George. Her father, the Marquis of Salisbury, who alone was not actively hostile to her, declared that he 'would have nothing to do' with her marital quarrels. Although her brother, Lord Cranborne, had been named one of her trustees (without his consent), he consistently urged her to caution and compromise and in the end found himself bitterly denounced by Emily as an enemy. Her first cousin, Lord Talbot, flatly refused to replace her brother as her trustee, or to have anything to do with her affairs. And in 1826 she broke off all relations with her elder sister.

---

[44] *Narrative of the Case*, 123, 135, 178, 181, 213.
[45] Ibid. A1, A2, 104, 129, 132, 133, 136, 137, 138; Stone, *Road to Divorce*, 369.

Her mother constantly advised Emily not to demand a private separation, and above all not to sue George publicly for a legal separation, her principal object being that 'their differences would be kept from the world'. But her advice was not only based on fear of scandal. She also regarded Emily as in no small measure responsible for the marital trouble by provoking George to lose his temper, and kept urging her to be 'more conciliatory' to him. When she eventually appeared in court as a witness, she openly criticized her own daughter, saying that 'she expressed her dislike of Lord Westmeath. She spoke as if she hated him.' This statement, and a later similar deposition before another court, caused a lasting and bitter breach between mother and daughter, which not even time could repair. When Emily visited Hatfield in 1823 to attend the funeral of her father, she rebuffed an appeal by the Rector of Hatfield for a reconciliation with her mother.[46] Brougham, who in 1819 acted as George's lawyer, observed in court of Emily that 'her temper was such that her mother who bore her could not endure it'. A family friend and relative, the Revd Valerian Wellesley, said that the quarrel 'is the fault of the daughter and not of the mother'. By the mid-1820s Emily had thus put herself in the position of not being on speaking terms with her husband, father, mother, brother, sister, and cousin, as well as her relatives the Wellesleys.[47] She was also, as we shall see, eventually to quarrel bitterly with her only child, Rosa.

There was also damaging evidence that Emily was a bully. When asked the cause of Emily's obstinate persistence in litigation against George, her friend and travelling companion, Miss Wood, replied: 'her ladyship has always succeeded in getting what she wished from him by bullying, and I suppose she is doing the same now.'[48] This comment is supported by the testimony of a servant. The footman who waited on them after the separation, when George was still living in the same house but meeting Emily only at dinner, observed that he 'appeared more than a little afraid of her. Her ladyship seemed to have her own way in everything.'[49] During a suit in 1825, George's counsel remarked sarcastically that the Marquis

had a foolish notion that he should be master in his own house. The Marchioness, however, had her own notion of this interesting subject. She is a genuine descendant

---

[46] *Eng. Rep.* 162: 1008, 1010 (*Westmeath* v. *Westmeath*, 1826); LPCA, D.2240: 1124, 1130, 1173–4; Hatfield House: 2M Gen., letter of 13 Jan. 1836 from Emily's sister, Lady Cowley, to her brother; *Sketch*, 38–9, 43; *Reply to the Narrative*, 7, 16–17, 34. There were even rumours that Emily had refused to see her dying father although she was in the house at the time (Hatfield House, Westmeath Papers).
[47] *Narrative of the Case*, 75–7, 84, 89, 91, 100–2, 105, 145, 149–50; *Reply to the Narrative*, 16–17, 54.
[48] *Eng. Rep.* 162: 1003 (*Westmeath* v. *Westmeath*, 1826), *Reply to the Narrative*, 74–5.
[49] LPCA, D.2240: 1207–211.

of the great Cecil, the minister and favourite of the glorious virgin queen [Elizabeth], and inherited from her progenitor a natural propensity to petticoat government.[50]

Thus everything points to the fact that Emily was by far the stronger character of the two, and that, by her nagging tongue and her insistence on having her own way, she gave George plenty of provocation for his outbursts of uncontrolled fury. George certainly had an abnormally short temper, but he had no staying power. Emily was much less irritable and temperamental, but also more dogged, more persistent, and more coldly calculating in pursuing her objectives. She may have loved George once, at the time of their marriage, but she no longer showed much affection for him after 1814, whereas George remained deeply attached to her until 1820.

George and Emily also differed widely in their attitudes towards sexuality. Forty years after the event, in 1857, Emily for the first time publicly disclosed a most curious and revealing story. In 1815–16, soon after the battle of Waterloo, the Duke of Wellington was living in Paris at the Élysée-Bourbon, the greatest hero in Europe, courted by royalty and aristocracy, and for whose favours many of the most beautiful women in Europe were fighting. Until Christmas the Westmeaths were also in Paris, as was George's mother, now divorced and remarried as Mrs Bradshaw. Emily had become convinced that George's plan, 'even at that time, was to benefit somehow or other, by fair means or foul, from the friendship the late Duke of Wellington had shown to me from my childhood', when he 'had spent much of his time, before and after his return from India, at Hatfield', where her mother, the hunting Countess, was not only an old friend but his second cousin. So fond was the Duke of Emily that as a wedding present in 1812 he had given her—at her request—'a complete and beautiful breakfast service in old plate . . . with his crest and my cypher'.[51]

Emily's story is that, taking her aside at a family dinner party in Paris in the winter of 1815–16, Mrs Bradshaw said to her: 'Now, my dear soul, you are very silly; there is but one step from friendship to love with a man for a pretty woman, and if you would make use of your prettyness as other women do, you might put Delvin [i.e. George] at the top of the tree.' To which Emily replied frostily, 'I am willing to consider this said by way of a joke, Mrs Bradshaw, but it is a very bad one, and I must request you never to mention such a subject to me again,' and promptly left the room. As soon as they got home that evening, Emily told George about his mother's suggestion that she advance the family fortunes by sleeping with

---

[50] RIA/HP 1342; 6 (*Westmeath* v. *Anne Connell et al.*, 1825).
[51] *Narrative of the Case*, 81.

the Duke. George, according to her, was 'not unwilling', and merely replied with amusement: 'Oh! My poor dear mother, she did not know what an old square-toes she was speaking to when she said that to you.'[52] The story may well be true. Emily swore that it was, and both her and George's remarks have a ring of truth to them. Mrs Bradshaw and George stood for the casual sexual ethics of the Regency, while Emily's prudery anticipated that of the Victorians. In the eyes of Mrs Bradshaw and George, Emily was passing up a good opportunity. In the eyes of Emily, she was being asked to prostitute herself.

Other and better-documented evidence of very different views about sexuality held by Emily and George all tend to support the hypothesis that the former was indeed 'an old square-toes'. For example, another of Emily's allegations about her husband's sexual immorality, which was also first dragged out into the open by her in 1857, was that George after her marriage had given her to read an allegedly risqué book entitled *Charles Faublas' Mémoires. Les Amours du Chevalier de Faublas* was indeed an erotic book, and George may perhaps have lent it to her in a vain effort to stimulate her sluggish libido. George hotly denied this accusation, claiming that before he got married he had carefully purged his library of 'a book or two of somewhat doubtful morality'.[53] Emily also complained about George's 'equally gross and indecent as well as unnatural conduct' after the birth of Rosa, 'in consequence, as he stated to me, of its being his determination for a time not to have any more children'. One can only guess what these 'indecent and unnatural' contraceptive practices adopted by George may have been, but it seems likely that she was referring to the rather messy business of *coitus interruptus* rather than sodomy. In 1828 George riposted by claiming that it had been Emily who did not want any more children. He said that she had told her friend Lady Talbot that she had refused to sleep with him any more in 1816 because childbirth 'spoils the shape'.

Another of his complaints was that she had used sexual blackmail to force him into agreeing to the deed of separation of 1817, by making acceptance of it a condition for the renewal of marital relations.[54] If Emily seems to have been sexually cold and very prudish, George was undoubtedly a warm sensualist, who by his own admission could not live without women, a fact that Emily seems to have exploited to get her own way. But he was not a promiscuous womanizer, and there is no conclusive

[52] Ibid. 81; *Reply to the Narrative*, 23–4.
[53] *Reply to the Narrative*, 90–1. A copy of the book is today still kept in 'L'Enfer' (the closed reserve for pornography) in the Bibliothèque Nationale in Paris (Annie Stora-Lamarre, *L'Enfer de la IIIe République: Censeurs et pornographes (1881–1914)*, (Paris, 1990), 17).
[54] *Sketch*, 54.

evidence that he was unfaithful to Emily as long as she continued to sleep with him.

But according to her George made sexual demands upon her with which she was unwilling to comply. She attributed many of their quarrels to her 'refusing to submit to the most indecent exposure of my person to him in a way I considered highly improper, and which he requested me to do', and that he had used language towards her 'the most indecent and disgusting'. Emily also claimed that on one occasion, when she refused to go to bed with him, he seized her and beat her 'in a most disgraceful . . . violent and indecent manner'—presumably on her bare buttocks—and when she complained said, 'I am happy I have so disgraced you.'

By her own account, these quarrels over sex were the cause of most of the beatings which she received from George.[55] At any period in history, most married women would not regard as 'indecent' either of the main bones of contention between them: a desire by a husband to get his wife to pose naked before him, and a desire to practise contraception. As in everything else, Emily was unwilling to compromise on these matters and her immaculate chastity after her breach with her husband at the age of 30 strongly suggests that she was more interested in parties, fashion, power, money, and the rights of women than in sex.

There was, however, another even more serious cause of disagreement between them. This was Emily's jealousy, resentment, and constant nagging, when in 1814 she discovered more of the truth about George's pre-marital liaison. She was justifiably mortified to find that George had conceived a second child by the woman just at a time when he had already begun to court herself, and when she had believed that he was deeply in love with her. She was more resentful still—again with justice—to find that after the marriage he still kept in touch with the woman and the two children, and that on one occasion George's mother, Mrs Bradshaw, had taken one of the children on a trip to France. She was also resentful—again with reason—to discover that George was supplying them liberally with money, at a time when he was keeping her on a very short allowance. She once said, a trifle implausibly, 'I am starved for them.' In 1814 George had arranged for the woman to be married to one Frank Irwin, and the correspondence between Emily and George contains angry accusations by Emily, and occasional grudging admissions by George, of a conspiracy by the Irwin ménage to extract the maximum financial support for themselves and their children.[56]

[55] LPCA, D.2240: 1023–33, 1043, 1140.
[56] The Irwins did not leave for France until 1818. LPCA, D.2240: 235, 247, 377, 411, 1148.

Westmeath v. Westmeath

This problem of how a wife should respond to the discovery that her husband kept a mistress was very unclear in the early years of the nineteenth century. The conventional wisdom of the eighteenth century had been that it was best to ignore it, since it was unlikely to last or to threaten the stability of the marriage. It was just something men did from time to time. The Victorian view was that adultery by either sex was a serious marital offence, although that of the husband was pardonable, whereas that of the wife was not, since it might bring spurious children into the family and upset the legal descent of property to the heirs of the body. In the case of George, the long duration of the liaison, the depth of his emotional attachment to his mistress and their children, and his financial generosity towards them, all created a special problem. George was behaving by eighteenth-century Irish rules, Emily by nineteenth-century English ones.

Emily's reaction to these discoveries combined a strong element of sexual and emotional jealousy with resentment that George's mistress seemed to be obtaining a greater share of his very limited financial resources than his wife. As early as 1815 she had made it clear to George that the liaison was threatening their marriage:

if you do not entirely get rid of the whole of that infamous gang, your good sense must tell you that it is impossible for us to live together without making ourselves miserable. If I were indifferent, or if I desired that you should have your objects and engagements separately from mine, I should, indeed, be more of a Madame Commode: but as you know well that I have no other object in the world but you, I cannot endure such a want of sincerity towards me. I must have all or nothing. You know my opinion in regard to your conduct before marriage; and God knows that that discovery was sufficiently afflicting to me, without having further to discover all that has since passed in that respect; but let us make an end to it; you have been the dupe of two wretches, the very dregs of mankind, and you and I have very nearly become the victims of our enemies, high and low, and this ought to be a lesson for us never to disguise anything.[57]

By contemporary standards, this was an entirely reasonable position for Emily to adopt. She wanted George never again to see the woman or her 'bastards', as she called them; to ship the latter off to America; and not to supply her or them with more than the bare necessities. To achieve this end she nagged at him incessantly, which caused him to lose his temper with her, abuse her, and occasionally beat her. But she kept at it, and this was a prime cause for the first marital separation in 1815. As we have seen, the key items in the reconciliation agreement of September in that year were a promise by George—which he did not keep—never to see or

[57] Ibid. 366, 411, 1023, 1138; *Eng. Rep.* 162: 1023 (*Westmeath* v. *Westmeath*, 1826).

communicate with them them again, in return for a promise by Emily never to mention them again.[58]

In the autumn of 1818, shortly before the birth of their second child, Emily persuaded George to go to France to see the mother, Mrs Irwin, and 'require her to deliver the care and custody of one of the natural children'.[59] But Mrs Irwin refused, and it is impossible to tell whether Emily's plan was to take the girl into her own care, or to ship her off to America.

George's side of the story is naturally very different. His letters of 1817 are convincing proof that, at least up to that time, he was still totally in love with Emily, while she was now almost entirely alienated from him. Emily's coldness towards him is confirmed by a maidservant in whom George confided in 1818. He complained to her that Emily 'does not care for me more than a dog, and is so reserved that I cannot bear it'. He also complained about her acidulated temper, and about her policy of blackmail by denying him sexual relations. George frankly conceded that because of sexual frustration he had gone back to his old mistress. He also admitted that the woman had certainly been 'very extravagant', and that she had recently extracted £700 from him. But he insisted that, despite his solemn promises to Emily in 1815, 'I will not abandon her. She is the mother of my children, and so long as I have a farthing she shall share it.' He bitterly contrasted Emily's coldness and indifference to him, with the tender and loving care he received from his mistress, saying 'she would go to the Devil for me'. He was a little ashamed of the liaison, confessing that, 'I know this woman is of the lower order, but still she loves me, and is thoroughly devoted to me.' He told the maid that he had never altogether severed relations with her, and that he had paid for her to be married in 1816. This marriage was apparently little more than one of convenience, since George started sleeping again with the new Mrs Irwin after Emily had denied him her bed in mid-1816. He frankly explained to the maid: 'I have not lived with my wife for two and a half years, and I cannot do without women.'[60]

George clearly found Emily's physical and emotional coolness very hard to bear, her habitual censoriousness extremely provoking for one of his combustible nature, and the interruption of all sexual relations for over two years after 1816 intolerable. But his return to the arms of his old mistress only made matters worse at home when Emily got to hear of it. There were thus clearly serious faults on both sides.

[58] LPCA, D.2240: 235, 247, 350, 366, 377, 411, 490–1, 1022, 1131, 1135, 1138.
[59] Ibid. 1145.
[60] Hatfield House, Westmeath Papers, Deposition of Julie Neville.

Westmeath v. Westmeath

Another cause of marital friction was lack of money. Emily complained not only of the lack of luxuries to which she had been accustomed, but even of simple necessities like fuel for the fires at Castle Clonyn in 1813–15. She also alleged—perhaps falsely—that George went to the point of refusing to pay for a wet-nurse after she gave birth to Rosa, despite the fact that after a very long and difficult labour she was too weak to nurse the baby. There is no doubt that George did indeed keep Emily extremely short of money in the winter of 1813–14, and that conditions in the draughty old castle at Clonyn were deplorable. But there is equally little doubt that George was extremely hard up, not only before his father died in 1814, but also afterwards.

Another cause of friction was a clash of preferred life-styles. The essence of this difference between them was put by an Irish lawyer with a fine rhetorical flourish at a trial in Dublin in 1825:

> The Marquis loved his native land; he delighted in his duties as a country gentleman; he cherished the seat of his noble ancestors, and his wish was to live at Clonyn. Her Ladyship had been bred in a court; she had been the ornament and the idol of the fashionable world, and it is not to be wondered at if she preferred the splendid glories of St James to the dull seclusion of an old Irish mansion-house.[61]

Emily had certainly lived in high London society and clearly delighted in clothes, parties, balls, and the other expensive and time-consuming social activities of circles around the Court. George, on the other hand, seems to have genuinely preferred to take part in the rough rural sports of the Irish countryside, to lord it over the County of Westmeath, and to live in his run-down castle of Clonyn. In 1825 he publicly boasted of 'my long residence in Ireland'.[62]

Given this clash of preferred life-styles, it is hardly surprising that George's genuine financial plight, which reached a crisis in 1815–16, exacerbated marital relations between him and Emily.[63] George could not afford to maintain her in the style to which she was accustomed. Irish rents were collapsing after the wartime agricultural boom, and his income was shrinking fast, so much so that in 1816 and 1817 he failed to pay Emily her pin-money of £500 a year.

Just how seriously Emily took the matter of money as the basis for a satisfactory marriage is shown by a remarkable letter of advice she sent to George in late 1817:

[61] RIA/HP 1342: 5–6. (*Westmath* v. *Anne Connell et al.*, 1825).
[62] Public Record Office of Northern Ireland, Parham Papers, letter of 5 Oct. 1825. (I owe this reference to Dr A. P. W. Malcomson.)
[63] LPCA, D.2240: 121, 347, 411, 973, 1041, 1191.

If I die and if you marry, do not think of doing so unless to some woman with plenty of ready money—very good sort of women are to be found, although they have large fortunes. And nothing, you may depend upon it, enables a man to do himself justice in the world and live comfortably at home as having plenty of money, dispending it carefully and properly.[64]

In her system of values, 'plenty of money' was a first priority. It was also the family view, to judge by the marriage four years later of her brother, the second Marquis, to the low-born but immensely rich Liverpool heiress, Mary Gascoigne. This was the marriage which caused the ancient Cecil family to change its name in perpetuity to Gascoigne-Cecil, in return for a huge injection of new capital and income—to say nothing of new genes to revive its flagging talents.

Even more serious than the quarrel about current expenditure, style of life, and place of residence, was that over the future settlement of the Nugent estates in Ireland. Before the old Earl of Westmeath died in 1814 he had urged his heir, George, to join with him in settling the estates on Thomas, the only surviving son of his second marriage after his divorce from George's mother, in the event that George failed to produce a legitimate male heir. But the latter had refused and the estates had been left unsettled.

When he inherited the estates in 1814, George was therefore free to dispose of them as he wished, and, during a passionate quarrel soon after the birth of Rosa, he threatened to settle them all, except for that set aside for Emily's £3,000 a year jointure, upon his half-brother, Thomas, to the exclusion of the new baby. He did not carry out the threat, but his alleged insistence on using contraceptive measures before he had begotten a male heir must have been particularly worrying to Emily so long as he delayed making any settlement of the estate. This failure to settle the Nugent estates had been a legitimate source of anxiety to her ever since the marriage, and in 1815 she had reminded George that, 'if anything should happen to you, recollect that Rosa and myself are beggars'.[65] As we have seen, it was not until the great domestic crisis of December 1817 that George was finally pressured into promising to settle the Nugent estates on the heirs of the body of himself and Emily, whether male or female, thus securing the inheritance to Rosa if they had no living male children.[66] This would cut out his half-brother, Thomas Nugent, as well as all his other male Nugent relatives, and even any son of his own by a second wife if Emily should die without a male child. By this promise, which was only

[64] Ibid. 961.
[65] Ibid. 377–8; *Eng. Rep.* 162: 1023, 1026 (*Westmeath v. Westmeath*, 1826).
[66] LPCA, D.2240: 133, 201–3, 367–8, 959, 1037.

finally fulfilled in 1822, there was a strong probability, which in fact occurred, that on George's death the Nugent estates would become separated from the Westmeath title.

In September 1817 Emily summed up in one bitter letter all her grievances against George, accumulated from the time of her marriage five years before:

You first took me away from all my friends, as good as shut me up in an obscure corner of the world, without horses or servants to stir out. In the bitter winter of '13 and '14 I was in a room not papered, sashes rotten, with child, and very ill; not allowed anything but green wood because turf was two shillings a kish instead of one. When my child was 12 hours in the world you told me you would be damned if you gave 25 guineas a year to a bitch of a nurse: 'Why the Devil could not I nurse her myself?', tho' the Dr told you I was unable. Three weeks after, the child was to be disinherited and settle everything upon Thomas. You took possession of my pin-money, would turn me out of doors if I dared to insist upon having it. You beat me. You endeavoured to place (I will call things by their proper names) a pimp's daughter as my own maid, her nephew a postmaster; and all this time, when I was undergoing all the privations I mentioned for want of money, you could find money for a prostitute. You could believe her word when she saddled herself and her children upon you and did you the honour to tell you they were yours. You dared tell me that you had injured her. You lived three years with me in constant deceit. At last you made an agreement with me, and bound yourself by all that was sacred that there should be an end of the business on conditions, God knows, to that woman's advantage enough. Last year you began again, and broke your most solemn word of honour [about not seeing his former mistress and her two children], and now you dare to tell me that you never thought of anyone but me. Remember your oath to me, and then ask yourself if you are to be trusted. Frankly speaking, I will never live with a man as his wife, who thought any other woman and her children had the slightest claim upon him. You and I are not intended for each other, and cannot understand each other. Rosa is very well, and sends her love.[67]

What is clear from the letter is the depth of resentment by Emily at her impoverished exile in a broken-down Irish castle, at the delay in settling the estate on Rosa, and above all at George's continued contacts with his mistress and illegitimate children. She had apparently married for love rather than money in the first place, and it was her views about the exclusive nature of marital obligations which caused at least some of the frictions which eventually shattered the marriage. Despite the hard-headed financial pragmatism she exhibited as the marriage turned sour, a good case can be

[67] Ibid. 955–8; there are printed extracts in *Eng. Rep.* 162: 1027 (*Westmeath* v. *Westmeath*, 1826).

made that she was in fact at least in part a victim of affective individualism and romanticism. First she allowed herself to fall in love with an impoverished Irish nobleman, and then she behaved towards him with unusual sexual possessiveness. And yet she treated him in bed with great sexual prudery, besides using the denial of sexual access to her body as a blackmail weapon against him. Taken together, this was a recipe for disaster.

At the time, George put a good deal of the blame for the failure of the marriage on Emily's personal maid, Sarah Mckenzie, for deliberately stirring up trouble between them. Later, in the 1820s, he mostly blamed Emily's trustee and personal adviser, Mr H. W. Wood, whom he referred to, in his usual extravagant style, as 'the hoary tyrant', 'the grand skulking instigator of these horrible scenes', and 'the fiend'. But above all he blamed Emily's own 'violence of temper and perverse conduct'.[68]

(iii) *The Struggle over Child Custody, 1819–1825*

It will be remembered that after the final breakdown of the marriage in May 1818 George continued to have a bedroom in Emily's house. It was there that in November Emily gave birth to a son, one of whose godparents was Emily's new relative, the Duke of Wellington, Emily's mother's second cousin and now the brother of her sister's new husband.[69] At Easter 1819 George began pressing Emily to surrender the two separation indentures of December 1817 and May 1818 which had given her and Rosa total independence of him, and had reduced him to a mere lodger in a house owned and run by her. This she refused to do, and fresh quarrels broke out. In April Emily informed George, in the most humiliating way by a message through the cook, that she would not allow him to dine with her any more, and as a precautionary measure began to remove some of her goods and chattels out of her house to that of her trustee and friend, Mr Henry Wood.[70]

George first appealed to Emily's friend, the Duke of Wellington, to act as arbitrator between them, in order to 'prevent these matters becoming a subject of public discussion'. But the positions of the two were unreconciliable: George wanted to preserve the marriage and to annul the two deeds of separation, which he said that he had been assured were worthless by 'the two most able conveyancers in London'. Emily was equally determined to separate, to retain the custody of the two children, to preserve their right of inheritance, and to enjoy the maintenance allowance of £1,300 a year, specified in the second deed of 1818. For four or five days

[68] *Sketch*, 35. [69] Hatfield House, Westmeath Papers.
[70] LPCA, D.2240: 1127.

the Duke came to the house, 'seeing Lord Westmeath in the dining-room, then coming up to me in the drawing-room, then down again to Lord Westmeath and generally walking out together by way of talking over all that had passed with me'.

The last interview with the Duke ended in an open quarrel, after which the hot-tempered George challenged the hero of Waterloo to a duel. After the Duke apologized, saying that he had no intention of wounding his feelings, George dropped the matter, but ordered the Duke never again to visit Emily in her house. The Duke denied any improper feelings towards Emily but insisted that, since George was separated from and suing her, she was free to entertain any friends she pleased in her own home. The next day, 14 June, the Duke again visited Emily, as a result of which there was an ugly scene. George burst into the room, said, 'You will be so good as immediately to leave this house', and by marching towards the Duke forced him to back out of the house so as to avoid being obliged to fight a duel with his brother-in-law.[71]

That afternoon, while Emily was out of the house consulting with Mr Wood, no doubt about what to do next, George abruptly summoned the housekeeper, dismissed her on the spot, and demanded the household accounts. She refused to accept the dismissal or to hand over the accounts, rightly claiming that she was an employee of Emily not of himself. He then summoned a constable to witness his exercise of his rights as a husband, and began breaking open presses. Alerted by a message from the housekeeper, Emily rushed home and confronted George, who was beside himself with rage. When she asked him what he was doing, he replied: 'I have been breaking open your presses and taking the house accounts, and I will do so again, for I will show you who is master in this house.' Emily retorted: 'If I am to be exposed to these horrors, I shall send for my solicitor for protection.'

While waiting for the latter to arrive, Emily withdrew with her maid to her bedroom and started packing her things, taking care to stuff as many important papers as she could into her pockets (including the love-letters written by George in 1817). George came storming into the bedroom, and when Emily said, 'I desire, Lord Westmeath, you will leave my room,' he retorted: 'I will come into your room as I please and stay as long as I please. I will have no more of these separate doings. I will be master in my own house.'[72]

---

[71] *Narrative of the Case*, 84–6; *Reply to the Narrative*, 24–33; Hatfield House, Westmeath Papers; *Sketch*, 10.

[72] *Eng. Rep.* 162: 1009 (*Westmeath* v. *Westmeath*, 1826); LPCA, D.2240: 144–7, 255–61.

When her solicitor arrived, Emily followed his advice and left the house. While all this was going on, the children were out for a walk with their governess, so Emily sent an urgent message to stop them from returning to the house and so falling into their father's clutches, and to direct them to take refuge at the town house of her parents, the Salisburys.[73] This episode marked the final break between George and Emily, and the start of a gigantic fifteen-year legal battle over the consequences, which began in 1819 and ended only in 1834.

There is reason to suppose that by now George was genuinely suspicious that Emily might have been committing adultery with her brother-in-law and old friend, the Duke of Wellington. We have seen how he lost his temper and challenged the Duke to a duel, and then lost his temper again and threw him unceremoniously out of the house. There is evidence that for a while he was seriously contemplating bringing an action against the Duke for crim. con. with Emily, a lawsuit which would have been the sensation of the decade. Later on, in the winter of 1820–1 Emily received a visit from her brother and trustee, Lord Cranborne, who solemnly warned her that, if she did not give way, and patch up the marriage, George was determined 'to bring an action against the Duke of Wellington about [her]'. Cranborne fully admitted that this was a blackmail device by George, but he warned her of the very uncomfortable position in which she would be placed if he carried out his threat. Regardless of the truth and of the ultimate result of the trial, the mere accusation of crim. con. and the demand for legal damages against the Duke would place Emily's reputation under a cloud for several months or even years. Emily retorted angrily that, 'if he does not succeed in proving that which he knows is false, I shall indict them all for conspiracy'.

Emily was just then struggling with George to retain custody of her child Rosa, and Lord Cranborne again warned her that, if she insisted on a custody fight, she ran the risk that George would tell the court that his reason for taking custody of Rosa was Emily's 'improper conduct with the Duke of Wellington'. Meanwhile Emily, who had taken to her bed with emphysema in shock at her loss of custody of Rosa, heard footsteps in the corridor of her house and whispering at the front door. She concluded that Rosa's pretty nursemaid was flirting with a suitor, and discharged her immediately. Later she allegedly discovered that the nursemaid was already working for George to try to entrap her. The maid was, she said, instructed to give George notice 'if the Duke of Wellington called on me'. Meanwhile George had hired a room nearby, where he posted two Irishmen, one of

[73] LPCA, H.365/2.

them a discharged footman of Emily. In the evenings Lord Westmeath came to Emily's door to talk secretly with the nursemaid about smuggling in the two men as soon as the Duke entered the house. Emily later concluded that she was only saved from a suit for crim. con. because she dismissed the nursemaid, and because, when the Duke came to see her, he was accompanied by Lord Cranborne and a solicitor. She claimed that 'had I ever been from home that evening, their purpose would perhaps have been ultimately attained', since the two Irishmen 'were prepared to swear anything and everything'.[74] How much credence should be given to this story is a matter of speculation, but, writing about it in 1857, Emily saw it as a preview of the fate which awaited her friend Mrs Norton many years later, when her husband prosecuted another Prime Minister, Lord Melbourne, for damages on grounds of his crim. con. with his wife.[75]

Even after the crim. con. action plan had been dropped, and George was suing Emily for restitution of conjugal rights, rumours of it continued to circulate. In 1823 there appeared in a Whig newspaper the following news item: '*Westmeath* v. *Westmeath*: this cause between the parties for infidelity, promoted by Lord Westmeath against Lady Westmeath, did not come on yesterday but was deferred until next term.' The shock of reading this caused Emily to suffer a brief nervous collapse. But she rallied and forced the reluctant newspaper to publish a retraction, stating that the suit was for restitution of conjugal rights, and not for separation because of infidelity. She was furious when her brother and trustee, Lord Cranborne, told her that she had made a grave mistake to quarrel with the newspapers, and that 'the press would be most inimical to me ever after'.[76]

Concurrently with this attempt by George to discover or invent a love-affair between Emily and the Duke of Wellington, he also sued in 1818 to remove Rosa and the baby boy from her custody, claiming that she had left him against his will, and that as their father he had legal right to custody of them.[77] Her solicitor, Mr Wood, fought back by obtaining a writ of habeas corpus to Chancery for delivery of the children to Emily under the terms of the deed of 1818. But in her own words

The Chancellor [Lord Eldon] decided they [the children] should be given over to him [George] on the ground, I believe, that as no man can refuse to perform his duties by his children, nor can he by deed or otherwise deprive himself of the care and maintenance over them. I have therefore lost them. This is a hurt and misfortune as makes me nearly unmindful of all the rest.[78]

---

[74] *Narrative of the Case*, 9.   [75] Ibid. 77, 102, 127–30.   [76] Ibid. 104–5.
[77] *Eng. Rep.* 102: 1035–36; RIA/HP 1342: 50–3 (*H. W. Wood* v. *Westmeath*, 1822).
[78] Hatfield House, Westmeath Papers.

The clause in the 1818 deed giving custody of the children to Emily was thus shown to be legally worthless. It was not the last time that she found that she had been given bad legal advice.

What she omitted to mention is that, when Lord Eldon asked Emily's mother, the Marchioness of Salisbury, to hold the children for a day or two while he thought the matter over, she replied, 'My Lord . . . I will keep no children from their father.' George believed that this was the remark which so enraged Emily that she never spoke to her mother again.[79] George made several offers of new terms of separation, but always insisted on the return and cancellation of the two deeds of 1817 and 1818. But Emily was determined never to surrender them, since they protected Rosa's claims to inherit George's estates, assured her of her separation allowance, and provided 'proofs of his ill-treatment of me'. She was also determined to come to no agreement which did not 'give me my daughter at least, if not both my children'.[80] After formal appeals by George for Emily to return to the house met with no response, he carried the children off with him to Clonyn in Ireland, and stopped payment of Emily's separation allowance of £1,300 a year.

But before either side could start litigation, news reached Emily in the summer of 1819 that her baby son was dangerously ill with water on the brain at Clonyn. She set out at once, accompanied by her brother, Robert Viscount Cranborne, who was her trustee and the only member of her family who, very reluctantly, allowed himself to be drawn even marginally into her marital affairs. By the time they arrived, the baby was dead. After Emily had viewed the body, George sent a message that he would like to see her. Lord Cranborne replied on her behalf that she refused to do so, since George had broken his word and had removed the children from her care, with the result that one was already dead. He asked if George was now prepared to hand Rosa back to her mother, the condition of acceptance by Emily being that George should promise never to demand her back again. George agreed, on condition that he was to approve the governess. Emily consented, and returned back to London with Rosa, who was a very delicate child in constant poor health.[81]

However, the verbal agreement which seemed to have been reached proved to be illusory. Emily understood it to mean that she was assured both personal financial independence and child custody for the indefinite future. But in November 1819 George told Lord Cranborne that

---

[79] *Reply to the Narrative*, 33-4.

[80] Hatfield House, Westmeath Papers; RIA/HP 1342: 50-3 (*H. W. Wood* v. *Westmeath*, 1822).

[81] RIA/HP 1342: 25-7 (*Westmeath* v. *Westmeath, Cranborne et al.*, 1821).

'presumed independence never entered into my brain in acting as I have done by assigning the charge of my daughter to her mother'. His motives, he said, had merely been to 'prevent her [Rosa] being miserable, and at the same time give her mother the comfort of her society. If you should unhappily have been presuming upon a point of law, I beg to be distinctly understood that the power over my child I do not surrender, nor ever will.'[82]

The inevitable show-down over the custody of Rosa occurred some eighteen months later, in early 1820. George spent the winter in London, and Rosa's governess had been in the habit of taking the child, now aged 6, on regular visits to her father. George had become convinced that Emily had 'used the utmost of her plausible talents to poison her infant mind against me'. And so when, on 12 March, the governess took Rosa to her father's house, he refused to let the child go. Emily immediately sought a writ of habeas corpus from the Court of Common Pleas to recover her beloved child, whose health, she claimed, would be endangered by her removal from her mother's care. So fast did she and her lawyers move that the case was heard the very next day. Doctors testified to Rosa's precarious health, and Lord Cranborne to George's verbal promise at Clonyn never to try to recover custody. Despite this promise and the clause in the May 1818 indenture, by which George had ceded custody to Emily, Lord Chief Justice Dallas followed ancient practice and declared that 'the father is in point of law entitled to the custody of the child'.[83] So Rosa was returned to her father, this time permanently.

Two days after taking possession of Rosa, George moved her to a country house belonging to his close friend and relative, the Duke of Buckingham and Chandos, at Avington in Berkshire, where she lived thereafter, with the Duke acting as her guardian. In order to 'save the child from perdition', George instructed all around her never again to allow Emily to see or communicate with the child.[84] For a while Emily managed to keep in touch with her daughter by smuggling letters to her in the laundry basket, but she only once managed to see Rosa again. One day in 1825, when she was ill and desperate, Emily entered the hall of Buckingham House in Pall Mall, where Rosa was then staying, and was only ejected after an ugly scene.[85] On another occasion in the same year, accompanied by a brawny

---

[82] Hatfield House: 2M Gen., 19 Nov. 1819.
[83] RIA/HP 1342: 24, 27–30 (*Westmeath* v. *Westmeath, Cranborne et al.*, 1821); *Reply to the Narrative*, 85–6; *Sketch*, 38; LPCA, D.2240: 793–5, 823–5, 894–7.
[84] LPCA, D. 795, 1152; H.365/2; for letters from George to the Duke of Buckingham, several about Rosa, see Huntington Library, Stowe MSS, Box 82 (23, 24, 28, 29).
[85] Hatfield House: 2M Gen., 1825.

footman, she forced her way into the house of a dancing mistress where Rosa was taking lessons, entered the upstairs room, locked the door, and spent the next hour trying to persuade, entice, shame, or bully the child into going home with her. The dancing mistress kept her head, and managed to send a message to a distinguished judge and barrister, Sir Edward Hyde East, to come and protect the girl and escort her back to Buckingham House. Meanwhile Rosa, who was then aged about 11 years old, wept bitterly, but steadfastly refused to kiss her mother or even shake her hand, much less go home with her. Some fourteen years later Emily recollected that Rosa had said to her, 'Papa and the Duke of Buckingham have pointed out to me what sort of woman you was. I never wish to see your face again.' In a bitter letter to Rosa, written much later in 1839, Emily accused George, his friend the Duke of Buckingham, and 'my relatives' (the Salisburys) of having 'succeeded in poisoning your mind towards your mother'.[86]

By then Emily had been driven by the injustice of her situation into political activity. Together with her friend Mrs Caroline Norton, she worked hard to promote Sergeant Talfourd's bill in Parliament to give custody of young children of a separated couple to the mother. The introduction of this bill enabled Emily to tell Rosa that, 'even in England, the power of unjustly torturing a woman through her best feelings is fast drawing to a close. Party, even the fury of party, has been laid aside to compass this.' Although the bill was defeated, Emily was (rightly) optimistic that it would soon become law. She went on: 'A mother, however, is long-suffering. She does not willingly give up the hope that some good feeling possibly still lurks in the heart of her only child. I once idolized you, Rosa, and was more attached to you that I ought to have been to anything of this world.' This is the letter of a deeply embittered woman, obsessed by her unjust sufferings at the hands of the law. On the other hand, this moral blackmail exercised upon a helpless child cannot but arouse disquiet. Fortunately Rosa was tough, and she coolly and briefly replied to her mother, denying 'cunning or hypocrisy on my part of my past or present conduct'.[87] In Emily's defence it has to be said that, throughout the lengthy legal battle with George, she defended Rosa's claim to be heiress to most of the Westmeath estates in Ireland, despite the fact that the latter was 'so long and cruelly estranged from me, and has been . . . brought up to detest her mother'.[88]

[86] Huntington Library: Stowe MSS, Box 82 (36); Hatfield House: 2M Gen., letter of 1839.
[87] *Sketch*, 43; for Sergeant's Talfourd's Child Custody Act, see Stone, *Road to Divorce*, 390. [88] *Narrative of the Case*, 174, 194.

(iv) *Litigation in the Secular Courts, 1820–1831*

This bitter struggle over child custody was merely the opening engagement in a prolonged legal battle between George and Emily, which dragged on for fifteen years, from 1819 to 1834. There were two main issues at stake, one fought out in the equity and the common-law courts for eleven years from 1820 to 1831 over the validity of the December 1817 and May 1818 separation indentures, which granted Emily her maintenance allowance; and the other, fought out for thirteen years from 1821 to 1834 in the ecclesiastical courts, over restitution of conjugal rights (by George) and over marital separation for cruelty and adultery (by Emily). Each suit gave rise to a series of appeals to higher courts, and also spawned subsidiary suits in other courts, so that there were at least seventeen lawsuits before eleven or more different tribunals, embracing all three legal systems. It was one of the most complex, most expensive, and most long-drawn-out legal battles of the age.

Litigation over the validity of the indentures of 1817 and 1818 was begun in the Court of Chancery in 1820, with a suit by George against Emily for an injunction to prevent her from distraining his Irish property for non-payment of her £1,300 annual maintenance allowance, due to her by the 1818 deed. This battle was waged by many suits in many courts for the next eleven years, until its final conclusion on appeal to the House of Lords in 1831.[89]

George's lawyers turned the suit into a test case to try to deny the legal validity of all private marital separation agreements, despite the fact that they had been accepted by the courts for several decades. George's lawyer, the Attorney-General, J. S. Copley, later Lord Lyndhurst, argued that such deeds were against public policy and morality, since *de facto* they made possible marital separation from bed and board by mutual consent. This was something which could by law only be granted by an ecclesiastical court on grounds of either adultery or gross cruelty by one of the spouses. Marriage, he argued, 'could not be dissolved by the consent of parties, much less at the caprice and whim of one of them', as was the case by the 1818 deed. Married couples, he declared, were 'disabled by public law from making it [marriage] a nullity by virtue of deeds creating private divorces'.

Lord Eldon, the Lord Chancellor, was well-known to be personally opposed to all marital-separation contracts, which was why Copley raised this general issue. His Lordship intervened to say that the 1817 document was unquestionably 'good for nothing', since it was conditional on a future

---

[89] *Eng. Rep.* 37: 797–804 (*Westmeath* v. *Westmeath*, 1820–1); RIA/HP 1342: 7–18 (*Westmeath* v. *Westmeath, Cranborne, et al.*, 1821).

separation, and that the sole issue was therefore the legal validity of that of 1818. After consulting two equity judges and two common-law judges, Lord Eldon issued his verdict. He reluctantly declared that thirty years before, as a common-law judge, he would have held 'all deeds of separation absolutely illegal and void'. But there had now accumulated so many precedents in case law in which so many eminent judges, including the highly respected Lord Kenyon, had declared them good, that he was obliged to admit that, rightly or wrongly, this was now the law of the land. Chancery would therefore do nothing to stop the Marchioness from suing at common law and distraining George's goods for payment of her £1,300 separation allowance.[90]

Buoyed by this victory, Emily sued George in an English common-law court—probably King's Bench—for her £1,300 a year annuity under the 1818 indenture, and won.[91] George still refused to pay her a penny, so she instructed her agents to distrain his goods in Ireland. In September 1822 some five hundred of George's tenants in County Westmeath were astonished to find their cattle being seized for payment of a debt allegedly due by their landlord to his wife in far-off England. George claimed that Emily's object was to 'sell up the whole of their property and means of existence', and thus to undermine the loyalty of his tenants. He tried to stop the seizures with writs of *replevin* from the Petty Bag Office in the Irish Chancery—at the cost of five and a half guineas each—but the sheriff, who was a trading partner of Emily's Irish agent, refused to execute them.[92] In order to save his goods and furniture at Clonyn Castle from being seized and sold, George hastily dismissed all the servants, and ordered the house to be shut up, the doors and gates locked and barred, and the windows boarded up, so that the under-sheriff and bailiffs were unable to gain entry in order to serve a process and seize his household goods. He took the precaution of having removed to the house of one of his staff in the Militia a chest containing the family plate (including most of the breakfast service given to Emily in 1812 by the Duke of Wellington as a wedding present). He also assured his agents that, 'if they try to break in, they [the bailiffs] may be shot'.[93]

This threat of distraint upon his Irish tenants galvanized George into further swift and ruthless action. He secured most of the landed property by getting prior liens on it by fictitious actions for debt by mortgages which took priority over Emily's claims. He also urged his tenants to 'resist them

---

[90] *Eng. Rep.* 37: 21–3; other associated suits in equity and common-law courts can be traced in ibid. 37: 797–803; 6: 622.
[91] LPCA, H.365/2, 10, 11.   [92] *Eng. Rep.* 5: 352; 6: 625.
[93] LPCA, D.2240: 833, 1257; *Narrative of the Case*, 141, 152.

[the bailiffs] and to treat them like robbers'. When the tenants did just that and were indicted for assault at the assizes, George used his influence to get the suit switched to the Quarter Sessions, which he largely controlled.[94] Thanks to this gross misuse both of the law and of his official posts as Governor and Colonel of Militia of the County, George was successful in preventing Emily's agent from seizing much, if any, of his Irish property. So from 1819, when George cut off her £1,300-a-year maintenance allowance under the 1818 deed, to 1827, when the ecclesiastical court ordered him to pay her temporary alimony, Emily received from George absolutely nothing except her £500-a-year pin-money, and even that fell into arrears for three years after 1823.

Defeated twice in the Court of Chancery in England in 1822, George also initiated an identical suit in the Court of Chancery in Ireland. But the Irish Lord Chancellor told George's lawyers curtly: 'You should never have come here. You had your opportunity in England'.[95] Meanwhile Emily ran up debts for necessities like food, clothes, rent, and household goods and arranged for one of her creditors to sue her husband in King's Bench for repayment. She won, George refused to pay, and from May to August 1822 he was 'confined in the King's Bench prison in consequence of a prosecution, instituted by Lady Westmeath, but brought by a creditor for payment of goods purchased by her'.[96] This forced the court to decide whether or not 'the defendant's wife Lady Westmeath was living apart from the defendant under a deed of separation valid at the time that debt was incurred'.

It was easy enough to prove that, although the separation deed was drafted in May 1818 and signed in August, George and Emily continued to live under the same roof until June 1819. George's lawyers demonstrated that they were living 'apparently under friendly terms, and apparently also as man and wife', only the footman and the maid knowing that in fact they slept in different bedrooms and that they met only at the dinner-table. It was also proved that, after the birth of their son in November 1818, to all external appearances George, who 'was then residing in the same house with her, and attending her with great affection, communicated the intelligence to his and her friends and relations, and received their congratulations on the event'. The couple also spent Christmas at Hatfield with Emily's brother, now Marquis of Salisbury, and her mother, the dowager Lady Salisbury, the latter of whom infuriated Emily by later appearing in court

---

[94] *Narrative of the Case*, 141–6.
[95] RIA/HP 1342: 24 (*Westmeath* v. *Westmeath, Cranborne, et al.*, 1821); *Eng. Rep.* 6: 625.
[96] LPCA, D.2240: 569, 577, 1185; *Eng. Rep.* 108: 427 (*Hindley* v. *Westmeath*, 1827).

to testify that she and George seemed to be 'living together on friendly terms, and in the usual manner as man and wife', occupying their usual apartment.[97]

The defence truthfully objected that what had occurred was not cohabitation and reconciliation at all. Emily had only very reluctantly been persuaded to allow her husband to retain a private suite in her house, with the status and authority of no more than a lodger. This was done merely in order to present to the world a false front of marital harmony. Both Emily's mother and George wanted the separation to be concealed from the world until Emily's child had been born, and until George had time to obtain for himself a post overseas or in a regiment. The Cecil family solicitor, Mr William Sheldon, had assured Emily that the lawyers on both sides had agreed that 'such permission should not, in any shape, impeach the deed of separation of the 30th of May 1818, or be deemed or construed to imply that any reconciliation had taken place or did take place'. The situation therefore 'could never be turned to her prejudice'.[98] But this interpretation had never been put in writing, and Mr Sheldon's advice was to come back to haunt him.

If George had, cunningly and with premeditation, set out to sabotage the deed of 1818, he could not have done it better than, first, by striking out the clause indemnifying him from responsibility for Emily's debts, and, secondly, by persuading her to allow him to stay on in her house. In fact, however, there is every reason to think that he had acted in all good faith, entirely ignorant of any possible legal benefits.

What nobody seems to have realized at the time was that the law was changing. In 1819 the two Chief Justices, sitting together with their brethren in the Court of Exchequer Chamber, had tried an important test case, in which they had formally declared that separation deeds, if followed by reconciliation, were indeed null and void at Common Law.[99]

In the light of this recent but authoritative ruling, in 1827 Chief Justice Abbott and his three fellow judges at last unanimously agreed that 'the deed if valid at the first . . . has been voided by what amounts to a subsequent reconciliation'. It was a stunning victory for George, and a stunning set-back for Emily, who lost her claim to £1,300 a year for life.[100]

It is easy to imagine the feelings of the Cecil family lawyer, Mr Sheldon, on hearing of this decision. He was so upset that, when he died three years later in 1830, he left £1,000 to Emily, as some small reparation for having,

[97] *Eng. Rep.* 5: 361; LPCA, D.2240: 1126–7.   [98] Ibid. 621, 623.
[99] *Eng. Rep.* 146: 1066–71 (*Durant* v. *Titley* [sometimes called *Titley* v. *Durant*], 1819).
[100] *Eng. Rep.* 108: 427–2 (*Hindley* v. *Westmeath*, 1827).

in his capacity as her family trustee, given her such catastrophically bad legal advice.[101]

In 1827 Emily encouraged another of her creditors to bring another collusive suit against George for necessary purchases by her. This time George appealed to the House of Lords.[102] In the brief to the House, George's lawyers stressed above all that the subsequent cohabitation had implied reconciliation, and therefore rendered the 1818 deed null and void. It was not until 1830 that the House of Lords finally took up the case, and not until 1831 that it came to a decision. Lord Chancellor Lyndhurst and the law lords had no difficulty in deciding that 'the circumstances of the parties being together after the execution of the deed was sufficient to impugn it, and set it aside as invalid'.[103]

In the end, therefore, the 1818 separation deed, which at the time had seemed so enormously advantageous to Emily, did her no good at all. She had lost custody of Rosa in 1820, and now, in 1831, after a twelve-year legal battle, waged at enormous cost, she had lost her claim to £1,300 a year for separate maintenance, which in fact had not been paid since 1819. Her repeated refusals to submit the various matters under dispute to arbitration were in the end to cost her dear. There had been at least five proposals for arbitration between 1819 and 1832, all of which had failed, due partly to Emily's refusal to compromise, and partly to George's extravagant demands.[104] The sticking-points for both of them were the validity of the £1,300 maintenance allowance and the custody of Rosa.

(v) *Litigation in the Ecclesiastical Courts, 1821–1834*

These protracted and expensive legal battles had been fought in most of the secular courts in both England and Ireland, and had ended in a crushing defeat for Emily. But they were carried on in parallel with an equally bitter and convoluted series of lawsuits in the ecclesiastical courts over the marriage itself. George had been the first to plunge into this second legal quagmire, when in 1821 he launched a suit in the London Consistory Court for restoration of conjugal rights, in direct violation of his promise in the 1818 separation deed never to do any such thing.

George's object in the suit was to obtain a legal injunction ordering Emily back under his roof and into his power. If he won but she refused to

---

[101] LPCA, H. 365/2, 11.

[102] *Eng. Rep.* 108: 427–32 (*Hindley* v. *Westmeath*, 1827); ibid. 5: 253 n. (*Westmeath* v. *Salisbury*, 1831); LPCA, D.2240: 365, 1185; *Sketch*, 14.

[103] *Eng. Rep.* 5: 349–78 (*Westmeath* v. *Salisbury*, 1831); 6: 619–29 (*Westmeath* v. *Westmeath*, 1830); Wharton, 396.

[104] *Narrative of the Case*, 85–7, 98–9, 100, 114–16, 145–50, 155 n. 166 n., 199, 203, 206–9.

return, he would no longer be responsible for her debts or maintenance. He would also be legally free, if he so wished, to seize her by force, carry her off to Clonyn, and keep her there indefinitely. In practice, however, Emily's residence in St James's Palace put her under royal protection, and therefore made any attempt at physical kidnapping extremely unlikely. A friend wrote to her: 'We feel quite happy that you are out of reach of Lord Westmeath by being in the palace.'[105] Emily was warned that it was hopeless to try to argue that George had promised not to sue under the terms of the 1818 deed, since it was generally agreed among the lawyers that 'such a deed as this is no bar to suit in the Ecclesiastical Court'.[106]

Emily was advised that the best defence was attack, that is to launch her own cross-bill for separation from bed and board, which could be granted on grounds of either cruelty or adultery or both. She could produce witnesses—mostly friends but especially her personal maid, Sarah McKenzie—who could testify to a great deal of verbal abuse and some occasional physical blows over the years between the marriage in 1812 and the separation in 1819. He had called her 'damned bitch', and threatened 'I will kick you to Hell'. He had once thrown a pitcher of water over her; and on several occasions he had kicked or pummelled her, two or three times severely, when in one of his rages. Only once, in 1814, had he injured her so badly that a surgeon had had to be called. On that occasion he had struck her a violent blow on the breast, which was passed off publicly as due to an accident arising from a fall on to a table with a raised edge.[107] None of these episodes was actually threatening to life, limb, or health, which were the traditional criteria of cruelty at canon law. Nor were they very frequent. On the other hand, this narrow definition of cruelty was in the process of being expanded to cover a persistent pattern of verbal and physical abuse that might threaten physical or mental health. As a result, her suit became a test case for a new definition of legal cruelty.[108]

But the issue was by no means a foregone conclusion, especially since several witnesses, including Emily's first cousin, Lord Arthur Hill, testified that 'Lord Westmeath at all times conducted himself in a kind, affectionate, and proper manner towards his wife.' Worse still for Emily was the fact that, by continuing to live with George until June 1819, she might be regarded as having condoned all his previous acts of cruelty. Informed of

[105] Hatfield House, Westmeath Papers.
[106] *Eng. Rep.* 162: 1006 n. a (*Westmeath* v. *Westmeath*, 1826); ibid. 5: 356 (*Westmeath* v. *Salisbury*, 1831).
[107] *Eng. Rep.* 162: 1002–6, 1019 (*Westmeath* v. *Westmeath*, 1826).
[108] LPCA, D.2240: 105–43; *Eng. Rep.* 162: 1010, 1011, 1016–27 (*Westmeath* v. *Westmeath*, 1826).

this situation, she was naturally terrified of losing her case, and of being obliged by law to return to George and to submit herself to possible banishment to Clonyn for the rest of her life.

Her response to this fear of defeat of her suit on grounds of cruelty was described in the following sarcastic terms by an eloquent Irish counsel speaking on George's behalf:

A case of adultery is suggested as the only possible defence now open to the Marchioness: a charge of adultery against the Marquis her husband, got up by an Irish agent, and to be supported by Irish witnesses to impose on the credulity of an English judge. Accordingly the plan is contrived, money is distributed.[109]

This was very close to the truth about what actually happened, although the insinuation that Emily deliberately encouraged perjury was never proven. As has been seen, Emily had good reason to suspect George's marital fidelity. Moreover, what she knew of George's sensual nature suggested to her that it was unlikely that he had remained celibate during the three years between 1819, when he and Emily finally parted beds, and 1822 when the investigation began.

The upshot of the enquiry into George's extramarital activities was that in 1822, a year after she had brought thirty-three charges of cruelty against her husband, Emily added twenty-five new ones of adultery.[110] She accused him of consorting with five different low women, two of whom he was alleged to have slept with in London, to help him to while away the time when he had been incarcerated in the King's Bench prison. But the evidence for both of these London episodes turned out to be very weak indeed, one of the women being described by her former employer the Countess of Glengall as 'a respectable elderly servant', whom the Countess herself had chosen to attend on George in prison.[111] The other three were Irish women George was alleged to have slept with in Clonyn or Dublin.[112]

To investigate George's sexual life in Ireland, Emily had turned for help to her attorney for Irish affairs, an energetic and aggressive man named Bernard McGuire, who entertained a lively hatred for the Marquis and whose power was such that he was said to be *de facto* sheriff of the county of Westmeath (where Clonyn is situated). What happened next is revealed by a bundle of private correspondence between Emily and McGuire, which by 1825 had somehow fallen into the possession of George. Either they were stolen, or the Marquis had bribed someone in the post office to remove

---

[109] RIA/HP 1342: 8 (*Westmeath* v. *Anne Connell et al.*, 1825).
[110] *Reply to the Narrative*, 57.
[111] LPCA, D.2240: 563–9, 577, 780–9, 809–10, 837–9.
[112] Ibid. 569–76, 831, 1393–5, 1493, 1511.

them, or, as he explained mysteriously, 'they came into my hands by the design of a good Providence'. It would seem that both sides were in the business of stealing each other's correspondence, since by 1827 Emily had somehow also gained possession of George's private letters to his land agent, Mr Hogg. All these purloined letters show that both Emily and George were prepared to reward and coach witnesses to help their cause.[113]

To obtain the necessary evidence, McGuire let it be known in the area around Clonyn that he was looking for information about adultery by the Marquis, the supply of which would be appropriately rewarded. He was soon approached by a local farmer and enemy of the Marquis, one John Monaghan, the son of a man who had been the Westmeaths' under-herdsman at Clonyn, and who was later described as 'the soul and centre of this conspiracy'.[114] In late August 1822 Monaghan, who had already been in contact with McGuire, wrote directly to Emily to offer her his services, and she was foolish enough to reply to him directly. She warmly thanked him for his good offices in locating a woman called Anne Connell, an alleged former mistress of the Marquis, and in persuading her to testify. She was anxious not to be outbid by the Marquis, and assured Monaghan:

I shall never forget the interest you have taken in putting me in the way of having justice done to me. I give you my word, and I am convinced you know that my word and Lord W.'s are two very different things, that the poor girl will, in fact, be far more secure than she is at present. . . . I am exactly informed by Mr McGuire of everything that goes on. . . . If you are requested not to keep letters, it is only what I am desired to do also, as lawyers advise. . . . You know me, Mr Monaghan, and believe me when I say that I never would ask or bribe any person, much less such a man as you, to tell me an untruth; but that I *never forget a kindness*, and repeat it. You have come forward voluntarily to assist a much injured person, and as long as I live I shall never forget it.[115]

It was clear from this revealing letter that the production of firm evidence of George's adultery would be well rewarded by Emily, and later evidence proved that indeed all the witnesses were well looked after. An ecclesiastical court judge later commented, with great self-restraint, that 'the information . . . has been collected or adopted with less caution than ought to be used in a matter so deeply concerning the honour and reputation of both the noble persons who are affected by it'.[116]

The following story was concocted by Monaghan, with the help of testimony from some disgruntled former servants whom the Marquis had

---

[113] *Reply to the Narrative*, 67, 91.   [114] Ibid. 71 n. *.
[115] RIA/HP 1342: 94–5 (*Westmeath* v. *Anne Connell et al.*, 1825).
[116] *Eng. Rep.* 162: 994 (*Westmeath* v. *Westmeath*, 1826).

discharged without references.[117] In 1815 a woman called Anne Connell, who by her own admission had given birth to children by four different men, came one day before George at Clonyn in his capacity as JP to swear to the paternity of yet another child she was carrying. He was attracted by her appearance, and, although she could neither read nor write, he offered her a written contract, which she accepted. The conditions were that she was to receive £15 a year, and £10 a year more for each child, and that in return she was to make herself sexually available to George whenever he visited Clonyn. According to her, she kept the document very carefully, sewn up in a hem of her petticoat, and continued for several years to sleep with George when called upon. Sometimes this took place in his bedroom at Clonyn—once on the very night of the death of his baby son in the house; sometimes in the adjacent woods; sometimes in a hotel in Dublin; and sometimes in a Dublin brothel. She claimed that she had two children by him, both delivered in the Dublin workhouse and baptized Nugent.

McGuire and Emily were very excited by this circumstantial and detailed story, particularly since it seemed that it could easily be proved by producing in court the written sexual contract and the two children. Part of Emily's letter replying to that of Monaghan was devoted to the urgent need to obtain possession of the contract before George got it back and destroyed it. But Anne Connell proved frustratingly evasive and dilatory in producing the contract, despite the handsome rewards and flattery lavished upon her. When she finally confessed she did not have it, the hunt turned to the children. 'Above all see the children,' wrote McGuire to one of his agents. But the children proved as elusive as the written contract, and Anne eventually declared that she could not remember their names, could not find them, and could not even produce any evidence of their existence. Meanwhile, McGuire and Monaghan were busy trying to find witnesses who were prepared to testify to seeing sexual intercourse between George and Anne taking place in the woods near Clonyn.[118]

Instead of abandoning the case at this point, McGuire decided to carry on, and to produce in court the testimony he had collected as proof of George's adultery. Anne Connell—decked out in a new mantle and bonnet with a plume of feathers—and the other witnesses were duly shipped over to London and kept in a safe house owned by a man called McKenzie, a discharged gardener of the Marquis and the husband of Emily's personal maid. The witnesses were kept confined for several weeks while being careful coached in what to say in court. They were also kept well away from

---

[117] LPCA, D.2240: 657–93, 729–53, 769–7, 829–31.
[118] *Eng. Rep.* 162: 86–90 (more purloined letters), 229–79.

any agents of George, who might attempt to bribe them to change their testimony, and McKenzie assured McGuire that he 'did not know where they could be in a more secure place then they are with me'.[119]

When she came to testify in court, Anne Connell told of the written contract, but claimed that George had not returned it to her the last time she had produced it in order to have an entry made that she had received her yearly payment. She also told about the two children, giving names and dates of birth, but claiming that they were both now dead. Under written cross-examination, however, her story collapsed. She was unable to describe in even the vaguest terms the Marquis's bedroom at Clonyn, where she said she had so often slept, nor how she had got to it, explaining that it was dark when she arrived in the evenings, and that when she left in the mornings the Marquis used to give her a stiff drink, which made her so tipsy that she lost all memory of her surroundings: 'By the Lord, I was so drunk, I don't know.' On the margin of the transcript of the interrogation, the examiner noted laconically, 'the witness is sober now'.[120]

When she was later tried for conspiracy, the prosecuting counsel had an enjoyable time pointing out how the Marquis had 'so happily adjusted the dose that she was just sober enough to find her way home, but too drunk to have remarked or known the way'. The same amnesia was revealed when she was cross-examined about the hotel in Dublin. Counsel sarcastically observed that 'she used to find herself in the Marquis's bedroom there; but how she got in, or where it was situated, she could not conjecture'.[121] To make matters worse, Anne Connell admitted to the court that Emily had promised her a position at a wage of £30 a year, as a reward for coming over to England to testify, and had sent her the money to buy the new clothes she wore when she set out from Dublin to London. She admitted being kept in the safe house, and refused to swear that she had not been coached about what to say. Her detractors described her to the court, with some justice, as 'a low prostitute, she is as base as a woman can be . . . a drunken impudent dirty prostitute'.

The witnesses to the other alleged adulteries made an almost equally poor showing. One ex-servant described how the Marquis had said to him, 'I want a girl,' and sent him off to find one, but admitted that he had been induced to testify in return for a place. Monaghan himself did rather better, but admitted that Emily had empowered him to offer an annuity to Anne Connell in return for handing over the sexual contract.[122]

[119] *Reply to the Narrative*, 68–9.
[120] LPCA, D.2240: 657–85; RIA/HP 1342: 9 (*Westmeath* v. *Anne Connell et al.*, 1825).
[121] RIA/HP 1342: 9 (*Westmeath* v. *Anne Connell et al.*, 1825).
[122] LPCA, D.2240: 699–712, 1241.

Westmeath *v.* Westmeath

Yet another witness, Patrick Furley, when later prosecuted for perjury, confessed that he had been induced to give false testimony for three reasons. First, after twelve years in the Marquis's service, he had been 'turned off without a discharge'; secondly, 'he would be well-paid for what he was doing'; and, thirdly, 'one of his lordship's forefathers destroyed the monastery of Foure at the time of the Reformation'—which last statement caused 'great laughter' in the courtroom.[123]

Based on this evidence of extensive collective perjury in return for money or promises, in 1825 George sued the witnesses for conspiracy before the Commission Court in Dublin. He made his preparations as carefully as Emily had done three years before when the witnesses for adultery were first being assembled. George was afraid that two, Connell and Monaghan, 'will be removed to England' to hide them from him and prevent them from giving evidence. He told his agent that 'everything must be prepared as well as we can', and as a result some of his witnesses were hidden in Roscommon, out of Emily's clutches. He offered to employ one of the witnesses after the trial, adding prudently: 'burn this letter'. Of another potential witness, he remarked, 'all I fear is that they will get her off out of the Kingdom [of Ireland]; all I want is to have her kept from doing anything'. George was made to pay heavily for all this damaging testimony and complained: 'I never saw such greedy people.'[124]

But he was hopeful that a conviction for perjury of the witnesses for adultery would lead to the discrediting also of Emily's witnesses for cruelty, and so to the collapse of her suit for separation. His hope was to have her agent, McGuire, convicted, since that would strongly suggest that Emily had also been a party to conspiracy to frame him. But he was also afraid, rightly, that Emily would come to court to defend herself and overawe his witnesses. Emily did indeed appear in person to support her witnesses and defend her reputation, dressed in the most sober of clothes to impress judge and jury. 'Her Ladyship wore spectacles. She was dressed in black, muff and tippet.' She took the witness stand and did not admit more than that she had coached one of the witnesses about dates so as to eliminate contradictions with other testimony.[125]

Despite the existence of undoubtedly suborned and perjured evidence, Emily's sober appearance seems to have impressed the judge, who, to George's great disappointment, went out of his way to exonerate both Emily and her attorney, McGuire, of any knowledge of the conspiracy.

---

[123] RIA/HP 1342: 25 (*Westmeath* v. *Anne Connell et al.*, 1825). In fact, the Nugents were granted the monastery in 1588.

[124] *Narrative of the Case*, 155, 158, 161, 162.   [125] Ibid. 158.

Carefully instructed by the judge, in a four-hour speech filled with racial slurs about the natural duplicity and untruthfulness of the Irish, the jury, after deliberating for an hour and a half, duly found Anne Connell, Monaghan, and Patrick Furley guilty and acquitted all the others. The judge sentenced the three convicted to be fined and to serve eighteen months in prison.[126] George arranged for the publication of a transcript of the evidence and sentence in the trial, in an appendix to which Emily later complained that he inserted 'garbled extracts from the evidence of a cause yet depending . . . palpably for the purpose of disparaging, by insinuation, the motives of the noble Marchioness'.[127]

Emily's plan to reinforce her suit in the Consistory Court against George for separation on grounds of cruelty, by producing evidence of her husband's adultery, thus backfired upon her. Her letters proved that she and McGuire had been, at the very least, naïvely reckless in their offers of rewards, which provided an obvious incitement to perjury. The judge might have reconsidered his exculpation of Emily and McGuire, if he had known that Monaghan and Furley had visited Emily in St James's Palace almost daily before the trial, or that, when Anne Connell was released from her prison sentence for perjury, she took refuge again in McKenzie's house in Faversham, where she was looked after at Emily's expense. The latter actually corresponded with Anne Connell after her release and expressed gratitude that she had 'come forward honestly and honourably to speak the truth'. Either Emily knew about the perjury and condoned it, or else she was obstinate enough still to believe in the veracity of her now wholly discredited witnesses.[128]

After the trial was over, Emily lobbied her dear friend and brother-in-law, the Duke of Wellington, to use his enormous influence to help her reward her dubious Irish witnesses and agents by finding them places in the government. At the end of his prison term in Dublin for conspiracy Monaghan wrote to Emily's patron the Duke of Clarence asking for a job. When this line of approach failed, Emily persuaded the Duke of Wellington to give him two places in the Ordnance Office. A year later the same happened to William McKenzie, the man who had hidden, bribed, and coached the perjured Irish witnesses before the trial. At Emily's request,

---

[126] RIA/HP 1342: 70–1 (*Westmeath* v. *Anne Connell et al.*, 1825); *Reply to the Narrative*, 60–2; Hatfield House, Newspaper Clippings, 1825.

[127] RIA/HP 1342: 5–6 (*Reports of Some Cases in which the Marquis and Marchioness of Westmeath have been Litigant Parties*, 1825).

[128] Hatfield House, Newspaper Clippings, 1825; *Reply to the Narrative*, 64–7, 94; the Earl presumably obtained these letters of Emily by buying them from Anne Connell; he used them to some effect in a subsequent Chancery case in 1825.

the Duke obtained for him a place as clerk in the Ordnance Office worth £80 a year. A newspaper, presumably tipped off by George, picked up this last story and commented acidly: 'we may remind our readers that Lady Westmeath's sister is married to the Duke of Wellington's brother. The Duke is Master General [of the Ordnance]. Truly it may be remarked that there are "wheels within wheels".' George asked 'how did the Duke of Wellington become acquainted with my discharged gardener', and why did he appoint a person who could not write English to a clerkship in his Department?[129]

In addition to these two jobs, the Duke also rewarded Emily's chief agent in the conspiracy, McGuire, with an appointment as government solicitor. The public exposure of all these acts of old-style corrupt patronage brought nothing but discredit upon the Duke, who wrote plaintively to Emily: 'I cannot conceive how Lord Westmeath could have known that I had a contemplation to appoint Mr McGuire solicitor.'[130] It seems that everybody was stealing or reading the enemy's correspondence.

Because of its complexity, the case in the London Consistory Court dragged on for years. It only came up for hearing in late 1825, and it was not until the spring of 1826 that the Chancellor of the Court, Sir Christopher Robinson, at last issued his sentence.[131] In his lengthy preamble, explaining his reasoning, Sir Christopher quickly dismissed the evidence that George was guilty of 'sundry acts of adultery' after the reconciliation of 1817.[132] Turning to the original charge of cruelty, he began by repeating what in the early nineteenth century was still the standard legal criterion for marital cruelty, namely 'reasonable apprehension of danger to life, limb or health'. He concluded that up to 1814 nothing more had occurred than 'the indulgence of a petty and peevish spirit, and of intemperance of speech, of which there are but too frequent indications and perhaps on both sides'.

Although the acts of physical violence in 1812–15 might have fallen within the new legal definitions of cruelty, Sir Christopher pointed out that in 1817 the couple had been reconciled, and 'reconciliation will supercede the grounds of complaint in these courts. . . . It is true, however, that past injuries may be revived' by new ones, so that the key question was whether or not George's behaviour subsequent to the reconciliation had been sufficiently violent to revive them.[133] The Chancellor decided that the post-1817 episodes could not justify a revival of the earlier acts of cruelty. He

[129] *Reply to the Narrative*, 70, 94–5; Hatfield House, Newspaper Clippings, 1825.
[130] Hatfield House, Westmeath MSS; *Sketch*, 27–8.
[131] *Eng. Rep.* 162: 992–1012 (*Westmeath* v. *Westmeath*, 1826).
[132] Ibid. 994, 999.   [133] Ibid. 1009.

therefore ordered Emily to return home to her husband and to restore to him his conjugal rights.[134]

Faced with this set-back, and the threat of forcible removal by George to Clonyn, Emily instructed her lawyers to lodge an appeal with the Court of Arches, where the case came to a hearing a year later, in 1827.[135] There the same story was told all over again, but the conclusions reached by the judge, Sir John Nicholl, in his three-and-a-half-hour speech, were now radically different from those of Sir Christopher Robinson. He agreed with Sir Christopher that Emily's charges about George's adulteries were totally lacking in proof. He also agreed that the half-dozen episodes between 1813 and 1816 in which George had kicked or struck Emily might have been sufficient to form legal grounds for separation on grounds of cruelty. But he also agreed that the subsequent reconciliation in 1817, proved by the renewal of cohabitation and sexual relations, formed a legal bar to separation because of these previous acts of cruelty.

The only remaining questions were whether the subsequent cohabitation under the same roof without sexual relations in 1818–19 was legally tantamount to a second reconciliation and condonation; and, if so, whether George's behaviour after the reconciliation, and especially the episode on 14 June 1818, when he forcibly broke open Emily's presses and refused to leave her bedroom when asked to do so, provided sufficient evidence of a potential threat to her health to permit the old condoned acts of violence of 1813–16 to be revived and taken into account. To deal with these issues, Sir John found it necessary to go over what he described as 'an immense mass of evidence', which had been built up over the five years of litigation concerning the seven years of the marriage from 1812 to 1819.[136]

In full realization that he was creating case law only loosely based on past precedents, he entered upon a lengthy disquisition about what constituted legal cruelty. He quoted the famous definition of cruelty by Sir William Scott, later Lord Stowell, as something 'that renders cohabitation unsafe, or is likely to be attended with injury to the person or to the health of the party'.[137] In Sir John Nicholl's eyes, this general definition had to be qualified by a consideration of the station and rank of the parties involved: 'Among the lower classes, blows sometimes pass between married couples who, in the main, are very happy and have no desire to part; amidst very coarse habits, such incidents occur almost as freely as rude or reproachful words:

---

[134] Ibid. 1009–12.
[135] Hatfield House, Newspaper Clippings; *Eng. Rep.* 162: 1012–37 (*Westmeath* v. *Westmeath*, 1826).
[136] *Eng. Rep.* 162: 1014–37 (*Westmeath* v. *Westmeath*, 1826).
[137] *Eng. Rep.* 162: 466–99 (*Westmeath* v. *Westmeath*, 1821).

a word and a blow go together.' On the other hand, 'if a nobleman of high rank and ancient family uses personal violence to his wife, his equal in rank, such conduct in such a person carries with it something so degrading in the husband, and so insulting and mortifying to his wife, as to render the injury itself far more severe and insupportable'. By this sociological interpretation of marital cruelty as something defined not by the objective acts of violence of the husband but by the subjective response to them of the wife, Sir John Nicholl was radically altering the traditional definition of marital cruelty, and anticipating the modifications finally established only later in the mid-Victorian period.[138]

This ominous preamble was clearly aimed directly at George, 8th Earl and 1st Marquis of Westmeath. On the other hand, Sir John conceded that George's behaviour sprang not from 'cold malignity or savage, continued, unfeeling, brutality of disposition; it is not that of satiated possession producing disgust and hatred'. He also admitted that the fairly rare acts of violence were 'not inconsistent with occasional kindness, with the existence and continuance of strong attachment, nay even with violent affection'. George's weakness was rather 'great irritability of temper, producing ungovernable passion, ending occasionally in acts of personal violence'.[139] This was a fair summary. Sir John catagorically declared that the cohabitation under the same roof, in 1818–19, when George was in the position merely of a lodger, formed 'no continued condonation'—in doing so contradicting four separate decisions made in English Chancery, Irish Chancery, the House of Lords, and the London Consistory Court.

He then proceeded to argue that after 1818 George's passions, instead of being brought increasingly under control, had become more 'domineering and despotic' to the point of subjecting Emily to 'the risk of personal injury'. To prove this, he cited George's tearing up of the original indenture in May 1818; a violent verbal quarrel just before their boy was born in November; his quarrels with Emily in which, trembling with rage, he demanded a cancellation of the deed of separation and his restoration as master of the house; the occasion when in Emily's bedroom he had 'stormed and raved like one mad . . . against Mr Wood; called him all sorts of names— a scoundrel, villain, blackguard, bogtrotter'; and his second explosive verbal attack on Mr Wood in his own house.[140] He concluded, 'I do think that she had a reasonable foundation for an apprehension of renewed personal violence,' which therefore fell into the legal category of marital cruelty as

---

[138] J. M. Biggs, *The Concept of Mental Cruelty* (London, 1962), 38.
[139] *Eng. Rep.* 162: 1017 (*Westmeath* v. *Westmeath*, 1826).
[140] Ibid. 1032–5.

defined by Lord Stowell. 'I must therefore reverse the sentence, pronounce that Lady Westmeath has sufficiently proved her first allegation, charging her husband with cruelty, and is, on that account, entitled to a sentence of separation.'[141]

Emily had won a spectacular victory, for which she was eternally grateful to Sir John Nicholl, and upon which she was warmly congratulated by her friends.[142] It was something she treasured to her dying day, and thirty years later, in 1857, she had the lengthy sentence reprinted in its entirety at her own expense. For George, however, the defeat rankled for the rest of his life. In 1828 he remarked: 'I cannot bring myself to believe any man from a British seat of justice ever delivered a sentence so wholly partial, to say the least of it.' To the end, he claimed that, by his sentence, Sir John Nicholl had for ever ruined 'my reputation and comfort in life'.[143]

Defeated in the Court of Arches, George took his grievance one stage further, a step taken only twenty-one times over a matrimonial case in the thirty years from 1800 to 1830.[144] He appealed the case to the Court of Delegates, on the grounds that the adultery charge had been abandoned; any possible cruelty before 1818 had been condoned by the renewed co-habitation in 1818–19; and his behaviour in June 1819 which induced Emily to leave the house was not marital cruelty according to Lord Stowell's classic definition of it, since there were no blows or even threats of blows. In 1829 the Court of Delegates, which was composed of an *ad hoc* body of distinguished common judges and some civilians, after hearing the evidence for five days, and deliberating for an hour and a quarter, finally issued its verdict. Supported only by a narrow majority of four to three, with the senior common-law judge in the minority, it upheld Sir John Nicholl's decree of marital separation in the Court of Arches, as well as the subsequent decree of alimony of £700 a year, and it assessed George with Emily's taxed legal costs of £1,600.[145]

The split vote proved that the legal profession was deeply divided on the justice of Sir John Nicholl's sentence, about which Lord Eldon had publicly expressed doubts in the privileged arena of the House of Lords. Under the circumstances, George was still unwilling to surrender, and

[141] Hatfield House, Westmeath Papers.
[142] *Narrative of the Case*, 1–75; *Eng. Rep.* 162: 1035–7 (*Westmeath* v. *Westmeath*, 1826).
[143] *Eng. Rep.* 162: 1035–7 (*Westmeath* v. *Westmeath*, 1826); *Reply to the Narrative*, 4–10, 57–8; T. C., Hansard, *Parliamentary Debates*, 3rd ser., 145 (1857), 479–80.
[144] *Report of the Commissioners Relating to the Ecclesiastical Courts, PP Eng.* (1831–2) 24, App. C., 360.
[145] *Eng. Rep.* 162: 987 (*Westmeath* v. *Westmeath*, 1826); PRO, Del. 1/720; Hatfield House, Newspaper Clippings, 1829; *Reply to the Narrative*, 89.

asked the King in Council to appoint a Commission of Review. This almost unheard-of request was rejected—a response which was hardly surprising, seeing that Emily not only possessed a close ally in the Duke of Wellington, who was then Prime Minister, but was also an intimate friend and Lady of the Bedchamber of the wife of the heir to the throne.[146]

By 1829 it looked as if at last George was beaten, but he still did not give up. He was condemned to pay all costs except those for the prosecution and defence of Emily's false charge of adultery. But he refused to pay the taxed costs of his wife's legal expenses in the appeal to the Court of Delegates. When Emily sued him in 1829 for contempt of court, George claimed immunity from arrest by virtue of his privilege as an Irish peer. The Court rejected the claim, found him in contempt for non-payment, and requested the Lord Chancellor to issue a writ for his arrest. It was then discovered, however, that a writ of contempt by an ecclesiastical court was not enforcible in law against a peer. In order to force George to pay up, an Ecclesiastical Court Powers Act had to be pushed through Parliament by Lord Brougham in 1832. Even this did not do much good, however, since as late as 1853 some of the legal costs still had not been paid and Emily was still being dunned for them.[147]

For several years George also used his privilege as a Representative Peer of Parliament at Westminster to avoid paying a penny of the £700-a-year alimony the ecclesiatical court had awarded Emily back in 1827.[148] She therefore sued him for her arrears, and in 1834 George went to law one last time, appealing to the newly constituted Judicial Committee of the Privy Council to reduce the size of the alimony. For reasons which will be explained, the Committee agreed that he had a case, reduced the alimony to £315 a year, but ordered George to pay £2,000 arrears from 1827 to 1833 at this new rate, as well as all costs of the litigation.[149]

(vi) *The Financial and Psychological Consequences*

And so at long last, in 1834, the great legal war between George and Emily finally came to an end. The key decisions were two. The first was the sentence by Sir John Nicholl in the Court of Arches in 1827, granting Emily separation from bed and board on the grounds of George's cruelty to her, thus formally severing the marriage, and making George responsible

---

[146] LPCA, H.365/4, 20.

[147] *Eng. Rep.* 162: 987–91 (*Westmeath* v. *Westmeath*, 1829); *Narrative of the Case*, 110.

[148] *Eng. Rep.* 162: 987 (*Westmeath* v. *Westmeath*, 1829); 5: 361 (*Westmeath* v. *Westmeath*, 1832); *Reply to the Narrative*, 42–3; LPCA, H.365/11.

[149] *Reply to the Narrative*, 42–3; *Greville Memoirs*, iii. 69–70, 75, 91; LPCA, H.365/15, 18, 19, 20.

for at least part of her legal costs, as well as for paying her alimony for life. This was Emily's greatest victory, won on very narrow, and indeed dubious, legal grounds. The second was the decision of both Chancery and the common-law courts, finally upheld by the House of Lords in 1831, that the separation deeds of 1817 and 1818, which granted Emily maintenance of £1,300 a year for life, were both invalid, each for a different reason. This, together with the loss of custody of her daughter Rosa, was Emily's greatest defeat.

Estimating the full legal cost to both parties of this prolonged struggle is not easy, since the 'taxed' costs by the court, which is all that is known for certain, only covered expenses after the initial citation in the court, placed a limit of two on the number of lawyers, controlled their fees and expenses, and excluded the costs of work done by solicitors and detectives, and much of the transport, care, maintenance, and rewards of the many witnesses carried to and from between Ireland and England to testify in the innumerable and long-drawn-out cases. By about 1827 George was complaining that he 'had been to a very enormous expense in various lawsuits in Ireland and England'. But this was not the end of the litigation, which ran on for another seven years, and for which George was ordered to pay costs, both for himself and for Emily. In 1834 George said he owed his Irish and English lawyers about £14,000, and much later, in 1857, he claimed that altogether the war had cost him £30,000.[150]

As for Emily, she claimed in 1831 that she had spent £12,000 on litigation, apparently in addition to the taxed costs paid by George. If their two claims were not grossly exaggerated, they had therefore between them spent at least £24,000 on legal fees and expenses up to about 1830, with probably another £6,000 or more to follow between 1831 and 1834, making a total of at least £30,000 and possibly more.[151] These enormous legal costs were a burden that impoverished both of them for decades to come, and explain the heavy debts with which they were both saddled by 1830.

Exactly how bad were George's finances after 1820 is very hard to determine, since the several statements he made varied widely. At the time of his marriage in 1812 he had claimed that his father owned 13,000 acres of Irish estates worth £10,000 a year, but he later scaled this down to about £5,000, arguing that Irish rents had fallen by a half.[152] When in 1836 Rosa came of age, he grumbled to his friend the Duke of Buckingham about the

[150] LPCA, H.365/2, 10, 11, 15, 20.
[151] LPCA, H.365/1, 10, 11; Hatfield House, Westmeath Papers, Will of Marchioness Emily drawn up in 1855; *Reply to the Narrative*, 47.
[152] LPCA, H.365/10, 11, 16; 365/20: 2; D.2240: 1132–3h; 363/20: 3; H.5/20: 3; H.365/10; D.2240: 1127, 1133.

cost of launching her in the London season, explaining that he was 'floundering in debt', although it was an expense 'which God knows I should not think of, if I was not persecuted by sharks'.[153] His financial troubles were further exacerbated by the Irish tithe reform instituted by the Whig government, which he claimed cost him £800 a year—a piece of legislation he characteristically described as 'the Tithe knavery'. The most comprehensive statement about George's financial troubles is provided by his declaration about his income, made on oath before the Court of Delegates in 1827–8. He put the gross income of his inherited estate at no more than £4,800 a year. From this, there had to be deducted £1,650 a year due to his creditors on a mortgage of £27,000; and £840 in annuities to relatives. This left him with a net spending income of only £2,300 a year.[154]

That he was extremely short of money in the 1820s is proved by the fact that for a while he shut up his Irish seat at Clonyn, and in 1836 was trying to rent it. He took up residence in London in an unfashionable end of town in humble rented houses owned by small tradesmen. At one lodging he was paying a mere two guineas a week for rent and another guinea for board and service. His landlords at other lodgings were a warehouseman and a tailor. He seems to have made do during these hard times with no more than a cook and a maidservant to look after him, while his daughter Rosa was living and being educated at the country house of Avington, in Berkshire, belonging to his friend the Duke of Buckingham.[155]

Emily's finances after the separation were hardly any better. During the first years of separation in the early 1820s she was very short of money, and ran up large debts because of her legal expenses. Thereafter, however, she was successful in exploiting her long and intimate personal ties to her brother-in-law, the Duke of Wellington, and to members of the royal family, especially Princess Adelaide of Saxe-Coburg, who in 1818 married George IV's brother and heir to the throne, William, Duke of Clarence, at which time Emily was appointed lady-in-waiting, at a salary of £250 a year. The Duchess was evidently on very good terms with Emily, congratulating her on the birth of her son, and addressing her first as 'l'aimable Countess of Westmeath', then 'ma chére Marquise', and finally 'ma chére amie' as their relationship grew increasingly intimate.

Soon after her separation from George, Emily was granted by King George IV a rent-free apartment in Saint James's Palace, quarters Emily later deprecatingly described as 'of very inferior description'. According to

---

[153] Huntington Library, Stowe MSS, Box 23 (28); Box 82 (29).
[154] LPCA, H.365/20: 2.   [155] LPCA, D.2240: 801, 803; H.365/10.

George, Emily obtained this favour from George IV by humiliatingly ob-sequious lobbying of the King's influential mistress, Lady Conyngham. After the Duchess became Queen in 1830, Emily became extra Lady of the Bedchamber, which was largely a sinecure but carried a salary of £275 a year.[156]

Emily also had a right to £500 a year pin-money due from George according to her marriage settlement of 1812, and about £350 a year as interest on the £12,500 she had inherited from Lady Anne Cecil on her father's death in 1823. During the 1820s, however, George never paid her a penny of the maintenance allowance of £1,300 a year due to her under the 1818 deed, nor any of her legal costs, nor the alimony awarded to her in 1827 by the Court of Arches. There was a bad period in 1823 when George also held up her pin-money for three years, and her inher-itance from Lady Anne Cecil had still not been settled. She later alleged that for three months she was reduced to living in St James's Palace off a diet of bread and cheese and barley water.[157] Although she was still running up huge debts to her lawyers and proctors, after 1826 she en-joyed free lodging in St James's Palace, and an income of about £1,100 a year.

After 1829 Emily's financial position improved, once more thanks to her influential connections. She put some quiet pressure on her friend Adelaide, Duchess of Clarence, by offering to resign her post as lady-in-waiting on the grounds that, thanks to the refusal of George to pay her her maintenance allowance or alimony, she was too poor to keep a carriage and generally live in the appropriate style. The Duchess passed the message on to the Duke of Clarence, the future William IV, who wrote on her behalf to the Prime Minister, her friend the Duke of Wellington. The letter was short and to the point:

This letter will be delivered to your Grace by our excellent and ill-used friend, the Marchioness of Westmeath. Her Ladyship is anxious to have a pension on the Irish establishment, and I trust the request is not unreasonable, and that it will be in your Grace's power to give the injured lady what she is so anxious to obtain and of which I know her to be much in want.

The Duke had been brought up in the old school, according to which a man of influence had a duty to reward his friends and relatives, by getting them appointed to lucrative offices at the disposal of the government. Thus he had lobbied hard in 1826 to obtain a bishopric for his brother, the Revd Gerald Valerian Wellesley. But Lord Liverpool refused to do it, perhaps in

---

[156] *Sketch.*   [157] *Narrative of the Case*, 107.

part because the Wellesley marriage was known to be on the rocks. So a year later the Duke obtained for him the rich church living of Bishop Wearmouth, and a prebend at Durham. As a result of this largesse directed in his way by his brother the Duke, the Revd Wellesley by 1832 was the second richest parson in England, with an income of £5,000 a year. What the Duke had done for Gerald, he could surely do for Emily. It should be remembered how the Duke had already looked after Emily's agents and witnesses, used in her attempt to prove her husband's adultery. So in 1829, when Emily was staying at Strathfieldsaye with the Duke, she used her influence and charm to persuade him to do something for her.

Prodded by this personal appeal and the letter from the Duke of Clarence, Wellington proposed to the ailing George IV that Emily be given a pension of £385 a year on the Irish list. But this blatantly improper lobbying by the heir to the throne and the Prime Minister on behalf of a personal friend of both of them caused a public outcry. Attitudes to 'Old Corruption' were changing, and Greville denounced the pension as 'a job' by the Duke of Wellington, and commented that it makes 'a great noise'. The Lord-Lieutenant of Ireland, the Marquis of Anglesea, strongly objected to it, writing that he would obey only on the express personal orders of the King, 'but I could not bear that it should stand as an act of mine'. Anglesea regarded the proposed pension as 'an instance of political corruption at Ireland's expense which had long been a grievance', and the matter caused a breach between him and the Duke which was never healed.[158]

In the face of all this opposition, the Duke was temporarily baffled, and publicly dropped the scheme for a while. But when the uproar had died down, he secretly slid it through thanks to a warrant under the royal sign manual, over the express wishes of the Irish administration. Thus in 1829 Emily found herself with a life pension on the Irish List of £385 (English) a year, for no other reason than that she was a close friend of the Duke and Duchess of Clarence and the Duke of Wellington. Years later Emily recalled bitterly 'all the horrible libels spread about by the Earl of Westmeath and his friends'—presumably that Wellington was merely paying off an old but still favoured mistress. She claimed that 'it was also immediately made a party matter', as a result of which 'there was no end to the attacks on the Prime Minister, with incessant and atrocious libels lavished with indefatigable perseverance on me'.[159]

[158] Ibid. 107–8; *Journal of Mrs Arbuthnot 1830–32*, ed. F. Bamford and the Duke of Wellington (London, 1950), 45, 80, 228, 313; Marquis of Anglesea, *One Leg: The Life and Letters of H. W. Paget* (London, 1961), 206; *Greville Memoirs*, i. 239, 242, 312; iii. 430; for the Revd Wellesley, see P. Virgin, *The Church in the Age of Negligence, 1700–1840* (Cambridge, 1989), 90. [159] *Narrative of the Case*, 108–9.

This was not the end of the affair, for when in 1833 the new Whig ministry set up a Committee to look into abuses in the pension lists, the whole matter came up again. Lord Grey, the Prime Minister, wrote to the Duke of Wellington to find out more details of just how and why this pension had been granted. He warned that 'much explanation will be expected on the subject of Lady Westmeath's pension, both from the magnitude of the sum and from her station and connections in society'. Lord Grey added that 'I am fearful of addressing Lord Westmeath, lest I do mischief and excite more family quarrels, besides which I do not consider him the most sensible of men.'[160] This sounded ominous, but somehow or other the Duke's influence proved sufficient to ward off the threat of cancellation, and Emily retained her Irish pension of £385 a year until her death twenty-five years later.

In the long run, however, this political job did her no good, since in 1834 George appealed to the Judicial Committee of the Privy Council for a reduction in the alimony she had been awarded by the Court of Arches by £385, on the grounds that account should be taken of her royal pension. According to Greville, who seems to have had little sympathy with either party, Emily tried to rush the case through the Committee in a hurry before the summer recess, using the good offices of her friend Lord Chancellor Brougham, but was blocked by Lord Lansdowne, the Lord President. When the case came up again in September, George won and the alimony was reduced by £385 from £700 to £315 a year.[161] So the Duke of Wellington's scandalous and politically damaging intervention on her behalf—which was in fact rather uncharacteristic of him—in the end did her no good at all.

Thanks to this governmental largesse and the settled alimony, Emily's gross income around 1836 was about £1,850 a year, plus a free apartment, and only fell to about £1,500 after the death of William IV in 1837.[162] Later on, in the 1840s, Emily was certainly comfortably off, investing in stocks, and living in her own house in Piccadilly, to which she was adding a ballroom.[163]

But the cost in time, money, spirit, and mental anguish of such protracted and complex litigation was very high indeed. The mental strain and financial burden of the litigation, together with her separation from Rosa, left her a deeply embittered woman, unforgivingly resentful not only of all the legal

[160] Hatfield House, Westmeath Papers.

[161] LPCA, H.365/11, 20; Hatfield House, Westmeath Papers; ibid., Newspaper Clippings; *Greville Memoirs*, iii. 69–70, 75, 91.

[162] LPCA, H.365/15, 18, 20: 2. [163] *Reply to the Narrative*, 43–6.

obstacles she encountered, but also of the lack of support from her family, who were above all anxious to avoid scandalous publicity. As George asked in 1828, in his usual rhetorical style: 'Was the spectacle of a married woman successfully employed in ruining her husband, against the wishes and sentiment of *all* her family, ever yet exhibited to the world in a Christian country?'[164]

She certainly had a grievance, because the Cecil family legal adviser, Mr Sheldon, had repeatedly given her bad advice. The first reconciliation in 1817, which was forced on her by her parents, was based on a deed drawn up by Sheldon, which allowed for a future separation at her discretion—something which was later judged to be void in law. The second private separation deed of 1818, also the work of Sheldon, lacked a clause indemnifying George for Emily's debts, and so turned out also to be possibly void in law. Worse still, it was Sheldon who helped to persuade her to let George stay in her house as a lodger to cover up the separation, a concession which was later judged to be legally an act of condonation, which voided the 1818 separation agreement and barred her from using in court any previous acts of adultery or cruelty by George. Thanks to Sheldon's wrong advice, she lost her £1,300 annuity and very nearly wrecked her case for judicial separation.

Although the Cecil family and Mr Sheldon meant well, their advice to Emily in the 1820s was thus the root cause of all her later legal defeats. Emily saw only the consequnces, misunderstood the motives, and became resentful, angry, and unforgiving, especially of her interfering mother and her timid brother. She was utterly convinced in her own mind that, if only she had ignored her family and had demanded a permanent private or judicial separation from George in 1817 or 1818, she would have been assured of both a comfortable maintenance for life and also custody of her daughter, Rosa. She would have avoided the loss of her daughter and the endless litigation which destroyed her life and her peace of mind and seriously undermined her finances.

By the 1830s Emily was a sick woman, worn down by anxiety and disappointments. In the late 1830s, 1840s, and 1850s she seems to have spent a good deal of time abroad for the sake of her health. Where she went we do not know, but once she was away from England for a period of six years, from 1834 to 1840, and on more than one occasion spent the winter in Florence. In addition to this chronic ill-health, she was clearly of a very nervous disposition. In 1820 she had taken to her bed on hearing that

---

[164] *Sketch*, 12 n.; letter of 13 Jan. 1836 from Lady Cowley.

George had kidnapped her daughter Rosa. In 1823 she had collapsed again on reading in the newspaper the erroneous claim that George was suing for separation on grounds of her infidelity.[165]

By the 1840s she was chronically sick, and increasingly deeply embittered, soured by a life which had gone tragically wrong, causing her decades of embroilment in fierce litigation with her husband, the loss of all contact with her only surviving child, and alienation from all her family. Her experience caused her to feel passionately about the need to reform the current laws concerning divorce, married women's property, the protection of an innocent mother's right to the custody of her younger children, and the abolition of the crim. con. action. She therefore became an ardent crusader for the rights of married women.[166]

When she was well and in England, she continued to circulate in high society, and to the end she retained her influential friends. The Duke of Wellington, who almost certainly was never her lover, stood by Emily until he died, and as late as 1853 he wrote a letter of introduction for her in which he described her as 'not only one of my oldest friends but a near relative'. Moreover judging from the surviving correspondence, Emily remained on equally good terms with the Duke and Duchess of Clarence, later King William IV and Queen Adelaide. She also became a good friend of two distinguished lawyers and later Lord Chancellors, Lords Brougham and Lyndhurst, who helped her to promote her feminist causes through law-reform legislation in the House of Lords; it was to them that she dedicated her pamphlet of 1857 about her legal sufferings.

Four episodes serve to illustrate the depths of her rage against the world and her deep sense of betrayal. The first was her obstruction of all attempts to submit to arbitration the litigation with George. Between 1819 and 1823 the latter offered to negotiate terms with her at least five times, only to be rebuffed, since his terms were too high. Her opening gambit was often what she herself called an 'ultimatum'. For example, in about 1825 she wrote to her brother Lord Cranborne:

For Lord Westmeath to talk of negotiating now with me, as if when once he had taken my child he had not done all he could do, is really ridiculous. I wish now to state most explicitly that, as to the treatment I have experienced respecting my child (to say nothing of other matters), no proposal shall ever originate with my advisers, or my *real* and *kind friends*, with my consent. I think it incompatible with what I owe to my character, and therefore *final* with me.

---

[165] *Narrative of the Case*, 76, 93, 100, 102, 104, 106, 117, 124.
[166] Ibid. 2, 102–3, 118, 123, 128, 132–3, 137–8.

When eleven years later, in 1836, George once more offered to discuss peace terms, Emily replied frostily: 'I never can, nor ever will, have any dealings with Lord Westmeath.'[167]

Secondly, Emily's treatment of her daughter Rosa was equally tinged with anger, resentment, and self-pity. So far as is known, she was excluded from all communication with Rosa after her abortive attempt in 1825 to lure the child away from her father during her dancing lesson. Until she was 21, Rosa was brought up in the household of George's close friend, the Duke of Buckingham. In 1839, when she was 25, she wrote the following letter to her mother: 'I am induced, with my father's consent, to write to you upon a subject in which my happiness is materially concerned.' She went on to explain that she had had an offer of marriage from Mr Fulke Southwell Greville, and concluded: 'I think in marrying him I have every prospect of future comfort and happiness. I have accepted him. I therefore hope you will approve of the marriage.'

Rosa's letter was undoubtedly cold and lacking in tact, making it clear that she was seeking no more than mere formal approval, not real consent. Her mother's reaction was explosive:

How much I lament, Rosa, since it seems at last to have occurred to you that you have a mother, that still you should not bring yourself to write in a less objectionable manner. As to natural affection, there is not an atom of that to be found in your letter. Have you ever in any one instance acted, since you came to the age of reason, as if you ever gave that a thought or felt any interest yourself towards me? The system pursued by those who educated you (and countenanced by my own family) must indeed have been a lamentable one since it produces such a result.

Emily concluded by recalling the words spoken by Rosa fourteen years before, at their last stormy encounter at the dancing school: 'I never wish to see your face again!' Her mother now commented bitterly: 'This from a little girl at that time about nine or ten setting herself up as a judge between her parents.'[168]

Emily had once loved both her husband and her daughter, but both had let her down, and were finally alienated from her. So, too, were the members of her own family, the Cecils. Emily's brother and trustee, Lord Cranborne (after 1823 the 2nd Marquis of Salisbury), was only anxious, like the rest of her family, to patch things up and get the washing of the family's dirty linen out of the public eye. For his pains he earned no more than Emily's

---

[167] Hatfield House, 2M Gen., 1822 [in fact *c.*1825]; *Narrative of the Case*, 75–6, 98–9, 100, 114–16, 145, 147–8, 150, 206, 208.

[168] Hatfield House, Westmeath Papers. For a genealogy of the Greville family, see J. C. Lyons, *The Grand Juries of Westmeath, 1727–1853*, 100–2.

lasting enmity. In about 1825 she still signed a somewhat truculent letter to her brother: 'yours affectionately, E. Westmeath'. By 1837, however, the tone had changed dramatically. She now reminded him of

the load of litigation intailed upon me by your sudden turning round upon me, and employing all the powers you had as my trustee to my detriment. . . . You then attempted to starve me into terms, by depriving me, through a legal quibble . . . for three years of my pin-money. . . . Your refused to pay me my father's legacy. . . . But all failed. I lived on bread and cheese when I could not procure meat, I drank water then, I could not afford wine. . . . At last came the blessed judgment of Sir John Nicholl. . . . It left me completely justified, and my family, who might have protected me, open to the query 'Why did they? Why would they wish to deliver their daughter, their sister, bound hand and foot, again into the power of such a man?' I leave them to answer that question to themselves and the world as best they can!!! . . . I shall not enumerate the various expensive litigations, under exercise of power and influence, that followed, and which finally succeeded in depriving me of a large portion of my just rights in the money way.

Ask yourself whether I possibly can, after all this, look upon your letter in any other light but adding insult to injury. You profess you wish to return to our former affectionate footing, but without any explanation. In truth this would indeed be most convenient for you.

She claimed that 'the concealed object' was 'of inducing me to countenance the above proceedings. This would indeed have been but poor reparation for all I have suffered.' Her brother's wife, the Marchioness of Salisbury, noted in her diary: 'The Duke [of Wellington] called here—told me all about Lady Westmeath's letters. A reconciliation is evidently out of the question. She is determined to persevere in her quarrels. However we have put ourselves in the right, so it don't signify.'[169]

When, nearly twenty years later, in 1855, Emily drew up her will, she had still neither forgiven nor forgotten, and raked up all her old grievances against her brother in his capacity as her trustee. She—quite unjustly— blamed him for the failure to obtain alimony for her between 1818 and 1828. She asked him to pay the £4,000–£5,000 legal fees still due to her Parliamentary agents after some twenty years, owing, she alleged, to his obstinacy. She mentioned that she had been told that in America there were new laws to protect married women and their property, and concluded with the savage hope that 'this case may prove a warning to any woman placed in my painful and trying position: let her avoid as a trustee a near relation or brother'.[170]

---

[169] Hatfield House, 2M Gen., 1836; C. Oman, *The Gascoigne Heiress: The Life and Diaries of Frances Mary Gascoigne-Cecil, 1802–39* (London, 1968), 200.
[170] Hatfield House, Westmeath Papers.

Westmeath v. Westmeath

The fourth episode which illustrates Emily's state of mind in her later years was her revival of all the old grievances once again in 1855–7, when Parliament was debating the divorce bill. This gave her the opportunity to get her revenge on all her enemies by publishing at her own expense a bitter pamphlet of 212 pages entitled *A Narrative of the Case of the Marchioness of Westmeath*.[171] It consisted of a reprint of Sir John Nicholl's judgment in 1826 in her favour, followed by a diatribe against all her enemies, real and imagined, including her husband, her daughter, the members of her own family, and the judges who had sided with her husband. She once more dredged up all the sordid details of her version of the story of her sufferings during her marriage some forty years back, and the injustices she had met with in the lengthy litigation that followed the marital breakdown. She claimed that she was bringing her story to public attention once again in order to 'obtain justice for a suffering class', namely married women under English law.

George did his best to answer his wife's accusations by publishing a ninety-seven-page pamphlet of his own, rebutting many of her facts and arguments point by point, and ignoring others. He asked, with good reason, 'whether the *Narrative* does not rather display the workings of malice and ill-will towards an individual than the breathings of a pure and benevolent spirit anxious only to promote the welfare of her sex'. He complained about the 'pain and anguish' caused by the publication, which obliged 'a man of near seventy-three years of age to recall the memory of events which have embittered his life and rendered his old age desolate'.[172] This last was something of an exaggeration, as we shall see.

In a wholly irrelevant speech in a Committee meeting of the House of Lords, George protested that Emily's pamphlet 'had been placed on the tables of the clubs, with a view to vilifying my character'. He told the Lords that the pamphlet had been followed up by an article in 'a most respectable newspaper'—an article planted, George assumed, by Emily—which, like the pamphlet, was full of 'the grossest perversions of . . . fact' and 'the most unjustifiable untruths'—all intended to blacken his reputation and make the world think that 'I was a villain'.[173]

After being reminded that the House of Lords was hardly the place in which to vent a personal grievance against a wife, he turned his attention to advocating the introduction of an identical divorce bill to cover Ireland, a proposal which was wholly impracticable in view of the implacable

---

[171] *Narrative of the Case.*   [172] *Reply to the Narrative*, 95, 97.

[173] Hansard, 3rd ser., 165 (1857), 479–80, 809–10; the newspaper was *The Globe*, 18 May 1857.

opposition to divorce of both the Irish Catholic Church and the Catholic laity.[174]

The best thing which happened to George after the marital separation was that in 1822 a Tory government promoted him from an Irish Earl to an Irish Marquis. In 1830 he was also elected a representative peer of Ireland with a seat in the English House of Lords, which provided him with an arena in which to propound his often eccentric and always unpredictable views on a wide variety of topics. With whom he lived between 1834 and 1858 is largely unknown. According to Emily, in the 1840s George openly kept a French mistress, and gave her and their offspring his family names and titles. There is no suggestion that George actually committed legal bigamy, but merely that he systematically ignored his first marriage and treated it as if it had never existed. In his will, he settled £600 a year as jointure on his French mistress, whom he called Lady Delvin, and gave £10,000 to his children by her, the eldest son being called by him 'Lord Delvin'. In 1857 Emily complained publicly that 'I am at this moment cruelly libelled with respect to the line of conduct Lord Westmeath has adopted of producing the children of his pretended second marriage as if born in lawful wedlock.'

For a while in the 1840s George called his new mistress 'Lady Westmeath' and Emily 'the Marchioness Dowager of Westmeath', a nomenclature which was even published in the official Court Guides. He also tried but failed to get his mistress presented at the Viceregal Court in Dublin under the title of Lady Delvin. Later he had two creditors sue his wife for debt in the Exchequer Court, in the name of 'Lady Emily Cecil'. This indignity infuriated Emily, who argued, rightly, that it was 'as if my marriage with Lord Westmeath had been dissolved, for misconduct on my part, by Act of Parliament'. George, she complained, 'is going about with impunity with another person living with him, and taking my name'. She tried to remedy the situation by placing advertisements in the newspapers claiming her rightful title, but all but the *Morning Post* politely refused to publish them, for fear of getting involved in a libel action.

As for the three bastard children to whom he left £10,000 in his will, in 1852 he lost his only son, and four years later one of his two daughters. A year later, in 1857, there appeared in *The Times* the following obituary notice: 'Died at Boulogne-sur-Mer, the Lady Mary Anne Nugent, daughter of the Marquess of Westmeath, aged 10 years.' By publishing this notice, asked Emily, does he not 'publicly admit that he is guilty of bigamy?'[175]

---

[174] Hansard, 3rd ser., 145 (1857), 480, 522; *Reply to the Narrative*, 95–6.
[175] *Gent's Mag.* (July–Dec. 1852), 214; *Narrative of the Case*, 118, 121, 124–7, 131.

Westmeath v. Westmeath

Right up to the day of Emily's death, George continued to struggle to free himself from her. In May 1857, over twenty years after the conclusion of the great legal battles between them, when the House of Lords was debating the divorce bill, George proposed to add a clause to allow remarriage of one party or both who had been legally separated for twenty years or more.[176] The reason was that, although now 72, and his French mistress presumably dead, George still preserved a lively interest in the other sex, and was waiting impatiently to marry another woman. The clause failed, but relief was near, since Emily died early the next year.

Within four weeks of her death, George, now aged 73, married again, to a woman very much younger than himself. But this second marriage turned out badly and four years later he had once more to resort to marital litigation—this time in the newly established Matrimonial Causes Court—in order to obtain a divorce because of his new young wife's adultery. Undeterred by this second unfortunate marital experience, George married yet again in 1864, a marriage which apparently lasted until he died in 1871, at the advanced age of 86.

His obituary in *The Times*, entitled 'A Tory of Tories', was frankly critical of his obstinate defence of the Protestant Establishment in Ireland: 'He strongly opposed Catholic Emancipation, the Repeal of the Test Act, the Reform Bill of 1832, the Maynooth Grant, and the Disestablishment of the Irish Church. . . . In fact to every liberal and enlightened measure of progress and improvement [he] offered the most constant opposition.'[177] As has been seen, this was an accurate assessment of his extreme political and religious views.

He was also an active supporter of some unexpected causes. Thus in 1857 he took the lead in promoting a Bathing Bill in the House of Lords. He denounced the 'unnecessary exposure taking place on the beaches of Margate and Ramsgate', where he claimed that it was 'the practice for women to go down to the sea-bathing places and dance in the water, without any covering whatsoever, to the great disquiet of the respectable inhabitants and visitors'. He therefore proposed a law that 'no one should be permitted to bathe in public without a decent dress'.[178] This was an unlikely crusade to be adopted by a man who forty years before had been complaining about his wife's refusal to pose for him in the nude.

Neither of George's two late marriages produced an heir, so that on his death his only legitimate child was Rosa, who at last inherited Clonyn Castle and the Nugent estates, an event for which her mother had been

---

[176] Hansard, 3rd ser., 145 (1857), 809. [177] *The Times*, 8 May 1871.
[178] Hansard, 3rd ser., 145 (1857), 1884.

plotting and fighting for half a century. Rosa's husband, who had recently been raised to the peerage as Lord Greville of Clonyn, and had assumed the name and arms of Nugent in 1866, inherited all the estates, while the empty title of 9th Earl of Westmeath went to a very distant cousin, descended from a younger son of the 2nd Earl of Westmeath of the late seventeenth century. Rosa and Lord Greville razed the decayed old Clonyn Castle and built a large new Victorian seat. Their timing was catastrophically wrong, however, for the end of the Protestant Establishment in Ireland was approaching, and by 1943 the house had long since been sold by the family to a Catholic nunnery, which was trying vainly to sell it again.[179]

(vii) *Conclusion*

This story of the legal wars between the Westmeaths includes examples of almost all the possible causes of marital breakdown, from cruelty to adultery; from disputes over money to quarrels over where to live; from incompatible attitudes to sex to occasional blows; from battles over child custody to struggles over the descent of property; from quarrels within the family to basic flaws in personal character and temperament.

The resolution of the various legal battles were of lasting importance in the changing of the law: for example, the sentence in the separation suit modified the previous legal definition of marital cruelty. The same suit was also a test case of what actions and behaviour amounted to condonation, and therefore acted as a bar to any subsequent suit for separation.

The litigation about George's alleged adultery and the distraint of his Irish property reveals unusually well-documented examples of encouragement given by both sides to the fabrication of false evidence, thanks to imprudent offers of rich rewards to impoverished witnesses. Other suits in the Exchequer show once again the potential power of a separated wife to make her husband legally responsible for her debts for necessary maintenance, even to the extent of getting him put in prison for them. Wood's case against George provides an early example of the common law at last actively intervening to punish challenges to duels among members of the élite, by condemning the challenger to prison.

The litigation over child custody reveals the continued inability, before the law was changed in 1839, of an innocent but separated wife and mother to recover care of or even access to her only child by a writ of habeas corpus from King's Bench. On the other hand, the grudging decision by Lord Eldon to recognize as legal the Westmeath private separation agreement was an important landmark in the validation of these documents. Even so,

[179] Information supplied by Dr A. P. W. Malcomson.

Westmeath *v.* Westmeath

Lord Eldon did manage to destroy the legality of several clauses in these deeds. One concerned the standard covenant not to sue in the ecclesiastical courts for restoration of conjugal rights, so as to force a spouse back into cohabitation against his or her will. In the Westmeath case the validity of the clause was denied, as indeed it usually had been. Another, much less common, issue was the validity of a separation deed drafted so as to come into effect sometime in the future, whenever the wife should choose. In an earlier test case, its validity had been upheld by Lord Chancellor Ellenborough, but it was now decisively rejected.

Many of the changes in legal interpretation and moral values which were occurring at this period were thus brought to the fore and decided in the many lawsuits between the Westmeaths in the 1820s and early 1830s. It is, therefore, hardly surprising that these suits were widely reported, since they made legal history. They formed what was probably the longest, the most expensive, the most complicated, and most famous war over marital separation of all time. It prepared the way for the abolition in 1857 of the powers over separation and divorce both of the ecclesiastical courts and of Parliament, and the abolition of the most scandalous and indefensible features of the common-law action for damages for crim. con.

In 1855 Mrs Caroline Norton, a personal friend of Emily, and like her a fighter for married women's rights, cited the Westmeath affair as conclusive evidence of the overwhelming power of patriarchy in the English courts of law. To her the treatment of Emily demonstrated the urgent need to reform the law, in order to make it more fair to separated women. In an open letter to Queen Victoria, she wrote a passionate paragraph about the legal and personal sufferings of her friend and fellow victim:

I have seen but one more resolute attempt at annulling the effect of the law on a woman's destiny; and I conceive even that to have failed. It was tried under the most favourable circumstances. Not, as in my case, in the reign of a Queen, but in the strong reign of a King; with the late Duke of Wellington for the lady's unflinching friend, the experiment of support was tried and failed. A pension of £380 a year on the Irish Civil List was granted to the maligned wife. She was afterwards made extra Lady in Waiting to Queen Adelaide; and all that great friends, great influence, and court favour could do for her was done. Her husband vainly attacked the Duke of Wellington in a published pamphlet for his interference in his domestic affairs; and deprecating what was done in defiance of himself, the lord and ruler of that broken home.[180] But set that woman's destiny to rights

---

[180] If such a pamphlet was ever published, no copy of it seems to have survived. But in a letter from the Duke to Emily, dated July 1819, he remarks 'as for the paragraph [in a newspaper], it is beneath contempt' (Hatfield House, Westmeath Papers). The date fits the period during which George was contemplating a crim. con. action against the Duke.

the Court could *not*, nor break her marriage; nor overrule what was determined by her husband as to her more intimate destiny—the dear tie of children or attacks on her reputation.

It is a glorious thing that the Law should be stronger than the Throne. It is one of England's proudest boasts. But it is *not* a glorious thing that being stronger than the Throne it should be weaker than the subject; and that that which even a king can only do within a certain limit (oppress or uphold) may be done with boundless irresponsible power in the one single relation of husband and wife.[181]

Given the important legal and moral issues raised by the wars between the Westmeaths, it is only fitting that they themselves should have played a role in the passage of the 1857 Divorce Act, by actively pamphleteering while the bill was under consideration by Parliament. The many legal and ethical problems associated with the breakdown of the Westmeath marriage pointed directly to the solutions adopted in the 1857 Divorce Act.

[181] C. Norton, *A Letter to the Queen* . . . (London, 1855), 101.

Index

347

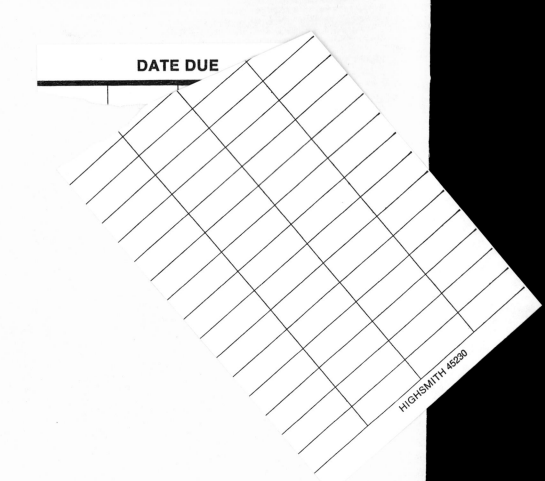

DATE DUE

HIGHSMITH 45230